"Without the Old Testament, the incredibly amazing and mys⎯
wouldn't make sense (or we may come to very strange conclusions).⎯
and wonderful thing to have Old Testament scholar Tremper Longm⎯   ⎯⎯⎯tary.
I seriously will never do a study on Revelation again without this b⎯   ⎯⎯⎯ry guide. It
brings us the lens of looking at Revelation through the original readers ⎯ ⎯⎯evelation."
—Dan Kimball, author of *How (Not) to Read the Bible*

"As a young Christian disciple, reading the book of Revelation was mystifying and puzzling—
and therefore ultimately discouraging! What did it all mean? I wish I'd had Tremper Longman's
volume as a reading guide. He presents the book's enduring message clearly, and lays out a rich
feast of Old Testament connections and Greco-Roman context. As an Old Testament scholar,
I learned much from this excellent contribution by a seasoned and thoughtful colleague; as a
Christian, my new understanding led to worship. This is a volume that pastors, scholars, and
laypeople will find a valuable companion to reading and studying the canon's final book."
—Lissa M. Wray Beal, Providence Theological Seminary

"The message of Revelation has been an important one in my own life. I have extensively studied
it and have taught it in non-academic settings. So I am pleased to recommend very highly this
unique commentary by seasoned Old Testament scholar Tremper Longman. His volume is a
rich, readable resource that will lead to a deepened understanding of this biblical book that
is saturated with Old Testament quotations, themes, images, allusions, and echoes. Longman
proves to be a sure guide on a book that many have ignored, misread, or found mystifying."
—Paul Copan, Pledger Family Chair of Philosophy and Ethics, Palm Beach Atlantic
University; and author of *Is God a Moral Monster?* and *Is God a Vindictive Bully?*

"It is almost a truism that it is impossible to understand the New Testament without
understanding the Old. Not so widely known is that the book of Revelation has more
Old Testament allusions than any other book in the New. It follows that the key for
understanding the symbols of Revelation is *not* the latest news cycle in the Middle East
(as claimed by many so-called 'prophecy experts'). It is the Old Testament! And there is no
more sure-footed guide to this mysterious book than a premier Old Testament scholar like
Tremper Longman. This exceptionally clear and cogent commentary will open your eyes
to this capstone volume of the New Testament like never before."
—Mark L. Strauss, University Professor of New Testament, Bethel Seminary

"In an age of increasing biblical illiteracy even in the church, and especially the lack of
knowledge of the Old Testament in the church, it is refreshing to have a whole series of
books dedicated to 'seeing the New Testament through Old Testament eyes.' Not only so,
but we are invited to see it through the eyes of excellent, seasoned Old Testament scholars
like Tremper Longman, who takes on the formidable task of reading Revelation in that
way. There are few scholars I'd rather have do such a sensitive and sensible reading than
Professor Longman. He is well aware of the nature of apocalyptic prophecy, understands
the back and forth of the Christological use of the Old Testament by New Testament
writers like John of Patmos, while at the same time doing justice to the way John has been
influenced in his interpretation of the Christ event by the Old Testament, especially Isaiah.
In short, to really get into a place where one can understand John's Scripture-saturated
mind (which involves many more allusions and echoes than Old Testament quotes) you
need a guide who himself has a Scripture-saturated mind. Tremper Longman is your man,
for he has labored long in the scriptural vineyard, and always provides us with the good
fruit of careful interpretation."
—Ben Witherington III,
Amos Professor of New Testament for Doctoral Studies, Asbury Theological Seminary

Through Old Testament Eyes

New Testament Commentaries

Series Editor: Andrew T. Le Peau

A BACKGROUND AND APPLICATION COMMENTARY

REVELATION

THROUGH OLD TESTAMENT EYES

Tremper Longman III

ANDREW T. LE PEAU
SERIES EDITOR

KREGEL
ACADEMIC

Revelation Through Old Testament Eyes: A Background and Application Commentary
© 2022 by Tremper Longman III

Published by Kregel Academic, an imprint of Kregel Publications, 2450 Oak Industrial Dr. NE, Grand Rapids, MI 49505-6020.

All rights reserved. No part of this book may be reproduced, stored in a retrieval system, or transmitted in any form or by any means—electronic, mechanical, photocopy, recording, or otherwise—without written permission of the publisher, except for brief quotations in printed reviews.

All Scripture quotations, unless otherwise indicated, are from the Holy Bible, New International Version®, NIV®. Copyright © 1973, 1978, 1984, 2011 by Biblica, Inc.™ Used by permission of Zondervan. All rights reserved worldwide. www.zondervan.com

Scripture quotations marked CSB have been taken from the Christian Standard Bible®, Copyright © 2017 by Holman Bible Publishers. Used by permission. Christian Standard Bible® and CSB® are federally registered trademarks of Holman Bible Publishers.

Scripture quotations marked ESV are from The Holy Bible, English Standard Version® (ESV®), copyright © 2001 by Crossway, a publishing ministry of Good News Publishers. Used by permission. All rights reserved.

Scripture quotations marked NAB are from the New American Bible. Copyright © 1970, 1986, 1991 by Confraternity of Christian Doctrine. All rights reserved.

Scripture quotations marked NLT are from the Holy Bible, New Living Translation, copyright © 1996, 2004, 2007 by Tyndale House Foundation. Used by permission of Tyndale House Publishers, Inc., Carol Stream, Illinois 60188. All rights reserved.

Scripture quotations marked NRSV are from the New Revised Standard Version Bible, copyright © 1989 by the National Council of the Churches of Christ in the U.S.A. Used by permission. All rights reserved.

Scripture quotations marked RSV are from the Revised Standard Version of the Bible, copyright © 1946, 1952, and 1971 by the National Council of the Churches of Christ in the U.S.A. Used by permission. All rights reserved.

ISBN 978-0-8254-4473-9

Printed in the United States of America

23 24 25 26 / 5 4 3 2

To my six beautiful granddaughters
Gabrielle Gagnon Longman
Mia Katherine Longman
Ava Rae Longman
Emerson Foster Longman
Samantha Tremper Longman
Lydia Eastwick Longman

CONTENTS

SERIES PREFACE

The New Testament writers were Old Testament people. Their minds were populated with Old Testament stories and concepts. Their imaginative world was furnished with Old Testament images, motifs, metaphors, symbols, and literary patterns. When Jesus came and turned much of their conventional wisdom on its head, they largely had Old Testament tools to understand what was going on in order to explain Jesus to others and to themselves. So that's what they used.

For many Christians the Old Testament has, unfortunately, become a closed book. It seems long, mysterious, and boring with a confusing history full of many strange, unpronounceable names. And then there are those sometimes bizarre prophecies populated with strange creatures. Yet my consistent experience in teaching the New Testament is that when I turn the attention of students to relevant Old Testament passages, the proverbial light bulbs go on. The room is filled with "aha"s. Formerly obscure New Testament passages suddenly make new sense in light of the Old. Indeed the whole of each book of the New Testament takes on fuller, richer dimensions not seen before.

The purpose of the Through Old Testament Eyes commentaries is to give preachers, teachers, and other readers this same experience. This series opens the New Testament in greater depth to anyone who wants to see fresh ways that Scripture interconnects with Scripture.

Scholars have long known that the Old Testament influenced the New Testament (an idea known as intertextuality). In fact, more than a millennia and a half ago Augustine famously proposed that we understand the relationship of the two testaments in this way: "The new is in the old concealed; the old is in the new revealed." Yet no commentary series is as devoted as this one is to seeing the richness of Old Testament allusions, references, echoes, and background to illuminate both puzzling passages and explain others in fresh ways.

Practices like baptism, meals, fishing, and fasting; concepts like rescue, faith, sin, and glory; and terms like "wilderness," "Sabbath," and "Lord" are just a few of the dozens of words in each New Testament book and letter with deep Old Testament resonances. Sometimes a narrative arc or an argument is also shaped by the Old Testament. An appreciation of this background enriches our understanding and helps us appropriately apply each passage.

In these commentaries you will find four repeating features which will enrich your encounter with the Scripture.

Running Commentary

Verse-by-verse or paragraph-by-paragraph commentary will include Old Testament background as well as other key information, to give readers an understanding of the text as a whole and to answer questions as they naturally arise.

Through Old Testament Eyes

Periodic summaries offer overviews of chapters or sections. These occasional pauses give the opportunity to step back from the detail to see the bigger picture of how Old Testament themes and motifs are being used by the New Testament authors.

What the Structure Means

New Testament authors often get their points across through the way they structure their material. The very organization of their writing conveys significant meaning in and of itself. How the events and teachings are linked makes a difference that, while not explicit, is an important part of the message. Again it is important to not take verses out of context as if they were timeless truths standing apart from their original settings, which affect how we understand them.

The authors of the New Testament also deliberately use, for example, repetition, contrast, hyperbole, metaphor, story, and other techniques so they can have the maximum impact on their readers. "What the Structure Means" will highlight these every so often and help us keep track of the overall flow of each book and letter so that the Old Testament background can be seen in its proper context.

Going Deeper

New Testament writers did not want merely to convey information. They wrote with the needs of the early church in mind. What should their attitude be toward family members who weren't Christians? How should they respond to challenges from Jewish or Roman authorities?

What about internal disputes within the church? These and many other issues were on their minds, and the New Testament addresses them and many more.

Through Old Testament Eyes commentaries will not only leave readers with an enriched understanding of the text but with enriched lives. In "Going Deeper" the authors will unpack the practical implications of each book and letter for Christians and churches, especially drawing from the Old Testament dimensions uncovered in the text.

As much as this series champions the importance of understanding the New Testament's use of the Old, two key points need to be mentioned. First, the Old Testament is not merely a tool for understanding the New. The Old Testament is important and valuable in its own right. It was the Bible of Jesus and the first Christians. They guided their lives by it. The Old Testament needs to be and deserves to be understood on its own terms, apart from the lens it provides for seeing the New Testament clearly. All the commentary authors in this series begin just here as they approach the text. In fact, our hope is that these commentaries will be a window into the Old Testament that will motivate many readers to look more deeply into what some have called the First Testament.

Second, the Old Testament is not the only interpretive lens we need to understand the New. Roman and Greek culture and history, for example, had a very significant influence on the New Testament era. So did the Second Temple period (from the start of rebuilding the temple about 537 BC to the destruction of the temple by Rome in AD 70). Where essential, these commentaries will reference such background material. But the emphasis will be on providing in-depth Old Testament background that readers too often overlook.

While these commentaries are grounded in solid scholarship, they are not intended primarily for an academic audience. For this reason many topics, approaches, and debates found in technical commentaries are absent. This series is for those who want to teach or preach, as well as any serious reader committed to understand Scripture.

The past is always present. The question is: Are we aware of how it affects us or not? The Old Testament was present with the New Testament writers. They knew that and treasured it. We can too.

—Andrew T. Le Peau
Series Editor

INTRODUCTION AND MAIN THEME OF THE BOOK OF REVELATION

Ask most people who read the Bible, casually or seriously, and a large percentage will say that the book of Revelation is hard to understand. Not only that, but they find it strange, even bizarre. In one sense, I can't blame them. The first three chapters are relatively "tame," but even in the introduction and the letters to the seven churches we read about one "coming with the clouds" (1:7), "the mystery of seven stars" and "seven golden lampstands" (1:20). The glorified Christ rebukes a group called the Nicolaitans (2:6, 15), a "synagogue of Satan" (2:9), those "who hold to the teaching of Balaam," 2:14), and "that woman Jezebel" (2:20). Churches that resist the temptation to compromise are promised "hidden manna" as well as a "white stone with a new name written on it" (2:17).

When readers reach the visions that start in Revelation 4 and extend to the end, the imagery seems overwhelming. A short list includes a seven-sealed scroll, four horsemen bringing destruction and death, 144,000 people with a seal on their foreheads, horselike locusts from the Abyss with scorpion tails and faces like humans, a woman battling a dragon, a beast from the sea and a beast from the earth, and a great prostitute called Babylon the Great. This constitutes just a few of the things that confound most modern readers of the book.

The difficulty, though, is not because of the complexity of the book of Revelation, but rather because we modern readers are unfamiliar with imagery that would have been known to its first readers. These images, for the most part, were not created out of thin air, but have a background not only in first-century-AD Greco-Roman culture but also in the Old Testament, which itself has its background in ancient Near Eastern literature.

Thus, it is important to familiarize ourselves with that background. This commentary has as its focus Revelation's Old Testament background. It's important to recognize that Revelation is not as esoteric as many assume, because some writers take advantage of a modern reader's (and often their own) lack of knowledge of the background to make all kinds of outlandish claims about the message of the book of Revelation. This includes those who might use the book as a source to predict the timing and nature of Christ's return.

Recent well-known popular treatments would include those by Hal Lindsey, Harold Camping, Tim LaHaye, and many Sunday morning TV preachers.

Truth be told, Revelation's main theme is as clear as day: despite present trouble, God is in control, and he will have the final victory. God wins in the end, even though his people at the present live in a toxic culture and are marginalized and even persecuted. This leads to a secondary theme: hope that leads to perseverance. Starting in the letters to the seven churches but continuing through the visions, the author's purpose is to engender hope in the hearts of his Christian readers so that they will have the resolve to withstand the turbulent present.[1] Of course, these messages are for those who respond to John's admonition to hear the book "and take to heart what is written in it" (1:3). Those who don't will find judgment or, as the glorified Christ warned the church of Ephesus, have their lampstand taken away (2:5).

Author and Date

The very first chapter of Revelation makes it clear that the book was written by John. He was the one who received the revelation that constitutes the contents of the book. God revealed the visions of the book "by sending his angel to his servant John, who testifies to everything he saw" (Rev 1:1–2). John then writes a letter to the "seven churches in the province of Asia" (Rev 1:4; the letters themselves in Revelation 2–3 come from the glorified Christ). He further discloses that at the time he received the revelation from God and wrote the letter, he was on the island of Patmos (Rev 1:9), presumably in exile because of his faith (see note at 1:9). In this verse, he identifies himself with the recipients of his letter as their "brother and companion in the suffering and kingdom and patient endurance that are ours in Jesus." At the end of the book, he summarily states, "I, John, am the one who heard and saw these things. And when I had heard and seen them, I fell down to worship at the feet of the angel who had been showing them to me" (22:8). Though John only appears by name in these four mentioned verses, he makes his presence known through many first-person references.

Thus, the book clearly claims to have John as its originator and author. But who is John? Or another way to ask this question is, "Which John?" After all, John was a popular name during the first century after Christ. Besides some minor characters, there are at least two and more likely three Johns who play a significant role in the New Testament, though only two are likely candidates.

The first John mentioned in the Gospels is John the Baptist, but he is certainly not the author of the book of Revelation. He was the herald who announced the coming of the Messiah at the beginning of Jesus' ministry (Mt 3). But John was executed by Herod before the crucifixion of Christ (Mt 14:1–12), so he was not alive at the time the book was written (see below).

Perhaps the most likely candidate for the authorship of Revelation is John the Apostle,[2] who is also credited with writing the Gospel of John, though he is not so named in the Gospel. John was part of the inner circle of disciples (Lk 8:51) and was a witness, along with Peter, of the transfiguration of Christ (Mt 17:1–13). He also played a leading role in the development of the church after the resurrection of Christ, even being arrested along with Peter for his public witness to Jesus (Ac 4:1–22).

But in the modern era the idea that John the Apostle wrote Revelation has been challenged, mainly on the grounds that the language of the Gospel of John and Revelation could not come from the same person.[3] Among those who reject the authorship of John the Apostle, many say that the book of Revelation was written by the author of the three letters of John, who is actually not named in these three letters beyond being called the "elder" (2 Jn 1:1; 3 Jn 1:1). Tradition, though, names the elder John, some thinking that John the Elder is the same as John the Apostle, and others who think they are two different people.

So who is the John who wrote Revelation? John the Apostle? John the Elder? A third man named John? No one knows for sure. Fortunately, the exact identity of John the author of Revelation is unimportant for the meaning of the book. We will simply refer to the author as John.

But when did John write Revelation? The answer to this question too is uncertain since no date is explicitly provided. Of course, since the church seems well established in western Asia Minor, as the reference to the churches in the seven letters in Revelation 2–3 make clear, we are talking some decades after the death of Christ. The book also indicates conflict between the church and Rome so that one of the main purposes of the book is to encourage its readers to persevere in the face of opposition and even persecution. Still there is no explicit mention of specific Roman emperors or specific historical events.

On the other hand, Revelation 13:18 (see commentary) informs the reader that the number of the beast is 666, which besides being a number of imperfection is suggestive of the name of Nero who ruled the Roman Empire from AD 54 to 68. In AD 64 a great fire broke out in Rome that Nero blamed on Christians, who were then persecuted. The Roman historian Tacitus wrote that Nero himself set the fire and used Christians as a scapegoat.

Nero died at the young age of thirty-one, likely having taken his own life. There then arose particularly in the eastern part of the Empire a myth that he would come back from the dead. Some scholars connect this Nero Redivivus myth to the statement that the beast "seemed to have had a fatal wound, but the fatal wound had been healed" (Rev 13:3).

Thus, some scholars believe that Revelation was written soon after the time of Nero, perhaps in the late 60s. But even if, as seems likely, these references in Revelation do allude to Nero, that does not require that the book be written that early.

An argument is also to be made that the book was written in the 90s during the reign of another persecutor of Christians, namely Domitian who ruled the Roman Empire from AD 81–96. The arguments in favor of this later date include the fact that emperor worship, about which John warns in Revelation, was more developed by this time. Also, as Metzger and deSilva point out, the church at Smyrna, according to the testimony of Polycarp who served as bishop in that city in the early second century, did not form until after Paul, making a date in the sixties unlikely. Also, they point out that Laodicea, described as wealthy in 3:17, suffered an earthquake in AD 61 and so it is unlikely that they regained their status as early as the end of that decade.[4] This view is the majority view not only today but among the leaders of the early church (e.g., Irenaeus writing around AD 180).

The weight of the evidence tilts toward a later date in the first century AD for the composition of the book of Revelation, though we cannot be dogmatic. Fortunately, as with the exact identification of the author, the specific date of composition also does not bear on the meaning of the book.

Genre Triggers Reading Strategy

Authors send signals to readers as to how to take their words. A commonly cited and obvious example of such a signal is a story that begins "once upon a time." Unless an author is trying to be mischievous, readers know that what follows is a fairy tale.

This is not the place to develop a nuanced genre theory which would take account of fuzzy boundaries between genres, the acknowledgment that literary texts actually participate in multiple genres (though some are more influential on our reading than others), the pros and cons of using modern literary categories to describe ancient genres, and so forth.[5] For our present purpose, it will suffice to focus briefly on the main genres of the book with a focus on how it affects our reading strategy. Interestingly, the book rather obviously communicates its genres through its form and through self-identification.

The form of the book is a letter. There are seven individual letters in which the glorified Christ writes to different churches in Asia Minor (Rev 2–3), but we should not miss the signal that the entirety of the book—the seven letters and the visions—is a letter written by John "to the seven churches in the province of Asia" (Rev 1:4), which has a benediction upon the recipients of the letter typical to letters of the time period. That the whole book is a letter is confirmed by the ending benediction on the reader, again typical of letters of the time.

That the book of Revelation is in the form of a letter is a reminder that the contents of the book address the existential issues of the church at the time of its writing. We can see also from the contents of the seven letters that the churches were marginalized and threatened by the wider culture. We also learn that some of the churches and individual Christians were tempted to give in to the pressure and compromise their faith. They needed to hear a message of hope and receive encouragement to persevere.

And that is where the second genre comes in. The very first verse of the book identifies it as a "revelation from Jesus Christ" (Rev 1:1). The word "revelation" translates the Greek word *apokalupsis* and gives us our English word "apocalypse." Revelation is an apocalypse. True, the book identifies itself as a "prophecy" (1:3; 22:7, 10, 18, 19), but an apocalypse is a prophecy of a distinct type. Revelation is such an apocalypse bearing formal and content similarities with Daniel and other Jewish and Christian apocalypses of antiquity.

Again, this is not the place to give a lengthy definition of the apocalyptic genre. Here I will just list the leading features of an apocalypse which we see manifest in the book of Revelation, followed by a brief statement of how that should guide our readerly expectations. We begin with the statement that an apocalypse like Revelation shares with other prophecy like, say, Jeremiah, an interest in the future. They also both are interested in the future not for its own sake but to generate a response from their contemporary readers. However, the reason for this future orientation differs between them. Jeremiah presents a picture of the future, which is largely conditional, with the hope that his hearers/readers will repent. John in Revelation presents the future, indeed including a much more distant future, to evoke hope in his readers who are in sore need of it.

Another feature of apocalyptic literature is how the future is portrayed, and this may be the most important matter for modern readers to keep in mind. As Revelation looks to the future, it pictures that future using highly figurative language, indeed much of it derived from the Old Testament and ancient Near Eastern mythic language (beasts from the sea and a divine figure riding a cloud are two obvious examples). Thus, it becomes important for readers to realize the figurative nature of the language to understand the message of the author. We do not need to dwell on this feature since that is the heart of this commentary: to recognize and explain how Revelation uses the Old Testament to communicate its important message.

Even though this discussion will be carried on in the commentary itself, it is important to provide a few general observations to prepare us for what follows. How are we to take the figurative language of the book of Revelation? There are three main options: literally, as symbols pointing to a concrete literal reality, or as pointing to a more general literal reality. To illustrate, I will refer to the description found in Revelation 9:3–11 of locusts that emerge from the Abyss when the fifth angel sounded his trumpet. These locusts are described as having the tails and power of scorpions. They wear crowns and have human-like faces with hair like women and teeth like lions. They have breastplates like iron and wings.

It stretches the imagination that this describes a literal locust plague considering the hybrid nature of these locusts and, as we will observe in the commentary proper, the figurative use of even ordinary locusts in the Old Testament. Some, though, believe that the metaphors of Revelation, including this one, point to a specific reference that bears what they consider to be similarities to these locusts. That these locusts fly, have hardened shells, and are here described as having stingers led Hal Lindsey to say that they predicted a future helicopter attack. This type of reading results from a faulty belief that the referent can be found at the time of the interpreter, in this case Hal Lindsey.

It is much more reasonable to understand the analogy in more general terms. These fearful, hybrid locusts stand for horrific devastation that could take many different forms. They could point to war or to environmental devastation or any number of things. The main teaching is that God will bring judgment on sinful humanity.

But is the book of Revelation talking about the past, the present, or the future? The short answer is yes. All of the above. While some people think that Revelation is all about the future and indeed all about the end times, the book speaks to its contemporary audience by describing what they are presently experiencing, namely marginalization and even persecution, and encouraging them to remain faithful and obedient in the present. While the letters clearly address the issues confronting John's contemporary church, the visions do as well. That said, Revelation is not all about the present and the past; the book does look to the future and indeed to God's final intervention in history to defeat evil and bring his church to himself.

Thus, the original readers would have recognized the relevance of the letters and the visions to their present situation even as John speaks about the future. But what about us? In particular, what about the church in the twenty-first century? One of the reasons why the church recognized Revelation as canonical, and thus part of our standard of faith and practice, is that the church knew that the book of Revelation would remain relevant throughout the ages.

Why? Because the church will always to the end of the history be under threat of marginalization and persecution. Christians have always and will always live in a culture that is toxic to their faith. Western, and particularly American, Christians sometimes lose sight of this because they live with the fiction that our culture or our nation or our government is or should be Christian. First, this belief is false as is becoming increasingly clear; and second, this belief is dangerous, as the wedding of political power and Christian faith has time and time again led not to the strengthening of the church but to its weakening.[6] Indeed, the message of Revelation is to not give up on the faith by falling in lockstep with the culture. This message, by the way, is not a call to culture war but rather to faithful living in the midst of the culture.[7] But of course, the church is global, not western. I start with the American church because that is my social location and will almost certainly be the location of most of my readers. I will simply say, though, that as Americans we should never lose sight of the fact that many of our brothers and sisters in other parts of the world live in a context that is more like that in which John lived. They live in nations where they are the minority and/or marginalized and perhaps even persecuted. They will not share the myth that they live in a Christian context. They know their culture is toxic and even dangerous to the faith. Revelation's message of present perseverance and future hope will be readily and encouragingly received.

OUTLINE OF REVELATION

Introduction to the Book and the Seven Letters (1–3)

Superscription and Blessing (1:1–3)

Greetings and Doxology (1:4–8)

The Glorified Christ Commissions John (1:9–20)

The Letter to the Church in Ephesus (2:1–7)

The Letter to the Church in Smyrna (2:8–11)

The Letter to the Church in Pergamum (2:12–17)

The Letter to the Church in Thyatira (2:18–29)

The Letter to the Church in Sardis (3:1–6)

The Letter to the Church in Philadelphia (3:7–13)

The Letter to the Church in Laodicea (3:14–22)

Christ Opens the Seven Seals of the Scroll (4:1–8:5)

The Lamb Worthy to Open the Scroll? (4–5)

The Heavenly Throne (4:1–11)

Who Is Worthy?—the Lion of Judah, the Root of David! (5:1–5)

The Lamb of God Takes the Scroll (5:6–7)

The Four Living Creatures and the Twenty-Four Elders Sing a New Song (5:8–10)

Thousands of Angels and Every Creature Join in the Worship (5:11–13)

Four Living Creatures and the Elders Say "Amen" (5:14)

The Seven Seals (6:1–8:5)

The First Seal (6:1–2)

The Second Seal (6:3–4)

The Third Seal (6:5–6)

The Fourth Seal (6:7–8)

The Fifth Seal (6:9–11)

The Sixth Seal (6:12–17)

Interlude: The 144,000 and the Great Multitude (7:1–17)

The Seventh Seal (8:1–5)

The Seven Trumpets (8:6–11:19)

The First Trumpet (8:6–7)

The Second Trumpet (8:8–9)

The Third Trumpet (8:10–11)

The Fourth Angel (8:12)

Interlude: An Eagle's Funeral Lament (8:13)

The Fifth Trumpet (9:1–11)

Interlude: One Woe Done; Two to Go (9:12)

The Sixth Trumpet (9:13–21)

Interlude: The Little Scroll (10:1–11)

Interlude: The Two Witnesses (11:1–13)

Interlude: Two Woes Done; One to Go (11:14)

The Seventh Trumpet (11:15–19)

The Woman versus the Dragon, the Land Beast, and the Sea Beast (12–13)

The Dragon Pursues the Woman (12:1–17)

The Sea Beast (13:1–10)

The Second Beast from the Earth (13:11–18)

The 144,000 (Again), Three Angels, Harvesting and Trampling (14)

The 144,000 Sing a New Song (14:1–5)

Warnings from Three Angels (14:6–13)

Reaping the Harvest (Salvation) and Trampling the Grapes (Judgment) (14:14–20)

The Seven Bowls of God's Wrath (15–16)

Presentation of the Bowls and Angelic Commission (15:1–16:1)

The First Bowl (16:2)

The Second Bowl (16:3)

The Third Bowl (16:4–7)

The Fourth Bowl (16:8–9)

The Fifth Bowl (16:10–11)

The Sixth Bowl (16:12–16)

The Seventh Bowl (16:17–21)

The Demise of the Great Prostitute (17:1–19:10)

The Great Prostitute Riding the Beast (17:1–6)

The Mystery Explained (17:7–18)

Lament over the Destruction of Babylon (18:1–3)

God's People Warned to Leave (18:4–8)

Three Woes over Destroyed Babylon (18:9–19)

The Kings of the Earth (18:9–10)

The Merchants (18:11–17a)

Sea Captains and Sailors (18:17b-19)

Rejoice! (18:20)

The End of Babylon the Great (18:21–24)

Hallelujahs over the Destruction of Babylon (19:1–10)

The Final Telling of God's Ultimate Victory (19:11–20:15)

Jesus the Warrior Wins the Final Battle (19:11–21)

The Dragon Bound a Thousand Years (20:1–6)

The End of the Devil (20:7–10)

The Final Judgment (20:11–15)

The Future World (21:1–22:5)

A New Heaven and a New Earth (21:1–8)

The New Jerusalem (21:9–27)

A Return to Eden—Only Better (22:1–5)

Conclusion (22:6–21)

Final Angelic Instructions (22:6–11)

Jesus' Final Announcements and Warnings (22:12–21)

Structure

The outline above makes clear the general contour and major sections of the book of Revelation. I have included the elements of this outline throughout this commentary to indicate key sections, but a few comments are in order as to how the various major parts relate to one another.

The book has a clear beginning, opening with a superscription (1:1–3) that names its genre or contents, a "revelation (or apocalypse) from Jesus Christ." The superscription also names the human intermediary of this revelation, since John received it from an angel. The opening concludes with a blessing pronounced on the one who reads the prophecy aloud and those who hear it and take it seriously. David deSilva highlights the fact that this book was supposed to be read out loud and heard rather than read.[8]

The opening then moves to a greeting by John to the addressees of the book, namely the seven churches in the province of Asia on which he pronounces a doxology. This introductory section ends with an exclamation that Jesus is coming on the clouds and a solemn first statement from the glorified Christ himself that he is the "Alpha and Omega . . . who is, and who was, and who is to come, the Almighty" (1:8).

John, as many prophets in the Old Testament do, also tells the reader the story of his divine commissioning, which intends to bolster his claim to authority (1:9–20). Like Moses at the burning bush (Ex 3), Isaiah in the temple (Isa 6), or Ezekiel by the Kebar River (Eze 1–3), John gives a vivid picture of his encounter with the glorified Christ on the island of Patmos where he is living, presumably in exile. Christ commissions him to write what he sees and send it to seven churches in Asia Minor.[9]

Not surprisingly, then, in the next two chapters (Rev 2–3), we read seven letters to churches in cities which, when plotted on a map, suggest the route a messenger would take to visit those seven cities. (For detail, see "What the Structure Means: The Letters to the Seven Churches [Rev. 2–3].") Since the seven churches were different in their responses to the faith challenges that they faced, the letters are quite different from each other in content, but all seven share a common purpose and a common structure. (See "What the Structure Means: The Outline of the Seven Letters [Rev. 2–3].") The purpose was to encourage the Christians in these churches with hope, while also exhorting them to remain faithful, or in some cases to repent.

A significant transition occurs between Revelation 3 and 4. The seventh and final letter is read to the church in Laodicea, and the remainder of the book contains visions that John has experienced. As we will remark again when we consider the closing of the book, it is clear, though, that these visions were also addressed to the seven churches. It is equally clear, thanks to the symbolic nature of the number seven which implies completeness or totality, that these seven churches represent the church universal of the time. These visions that show God's ultimate victory over evil serve to encourage the churches to remain faithful.

In terms of contents, the transition from letters to reports of visions is abrupt and marked by a simple connective "after this" (4:1). Still the visions themselves support the main message that runs throughout the book, which is that despite present troubles God is in control, and he will have the final victory. Therefore, persist in your faith and remain obedient to God. Don't succumb to the evil forces in the world.

Right away John is caught up into the heavenly throne room, which he describes in its magnificence. God's throne is in the center of the picture, surrounded by four living creatures and twenty-four elders (representing the Old Testament and New Testament people of God). They give God honor and full-throated worship (Rev 4). The throne is the control center for all the activity that the visions describe.

After taking all this in, John's attention is drawn to the right hand of God which holds a scroll. A mighty angel asks whether there is one who is worthy to open the scroll that has seven seals. While at first John believes that no one will be found, one of the elders tells him to look at the Lion of the tribe of Judah, the Root of David (5:5). His worthiness is rooted in his triumph, which points to his death and resurrection. When John sees him, he calls him, not the Lion of Judah, but the "Lamb, looking as if it had been slain" and standing at the center of the throne, thus closely identified with God who is sitting on the throne, and receiving worship (5:6–14).

At that point, the Lamb opens the seven seals one by one. With the first four seals, judgment comes on the earth via the famous four horsemen with increasing in intensity. The opening of the fifth seal does not bring judgment, but a description of the martyrs who cry out for justice (6:9–11), followed by the sixth seal (6:12–14), the opening of which results in territorial and cosmic convulsions leading to fear on the part of the wicked. Surprisingly, an interlude occurs between the sixth and the seventh seal. Revelation 7 speaks of the 144,000 from all the tribes of Israel who receive a seal on their forehead to preserve them from the judgment. After this John looks and he sees a great diverse multitude before the throne and the Lamb worshipping God. These were those who persisted in "the great tribulation" (7:14) and now are with God and the Lamb. In the commentary we will present arguments that suggest that the 144,000 and the "great multitude" are the same group of people, God's faithful followers.

After this interlude, the Lamb opens the seventh climactic seal (8:1–5). But notice that before the seventh seal is opened, John saw "seven angels who stand before God, and seven trumpets were given to them" (8:2). In this way, John presages the next major section, raising the question of how the trumpets relate to the seals. Once the glorified Christ opens the seventh seal there is momentary silence before an angel throws a censor to the earth which produces "peals of thunder, rumblings, flashes of lightning, and an earthquake" (8:5)

By narrating the emergence of the seven trumpet-bearing angels before the seventh scroll, we see that there is overlap between the picture of judgment: as the unsealing of seven scrolls, and as the blowing of seven trumpets. Indeed, it is best to understand the trumpet judgments not as seven additional and subsequent judgments but as a recapitulation of the same judgments (not new ones)—but perhaps moving closer to a crescendo. This understanding is furthered by some parallels found between the seal and the trumpet judgments, including the first four trumpets forming a unit, the presence of interludes, as well as similarity in the seventh judgment.

Like the first four seals picturing the emergence of the four horsemen, the judgments following the blowing of the first four trumpets are briefly told and form a unit (8:1–12). This section is also separated from what follows by an interlude of an eagle announcing the woes of the following three trumpet blasts (8:13).

The fifth trumpet announces a star that represents an angel that falls into the sea, who opens the Abyss, loosing fearful hybrid locusts that torture those they sting with their scorpion-like tails (9:1–11). John announces that this is the first of the threefold woes announced by the angel, with two more to come (9:12). The sixth trumpet blast announces the release of four angels who kill a third of mankind. They bring three plagues on humankind (9:13–19); even so, the survivors chose not to repent (9:20–21).

As we saw with the seals, interludes delay the reporting of the seventh trumpet blast. In the first interlude John sees an angel come down from heaven with a little scroll in his hand. After declaring that there will be no more delay, the angel gives John the scroll and obeys the angel's instructions to eat it, thus signifying that John will prophesy to the diverse peoples of the earth (10:11).

Next comes a second interlude concerning two witnesses who represent the church as it testifies to the world (11:1–13). They have great power, but still a beast that comes up from the Abyss is able to kill them. However, though their bodies are put on display to the joy of those against whom they spoke, they were soon raised from the dead, like their Lord, and taken up into heaven.

After this vignette, we hear that the second woe (referring back to the sixth trumpet) has passed and the third woe comes soon (11:14). The seventh angel then blew his horn followed by worship (rather than the silence of the seventh seal). But like the seventh seal, the seventh trumpet produces "flashes of lightning, rumblings, peals of thunder, and earthquake and a severe hailstorm" (11:19). The similarity supports the idea that the relationship between the seals and the trumpets is that the judgments are being recapitulated.

Revelation 12–13 presents what appears to be a separate and discrete vision that connects to the previous section with a simple "and" (*kai*; 12:1). But it bears similarities to the vision of the two witnesses that served as an interlude between the sixth and seventh trumpet blasts (Rev 11:1–13). The two witnesses represent the church who come under attack from the beast that comes up from the Abyss. While not escaping suffering or even death, the two witnesses are ultimately protected by and cared for by God and those who celebrated their demise were punished. In the vision found in Revelation 12–13 a pregnant woman described in cosmic terms now represents the church. Her evil adversary is a seven-headed red dragon with ten horns and seven crowns who represents Satan (12:9). As the woman (who may also stand for Mary) gives birth to a male child, representing Jesus, the dragon tries to devour the child. God takes the child into heaven and sends the woman to a safe place he prepared for her in the wilderness.

Revelation 13 turns attention to the emergence of beasts that are allies with the dragon in its war against God's people. The first is a beast from the sea, also with multiple heads, horns, and crowns (13:1–10), which represents Rome and other worldly powers. This beast will wage war against "God's holy people" as it rules over "every tribe, people, language and nation" (13:7). This beast becomes the object of worship (13:4).

The second beast emerges from the earth. It had a benign appearance ("two horns like a lamb"), but "it spoke like a dragon" (13:11). Later in Revelation this second beast is called a false prophet (16:13; 19:20; 20:10). The false prophet's goal was to compel people to worship the sea beast, for whom he erected an image which he then animated, and marking converts by putting a mark on their right hand or forehead that would allow them to participate in the economic life of the community. As explained in the commentary, the dragon, the sea beast, and the earth beast form a kind of unholy trinity, mimicking the Father, the Son, and the Holy Spirit.

Revelation 14 provides a counter-picture to the description of those who follow the unholy trinity and in particular worship the image of the sea beast. Rather than the mark of the beast on their hand or forehead, the 144,000 who worship the Lamb on Mount Zion have the Lamb's name and the Father's name written on their foreheads (14:1–5). Three angels then fly across the sky, the first calling on people to fear God in the light of the coming judgment, the second announces the fall of "Babylon the Great," a soon-to-be developed symbol for Rome and other evil human kingdoms (16:19; 17:1, 5; throughout 18), and the third announcing fearsome judgment against those who worship the beast and his image and receive his mark (14:6–13). The chapter ends with two heavenly beings each with a sickle, the first reaping the harvest (a positive image of gathering the faithful), while the other gathers clusters of grapes and throws them into the winepress out of which blood freely flows (a negative image of judgment).

We come to the third and final cycle of seven judgments, this time depicted as angels who pour out the contents of their bowls that lead to devastation. The second cycle (trumpets, 8:6–11:9) followed quickly on the heels of the first (seals, 6:1–8:5). They were also linked by the angels, with trumpets coming out immediately before the opening of the seventh seal. However, the cycle of seven bowls does not come right after the trumpets but after a separate vision. Still there are connections of this third cycle with the first two, as we will see. There is also a link with the immediately previous vision when it is introduced as "another great and marvelous sign," which refers back to the "great sign" that introduces the vision of the pregnant woman and the dragon and his beastly underlings (12:1; 15:1).

This third cycle recapitulates the judgments of the first two cycles in a kind of spiral fashion. In other words, they are not twenty-one separate sequential judgments, but rather a rehearsal using different imagery of the same judgment, though the case can be made that this third sequence of seven does take matters further. First there are no delaying interludes, giving the impression of rapidity. Further, we read by way of introduction that these are "the seven last plagues—last because with them God's wrath is completed" (15:1) and with the pouring of the seventh bowl, we hear a loud voice from the heavenly throne, presumably God's, announcing "It is done!" (16:17).

Just before the angels initially come with their bowls, those saints who had persisted despite their persecution worship God (15:3–4). Afterward, they pour out the contents of their bowls one by one. Similar to the first four seals and trumpets, the first four bowls form a unit by virtue of their brief narration (though the third is a little longer) and by the sequence of bringing harm to the earth, sea, rivers and springs, and celestial bodies, similar to the trumpets.

The fifth angel poured out the contents of his bowl on the throne of the beast (another linkage to the previous vision), so that its kingdom was plunged into darkness and its worshippers suffered agonizing pain. Still they did not repent (16:11; cf. 9:20–21). The pouring out of the contents of the sixth bowl dried up the Euphrates (the river that at the time separated the Roman Empire from the feared Parthians). Three frogs then come out of the mouth of the dragon, the beast, and the false prophet. These demonic spirits perform signs that result in the gathering of the kings of all the earth to a place called Armageddon, "for the battle of the great day of God Almighty" (16:14).

The seventh bowl produces meteorological and terrestrial convulsions reminiscent of the seventh seal and the seventh trumpet: "there came flashes of lightning, rumblings, peals of thunder and a severe earthquake" (16:18). However, there is an escalation in the damage that these phenomena cause on the earth.

The next vision is simply introduced in the Greek (not translated by the NIV) by *kai* ("and" or "then"). Still, the link to the previous episode of the pouring of the seven bowls is provided when John tells the reader that "one of the seven angels who had the seven bowls" served as his guide during the vision.

The vision, the subject of 17:3–6, starts with a description of a decadent prostitute, who is later identified as Babylon the Great, a cipher for Rome. Revelation 18 contains reactions to the fall of Babylon the Great (and is connected to the vision by the simple "after this"). An angel first announces the fall followed by another voice from heaven, likely the glorified Christ, urging his people to leave the city and thus avoid being collateral damage (18:1–8). A second and much different negative reaction comes from those kings, merchants, and sea captains who benefited from the prostitute who represents Babylon the Great, which represents Rome (18:9–17). The tone changes yet again from sadness to joy as we hear the heavenly and earthly followers of God rejoice over her downfall (18:20). Then an angel picks up a boulder and throws it into the sea to doom Babylon the Great (18:21–24).

The transition from Revelation 18 to 19 is again marked by a simple "after this," which then leads to a great multitude in heaven singing praises; they are joined by the twenty-four elders and four living creatures (19:1–8). At the end of this section an angel blesses those who are invited to the wedding supper of the Lamb (19:9–10).

But the wedding supper does not take place immediately.[10] The scene shifts, marked by John saying, "and I saw," to a new vision of the final battle between Christ and the combined forces of evil (19:11–21). In Revelation 12 the dragon was defeated in heaven after which he was hurled to earth, where he enlisted the sea and earth beasts in his unholy cause (13). Now we learn Christ's victory on earth as he rides out on a white horse, leading his angelic army and defeating the evil people and evil spiritual powers, represented by the beast and the false prophet being thrown into the lack of fire.

Attention then shifts to the dragon, representing Satan (20:2), who is initially seized and imprisoned in the Abyss. After a thousand years he is freed, but then he is judged and thrown into the lake of fire (20:7–10), followed by all the dead and even death and Hades themselves being thrown into the lake of fire. Evil is once and for all definitively defeated (20:11–15).

After this final and climactic picture of judgment, the next sections present three major pictures of life for God's people after the eradication of evil. The first, drawn especially from Isaiah (see commentary), speaks of the new heavens and the new earth (20:1–8). In this context we also return (see 19:7–9) to wedding imagery (21:2), as we do in the second picture of a New Jerusalem (21:9–27, for wedding imagery see 21:9). The third picture surrounds that of a new restored Eden, only this Eden is better than the original (22:1–5).

The conclusion of the book of Revelation has two parts. First (22:6–11), John's guiding angel gives him final assurance of the truthfulness of the visions and the command to not "seal up its words" (22:9) because the time is near. John, tempted to worship this glorious heavenly creature, is told to worship only God. Then second, Jesus himself announces that he is coming soon to judge and confirms that he is the one who sent the angel to John (22:12–21). The book signs off with a benediction typical of a letter, thus reminding us that the book as a whole is a letter to the churches.

COMMENTARY

REVELATION 1

Introduction to the Book and the Seven Letters (1–3)

Superscription and Blessing (1:1–3)

1:1 *The revelation from Jesus Christ.* The term "revelation" translates the Greek word *apokalupsis*, which modern scholars have used as a genre label for books like Revelation, most notably the book of Daniel that provides an Old Testament background to many of the themes, motifs, and metaphors in Revelation, as we will note in the commentary to follow. In addition to Daniel and Revelation, some other noncanonical books (including 2 Esdras; Book of Enoch; 2 Baruch) have been identified as apocalyptic or as having apocalyptic features (Jubilees). Apocalyptic books speak about God's judgment in the future, and ultimately the end of time, as a way of providing hope during present circumstances. The authors of these books present their visions to the faithful to comfort them during their struggles. Apocalyptic books utilize vivid figurative language in part because they are speaking about the distant future and in part to capture the readers' attention. Many of the metaphors and similes of Revelation have a background in the Old Testament and the broader ancient Near East. The noun *apokalupis* is in genitive relationship with the name Jesus Christ ("the revelation of Jesus Christ"), and the NIV has rightly caught the correct sense of the genitive that it indicates this is a revelation from Jesus, not really about Jesus—though of course Jesus will play a central role in this vision of the future.

What must soon take place. As in Daniel 2:28–29: "there is a God in heaven who reveals mysteries. He has shown King Nebuchadnezzar what will happen in days to come. Your dream and the vision that passed through your mind as you were lying in bed are these: 'As your Majesty was lying there, your mind turned to things to come, and the revealer of mysteries showed you what is going to happen." As Osborne puts it, "the prophecies of Daniel are seen throughout the book as coming to final fulfillment."[1] In other words, what was in the distant future to Daniel now has a sense of immediacy to it.

By sending his angel to his servant John. In Old Testament prophecy, God spoke directly to the prophet who then was tasked with taking the message to the people with the purpose of eliciting repentance. In Revelation, and Daniel before it, God gave his apocalyptic seer a vision and then sent an angel to provide an interpretation (e.g., Dan 9:21–22). The purpose of the vision was to comfort the faithful.

1:3 *Blessed is the one.* The conferring of blessings of this sort may be found in the wisdom literature of the Old Testament (Pr 3:13; 8:34; 28:14, see also Ps 1:1) and encourages wise behavior and attitudes with the inducement of benefits. (See "Revelation Through Old Testament Eyes: Psalms" at Rev 12:5.) There are seven blessings conferred in the book of Revelation, starting with this one (see also Rev 14:13; 16:15; 19:9; 20:6; 22:7, 14). Perhaps there is significance that the blessing-sayings intensify toward the end of the book as it works through judgment toward a description of the new heavens and earth.

The words of this prophecy. In the immediately previous section we mentioned the difference between Old Testament prophetic books and apocalyptic books like Daniel and Revelation. Here "prophecy" is used in the broad sense concerning matters pertaining to the future, both near-term future as well as the more distant future.

Because the time is near. At the end of the book of Daniel, after Daniel had received four visions concerning the future, an angelic figure tells him, "Go your way, Daniel, because the words are rolled up and sealed until the time of the end" (Da 12:9). "The time" that is said to be near in this verse is clearly the "time of the end." No longer are the words to be "rolled up and sealed" as at the time of Daniel, but now are to be read aloud and heard.

What the Structure Means: A Letter, an Apocalypse, and a Prophecy (Rev 1:1–8)

Revelation 1:4 sounds like the opening of other New Testament letters. Compare Paul's letter to the Galatians as an example. The letter begins when Paul identifies himself as the writer of the letter (Gal 1:1) and then identifies the recipients of the letter ("to the churches in Galatia," 1:2). Then he confers a benediction on the Galatians by saying "Grace and peace to you from God our Father and the Lord Jesus Christ" (1:3). In the same way, after an opening superscription and blessing to be discussed in a moment, John identifies himself as the writer and goes on to identify the recipients of his letter ("to the seven churches in the province of Asia"). He follows this with a benediction like the one found in the letter to the Galatians, "Grace and peace to you" (Rev 1:4).

Unlike the letter to the Galatians and other letters in the New Testament, this epistolary opening does not begin the book of Revelation. Rather, the book starts with a superscription and a blessing. The superscription identifies the book as a "revelation from Jesus Christ" (1:1) and explains that God made it known to John by sending an angel to him. The Greek word here translated "revelation" is *apokalupsis*, and as explained in the note to 1:1 gives its name to a genre of literature called apocalyptic. Thus it's not sufficient to call Revelation a letter like all other letters in the New Testament. The opening also signals to us that it is an apocalypse, a highly symbolic depiction of the future, most similar to the book of Daniel. Though specifically an apocalypse, the book uses what might be considered a broader term, "prophecy," to refer to the contents of the letter (1:3). A prophecy is a vision of the future, usually a more near-term future, to speak to the issues of the prophet's contemporary audience. For that reason, the prologue here pronounces a blessing on those who hear and "take to heart" (1:3) the message that is communicated by this book.

That said, this apocalypse/prophecy is communicated to the seven churches in a letter. So we are not surprised that Revelation ends like most other New Testament letters with another benediction. Galatians ends when Paul writes: "The grace of our Lord Jesus Christ will be with your spirit, brothers and sisters. Amen" (6:18), and Revelation ends by saying: "The grace of our Lord Jesus be with God's people. Amen" (22:21).

Greetings and Doxology (1:4–8)

1:4 *John, To the seven churches in the province of Asia.* After the prologue to the book (1:1–3) which speaks in the third person, John now begins his letter with what is a recognizable salutation to his intended readers, the seven churches in the provinces of Asia. In the Old Testament, seven is the number of completion or perfection. These seven churches may be representative of the larger number of churches in Asia. The location of these churches indicates that Asia refers to what we call Asia Minor, present-day Turkey, particularly on the western side.

From him who is, and who was, and who is to come. God exists in the present, the past, and the future. As often pointed out, the background appears to be God's revelation of his covenantal name, Yahweh, at his meeting with Moses at the burning bush. At that time, God responds to Moses' request for his name by saying, "I am who I am. This is what you are to say to the Israelites, 'I am has sent me to you'" (Ex 3:14). John here reflects the Septuagint rendering of "I am" (*ho on*; I am the One who is").[2] One might expect the order, past ("who was"), present ("who is"), and then "future" ("who is to come") like at Rev 4:8), but here the emphasis might be on the present as a note of assurance to the immediate recipients of the letter. See also note at 1:8.

The seven spirits before his throne. The NIV footnote suggests that rather than seven spirits, we should think "seven spirits" is a reference to the "sevenfold Spirit," namely the Holy Spirit in all his magnificent perfection and completion. Many commentators believe that there is a reference here to Isaiah 11:2, which lists seven attributes of the spirit of God. From this comes the suggestion of a trinitarian reference in this verse and the next.[3] However, more likely is Metzger's view that this is a reference to seven angels, who according to Tobit 12:15 are in the immediate presence of God.[4] (See "Revelation 4 Through Old Testament Eyes: God on His Throne.")

What the Structure Means:
The Number Seven in Revelation

The number seven permeates the book of Revelation. There are seven letters to seven churches (1:4; 2–3), seven spirits before the throne (1:4), seven golden lampstands (1:12), seven stars in the glorified Christ's right hand (1:16, 20), a scroll with seven seals (6:1–8:5), a Lamb with seven horns and seven eyes (5:6), seven angels blowing seven horns (8:2; 8:6–11:19), seven bowls filled with plague (15–16), seven thunders (10:4); a dragon with seven heads and seven crowns (12:3), a sea beast with seven heads (13:1), seven blessings (1:3; 14:13; 16:15; 19:9; 20:6; 22:7, 14), a city with seven hills (17:9), and seven kings (17:10).

This symbolic use of the number seven has an Old Testament background and signifies completion, totality, and/or perfection. The root of this Old Testament symbol is most likely found in the seven-day week of creation (Ge 1) that becomes one way Hebrews determined a particular period (that continues to today). Examples of the symbolic use of seven in the Old Testament signifying completion, totality, perfection include the seven good cows and the seven ugly cows that represent seven years of plenty and seven famine in Pharaoh's dream (Ge 41:25–27), sprinkling the blood of a sin offering seven times on the Day of Atonement (Lev 16:14, 19), and the Israelites under Joshua marching around Jericho for seven days and seven times on the seventh day (Jos 6:3–4).

The use of symbolic numbers like seven is particularly common in apocalyptic literature. Symbolic numbers should not be pressed literally in a quantitative sense. Communicating the idea of completion leaves ambiguous whether only seven churches were the intended recipient of this letter, or whether there would only be three cycles of seven discrete judgments.

1:5 *From Jesus Christ.* The Greek title Christ is equivalent to the Hebrew *mashiah* or Messiah, and points to Jesus as the fulfillment of the anticipated anointed king who came to rescue his people (2 Sa 7:16–17).

The faithful witness. As Tabb points out, Psalm 89:37 points to the moon as the "faithful witness in the sky" whose testimony is that God will assure that David's line will endure "before me like the sun" (Ps 89:36). Tabb goes on to say that "John goes further than Psalm 89 by identifying the risen King Jesus himself as the faithful witness,"[5] since he is also the one whose very self assures that David's line will endure forever.

Firstborn from the dead, and the ruler of the kings of the earth. In Colossians 1:15, Paul calls Jesus "the firstborn over all creation," an obvious allusion to Proverbs 8:22–26. But here he is called the firstborn of the dead, not because he was the first person to die but because he was the first person to die and be "born" from the dead through the resurrection (see also 1 Co 15:20; Col 1:18). While Jesus had brought Lazarus back from the dead to show his divine power over death (Jn 11:38–44), Lazarus, unlike Jesus, died again.

The reference to Jesus as "the ruler of the kings of the earth" seems to be a reference to Psalm 89:27, where the psalmist remembers the divine announcement that David would be "the most exalted of the kings of the earth" after saying that David was appointed as God's firstborn (and thus also providing a background to the reference to firstborn in this verse). The psalm is actually a lament bemoaning the decline of the Davidic monarchy, calling on God to restore their fortunes. Of course, neither David nor any of the kings in his line who ruled from Jerusalem were ever considered the most exalted of kings except perhaps in God's eyes. But it is Jesus, David's greater son, who assumes that privilege due to his death and resurrection.

1:6 *Has made us to be a kingdom and priests to serve his God and Father.* At Mount Sinai, God told Moses, "although the whole earth is mine, you will be for me a kingdom of priests and a holy nation" (Ex 19:5–6). Israel's special status was not to special privilege but to serve God and be priestly intermediaries to the rest of the world. John here states that the seven churches of Asia (and those that they represent) now constitute God's kingdom and have the priestly responsibility to serve God on behalf of the rest of the world. The church, now made up of Jews and Gentiles, is a spiritual kingdom that is set apart for holy service. That position comes as a result of Christ's death, which has "freed us from our sins by his blood" (Rev 1:5).

1:7 *Look, he is coming with the clouds.* The picture of Christ returning with the clouds has an Old Testament and ancient Near Eastern background. In the ancient Near East, cloud-riding was associated with storm gods like the Canaanite Baal, who is repeatedly called "the rider on the clouds" in the mythology of the Canaanites. Because of its association with the storm, we should picture this cloud here and in the biblical texts not as a white fluffy cloud but as a dark storm cloud (Ps 18:9, though see Rev 14:14). The Old Testament poets and prophets on several occasions picture God riding a cloud into battle to rescue his people. In the magnificent and powerful description of God in Psalm 104, for example, we read that "he makes the clouds his chariot and rides on the wings of the wind" (v. 3). When the psalmist calls to God for help in the face of formidable enemies, we hear in response that God "parted the heavens and came down; dark clouds were under his feet. He mounted the cherubim and flew; he soared on the wings of the wind" (Ps 18:9–10). In a prophecy against Egypt, Isaiah exclaims, "See, the LORD rides on a swift cloud and is coming to Egypt. The idols of Egypt tremble before him, and the hearts of the Egyptians melt with fear" (Isa 19:1–2). In the opening to Nahum's oracle against the Assyrian city of Nineveh, we read that God the divine warrior's "way is in the whirlwind and the storm, and clouds are the dust of his feet" (Na 1:3).

But John here cites a different, specific passage from the second scene of Daniel's first vision, namely Daniel 7:13: "In my vision at night I looked, and there before me was one like a son of man, coming with the clouds of heaven." Daniel's opening scene (Da 7:1–8) pictures four horrifying beasts emerging from a chaotic sea. The sea and the monsters that are in it, or in this case emerge from it, are symbols of anti-creation forces of chaos and evil. Later in the chapter, an interpreting angel will announce that these beasts represent "four kings that will rise from the earth" (Dan 7:17). They will ravage the earth and in particular the people of God. The second scene (7:9–14) changes the setting to a court room in which sits the Ancient of Days, a figure clearly to be identified with God, who is ready to issue judgments against the kingdoms represented by the beasts. Into his presence there arrives the one like the son of man riding a cloud. He is the one who will execute the Ancient of Days' judgment on the forces represented by the beasts and the horns that emanate from the fourth beast.

What is particularly striking about this passage is that it presents two figures, in ways that associate them both with divinity. As mentioned, the Ancient of Days can only be God, but then only God can ride the cloud into battle. That this cloud-riding figure is called "one like a son of man" is particularly intriguing. In the Old Testament, "son of man" always means human being, but this figure is not a son of man, but "like a son of man." Thus, we have a humanlike figure riding the cloud, a prerogative of God alone, into the presence of the Ancient of Days. No wonder John saw this figure as suggestive of Jesus at the end of time, when he will come to bring judgment on evil people and spiritual powers. And John was not the only one. The Gospels also picture Christ riding a cloud when he returns again at the end of time (Mt 24:30; Mk 13:26; Lk 21:27).

"Every eye will see him, even those who pierced him"; and all peoples on earth "will mourn because of him." After citing Daniel 7:13, John quotes Zechariah 12:10[6] and applies it to Christ, who will return on the clouds. Let's begin by turning our attention to the meaning of Zechariah 12:10 in its original context. Zechariah 12 begins with the announcement that it is "a prophecy. The word of the LORD concerning Israel" (12:1). Zechariah's prophecy begins by announcing that in the future all the nations of the earth will gather against Jerusalem and that God will watch over his people and "will set out to destroy all the nations that attack Jerusalem" (12:9). The next section of the prophecy (12:10–13) begins by describing how God will transform his people by "pour[ing] out on the house of David and the inhabitants of Jerusalem a spirit of grace and supplication" (12:10). As a result, God's people will look to God, who is identified as "the one they have pierced" and will mourn him. The idea that they have pierced God is metaphorical for their rebellion against God that led to their judgment in the first place, a judgment that is now going to be followed by their restoration. Their mourning will be intense, like the mourning of an only child or the weeping "of Hadad Rimmon in the plain of Megiddo" (12:11). The latter reference is obscure, but according to Boda, is likely a reference to weeping over Baal (often referred to as Hadad) whose adherents wept at his supposed death at the hands of the god Mot.[7] If true, this reference is not an affirmation of the mythological elements of the story, but rather is simply pointing to an example of intense mourning.

The New Testament saw a deeper meaning to the reference to the "piercing of God" in the crucifixion of Jesus.[8] John reports that to hurry the death of Jesus and the two other men crucified along with him that the soldiers decided to break their legs. But when they came to Jesus, they did not break his legs but rather pierced his side with a spear. John ends the description of the crucifixion by citing Zechariah 12:10: "they will look on the one they have pierced" (Jn 19:37).

We can now see how appropriate it is to cite this verse at the beginning of the book of Revelation. John recognizes that this day is the day anticipated by the prophecy of Zechariah 12, the day when God would defeat the amassed enemies of his people. Jesus, the one who was pierced, is the one who will come to defeat those enemies and save his people. Interestingly, Revelation notes that it is "all peoples of the earth" rather than just the house of David and the inhabitants of Jerusalem, as in Zechariah 12, who will look on the pierced one and mourn. As Köstenberger points out, "John in Rev 1:7 . . . transforms Zec 12:10–14 to show the fulfillment of the Abrahamic blessing of the nations through the suffering and reigning messianic seed."[9]

In this dual reference to Daniel 7 and Zechariah 12 we have an important theme that will reoccur in the book of Revelation. The divine warrior (the one coming with the clouds) is none other than the suffering servant of God (the one who was pierced).

Revelation Through Old Testament Eyes: Daniel

Perhaps no book of the Old Testament has a bigger impact on the book of Revelation than Daniel, particularly Daniel 7–12. We should not be surprised at this similarity, given that Daniel 7–12 and Revelation are the only true apocalypses in the canon.

The book of Daniel was written toward the end of the Old Testament period[10] and addressed God's people when they were living under the domination of a foreign power. During Daniel's life, Jewish people were vassals under Babylon and then Persia. The book anticipates that later nations will succeed these two, anticipating at least Greek domination (Da 8 and 11) but also beyond. By the time of the book of Revelation, the Romans had replaced the Greeks as the empire that controlled Jerusalem and Judah.

Both books looked forward from their present circumstances where it appeared that evil forces were in control. And into that situation, God gave both Daniel and John the same message. Despite present troubles, God was in control, and he would win the final victory. This message was one of hope amid potential despair. In addition, God spoke through Daniel and John to encourage their contemporary readers to persist amid trouble. Both Jews at the time of Daniel and Christians at the time of John lived in a culture toxic to their faith. Receiving this message of hope intended to give them the strength to resist caving into the culture.

It did not mean that they would avoid suffering, but it did inform faithful readers that their suffering would have meaning in that it would lead to a better future. But not only a better future—God was also working in the present. He was in control despite present appearances.

Daniel looks to the end of history when God will come and bring evil to an end decisively, once and for all. In Daniel 2 Nebuchadnezzar has a dream that reveals a succession of kingdoms and culminates in the rock which represents "a kingdom that will never be destroyed" (2:44). That kingdom is none other than the kingdom of God.

Grant Osborne clearly expresses the reason why the book of Revelation echoes the book of Daniel so often when he states that "the prophecies of Daniel are seen throughout the book as coming to final fulfillment."[11] It's not that Daniel did not foresee more events soon, but the book looked forward to the very end of history, which Revelation also anticipates. Both books announce God's final victory over evil to encourage God's suffering people during a difficult present.

While God revealed to Daniel and through Daniel to his faithful people that God was going to win at the end, there is also the sense that this anticipated victory would not happen soon. At the end of the book an angel, probably Gabriel, first instructs Daniel to "roll up and seal the words of the scroll until the time of the end" (12:4) and then to, "Go your way, Daniel, because the words are rolled up and sealed until the time of the end" (12:9). That they are sealed to the end does not mean that they are not able to be read; after all, we hear these instructions after reading the book of Daniel, including its four visions and their interpretation. But what it means is that it is not yet time for the events of the end to take place.

The book of Revelation, in contrast, was written after the first coming of Christ. He had died and been raised and then ascended into heaven. In his great redemptive acts he had defeated the powers and the authorities (Col 2:13–15), but it was an already-and-not-yet victory. Christ's act on the cross assured the final victory, but the complete realization of that victory will take place, according to the witness of the New Testament and in particular Revelation, at the time of his second coming.

The book of Revelation testifies that with the first coming of Christ we have moved into the end times that will be fully realized when Christ comes again. Therefore, whereas for Daniel the end was far off, now for John in Revelation "the time is near" (Rev 1:3) and the end is not something far off, but something that "must soon take place" (Rev 1:1). The mystery that Daniel foresaw is something that will be accomplished according to the visions of the book of Revelation (Rev 10:7).

The scroll that had been rolled and sealed (Da 12:4, 9)—in other words, that proclaimed the final judgment on evil and the rescue of the faithful— would now be unsealed by the Lamb who was worthy (Rev 5–8).

1:8 *I am the Alpha and the Omega . . . who is, and who was, and who is to come, the Almighty.* The greeting and doxology end with the Lord God's self-identification in three parts. As typical of self-identifications, he begins by asserting "I am," evoking memory of God's revelation of his name to Moses at the burning bush as "I am who I am" (*'ehyeh 'asher 'ehyeh,* Ex 3:14, see note at 1:4).[12] He then goes on to state that he is the Alpha (the first letter of the Greek alphabet) and the Omega (the last letter).[13] God thus says that he is the beginning and end, the first and the last (see also 1:18). Of course by claiming the beginning and the end, he also claims everything in between. In this assertion, we can see a reflection of Yahweh's proclamation recorded in Isaiah 44:6 (see also 41:4; 48:12): "I am the first and I am the last; apart from me there is no God." In Isaiah, God asserts this claim over against the pretensions of the false gods whom the Israelites found so tempting to worship. In other words, there is only one God. R. H. Mounce provides a Greco-Roman background that suggests that perhaps this expression of God's eternality targeted a particular contemporary false God, namely Zeus. According to Mounce, "in the Greek world, similar titles for the gods are found. In the song of the doves at Dondana we read about 'Zeus who was, Zeus who is, and Zeus who will be,' Pausanias x.12."[14]

In Revelation, Jesus has died to free us from our sins so that we might serve his God and Father as citizens of his kingdom and priests. Then by citing Daniel 7:13, which associates Jesus with the one like the son of man riding the cloud (an implicit claim to divinity), and by saying that Jesus is the one who was pierced, citing a passage from Zechariah that referred to Yahweh, this passage associates Jesus with divinity. Thus, when the Lord God proclaims that he is the sole God (the Alpha and the Omega) we should not think this a proclamation of the Father alone, but also of the Son and the Spirit.

We should also hear an assertion of eternity that is made explicit in the following statement that he is the one who is (the present), and who was (the past), and who is to come (the future). He thus spans all time. God, therefore, exclusively fills the category God (the Alpha and the Omega, the first and the last); he also completely fills the category of time.

Finally, he is the Almighty (*pantokrator*), the Greek equivalent[15] to the Hebrew *yahweh sebaòt*, the Lord of Hosts. The Hosts refer to God's heavenly army, and the use of "Almighty" contributes to the heavy emphasis on the triune God's role as warrior who comes to save his people.

What the Structure Means:
The Glorified Christ Commands John to
Write the Seven Churches (Rev 1:9–20)

In the previous verses, John addressed his letter to the seven churches of Asia (1:4a). He then channeled a benediction from God and Jesus on the recipients of the letter (1:4b-5) and followed that with a dedication to Jesus and a call to be on the lookout for his return (1:6–7). Jesus himself then provides a brief description of himself as the "Alpha and the Omega," the one "who is, and who was, and who is to come, the Almighty" (1:8).

Between the introduction of the letters and the letters themselves in chapters 2–3, John tells us that he met the glorified Christ, who commands him to write to the seven churches. Specifically, he exhorts him to "write on a scroll what you see and send it to the seven churches" (1:11) and then again later "write, therefore, what you have seen, what is now and what will take place later" (1:19). At the heart of this section John describes his encounter with the glorified Christ in all his mysterious splendor (1:12–16). In Christ's appearance to John and his command to write, we see his commission to his prophetic task like those that the Old Testament prophets experienced.

Moses, the paradigmatic prophet (Dt 34:1–12), received his prophetic calling at the burning bush. There he met God who commissioned him to go to Egypt to press Pharaoh to release the Israelites from their bondage (Ex 3). We might also think of Isaiah, who through a vision saw God enthroned in the temple where he accepted God's call to send someone to his people to call his people to repentance or face the threat of judgment. However, the closest parallel in this section, as will be detailed, is to Ezekiel's call to his prophetic task (Eze 1–3). Like Ezekiel, John was "in the Spirit" when he encountered the glorified Christ (see note to 1:10) and the description of Christ bears close analogy to what Ezekiel saw at the time of his prophetic commission (see note at 1:13–15). The similarities between the calling of John and the Old Testament prophets establishes his divinely given credentials as he writes to the churches.

The Glorified Christ Commissions John (1:9–20)

1:9 *On the island of Patmos.* After his epistolary greeting, John now describes to his audience, the seven churches of Asia, how the glorified Christ instructed him to write to them. He tells them that he is on the island of Patmos, a small island (approx. thirty-four square miles) off the coast of Asia Minor (today Turkey) where the seven churches were located. John has likely been exiled there "because of the word of God and the testimony of Jesus," and so considers himself a "companion in the suffering" with those whom he is writing.

1:10 *On the Lord's Day.* John is about to recount his encounter with the glorified Christ, and he first tells the audience that it happened, appropriately enough, on the Lord's Day, a day set apart by the church for fellowship and worship. The background in the Old Testament is the Sabbath, the seventh day of the week, during which God's people were to cease their regular work. The Sabbath was established at the time of the creation (Ge 2:1–3), mandated by the fourth commandment (Ex 20:8–11; Dt 5:12–15), and considered the "sign" of the Mosaic covenant (Ex 31:12–18). Thus, the Sabbath was to be strictly observed during the time of the Old Testament, though we have accounts of disobedience and the judgment that followed (Nu 15:32–36; Jer 17:19–27).

Surprisingly, however, Jesus suggests a change is forthcoming when during his life he flaunts contemporary Sabbath laws. His actions go beyond simply ignoring contemporary legalistic understanding of these laws to violate certain Old Testament requirements. We see this, for instance, when he allows his disciples to pick grain on the Sabbath (Mk 2:23–28), a practice clearly prohibited during the Old Testament period (Ex 34:21; see also Ex 16:25–29).

Paul reflects theologically on the transition that takes place at the time of Jesus' coming. He tells the church, "therefore do not let anyone judge you by what you eat or drink, or with regard to a religious festival, a New Moon celebration or a Sabbath day. These are a shadow of the things that were to come; the reality, however, is found in Christ" (Col 2:16–17). Now that Christ has come, no longer is there a need for a special set-apart (holy) time, now all time is holy.[16]

But what then does Paul mean by the Lord's Day? Even though a Sabbath Day is no longer required by law, wisdom suggests that a day be set apart so that believers can gather for fellowship and worship. Hints from the New Testament strongly suggest that by the time John is writing Christians were in the habit of meeting not on the seventh day (the Jewish Sabbath, from Friday sundown to Saturday sundown), but rather the first day (Sunday; see Ac 20:7; 1 Co 16:2; see also Jn 20:19–26).

I was in the Spirit. John recognizes that the vision that he is about to recount is not the result of simply natural experience but of being "in the Spirit." The Holy Spirit, in other words, enables his hearing the heavenly voice and conveying its message. In this way, John likens himself to Old Testament prophets like Ezekiel who also speaks of the Spirit's enablement of his ministry (Eze 3:12–15; 11:24; 37:1, see also Mic 3:5–8). He is speaking under divine inspiration. This phrase, "in the Spirit," occurs in three other strategic locations in Revelation (see 4:2; 17:3; 21:10).

A loud voice like a trumpet. John heard a voice that sounded like a trumpet which causes him to turn around where the exalted Christ's presence overwhelms him. In the Old Testament, the sound of trumpets often accompanied God's appearance, notably at Mount Sinai (Ex 19:13, 16, 19). On the seventh day of marching, after circling the city of Jericho seven times on that final day, the Israelites, announcing the manifestation of God in his great power resulting in the collapse of its walls (Jos 6:20–21; see also Lev 25:9; Nu 10:1–10; Zec 9:14). The blare of a trumpet may specifically mimic thunder, presaging the storm. Storm imagery surrounds the appearance of God the warrior (see comment at Rev 1:7). In this passage, the voice, which we will soon learn belongs to God himself, sounds like a trumpet, announcing his own appearance. A loud voice is commanding, demands attention, and expresses authority.

1:11 *Write on a scroll.* The trumpetlike voice begins with a command that John write down what he sees on a scroll. In biblical times, scribes wrote on scrolls, rolled up writing surfaces of parchment, leather, or papyrus. We hear a similar divine demand directed to the prophet Jeremiah when after years of speaking God's word to the people calling them to repentance, God tells him to "take a scroll and write on it all the words I have spoken to you" (Jer 36:2). Writing down the prophecy gives it more permanency. Though King Jehoiakim took Jeremiah's scroll and burned it, that did not thwart God's purposes because afterward "Jeremiah took another scroll" and had his scribe Baruch write down the words once again "and many similar words were added to them" (Jer 36:32). Also relevant are the words spoken by God's angelic messenger to Daniel after he had received his visions and their interpretation: "But you, Daniel, roll up and seal the words of the scroll until the time of the end" (Da 12:4). Both Daniel and John, recipients of apocalyptic visions, record them on scrolls for posterity, though there is a sense of concealment in the instructions to Daniel that we don't find given to John, because now that Christ has come "the time is near" (Rev 1:3).

To the seven churches. What John writes was to be sent to seven churches, all of which are in western Asia Minor. They are listed in an order (Ephesus, Smyrna, Pergamum, Thyatira, Sardis, Philadelphia, and Laodicea) that, starting with Ephesus, moves to the north and then, with a turn to the east, around in almost a circle to the south. It is between thirty to forty-five miles from each city to the next, suggesting that perhaps the scroll was taken by messenger from one church to another. For the number seven and its symbolic significance in reference to the churches, see comment at 1:4. Even though the letter is addressed to these seven churches, the message of the book is relevant to all the churches. As Tabb points out, "the Muratorian Fragment (c. AD 170) states, 'John . . . though he writes to seven churches, nevertheless speaks to all' (lines 57–60)."[17]

1:12 *Seven golden lampstands.* John heard the voice that sounded like trumpets behind him, so he turned to see who was speaking to him. He first reports seeing seven golden lampstands, which we will later learn represent the seven churches listed in 1:11 (see 1:20). In the Old Testament, a lampstand (*menorah*) illuminated the interior of the tabernacle (Ex 25:31–40). This lampstand was styled like a tree with cups shaped "like almond flowers with buds" (Ex 25:33), clearly a tree symbol. A tree in the place where God made his presence known evokes memory of Eden, when humans and God dwelt together in harmony (see Ge 1:11–12, 29; 2:9).[18] This lampstand had six branches extending from the center branch for a total of seven lamps (Ex 25:37). Even though in our passage in Revelation we have seven separate lampstands rather than a single lampstand with seven separate lights at the end of each branch,[19] we find God making his presence known in their midst.

1:13 *Someone like a son of man.* The unnamed figure that John sees as he turns around is clearly the glorified Jesus. Jesus is the one "like a son of man," an allusion again (see 1:7) to Daniel 7:13–14. Jesus is the divine warrior who rides the storm cloud into battle. As explained at 1:7, "son of man" means human being, but he is "like" a human being, while riding the cloud is the prerogative of deity. See "Going Deeper into Jesus the Divine Warrior who Defeats Evil" after Revelation 22.

1:13–15 *Dressed in a robe down to his feet and with a golden sash around his chest. The hair on his head was white like wool, as white as snow, and his eyes were like blazing fire. His feet were like bronze glowing in a furnace, and his voice was like the sound of rushing waters.* Thus, John describes his vision of the one like a human being, whom we know is the glorified Christ. The description of his clothing, body, and voice echo various descriptions of visions of Yahweh in the Old Testament. Ezekiel reports his vision of the glory of God (Eze 1:24–28; see also 8:2). This description includes elements of glowing metal and hearing a voice "like the roar of rushing waters" (Eze 1:24, said of cherubim whose wings are said to sound like the "voice of the Almighty"; see also 43:2, said of God's voice). In Daniel 7:9 the hair of the Ancient of Days, clearly representing Yahweh, is said to be "white like wool," a description that is here applied to the glorified Christ. In the introduction to his fourth and final vision, Daniel also recounts a vision of God filled with imagery of fiery brightness and a resonant voice ("like the sound of a multitude," Da 10:4–6). While none of these Old Testament descriptions of the appearance of Yahweh are exactly identical to John's vision of the glorified Christ, they all echo elements of it and share similarities. All these descriptions communicate magnificent splendor and evoke awe. For the golden sash, see note at 15:6. See also "1. The Depiction of the Glorified Christ" in "Revelation Through Old Testament Eyes: Ezekiel" at 20:7.

1:16 *In his right hand he held seven stars, and coming out of his mouth was a sharp, double-edged sword.* The right hand represents control and power in the Old Testament, since the presumption in antiquity was that people were right-handed. God delivered Israel from Egypt by the power of his right hand (Ex 15:6, 12).

On occasion, the Old Testament, as Johnson points out,[20] associates stars with angels (Job 38:7), seven again being a number of completeness and perhaps again a reference to the seven angels who stand in the immediate presence of God (see 1:4). The identification of the stars with angels is made explicit in Revelation 1:20. Out of his mouth comes a double-edged sword (see also Rev 2:12; 19:15). The closest analogue in the Old Testament is the picture of the "shoot" that "will come up from the stump of Jesse" (Isa 11:1, commonly taken as an anticipation of the future Davidic king [messiah]). This one "will strike the earth with the rod of his mouth; with the breath of his lips he will slay the wicked" (Isa 11:4). The image of a lethal weapon coming from the mouth of the glorified Christ in Revelation, with its background in Isaiah 11:4, indicates that this one has the power to kill the wicked by means of his words. The description in Revelation anticipates that Jesus returns to bring violent judgment against the wicked and leads us to reject recent attempts to take the reference to the sword as having a nonviolent meaning.[21] We might also think of Isaiah's description of God making the mouth of the servant (representing the remnant of Israel and ultimately Christ himself) "like a sharpened sword," in other words like a weapon (Isa 49:2; see also note at 19:15).[22]

His face was like the sun shining in all its brilliance. The glorified Christ's face shines brilliantly like the sun. Yahweh is said to be "a sun and shield" in Psalm 84:11. Isaiah proclaims the sun will no longer be needed because "the LORD will be your everlasting light" (Isa 60:19–20).[23]

Going Deeper into the Glorified Christ: Revelation 1:12–16

Jesus is the very picture of who God is. According to the author of Hebrews, "the Son is the radiance of God's glory and the exact representation of his being" (1:3). Paul speaks of Jesus as the very "image of God" (2 Cor. 4:4; Col 1:15). Jesus himself claimed that "anyone who has seen me has seen the Father" (Jn 14:9).

To know Jesus is to know God. As we reflect on this truth, our minds often and rightly go to the Gospels, where we see Jesus choosing the way of suffering and service to others. We marvel at his humility. We see that he chooses to die on a cross for our sins and not for his own. Paul captures Jesus beautifully when he says that he:

> Being in very nature God,
>   did not consider equality with God something to be used to
> his own advantage;
>   rather, he made himself nothing
>   by taking the very nature of a servant,
>   being made in human likeness.
>   and being found in appearance as a man,
>   he humbled himself
>   by becoming obedient to death—
>   even death on a cross. (Php 2:6–8)

However, this description of Jesus does not exhaust the New Testament's portrait of him. The Gospels aren't the only place that we meet Jesus, of course. The book of Revelation also informs us about Jesus. Here we meet the triumphant, glorified Christ. At the first introduction, we hear he is "the faithful witness, the firstborn from the dead, and the ruler of the kings of the earth" (1:5) and that he was the divine warrior who was coming with the clouds (1:7) expected since the time of Daniel. In 1:12–16 we read a magnificent and powerful figurative depiction of Christ, drawn from imagery describing Yahweh in both Ezekiel and Daniel (see details at commentary). You may have seen some Sunday-school art that tries to illustrate this picture of Christ in a literal fashion. But that's not how apocalyptic literature works. What John seeks to emphasize through these images is not what Jesus looks like in heaven but aspects of who Christ is—a divine warrior and judge who comes with power and authority. Revelation, in other words, right from the start pictures the post-resurrection, post-ascension glorified

Christ, whom Paul also describes in the second part of the magnificent song/poem in Philippians 2:

> Therefore, God exalted him to the highest place
>   and gave him the name that is above every name,
>   that at the name of Jesus every knee should bow,
>   in heaven and on earth and under the earth,
>   and every tongue acknowledge that Jesus Christ is Lord,
>   to the glory of God the Father. (Php 2:9–11)

Of course, the Gospels are not devoid of Christ's glory. We might think, for instance, of the Transfiguration (Mt 17:1–8; Mk 9:2–8; Lk 9:28–36) about which Peter later says that the accompanying disciples "were witnesses of his majesty" (2 Pe 1:16). And, not only in Revelation, but what Jesus himself said of his triumphant return when "people will see the Son of Man coming in clouds with great power and glory" (Mk 13:26). For these reasons the Nicene Creed proclaims:

> He ascended into heaven
> And is seated on the right hand of the Father.
> He will come again with glory
> To judge the living and the dead.
> His kingdom will never end.

No wonder worship breaks out when Jesus makes his appearance in the book of Revelation. We see this most dramatically in Revelation 5, when the one who is worthy steps forward to take the seven-sealed scroll to open it. Today, our own worship of Jesus should encompass not only the Savior who emptied himself and died on the cross, but also the triumphant resurrected Christ who sits at God's right hand and who will come to save his people and judge all evil spiritual and human powers.

1:17 *I fell at his feet as though dead. . . . "Do not be afraid."* In a scene reminiscent of Moses at the burning bush (Ex 3:5–6) and, even more closely, Daniel's experience of coming into the very presence of God (Da 10:7–11), so John responds to his vision of the glorified Christ with great fear, so that he falls at his feet "as though dead." An angel approaches the fallen Daniel, touches him so that he might come to his feet trembling. He then encourages Daniel, "Do not be afraid, Daniel" (Da 10:12). In John's case, it is none other than the glorified Christ that so encourages him (Rev 1:17). Though overwhelmed by the divine presence, Christ gives him the strength that he needs to carry out the task for which he has been commissioned (see 1:19–20).

He placed his right hand on me. See note at 1:16.

I am the First and the Last. Jesus again claims to be the first and the last, implying everything in between (see note at 1:8 on Alpha and Omega).

1:18 *I am the Living One. . . . I hold the keys of death and Hades.* In yet another "I am" saying (see 1:8), Jesus claims for himself the divine title "the Living One" (see Jos 3:10; Ps 42:2; Hos 1:10). He asserts this claim in the light of the resurrection, "I was dead, and now look, I am alive for ever and ever!" Due to the resurrection and his divine status, he possesses "the keys of death and Hades." Hades is the equivalent of the Old Testament Sheol, a name that typically denotes simply the grave, but sometimes implies the netherworld, the place that all people go after death (Ge 37:35; Dt 32:22; Ps 30:3; 86:13; Eze 31:14–17).[24] As holder of the keys, Christ can open the gate of the netherworld to let those who would otherwise be locked in to come out. While the keys to death and Hades are never mentioned in the Old Testament, both Job (Job 17:16) and Hezekiah (Isa 38:10) speak of the "gates of death," and Psalm 9:13 and 107:18 do also."

1:19 *Write, therefore, what you have seen, what is now and what will take place later.* See note at 1:11. Here Christ commands John to write down not only what is now, but what will take place in the future. The most natural understanding of this verse is that it refers to the contents of the book of Revelation itself, which thus concerns present conditions that the church faces as well as an eschatological (or future-oriented) perspective. The idea that the book of Revelation only speaks of the past or only of the present or of the future does not conform with the nature of this command.

1:20 *The mystery of the seven stars . . . the seven golden lampstands.* A mystery is something not fully grasped until further revelation removes the shroud over our understanding and makes it clearer. For the significance of the stars and the lampstands, see notes at 1:12 and 1:16 respectively. When Daniel told Nebuchadnezzar the contents of his dream and its interpretation, Daniel called God as the "revealer of mysteries," who was able to show him "what is going to happen" (Da 2:29). Christ here is the divine revealer of mysteries, which are hitherto shrouded truths about the future.

REVELATION 2

What the Structure Means:
The Letters to the Seven Churches (Rev 2–3)

In the previous chapter, the glorified Christ commissioned John to write to seven churches, all located in the western part of Asia Minor, now Turkey. He begins by writing them separate letters (Rev 2–3); but the rest of the book, also part of the letter format of the book (see "What the Structure Means: A Letter, an Apocalypse, and a Prophecy [Rev 1:1–8]"), is intended for all of them.

There are seven letters written to seven churches. Seven is a number found throughout the book and should be taken in its symbolic sense, meaning complete or total. Though a symbolic number, these letters were written to seven actual churches; still, their message and the message of the whole book was not just meant for them but for all the churches both in Asia Minor and throughout the world of the time. The letters specifically address what was happening in those churches, but still all churches could hold their own situation up to the mirror of these seven and feel challenged or encouraged or both by Christ's words. As we take these letters as a whole, we find first, words of comfort to those who suffer; second, exhortation to maintain faith in the face of those who were hostile toward the faith or even actively persecuting it; and third, calls to repentance for those Christians who were not passionate about their faith or who were even participating in the pagan customs of their city. Just like other churches of the day could hold the mirror of these letters up to themselves, so can churches and individual readers of Revelation today.

At the time of writing, John was in exile on the island of Patmos (see note at 1:9), a few miles off the southwest coast of Asia Minor. The first letter is addressed to Ephesus, the city closest to Patmos on the mainland. After this, the respective cities form a rough circle going up the western coast (to Smyrna and then Pergamum) before moving inland toward the east (from Pergamum to Thyatira) and then going south (to Sardis, Philadelphia, and then Laodicea). The final church, Laodicea is directly east of the starting point in Ephesus. The order of churches, in other words, appears to follow a route that a person would take to deliver the letters to these churches.

The first city is *Ephesus* (see description at 2:1) across the water from John on Patmos. The letter to the Ephesians starts out on a very encouraging note. After identifying himself (2:1), Christ praises their perseverance in the light of the persecution they were experiencing and because they do not tolerate wicked people. Rather, they have been careful to test people who claim to have apostolic authority. Though they are doing the right things, Christ criticizes them because they don't have their original passionate love toward him. This "fall" threatens their relationship with Christ. Still, they reject the practices of the Nicolaitans also mentioned in the letter to the church in Pergamum (2:15). Unfortunately, we do not know precisely what these practices consist of, and the idea that it refers to participating in the local cult has no concrete basis, though it may still be true. We just don't know for sure. Whatever these practices are, the fact that the Ephesian church rejects them (while some in Pergamum did not) is a mark in their favor. The letter ends with a call to listen and obey, with the promise of victory.

The city of *Smyrna*, an ancient city, was thirty-five miles to the north of Ephesus. In contrast to the church in Ephesus, Christ has no criticism of the church in Smyrna. After introducing himself (2:8), he commends them for their perseverance in the light of the slander of the Jewish community. They may be socially and economically poor, but they are rich in their life with God through Christ. He warns them that they will experience further suffering and encourages them to continue in their perseverance, with the sure knowledge that they will be rewarded.

Fifty miles to the north of Smyrna was the city of *Pergamum* and the recipient of the third letter from the glorified Christ. After introducing himself (2:12), Christ praises the church at Pergamum for their consistent witness in the face of opposition even when the persecution was particularly severe in connection with a man named Antipas, who is called a "faithful witness" (2:13). We do not know the specifics, but the reference to Antipas as a "faithful witness" suggests that he stayed firm in his faith in the light of some threatening challenge that led to his death. The commendation of the church indicates that they too stayed firm in their faith. Presumably they too could have lost their lives by their perseverance. The animosity that the city of Pergamum demonstrated toward God's people there reveal that it is a city "where Satan lives" and "has his throne" (2:13).

Nonetheless, the church at Pergamum also had substantial failings. Christ chastises them for following "the teaching of Balaam" (see below on 2:14) and the "teaching of the Nicolaitans" (for which see note at 2:6). If they listen and respond in faith and obedience, Christ will reward them (see below on 2:17).

The sequence of the seven churches, we have suggested, follows the likely route that the messenger who bore the letters followed to deliver them. From Ephesus to Smyrna to Pergamum involved movement to the north along the western side of Asia Minor, but the road to *Thyatira* from Pergamum moved to the south and east on the way to Sardis, the recipient of the next letter. The distance from Pergamum to Thyatira was about forty-five miles.

The letter starts out positively, commending the church's deeds, faith, and perseverance, even highlighting its growth over time. But then the church is severely chastised for listening to a prophet whom the letter refers to by the name of Jezebel, the wicked, idolatrous queen of the northern kingdom at the time of King Ahab. Whatever her real name, she has convinced some to participate in acts that are idolatrous as well as sexually immoral. The letter, though, acknowledges that not all the members of the church have followed her teaching, and so the letter goes on to tell them to persevere.

Next comes the letter to *Sardis*, located approximately thirty miles south of Thyatira. The members of the church of Sardis are divided between those who have lost their passion and participated in sin and those who have not. Focused attention is given to the former. They are falling asleep in their faith and deeds, and Christ calls them to "wake up" or else suffer the consequences (3:2). To wake up is equivalent to repenting of their spiritual sloth. On the other side, those who have remained faithful will be rewarded.

After Sardis, the next letter goes to the church in *Philadelphia* approximately thirty-five miles further southeast. Christ only has good things to say about the church in Philadelphia. They have been through many difficulties and have been weakened by their experiences, but they have still endured and because of their persistence Christ will preserve them through the coming trial.

The seventh and final church is *Laodicea*, about forty-five miles south of Philadelphia and one hundred miles to the east of Ephesus. The route from Ephesus to Laodicea was an almost completed circle that moves first up north and then to the east and the south.

While Christ has nothing bad to say about the church in Philadelphia, he has nothing good to say about the church in Laodicea. They are lukewarm, neither hot nor cold, in their faith. They think they are rich, but they are really poor. Perhaps they are materially rich, but they are spiritually poor, and that is what counts. Christ threatens to spit them out like one would spit out lukewarm water. He encourages them to change their behavior and repent.

As we look back over these seven letters, we see that Christ encourages and comforts some, and he rebukes others and calls them to repent. In some letters we see a mixture of both. The letters describe churches that live in a toxic culture and have both positive and negative reactions to the hostility and persecution that threatens them. The visions in the following chapters will continue to challenge and comfort the church.

The Letter to the Church in Ephesus (2:1–7)

2:1 *To the angel of the church in Ephesus write.* Ephesus was the most significant city of the Roman Empire in this list of seven, having a population of approximately a quarter of a million people serving as a major commercial hub in the region. Indeed, it was the fourth largest city in the Roman Empire after Rome, Syrian Antioch, and Alexandria. Ephesus also boasted in a number of temples to the emperor cult as well to the famous temple to Diana (Artemis). The latter temple featured in an earlier episode mentioned in the book of Acts. In Acts 19, we read about Paul going to the city of Ephesus during his third missionary journey. When he arrived in the city, the people there, who had experienced "John's baptism," a "baptism of repentance" (19:4), had not yet received the spirit. Paul placed his hands on twelve men, and they received the Spirit. Then Paul went into the local synagogue to preach, but after receiving a tepid reception at best he began to give daily discussions in a lecture hall. He did this for two years. Miracles accompanied his teaching with wonderful results. However, a silversmith named Demetrius who made his money by making silver shrines of Artemis provoked a backlash based on their diminished business and the implied disparagement of the great temple to Artemis. A near-riot broke out, but calming words by the city clerk managed to quiet them (19:35–41). After this incident, Paul left Ephesus never to return. However, toward the end of his life when he returned to Jerusalem, while not going to the city of Ephesus, he sent for the elders of Ephesus to meet him in Miletus where they prayed for him before he continued his journey (Ac 20:13–38). One of Paul's most powerful letters was sent to Ephesus and bears the name of that city. In addition, Paul wrote his disciple Timothy in Ephesus and commissioned him to speak against certain false teachers who were in the city (see 1 Ti 1:3, and the note on Rev 2:2 below).

These are the words. Old Testament writers use a similar formula to introduce a divine communication (Dt 1:1; 29:1 ESV; Jer 29:1 ESV; 30:4, etc.).

The seven stars . . . the seven golden lampstands. The glorified Christ holds the seven stars that represent the angels of the seven churches, which are themselves represented by the seven golden lamp stands among whom he walks (see notes at 1:20 as well as 1:12 and 1:16).

2:2 *I know your deeds.* Psalm 62 concludes with two affirmations concerning God, the second being "You reward everyone according to what they have done." This emphasis on good deeds runs throughout the letters to the churches as well as in later parts of the book of Revelation, but as we can see from Psalm 62 has a background in the Old Testament. For more, see "Going Deeper into 'I Know Your Deeds': Revelation 2:2, 19; 3:1, 8, 15."

You have tested those who claim to be apostles but are not, and have found them false. Paul had earlier warned the Ephesians that people would attack them like "savage wolves" attack a flock of sheep. These wolves "distort the truth in order to draw away disciples after them" (Ac 20:29–30). Not everyone who says they are apostles are truly apostles. Those who claim to be apostles need to be tested like the people of Israel needed to test those who claimed to be prophets (Dt 13:1–5; 18:14–22). Unlike the test for false prophets which stated criteria (must speak in the name of the Lord, and what they say must come true), nowhere do we learn the nature of the test administered by the Ephesian church, but Christ is pleased that they were able to discern the difference.

2:4 *The love you had at first.* The prophets often spoke of Israel's first passionate love for Yahweh (Jer 2:2; Hos 2:14–15) as they decried how they had lost their love and turned against God, thus bringing God's judgment on them (see note at 19:7 regarding "the wedding of the Lamb").

2:5 *Your lampstand.* See note at 1:12.

2:6 *The practices of the Nicolaitans.* Early tradition names Nicolas one of the first deacons (Ac 6:5), and some believe he was the founder of this problematic group. However, Nicolas was a common name, and so such an association is uncertain and probably unlikely. Many think they "advocated accommodation to pagan society by eating food sacrificed to idols and engaging in sexual immorality."[1] Such a description of the Nicolaitans may indeed be true but depends on an identification between them and those "who hold the teaching of Balaam, who taught Balak to entice the Israelites to sin so that they ate food sacrificed to idols and committed sexual immorality" (see below on 2:14). Perhaps a further argument, though, can be made based on the name Nicolas, which means, according to Bauckham, "conquer the people" and provides a connection to the word *victory/victorious* that concludes all seven letters. Thus, Bauckham suggests, "their teaching made it possible for Christians to be successful in pagan society, but this was the beast's success, a real conquest of the saints, winning them to their side, rather than the only apparent conquest he achieved by putting them to death."[2]

Going Deeper into "I Know Your Deeds": Revelation 2:2, 19; 3:1, 8, 15

Paul could not be clearer. We are saved by faith not by works:

Therefore no one will be declared righteous in God's sight by the works of the law. (Ro 3:20)

For we maintain that a person is justified by faith apart from works of the law. (Ro 3:28)

Know that a person is not justified by the works of the law, but by faith in Jesus Christ. (Gal 2:16)

For it is by grace you have been saved, through faith—and this is not from yourselves, it is the gift of God—not by works, so that no one can boast. (Eph 2:8–9)

But in the letters to the seven churches, the glorified Christ puts the deeds of Christians in focus. In five of the letters, he states "I know your deeds" (2:2, 19; 3:1, 8, 15) and evaluates them. He praises the deeds of the Ephesian church particularly "your hard work and your perseverance" (2:2). He compliments the deeds of the church in Thyatira, "your love and faith, your service and perseverance, and that you are now doing more than you did at first" (2:19). To this church as well, he reminds them that he is the one who "searches hearts and minds" and "will repay each of you according to your deeds" (2:23). When it comes to the church in Sardis, Jesus knows their deeds are not good. They have a reputation for being alive, but they are dead. Thus, they get the admonition, "Strengthen what remains and is about to die, for I have found your deeds unfinished in the sight of my God" (3:2). Christ also knows and evaluates the deeds of the churches in Philadelphia (3:8) and Laodicea (3:15) and even though he does not preface his comments by saying "I know your deeds," Christ also evaluates the deeds of the churches at Smyrna and Pergamum.

But it is not only in the seven letters that the book of Revelation makes clear that the deeds of people matter to God. In Revelation 14, we hear a voice from heaven say, "Write this: Blessed are the dead who die in the Lord from now on" with a response from the Spirit announcing, "Yes . . . they will rest from their labor, for their deeds will follow them" (14:13). In the climactic judgment at the end of the book, when the dead stand before God's throne where he declares judgment, we read that "another book was opened, which is the book of life. The dead were judged according to what they had done as recorded in the books" (20:12). At the very end of the book, Jesus speaks about his future return with the warning that he is coming soon, and that "my reward is with me, and I will give to each person according to what they have done" (22:12).

The book of Revelation makes it clear that our deeds are important to God. How does this reconcile with Paul's teaching that we are not saved by works but rather by our faith?

To answer this question, we turn to the book of James where he addresses the relationship between faith and deeds. He is writing to people who seem to have taken the Pauline teaching too far, further than Paul himself would take it. Paul would never think that deeds are unimportant, though he definitely wanted to make it clear that we do not earn our salvation. James' point is that true faith will always result in good deeds. To make his point, Paul often cited Genesis 15:6 where "Abram believed the LORD, and he credited to him as righteousness." His scriptural argument was that Abraham was justified even before circumcision became a covenantal requirement in Genesis 17. And this sequence was significant because there were some Judaizing Christians who wanted to impose circumcision on Gentile converts to Christianity.

But Paul did not mean to minimize the importance of works in the Christian life. He was the one, after all, who said that "we are God's handiwork, created in Christ Jesus to do good works" (Eph 2:10). He exhorted his readers to "continue to work out your salvation with fear and trembling" (Php 2:12). And of course Paul knew the Abraham story, about which James reminds his readers.

After the birth of Isaac, the child of promise, God told Abraham to take him to Mount Moriah to sacrifice him. As readers we are told right from the beginning that this was a test (Ge 22:1), though Abraham would not have known this. God was testing Abraham to see if he had finally come to a place of complete trust in him, and as we read the story, we see that the answer was yes, Abraham was willing to follow through on this divine demand, though God kept him from doing so. What captures James' attention is what the Lord tells Abraham at the end of the story: "because you have done this and have not withheld your son, your only son, I will surely bless you and make your descendants as numerous as the stars in the sky and as the sand on the seashore . . . and through your offspring all nations on earth will be blessed, because you have obeyed me" (Ge 22:16–18). James concludes from this "you see that a person is considered righteous by what they do and not by faith alone" (Jas 2:24). We are saved by faith, but that faith will always show itself by good deeds; and if not, then it is not true faith: "faith without deeds is dead" (Jas 2:26). Again, this viewpoint does not conflict with Paul who himself reported to "those in Damascus, then to those in Jerusalem and in all Judea, and then to the Gentiles, I preached that they should repent and turn to God and demonstrate their repentance by their deeds" (Ac 26:20). As the Reformation formula puts it, "We are justified by faith alone, but the faith that justifies is never alone."

2:7 *Whoever has ears, let them hear what the Spirit says to the churches.* Thus will end all seven letters sent to the churches of Asia Minor. As Beale points out, this pronouncement echoes the words of the prophets of the Old Testament (Isa 6:9–10; Jer 5:21; Eze 3:27; 12:2) and "refers to the fact that Christ's message will enlighten some but blind others."[3] In such contexts "hearing" means not just listening but also obeying. John would have also been mindful that Jesus used this formula himself (Mt 11:15; Mk 4:9, 23; Lk 8:8).

To the one who is victorious. All seven letters end with an enticing reward for those who will win the victory (see also 2:11, 17, 26; 3:5, 12, 21; also 15:2; 21:7). Victory "is an athletic and military metaphor that connotes superiority and victory over a vanquished foe."[4] Osborne goes on to say that in the New Testament the term is primarily military, and suggests that meaning here. But how does one achieve the victory to which the glorified Christ calls his people? By remaining faithful in the light of persecution. This victory is not won by physically fighting another, but patiently enduring suffering at the hands of others. In this way, his people join in the victory of Christ on the cross, not won by killing but by dying.

I will give the right to eat from the tree of life, which is in the paradise of God. Christ encourages the Ephesian church to rekindle their first love and stay faithful amid challenges by promising them life in God's future "paradise" (see Rev 21–22 and the Edenlike description of the New Jerusalem), the Greek word used to refer to Eden in the Septuagint. The tree of life represented life in the presence of God in Genesis 2, but because of their rebellion, Adam and Eve were forced to leave Eden. Since they were no longer able to eat from the tree of life, death was the eventual result.

What the Structure Means:
The Outline of the Seven Letters (Rev 2–3)

The seven letters are all different in content, but they all share a fairly set form composed of six parts:

Addressee: Each letter begins "to the angel of the church of x." As we learned from 1:20 each church had an angel associated with it. To address the angel was to address the church at large. In the Old Testament, we do get occasional glimpses of the role of angels as servants of God. Deuteronomy 32:8 for instance is best rendered "when the Most High gave the nations their inheritance, when he divided all mankind, he set up boundaries for the peoples according to the sons of God,"[5] where "sons of God" is a common way to refer to angels. For the idea that God assigned angels to nations we can cite Daniel 10 where the angel Gabriel refers to a conflict between Michael, whom later Gabriel refers to as "the great prince who protects your people" (12:1), and the "prince of Persia" and the "prince of Greece" (10:13, 20–21). Here the angel is probably the messenger (another possible translation of the Greek *angelos*) to the church since the contents of the letters are clearly directed to the human members.

Introduction of the Speaker: In all seven cases, the glorified Christ is the one speaking to the church. The formula for introducing him always begins "these are the words of . . .," but then the speaker designates Christ by a series of different epithets that glorify and exalt him as he begins to address the church.

Evaluation: Christ evaluates each church, introducing his comments by "I know . . .". Most churches received positive and negative comments, but two churches (Smyrna and Philadelphia) hear only positive comments and one church receives only negative evaluations (Laodicea).

Required Responses: After the evaluation, Christ calls the churches to some type of response. This response might be to repent of their sin or to wake up their dormant faith or to continue to endure in their faith despite the challenges that they face. Occasionally, the call to repent is accompanied by threats of judgment that intend to urge the church toward repentance. (See also "Going Deeper into Repentance: Revelation 9:20–21.")

Call to Pay Attention: Each letter contains a call to pay attention at the end of the letter: "Whoever has ears, let them hear what the Spirit says to the churches." Sometimes it precedes the promise of reward but sometimes follows it. The formula challenges those who read the letter to respond with obedience and puts the responsibility on them if they choose to ignore the warnings of the letter.

Reward: The letters also end by noting the reward that will come "to the one who is victorious," that is those who remain faithful and obedient to the very end.

The Letter to the Church in Smyrna (2:8–11)

2:8 *To the angel of the church in Smyrna write*. Smyrna was also a commercially successfully city that boasted significant temples. Metzger and deSilva mention two: a temple to the goddess Roma that was built in 185 BC and a temple to the emperor Tiberius built in AD 26.[6]

    These are the words. See note at 2:1.

    The First and the Last. See notes at 1:17 and 1:8. The reference is to Jesus "who died" (was crucified) "and came to life again" (was raised from the dead).

2:9 *A synagogue of Satan*. The local synagogue apparently has harassed, or worse, the local Christians and thus show themselves to be in league with Satan (referred to as the devil in v. 10, see note at 12:9). While the devil who is also known as Satan (from the Hebrew/Aramaic word that means "to accuse" or "to be an adversary" or perhaps "to execute"[7]) has been around even before humanity, the Old Testament does not mention him. References to "the Satan," the accuser in Job (1:6–9, 12; 2:1–7), and Zechariah (3:1–2) are clearly not a personal name since they have the definite article prefixed to the word *satan*. While 1 Chronicles 21:1 does not have the definite article, the similar dynamic between God and this figure as we have in Job (that this figure carries out the work of God [compare 1 Ch 21:1 with 2 Sa 24:1]) suggests that these references to the accuser are actually to an angel who does God's work on his behalf).

2:10 *Your victor's crown.* NLT and ESV are more faithful to the Greek, rendering the phrase "the crown of life." The picture of a crown being a reward for godliness may be seen as early as Proverbs (4:9; 10:6). Paul tells the Corinthian church that their spiritual efforts will result in "a crown that will last forever" (1 Co 9:25). James speaks in terms even closer to that of Revelation when it promises that the one "who perseveres under trial" will receive the "crown of life" (Jas 1:12).

2:11 *Whoever has ears.* See note at 2:7.

The one who is victorious. See note at 2:7.

Will not be hurt at all by the second death. While those who are victorious will suffer death, they won't suffer at the time of the final judgment (see note on "second death" at 20:6). The letter began by describing the glorified Christ as the one "who died and came to life again" (2:8), and now he promises that those who follow him will follow in his wake.

The Letter to the Church in Pergamum (2:12–17)

2:12 *To the angel of the church in Pergamum write.* Like the previous two cities, Pergamum was known for its many altars dedicated to the Greek gods and to the Roman emperors. According to Metzger and deSilva, when Christ refers to Pergamum as the place "where Satan has his throne" (2:13), the most likely referent is a tremendous altar dedicated to Zeus (the chief god of the Greeks and Romans and therefore appropriately identified with the chief of the demons) that was in Pergamum.[8]

These are the words. See note at 2:1.

Who has the sharp double-edged sword. See notes at 1:16 and 19:15.

2:13 *Where Satan has his throne . . . where Satan lives.* Probably a reference to the large altar dedicated to Zeus mentioned above. For Satan, see note at 2:9.

2:14 *The teaching of Balaam.* Numbers 22–25 tells the story of Balaam, and the specific reference here is to Numbers 25. In the first part of the story, the king of Moab, a man named Balak, was concerned because the Israelites were about to enter their territory on their way to the Promised Land from Egypt. He worried that they would eat up their resources and "lick up everything around us, as an ox licks up the grass of the field" (Nu 22:4). In response, he calls on the services of a diviner named Balaam, who lived at Pethor, near the Euphrates River (22:5). The king wanted to pay him to curse the Israelites as they passed through. At first Balaam refuses because Yahweh told him that he would not allow him to curse the Israelites. When the Moabites persisted, Yahweh told the diviner that he could go but only say what Yahweh would tell him to say. As he left for Moab, an angel of the Lord opposed him. While Balaam could not see the angel, the donkey could and refused to move. Balaam beat the donkey three times before the donkey spoke to tell him about the opposing angel in is path. Apparently, the donkey was more spiritually aware than the diviner, and Yahweh was intent on driving home his point that Balaam could only say what Yahweh himself told him to say.

When Balaam arrived, four times God told him he could not curse the Israelites but only bless them, thus greatly frustrating Balak. Balaam told him he could only do what Yahweh wanted him to do. Thus, he was only able to bless and not curse the Israelites. He even announced curses toward some of Israel's enemies including Amalek, the Kenites, Ashur, and Eber (Nu 24:2–25).

One would think that Balaam's refusal to curse the Israelites would end the story, but apparently Balaam was interested in getting paid for bringing harm to Israel as they passed through Moab. The next chapter describes how Moabite women seduced some Israelites to sacrifice to false gods and eat a meal made of the food sacrificed to these false gods. God was intensely angry with Israel and commanded Moses to execute those who so allied with the false god, "the Baal of Peor" (Nu 25:3–4). After this divine command was given, an Israelite named Cozbi brought a Midianite woman (apparently allied with the Moabites at this point) into the camp. The priest Phinehas chased after them and with one thrust of his spear killed both, indicating they were copulating at the time. When Phinehas executed the pair, the plague that God had sent into the camp stopped, earning the priest great praise and "a covenant of a lasting priesthood, because he was zealous for the honor of his God and made atonement for the Israelites" (25:12–13).

Balaam is not mentioned even once in Numbers 25. But later when the Israelites fought the Midianites, Moses calls for punishment against the whole population because "they were the ones who followed Balaam's advice and enticed the Israelites to be unfaithful to the LORD in the Peor incident, so that a plague struck the LORD's people" (Nu 31:16).

Balaam's crime was motivated by greed. Thus, Jude connects false teachers at this time with Balaam by saying that they "have rushed for profit into Balaam's error" (v. 11; see also 2 Pe 2:15). And the glorified Christ associates those in Pergamum who were eating food offered to idols and committing sexual immorality with this detested Old Testament character.

2:15 *The teaching of the Nicolaitans.* See note at 2:6.

2:16 *The sword of my mouth.* See note at 1:16.

2:17 *Whoever has ears.* See note at 2:7.

To the one who is victorious. See note at 2:7.

The hidden manna. When the Israelites were in the wilderness, God supplied them with manna, described as "bread from heaven" (Ex 16:4). When God first supplied this "bread" and the people saw it on the ground, they asked "what is it?" which in Hebrew is *man hu'*, giving manna its name (Ex 16:15). It was "white like coriander seed and tasted like wafers made with honey" (Ex 16:31). Manna thus was God's miraculous provision of food in the desert, and so the potential reward of "manna" to the victorious Christians of Pergamum is a way of suggesting God's provision. At the moment the manna is "hidden," perhaps a reference to the later Jewish idea that the ark of the covenant (with its jar of manna, Ex 16:32–34; see also Heb 9:4) was hidden before the Babylonians burned down the temple (2 Macc. 2:4–8; 2 Bar. 6:8). Most likely, the manna described here is not literal food, but rather a symbol of God's provision in a broader sense. The symbolism may be particularly relevant in contrast to the food sacrificed to idols in 2:14 that Christ calls on his people to forgo.

A white stone with a new name written on it. An inscribed white stone is the second reward promised to victorious Christians from the Pergamum church. We can discern no Old Testament background to the white stone as such. According to Metzger and deSilva, the background was more recent but still "ancient" in that "a white stone was greatly prized, either as an amulet, especially if the name of some deity was engraved upon it, or as a mark of membership in a special group."[9] The white stone will have a "new name written on it," indicating a new identity because of God's reward. In Isaiah, vindicated Israel "will be called by a new name that the mouth of the LORD will bestow" (Isa 62:2). Alternatively, this "new name" may refer not to a new name for the victorious individual, but a new name of Jesus that would grant a deeper insight into his nature (see note at 19:12). See also note at 3:12.

The Letter to the Church in Thyatira (2:18–29)

2:18 *To the angel of the church in Thyatira write.* Thyatira was a commercial hub with many trade guilds.[10] Trade guilds would have meetings and banquets that were held in temple precincts. Participation in them would have created a theological and ethical problem for the Christians in the city.[11]

These are the words. See note at 2:1.

Whose eyes are like blazing fire and whose feet are like burnished bronze. See note at 1:13–15.

2:20 *That woman Jezebel.* The glorified Christ singles out a woman whose false teaching and practices threatens the well-being of the church in Thyatira since the Christians there "tolerate" her. She is a self-appointed prophet who advocates sexual immorality and eating food sacrificed to idols. In the letter to the church at Pergamum these specific sins were linked with the Old Testament story of Balaam. In this letter, the same sins are associated with the story of Jezebel.

Ahab, king of the northern kingdom of Israel (871–852 BC), married Jezebel, the daughter of the king of Sidon, who brought her form of Baal worship to the kingdom. Ahab constructed an altar to Baal in the northern kingdom, thus bringing on God's anger (1 Ki 16:31–33). God responded by commissioning his prophet Elijah to confront Ahab and Jezebel, leading to the dramatic scene on Mount Carmel where God lit the altar fire after the Baal prophets' failure to do so (1 Ki 18). Jezebel was thus a paragon of false worship and its associated practices, and thus was an effective analogy for a woman in the church at Thyatira who was also advocating false religious ideas and practices.

2:23 *I am he who searches hearts and minds, and I will repay each of you according to your deeds.* The glorified Christ asserts his right to judge people based on his intimate and sure knowledge of their inner life. This ability and right are divine, reflecting the claims of Yahweh in the Old Testament. In Jeremiah, for instance, we read, "I the LORD search the heart and examine the mind, to reward each person according to their conduct, according to what their deeds deserve" (Jer 17:10; see also 11:20; Ps 7:9; 139:1–2, 23).

2:26 *To the one who is victorious.* See note at 2:7.

2:27 *Will rule them with an iron scepter and will dash them to pieces like pottery.* The glorified Christ promises the persecuted Christians, who resist false teaching and evil practices, that they will go from being the oppressed to being people in authority, able to counter those who try to harm them.

Such a promise, while off-putting to comfortable and secure people today, would be greatly encouraging to the original recipients of the letter. The quotation comes from Psalm 2 (specifically v. 9). This psalm warns those who resist God and his "anointed" that God's judgment would come on them since they threatened the people of God. In its original setting, God's anointed was the Davidic king, who was God's representative on earth and who had a special relationship with God. God had made a covenant with David proclaiming that his descendants would be his sons and that he would be their father (2 Sa 7:14). God further assured David that "your house and your kingdom will endure forever before me; your throne will be established forever" (2 Sa 7:16).

During the monarchical period, Psalm 2 was almost certainly used as a hymn celebrating the inauguration of a new Davidic king.[12] But, due to the sin of God's people as well as David's descendants, the last king to sit on the throne in Jerusalem was Zedekiah, whose reign ended with the Babylonian defeat of that city (586 BC). At that point, the faithful came to understand Psalm 2's latent eschatological sense as they started to look forward to a future descendant of David who would be the Messiah. For this reason, in the aftermath of the resurrection, the New Testament authors knew that Jesus was the fulfillment of that anticipation and thus often quoted Psalm 2 in reference to him (Ac 4:25–26; 13:33; Heb 1:5; 5:5). Indeed, the reference here won't be the last time John quotes or alludes to Psalm 2 (see "Revelation Through Old Testament Eyes: Psalms" at Rev 12:5, and note at Rev 19:15, "He will rule with an iron scepter") in connection with the glorified Christ who will judge the godless and save his people.

The citation here, though, is slightly different in that Christ promises the victorious Christians at Thyatira that they will be the ones who exercise judgment on those who oppress them. In other words, God's people will join their Lord in bringing an end to the evil of the world (Rev 20:4–5). Christ has received the authority for judgment from the Father ("just as I have received authority from my Father"), but the people will participate in this great work.

2:28 *The morning star.* Christ promises that those who are victorious will receive the morning star. The morning star, perhaps a reference to Venus (actually a planet, but shining like a star in the sky), would be the brightest light in the sky. We have already mentioned (see note at 1:16) that in Scripture, including the Old Testament as well as Revelation, stars represent celestial beings like angels. Jesus will later identify himself as the "bright Morning Star" (Rev 22:16). So here Jesus may be offering himself as a prize to the victorious or as Metzger and deSilva put it, "Christ is pledging to give himself.

The ultimate reward enjoyed by Christians is to be with their Lord."[13] As Ian Paul points out,[14] there may also be a connection here with the fourth oracle of Balaam (Nu 24:15–19) where we also have a mention of a star (but not specifically the morning star) and a scepter, as well as crushing the enemy. Perhaps the connection was made because this fourth oracle was widely regarded as having messianic import in Jewish circles of the time. As Keener suggests, Christ giving the morning star to the victorious people of Thyatira "suggests that he will share not only victory in an abstract sense (2:26) but himself as the morning star with his people (2:28)."[15] The only other time "morning star" is mentioned in the Old Testament, it is used in a negative sense (Isa 14:12)

2:29 *Whoever has ears.* See note at 2:7.

REVELATION 3

The Letter to the Church in Sardis (3:1–6)

3:1 *To the angel of the church in Sardis write.* Sardis, like Thyatira, was a busy commercial hub. Sardis had a storied past by the time the letter arrived in the city, having been the capital of Lydia when the famed and wealthy Croessus was its king in the sixth century BC. His kingdom came to an end when Cyrus the Great defeated the city in 546 BC, even before that Persian king defeated Babylon in 539 BC. Sardis had never again resumed its former glory but was still a substantial city in the first century AD.

The seven spirits of God. See note at 1:4.

And the seven stars. See notes at 1:20; 2:1.

3:2 *Wake up!* Christ rebukes the church in Sardis for being spiritually asleep. The prophet Joel also instructed his audience to wake up, characterizing them as drunkards (Joel 1:5). In their case, however, they were to wake up to wail because new wine has been taken from them. In other words, they were to wake up to experience the punishment that was coming on them. In the case of the church at Sardis, they were to wake up so that they could strengthen what was about to die, namely their spiritual passion.

3:3 *I will come like a thief.* Jesus warns them that if they don't wake up in their spiritual life, then he will come on them as a thief, in other words with stealth (Job 24:14) and suddenly (Pr 6:11). The idea of Jesus coming back like a thief is reminiscent of 1 Thessalonians's warning that "the day of the Lord will come like a thief in the night" (5:2). Paul urges the Thessalonian church to "not be like others, who are asleep, but let us be awake and sober" (5:6).

3:4 *Not soiled their clothes . . . dressed in white.* In one of his night visions (Zec 3:1–10), the prophet Zechariah sees the High Priest at the time dressed in filthy clothes with an accuser next to him making accusations. The angel of the Lord (who is the Lord himself) rebukes the accuser, telling him that Joshua is like a stick rescued from a burning fire. He then orders that the filthy clothes be removed and that he be given a clean turban. He then calls on Zechariah to be obedient, and in return the angel says that he will govern "my house and have charge of my courts" (confirming the connection between the angel and the Lord, Zec 3:7).

Filthy clothes, of course, are symbolic of sin (see also note at 7:13–14). Since some in Sardis have not soiled their clothes, that means at least a few have not participated in the sins which led the glorified Christ to say most of them are "dead" and need to "wake up" (3:1–2). They will wear white garments, indicating that they are pure and victorious and associated with the heavenly realm (see note on "white clothes" at 3:18).

3:5 *The one who is victorious.* See note at 2:7.

From the book of life. In the imprecation of Psalm 69, the psalmist calls on God to blot out of the book of life the names of those who falsely accuse him (v. 28). In its Old Testament context, this request is simply that they die. This is the book that Moses also refers to when, in the aftermath of the sin with the golden calf, he intercedes by saying, "Please forgive their sin—but if not, then blot me from the book you have written" (Ex 32:32). In the Old Testament it is only in the book of Daniel that we have a reference to a "book" that registers whose who will participate in the afterlife: "At that time Michael, the great prince who protects your people, will arise. There will be a time of distress such as has not happened from the beginning of nations until then. But at that time your people—everyone whose name is found written in the book—will be delivered" (Da 12:1). In our passage, the idea is that people who are alive are in the book of life and that those Christians who persevere will continue to be in the book of life even after present physical life.

3:6 *Whoever has ears.* See note at 2:7.

Going Deeper into the Victorious Life:
Revelation 2:7, 11, 17, 26; 3:5, 12, 21

All seven letters to the churches promise a reward to "the one who is victorious." But what exactly does it mean to live the victorious life according to the book of Revelation?

In the first place, victory is in the future for those addressed in the letters. At present, the Christians in the seven churches live in contexts where their faith is belittled and perhaps even persecuted. As a result, many are tempted to give in and give up on their faith. Therefore, victory comes as one perseveres and stays faithful in the face of temptation and suffering, which will never go away in this life. Indeed, the only ones in the book of Revelation who have presently and definitively achieved victory are those who have died already. A heavenly voice commends the martyrs because:

> They triumphed over him [the dragon who represents the devil]
>> by the blood of the Lamb
>> and by the word of their testimony;
> they did not love their lives so much
>> as to shrink from death. (Rev 12:11; see also 15:2)

Victory, therefore, comes at the end after living a faithful life. Victory does not mean escaping suffering in this life; indeed, as the martyrs can testify, victory might mean dying a gruesome death, but as the glorified Christ says to the church at Smyrna, "the one who is victorious will not be hurt at all by the second death" (2:11).

The rest of the New Testament agrees that life from beginning to end is a struggle. No one escapes trouble. Complete victory is in the future. But that does not mean Christians cannot experience glimmers of that future victory in our present life amid suffering. Jesus told his disciples that "in this world you will have trouble." Yet we can still have peace not because there will be no turmoil, but because, Jesus says, "I have overcome the world" (Jn 16:33). Paul too spoke to the Christians at Rome as people who would experience "trouble or hardship or persecution or famine or nakedness or danger or sword" and then applied Psalm 44:22 to his readers: "For your sake we face death all day long; we are considered as sheep to be slaughtered" (Ro 8:35–36). Even so, he can call Christians who experience such difficult things "more than conquerors through him who loved us" (Ro 8:37). Why? Because nothing "will be able to separate us from the love of God that is in Christ Jesus our Lord" (Ro 8:39).

What then is the victorious life? It is a life lived in faith that (despite our present suffering) God will have the final victory. Because of this we can live a life, even one beset with trouble and temptations, with peace and joy. The book of Revelation reminds us that the truly victorious one is not only the one who lives in faith and obedience today, but all the way to the end.

The Letter to the Church in Philadelphia (3:7–13)

3:7 *To the angel of the church in Philadelphia write.* Philadelphia was named after the king who established this city, the king of Pergamum at the time, Attalus II Philadelphos ("lover of his brother"), who himself was named because of his attachment to his brother Eumenes. The city had been periodically damaged by earthquakes, with one particularly severe earthquake in AD 17. However, by the time the church there received its letter, the city had been rebuilt.

These are the words. See note at 2:1.

Who holds the key of David. The reference to the key of David takes us to Isaiah 22 and a comparison between the then palace administrator Shebna and a person named Eliakim who will succeed Shebna in that position. God announces the future removal of Shebna because he is more concerned about his tomb than he is about caring for the people of God. The palace administrator, a powerful position, influenced both the material and spiritual health of the people.[1] He held the "key of David," so that "what he opens no one can shut, and what he shuts no one can open" (Isa 22:22). In other words, as palace administrator, he could bring people into the presence of the king or keep them shut out. That Christ possesses the "key of David" is a way of saying that he controls who has access to God and who does not. For the Philadelphians, Christ has "placed before you an open door that no one can shut." He thus encourages the members of this church who "have little strength, yet . . . have kept my word and have not denied my name" (3:8).

3:9 *The synagogue of Satan.* See note at 2:9.

Make them come and fall down at your feet. To fall at someone's feet is a gesture of submission and lower status (1 Sa 25:24; 2 Sa 22:39–40; 2 Ki 4:37; Ps 18:38).

3:11 *Your crown.* See note at 2:10.

3:12 *The one who is victorious.* See note at 2:7.

A pillar in the temple of my God. Those who stay faithful in the face of persecution (are "victorious") will be made pillars in the temple of God. In the Old Testament temple stood two prominent pillars named Jachin ("he will establish") and Boaz ("by strength"; 1 Ki 7:15–22). These pillars, a temple innovation compared to the tabernacle which did not have pillars, reinforced the idea that God had established his people in the land after the defeat of their internal enemies through the leadership of David, the conquest completer.[2] The temple represented the presence of God on earth during Old Testament times, so to be a pillar in the temple means that these faithful Philadelphians would live forever in God's presence: "never again will they leave it."

I will write on them the name of my God and the name of the city of my God, the new Jerusalem, which is coming down out of heaven from my God; and I will also write on them my new name. The faithful in Philadelphia will be inscribed with the names of God, the New Jerusalem, and Christ's new name. Writing a name on something signifies ownership. Jerusalem was the city of Zion, where God made his presence known. The new Jerusalem from heaven will be further described at length in the final two chapters of Revelation (particularly 21:9–21), but represents the kingdom of God, heaven itself, where people live in God's very presence. Williamson points out that in the Old Testament "only the high priest bore God's name (inscribed on the gold band of his turban, Ex 39:30–31)."[3] Priests were those who lived in the very presence of God, thus in the new Jerusalem all God's faithful people are priests. Christ's "new name" refers to his new status as the glorified Christ after the resurrection and ascension. We might also see a connection here with the third commandment, traditionally understood to prohibit using God's name in vain; but according to Carmen Imes, it has a larger meaning, that would also effectively prohibit a misuse of the name. She translates "you must not bear (or carry) the name of Yahweh, your God in vain, for Yahweh will not hold guiltless one who bears (or carries) his name in vain."[4] Here, the faithful are pictured as bearing God's name, which means living and representing God faithfully to the world.

3:13 *Whoever has ears.* See note on 2:7.

The Letter to the Church in Laodicea (3:14–22)

3:14 *To the angel of the church in Laodicea write.* The city was named after Laodice the wife of its founder the Seleucid ruler Antiochus II. Laodicea was a wealthy textile town, known for its soft, black wool. The city was noted for its medical facilities, including an ointment to treat eyes.

These are the words. See note on 2:1.

Of the Amen, the faithful and true witness, the ruler of God's creation. The glorified Christ is the Amen, which comes from the Hebrew, meaning "so be it." His work on the cross and his coming judgment will be the final word, bringing to full completion God's redemption of his people.

Witness is a legal term, in the Bible often associated with the covenant, which is a legal metaphor of God's royal relationship with his vassal people.

The witness testifies to the validity of the relationship and ensures the fulfillment of the terms. Jesus is a "faithful and true witness" (see also 19:11), thus assuring the church in Laodicea that the divine promises will surely come to fruition.

Finally, in this verse Jesus is the "ruler" (*arche*) of God's creation. The NIV rendering is idiosyncratic and obscures certain connections. Other English versions provide a superior translation "beginning" or "originator" of creation (see NLT, ESV, CSB, and more). Jesus is also said to be the "beginning" (even NIV renders *arche* as "beginning") in Colossians 1:18, in a context that also proclaims Jesus "the firstborn over all creation" (Col 1:15). Here we see a connection back to the picture of Woman Wisdom in Proverbs 8:22–31. Thus, Paul in Colossians, John in Revelation, and see also Matthew 11:18–19 and John 1:1–3, associates Jesus with Woman Wisdom to assert that Jesus not only observed but also participated in the creation of the world.[5]

3:16 *Because you are lukewarm.* This vivid analogy between the church in Laodicea and lukewarm water likely comes not from the Old Testament but from the local region itself. As often pointed out, the city of Laodicea brought in its water from the nearby hot springs at Heliopolis. While hot at its source, by the time the water arrived in Laodicea, it was lukewarm and so filled with minerals that if one would drink it without waiting for the water to cool, they would vomit it up. In this way, the glorified Jesus describes the tepid "deeds" of the church as repulsive to him.

3:18 *Buy from me gold refined in the fire.* In the previous verse, Christ has criticized the Laodicean church for becoming materially wealthy and claiming they need nothing. But in reality they are spiritually poor and pitiful. They need to understand that true wealth is measured in their devotion to God. They need to trade their material wealth for true spiritual wealth that can only come from God. In Jeremiah, God describes himself as the one who will refine his people, whose sin is likened to the dross which destroys the high quality of precious metals (Jer 6:29; Zec 13:9; Mal 3:2–3).

White clothes to wear, so you can cover your shameful nakedness. According to 3:17 the Laodiceans, who thought they were rich, were actually "wretched, pitiful, poor, blind and naked." Their present spiritual state is here described as "shameful nakedness." Originally there was nothing shameful about nakedness; indeed, the second creation account ends by describing the first man and woman as "both naked, and they felt no shame" (Ge 2:25). In the very next chapter, though, they rebel against God by eating of the forbidden fruit of the tree of the knowledge of good and evil with the result that their harmonious relationship with God is shattered, as is their intimate relationship with each other. The result is that they no longer stand naked before each other without feeling shame. While God judges them by expelling them from the garden, he shows his grace to them by giving them clothes (3:21).[6] Thus, Israel's poets and prophets will later describe Israel's sinful condition by referring to their shameful nakedness (La 1:8; Mic 1:11; Na 3:5).

If they turn to Christ and acknowledge their state, then he will clothe them so their nakedness will no longer be seen. Specifically, he will clothe them with white clothes. The only Old Testament precursor to this may be seen in the clothes of the Ancient of Days, God himself, in Daniel's first vision, but that seems to connect with the New Testament's use of white clothes with those associated with heavenly realities. At the Transfiguration, for instance, Jesus' clothes became white (Mt 17:2; Mk 9:3). Angel's garments are also described as being white (Mt 28:2–3; Mk 16:5; John 20:12; Ac 1:10). The most frequent mention of white clothes comes in the book of Revelation where, like in this passage, white signifies heavenly associations for glorified saints and angels alike (3:4, 5; 4:4; 6:11; 7:9, 13–14; 19:14).

Salve to put on your eyes. In 3:17, the Laodiceans were called blind. They thought they were rich, but in reality they were poor. In other words, their blindness was not physical, but refers to their lack of self-awareness of their true spiritual state. In verse 18 Christ tells them that he will provide them with salve that will cure their blindness if they buy from him refined gold (representing true wealth; see above comment). The Old Testament uses blindness as a metaphor for lack of perception and discernment on several occasions (Isa 43:8; 44:9–10). Only God can heal this type of spiritual blindness (Isa 29:18; 42:16).

The specific reference to salve as an agent of healing has, according to some commentators, a more local significance. Osborne, basing his comments on Hemer, mentions that Laodicea was known for "their medical center and the eye salve it developed."[7]

3:19 *Those whom I love I rebuke and discipline.* The glorified Christ assures the Laodicean church that his criticisms are for their good, not their destruction. He hopes that by pointing out their faults that they will repent. The sages taught similarly that God rebukes those whom he loves, as we note in Proverbs 3:11–12: "My son, do not despise the Lord's discipline, and do not resent his rebuke, because the Lord disciples those he loves, as a father the son he delights in."[8] See also "Going Deeper into Repentance: Revelation 9:20–21."

3:20 *I stand at the door and knock.* Jesus' rebuke of the Laodicean church has its intention to lead them to repentance. He is inviting them to a more intimate relationship with him. But he will not force himself on them. He stands at the door and is knocking. They need to open the door (respond to his invitation). Despite attempts to connect this image of Christ at the door seeking entry with the man in the Song of Songs, requesting that his beloved open her door to allow him to enter (SS 5:2), there seems to be no substantial connection. The analogy depends on an allegorical reading of the Song, where the man stands for God or Christ and the woman represents the people of God or the church. Those, like myself, who see the Song as a love poem interpret the request of the man to be sexual in nature.

And eat with that person. Even today, to eat with someone is to participate in a deeper relationship. In the ancient world, to share a meal was a sign of friendship. In the Old Testament, Woman Wisdom invites all the men (who represent the readers of the book of Proverbs) to share a meal she has prepared for them. Woman Wisdom is a personification of Yahweh's wisdom and ultimately stands for God himself. After arriving at Mount Sinai, Moses and other leaders "saw the God of Israel" and responded by eating and drinking in celebration (Ex 24:10–11).[9] In our present passage, Jesus seeks entry into the house of those whom he wants to repent to have a relationship with them. To eat with Christ is to "participate in God's salvation in Christ" and has overtones of "the Lord's Supper, in which believers eat the bread as symbolic of sharing in Christ's bodily death (1 Cor 11:23–29)."[10] To eat with Christ is to celebrate, enjoy his hospitality (Ps 23:5), and friendship.

3:21 *To the one who is victorious.* See note at 2:7.

I will give the right to sit with me on my throne, just as I . . . sat down with my Father on his throne. Those who are victorious, namely those who stay faithful in the face of persecution, will share the throne with the glorified Christ as he, who stayed faithful in the face of death, shares the throne with the Father. Written at a time when kings sat on thrones, this image of authority would be immediately understandable to the original audience of these letters. In the Old Testament, God the king was often pictured as sitting on a throne. For two of many examples, we might think of Psalm 47 where God ascends his throne or the picture in Daniel's first vision where the Ancient of Days (Da 7:9). The letter opened with a description of the glorified Christ as the "ruler of God's creation" (3:14), and now we see that Christ will reward his faithful followers by allowing them to share in his rule. (See "Revelation 4 Through Old Testament Eyes: God on His Throne.")

3:22 *Whoever has ears.* See note at 2:7.

What the Structure Means:
From Letters to Visions of the Future

From a structural point of view, the move from the first three chapters of Revelation to what follows seems abrupt. The same might be said from a generic perspective. We move from letters to visions, with the only transitional comment being the rather vague "after this" (4:1).

But we should look closer particularly at Revelation 1 (see notes at 1:4–6, 11) and the end of 22 (see note at 22:20–21), which begin the book and end it as a letter. Revelation in its entirety is a letter written to the seven churches and through them to all Christians. Also, right from the start John is called a prophet and what he was to write was a prophecy (1:3) which includes "the revelation from Jesus Christ, which God gave him to show his servants what must soon take place" (1:1). Finally, when Christ commissions him as a prophet he tells him to write "what you have seen, what is now and what will take place later" (1:19), something that is not fulfilled simply in the seven letters found in chapters 2 and 3.

As we turn from Revelation 3 to 4, we move from seven letters to a series of apocalyptic visions. But we should not lose sight of the fact that these visions are included in the letter.

REVELATION 4

Christ Opens the Seven Seals of the Scroll (4:1–8:5)

The Lamb Worthy to Open the Scroll? (4–5)

The Heavenly Throne (4:1–11)

4:1 *Before me was a door standing open in heaven.* Doors (and gates) represent points of entry into different areas or realms, whether the door of a house through which one can pass from the outside in or inside out or figuratively as in this verse where the door stands for the transition point between heaven and earth. A closed door excludes entry and departure, while an open door allows access. Here the door to heaven stands open so that John can be brought up to heaven into the very throne room of God.

When Jacob fled his brother into Paddan-Aram, he stopped for the night to rest. During the night, he had a dream "in which he saw a stairway resting on the earth, with its top reaching heaven, and the angels of God were ascending and descending on it" (Ge 28:12). After the dream, Jacob exclaimed, "This is none other than the house of God; this is the gate of heaven" (28:17). He thus named the place Bethel, the house of God. Furthermore, Tabb believes that this passage hearkens back to the first verse of Ezekiel where the prophet tells us that "the heavens were opened and I saw visions of God" (Eze 1:1).[1] These Old Testament passages indicate that the idea of an open door to heaven provides access to a more immediate experience of God's presence.

Speaking to me like a trumpet. See note at 1:10.

"Come up here, and I will show you what must take place after this." A heavenly voice, like that of an angel who is perhaps the gatekeeper to

heaven, calls through the open door to invite John to enter the heavenly court. Isaiah began his prophetic ministry after he finds himself in the presence of God on his throne (Isa 6). Isaiah's experience was of God on his throne in the temple (6:1, 4; and see Rev 4:2), but the temple was considered heaven made manifest on earth.

4:2 *I was in the Spirit.* See note on "I was in the Spirit" at 1:10. Besides here and in 1:10, this phrase is used two additional times (17:3 and 21:10) at moments of transition in the structure of the book. Here we move from the letters to the seven churches to the vision of God in the heavenly throne room and the undoing of the seven seals of the scroll.

A *throne in heaven.* See note at 3:21. As we read on, we will see that the throne on which God sits is at the center of everything and everything is oriented in relationship to the throne. As Tabb puts it, "the throne is dominant feature of John's heavenly vision."[2]

4:3 *One who sat there had the appearance of jasper and ruby.* The one who sits on the throne is none other than God, but John's description of him is appropriately vague and majestic at the same time. Today jasper is considered a semiprecious stone, which can come in a variety of colors (red, green, yellow, brown) and ruby is a precious red stone or jewel. We don't know what color jasper John saw in his vision of God, but what we do know is that these are breathtaking and expensive stones. The mention of these stones may draw our attention to the description of the breast piece of the High Priest which is adorned with twelve precious and semiprecious stones (Ex 28:17–21; 39:8–14), but the precise identification of these stones is difficult and uncertain.[3] What is certain is that the Old Testament connects the spiritual realm with semiprecious and precious stones.

A *rainbow that shone like an emerald encircled the throne.* The first rainbow mentioned in the Bible came after the waters of the flood receded and was a sign of God's covenant with Noah assuring the continuation of creation (Ge 9:13). Ezekiel had a vision of God, whom he describes as having the "appearance of a rainbow in the clouds on a rainy day, so was the radiance around him" (Eze 1:28). John's description of the rainbow as shining like an emerald and encircling the throne is like no other rainbow in Scripture or in nature. Rainbows present the colors of the spectrum, not simply green. Perhaps the mention of the emerald is motivated by the fact that it too was found on the front of the High Priest's breast piece (Ex 28:18; 39:11). According to Tabb, "the rainbow in Revelation 4:3 and Ezekiel 1:28 thus conveys the Creator's faithfulness and commitment to his creation, which he will demonstrate by 'destroying the destroyers of the earth' [Rev. 11:18; cf. Gen. 6:11–13] and ushering in the new creation free from the threat of evil (Rev. 21:1, 8)."[4]

Revelation 4 Through Old Testament Eyes: God on His Throne

Following the letters to the seven churches, Revelation 4 turns to John's first vision. He sees a door open in heaven and hears a trumpetlike voice inviting him in so he could see and hear "what must take place after this" (4:1). Suddenly he "was in the Spirit" where he saw "a throne in heaven with someone sitting on it" (4:2). While mentioned earlier in 1:4, John sees the throne for the first time, and it immediately becomes clear that the unnamed occupant is God himself. This throne features centrally in this initial vision of the unsealing of the seven scrolls in Revelation 4–5 but is also mentioned throughout the remainder of the book (6:16; 7:9–11, 17; 8:3; 11:16; 12:5; 13:2; 14:3; 16:17; 19:4–5; 20:11–12; 21:5; 22:1, 3). The throne plays a central role in the book; it is the place from which God directs the action, saving his people and judging their oppressors. The throne is a metonym for God's kingship. He is king over all, and it has connections both with the Old Testament as well as providing a polemic against contemporary understanding of power.

In the Old Testament God is seated on the throne and is king of all. God allowed his prophets to see him on his heavenly throne. The first we hear about is the prophet Micaiah, who begins his prophetic utterance to King Ahab by saying, "Therefore hear the world of the LORD: I saw the LORD sitting on his throne with all the multitudes of heaven standing around him on his right and on his left" (1 Ki 22:19). Then there was Isaiah, who at the time of his prophetic commissioning "saw the Lord, high and exalted, seated on a throne; and the train of his robe filled the temple" (Isa 6:1). Ezekiel too when God called him reports that he saw "what looked like a throne of lapis lazuli, and high above the throne was a figure like that of a man" (Eze 1:26). In a passage that reverberates through Revelation, we hear that Daniel (7:9) too looked as "thrones were set in place, and the Ancient of Days took his seat."

God's throne in the Old Testament was known to be in heaven (Ps 103:19), but because the temple was "heaven on earth," he was also thought to be in that building in Jerusalem:

> The LORD in his in holy temple;
> > the LORD is on his heavenly throne. (Ps 11:4)

God's throne and thus his kingship is closely connected with judgment as it is in the book of Revelation:

> The LORD reigns forever;
> > he has established his throne for judgment.
> He rules the world in righteousness
> > and judges the peoples with equity. (Ps 9:7–8)

God on his throne evokes fear in those who resist him and fight his people, but God on his throne evokes worship from the angels and from his people (see "Going Deeper into Worship: Revelation 4–5").

We see there is a close connection between God the king on his throne in the Old Testament and in the book of Revelation. However, there are also differences. Ian Paul, based on the work of Aune, cites the following differences:

1. Rather than priests, twenty-four elders wearing white, like pagan priests, surround the divine throne.

2. They sing "repetitive choruses of exaltation, rather than using the language of the psalms."

3. The cry of "worthy" is not typical of the psalms, but rather "relates to the notion of the *consensus omnium*, according to which, despite appearances of despotism, the emperor[5] actually rules by the will of all and for the good of all."[6]

At the time of the book of Revelation, the Roman emperor demanded total obedience and brooked no rivals. The central role played by God's throne makes it clear that there is one and only one God who deserves our obedience and worship. (See also "Revelation 11:1–2 Through Old Testament Eyes: The Temple" and "Revelation 21 Through Old Testament Eyes: The Heavenly Temple.")

4:4 *Twenty-four other thrones, and seated on them were twenty-four elders.* Moving out from the throne on which God sits are twenty-four other thrones, on which sit twenty-four elders. Their proximity to the divine throne indicates their importance, but the identities of the elders remain something of a debate, starting with the question of whether these are spiritual beings or human. Elder is never used of angels elsewhere, but their closeness to God indicates to some that they must be spiritual, not human. That said, as the psalmist exclaims, "What is mankind that you are mindful of them, humans beings that you care for them? You have made them a little lower than God[7] and crowned them with glory and honor" (Ps 8:4–5). But why twenty-four? Twelve is a number of great significance, being the number of tribes of Israel as well as the number of disciples, and here is likely where the number twenty-four comes to play. That is, perhaps the twenty-four elders represent the twelve tribes of Israel and the twelve disciples being the foundation of the church. This picture suggests the unity and continuity between the Old Testament and the New Testament peoples of God. In Jesus, the division or "wall of hostility" between Jews and Gentiles is torn down since "his purpose was to create in himself one new humanity out of the two, thus making peace" (Eph. 2:15).

Dressed in white. See note at 3:18.

4:5 *From the throne came flashes of lightning, rumblings and peals of thunder.* Storms accompany the appearance of God in the Old Testament as well, influenced by ancient Near Eastern storm god imagery (Ex 19:16; 20:18; 2 Sa 22:14; Ps 18:12, 14; 29:7, etc.). Typically these meteorological phenomenon indicate the divine presence particularly pointing to God's wrath and readiness to judge evil (Isa 30:30; Jer 23:19; 25:32; 30:23). This description anticipates such language relating to the opening of the seventh seal (8:5), the sounding of the seventh trumpet (11:19), and the pouring out of the seven bowl of God's wrath (16:18). This repetition is a key indicator that these three cycles of seven are not giving a sequence of twenty-one judgments, but rather that each cycle recapitulates the previous one, though the last cycle does have a sense of finality to it. See "What the Structure Means: Seals, Trumpets, and Bowls (Rev 6:1–7:5; 8:7–11:19; 15:1–16:21)" at the end of Revelation 16.

The seven Spirits of God. See note on "the seven spirits before his throne" at 1:4.

4:6–8 *What looked like a sea of glass, clear as crystal.* Nothing quite like this occurs elsewhere in Scripture at least outside of the book of Revelation (see 15:2), but there are some connections still to be made. First, the mention of a sea before the throne of God resonates with the fact that the temple had a huge laver of water (holding 11,000 gallons) in front, which was named "the Sea" (1 Ki 7:23–26). The sea was often an image of chaos and even evil, which is controlled and ruled over by God (Ge 1:2; Job 7:12; 26:12; 38:8–11; Ps 74:12–14; 89:9–10; Isa 27:1; Jer 5:22; Da 7:2–3). But the temple water laver called the Sea represented the containment and restraint of these anticreation powers. We can find ourselves in dangerous interpretive territory when we take images like this literally instead of focusing on their metaphorical meaning. In this case we would be closer to its true sense by noting that a calm, "glassy" sea before the throne of God would represent his subduing of the powers of chaos.

Though not symbolically representing the sea, other visions of God's appearance speak of a jeweled platform under his feet (Ex 24:10). Then finally we can see elements like Ezekiel's vision of God in the opening chapter of his prophecy. He first mentions a storm (Eze 1:4), then beings, likely the cherubim, the most powerful God's angelic attendants. Above the living beings "was a surface like the sky, glittering like crystal" (1:22 NLT). And on this surface was "a throne made of blue lapis lazuli" on which sat a figure, surely representing God, whose body is compared to "gleaming amber, flickering like a fire" (1:26–27 NLT), while surrounding him "was a glowing halo, like a rainbow shining in the clouds on a rainy day" (1:28 NLT). This rich metaphorical description in Ezekiel communicates God's grandeur and intends to elicit awe.

In the center, around the throne, were four living creatures. In the previous note we mentioned the four living creatures in Ezekiel's opening vision to be identified with the cherubim. Ezekiel's four living creatures had four faces each: human, lion, ox, and eagle. The four living creatures in Revelation have one face each, one of a human, the others a lion, ox, and an eagle. The lion (wild beast), ox (domesticated beast), and the eagle (bird) represented the most powerful of their class of living creature and of course humans were the pinnacle of all living creatures. While in Ezekiel's vision eyes covered the wheels of what should likely be considered the divine chariot propelled by the four living creatures, in Revelation the four living creatures themselves were covered with eyes all over their bodies, allowing them to see in all directions. While the living creatures of Ezekiel had four wings, those in Revelation had six, like the seraphim, another type of powerful heavenly creature (see next note).

Holy, holy, holy is the Lord God Almighty. In Isaiah's commissioning vision, he sees the seraphim with six wings each (Isa 6:2) and hears them calling out, "Holy, holy, holy is the LORD Almighty" (Isa 6:3). In Revelation 4, the author seems to be taking elements from both Isaiah and Ezekiel's opening visions to give shape to his experience of God's appearance. In this way, he communicates the majesty of God, as well as his ineffability, with the aim of provoking reverence and worship.

The Lord God Almighty, who was, and is, and is to come. See notes at 1:4 and 1:8, though note the new order: past, present, future.

4:9-10 *The living creatures give glory, honor, and thanks . . . the twenty-four elders fall down before him.* The living creatures, representing the pinnacle of spiritual power, and the twenty-four elders, representing the Old and New Testament people of God, combine in their worship of God who sits on the throne. The elders lay their crowns before God, showing that, though they have power and authority of their own, it derives from God and is subordinate to his.

4:11 *You are worthy.* See note at 5:9 on "you are worthy."
   For you created all things, and by your will they were created. The twenty-four elders acknowledge that everything, including the living creatures and all humanity, were created by God, which provides the foundational story of the entire Bible (Ge 1–2).

What the Structure Means: The Glorified Christ Opens the Seven-Sealed Scroll (Rev 4:1–8:5)

After the introduction to the book and the letters to the seven churches (chapters 1–2), John presents a series of visions, beginning with the opening of seven seals of a previously closed scroll that announces judgment on evil and rescue for God's beleaguered people.

Before the description of judgment that follows the opening of each of the seals, an angel brings John into the heavenly room where God sits on his throne. This dramatic opening informs us that the action that follows is initiated and controlled from God as he sits on his throne. From the throne came "flashes of lightning, rumblings and peals of thunder" (see note at 4:5), meteorological phenomenon that indicates the divine presence particularly pointing to God's wrath and readiness to judge evil.

God is not alone in heaven. We first hear that there are twenty-four elders, representing the Old Testament and the New Testament people of God (see note at 4:4) also sitting on thrones surrounding God's throne. There are also the "seven spirits of God" in front of the throne, most likely referring to seven angels (4:5, see note at 1:4). In addition, there are "four living creatures" most likely referring to the cherubim, the most potent members of God's heavenly army (see note at 4:6–8).

We should take special notice of the worship offered to God in description of the throne room. Revelation 4 thus ends with praise: "You are worthy, our Lord and God, to receive glory and honor and power, for you created all things, and by your will they were created and have their being" (4:11).

Now that we have heard the description of the scene, John next narrates the action that takes place in the throne room. We hear first that God, the one "who sat on the throne" (5:1) held a scroll in his right hand. This scroll had writing on both sides and had seven seals.

An angel then poses a question that might be taken as a challenge: "Who is worthy to break the seals and open the scroll?" (5:2). At first, it looked to John as if no one on heaven and earth was worthy for this task. This saddened him, until one of the twenty-four elders informed him that there was one who indeed was worthy for this task. The elder names him "the Lion of the tribe of Judah, the Root of David" (5:5). And then John sees the designated one standing at the center of the throne. But rather than a lion, he tells the reader that he saw "a Lamb, looking as if it had been slain" (5:6). All these epithets, of course, refer to Jesus as the one who was worthy to open the seals.

Jesus accordingly takes the scroll from the right hand of God. As a result praise erupts. First the four living creatures and the twenty-four elders proclaim:

> You are worthy to take the scroll
>> and to open its seals,
> because you were slain,
>> and with your blood you purchased for God
>> persons from every tribe and language and people and nation.
> You have made them to be a kingdom and priests to serve our God,
>> and they will reign on the earth. (5:9–10)

The living creatures and elders are then followed by a multitude of angels, who also acknowledge Christ's worthiness to open the seals:

> Worthy is the lamb, who was slain,
>> to receive power and wealth and wisdom and strength
>> and honor and glory and praise! (5:12)

Then, finally, every creature in heaven and earth chime in:

> To him who sits on the throne and to the Lamb
>> be praise and honor and glory and power
> for every and ever! (5:13)

The four living creatures have the last word when they exclaim "Amen!" ("so be it"), giving final affirmation to the whole occasion.

At this point Christ proceeds to open the seals one by one. The first four form a unit in that as each is opened a living creature announces, "Come!" And horses of a certain color (white, black, red, pale green) each take center stage, bringing some form of devastation (war, internal conflict, economic disaster, and death).

The opening of the fifth seal does not bring judgment and devastation, but rather reveals those who have been martyred for their testimony under the heavenly altar, calling for justice against those who had perpetrated such harm against them. They are told that they must wait for a bit longer and that there were more who would have to suffer the fate that they had.

The opening of the sixth seal results in terrestrial and celestial convulsions. The powerful and the not-so-powerful react with fear. They try to hide from the devastation coming from God and the Lamb, but to no avail since "the great day of their wrath has come" (6:17).

All that then remains is the opening of the seventh seal, but rather than proceeding directly to that climactic moment, John provides an interlude. We will see that interludes will also occur between the sounding of the sixth and seventh trumpets (10:1–11:14), but not with the conclusive final cycle of seven, the pouring out of God's bowls of wrath.

The interlude between the opening of the sixth and seventh seals serves to build up the dramatic tension. It also informs us that, like the Israelites at the time of the Egyptian plagues, so those who follow God and the Lamb will be spared from the judgment. God directs his angels to place a mark on 144,000 from the twelve tribes of Israel and then we hear of a white-robed multitude who are "they who have come out of the great tribulation" (7:14). A close reading of this section, as we will see, reveals that these two groups are in actuality one.

After this interlude, Christ opens the seventh seal. For a "half an hour" (8:1), silence settles on heaven and earth. Then an angel carries a censer with the prayers of God's people, which rose to God like smoke. Afterward, the angel filled the censer with fire and threw it on the earth, "and there came pleas of thunder, rumblings, flashes of lightning and an earthquake" (8:5). The judgment that comes with the blowing of the seventh trumpet (11:19) and the pouring of the seventh bowl (16:17–21) will be similar.

John will then move on to the next vision, also a seven-part description of judgment in this case announced by an angel blowing a trumpet. We should observe, though, a subtle connection between the seals and the trumpets, since during the half-hour period of silence before the casting of the censer we are introduced to the seven angels being given trumpets before the narration of the seventh seal (8:2), thus linking the two cycles.

REVELATION 5

Who Is Worthy?—the Lion of Judah, the Root of David! (5:1–5)

5:1 *In the right hand.* See note at 1:16.

A scroll with writing on both sides and sealed with seven seals. In biblical times, scribes wrote on scrolls, rolled-up writing surfaces of parchment, leather, or papyrus. They were closed and secured by seals—sometimes, as we have here, multiple seals, seven being a symbolic number for completeness or totality. Daniel's words were sealed and not to be opened (Da 12:4, 9), but this scroll needed to be opened. The writing on both sides of a scroll is unusual. These rare scrolls have the technical name of *opisthograph*. The writing on both sides also reminds us of the scroll that the prophet Ezekiel was given (Eze 2:9–10). He was told to ingest this scroll and then speak its words (3:1–9; see Rev 10:9–11). The connection with Ezekiel shows that John is standing in the tradition of the Old Testament prophets. The scroll that Ezekiel was given contained "words of lament and mourning and woe" (2:10), providing another connection to the judgments represented by the seals. As the vision continues, we will see that it is the seals themselves that take center stage beginning with the question of who is able to "open the scroll and its seven seals" (Rev 5:5). It is not certain whether the scroll itself contains the prophecy to follow or some other content.

5:2 *Who is worthy to break the seals and open the scroll?* We have already heard that God is worthy in the praises of the twenty-four elders (4:11). That is, God is worthy to receive their glory and honor and power. But who will be worthy to open the scroll? As of yet, we are not aware of what constitutes worthiness in this matter, but we are told that "no one in heaven or on earth or under the earth" was capable of opening the scroll or seeing what was written inside.

5:5 *The Lion of the tribe of Judah, the Root of David, has triumphed.* Attention now turns to the one who is judged worthy to open the scroll. He is identified first as the Lion of the tribe of Judah. These titles of the one who will be described as the slain lamb (5:6) are ascribed to none other than Jesus, and the titles derive from the Old Testament. Here the triumph of God in Christ is already proclaimed, even before we see many of the other dramatic events found in Revelation. This theme, repeated throughout the book, assures us that despite present or future trouble, God is in control. The final victory is his.

At the end of his life, Jacob confers blessings and curses on his various sons. In connection with the blessing of Judah, we hear that Judah is "a lion's cub . . . you return from the prey, my son. Like a lion he crouches and lies down, like a lioness—who dares to rouse him?" (Ge 49:9). The lion was the most powerful of the wild animals, the comparison suggests that Judah will be a dominant tribe. Indeed, the very next verse of Jacob's blessing anticipates the rise of kingship in the tribe of Judah: "the scepter will not depart from Judah, nor the ruler's staff from between his feet, until he to whom it belongs shall come and the obedience of the nations shall be his" (49:10). And, after an abortive first king from the tribe of Benjamin, namely Saul, kingship takes root in the dynasty of David, a descendant of Judah. David is the one whom God promised an eternal kingship (2 Sa 7:11b-16) which finds its ultimate realization in Jesus Christ, David's descendant, the "anointed king" or Messiah. He is thus the lion of Judah, as he is also the root of David.

Isaiah anticipates that "a shoot will come up from the stump of Jesse; from its roots a Branch will bear fruit" (11:1). This anticipation of a future descendant from the line of Jesse, David's father, comes with hope that he will lead God's people with wisdom and righteousness, ridding the land of wickedness and helping those who are vulnerable, thus leading to a world without conflict (11:2–9). With this background, Isaiah writes "in that day the Root of Jesse will stand as a banner for the peoples; the nations will rally to him, and his resting place will be glorious" (11:10). Paul cites this verse in its Septuagint form in Romans 15:12 and applies it to Christ. Here the book of Revelation changes "Jesse" to his son "David," perhaps to enhance the royal aspect of the title. Jesus is the expected descendant of David, who far exceeded the expectation of a human king who would deliver God's people from their enemies. He is the one who through his death and resurrection will judge the wicked and bring his people to himself.

Going Deeper into Worship: Revelation 4–5

Earlier we explored how the throne in heaven stood for God's kingship (see "Revelation 4 Through Old Testament Eyes: God on His Throne").

God executed his judgment from his throne, punishing the wicked and rescuing his people. Thus, we are not surprised that the throne of God elicits worship from those who surround the throne. In Revelation 4, we hear of the powerful spiritual beings called living creatures repetitively proclaiming: "Holy, holy, holy is the Lord God Almighty, who was and is, and is to come" (4:8). In this way, they give God "glory, honor and thanks" (4:9) and are called by the twenty-four elders who fall down and place their crowns before the throne and announce:

> You are worthy, our Lord and God,
>> to receive glory and honor and power,
> for you created all things,
>> and by your will they were created
>> and have their being. (4:11)

In Revelation 5, worship is now directed at the glorified Christ, who is described as "a Lamb, looking as if it had been slain" and who himself, we learn, is "standing at the center of the throne" (5:6). Like God he is surrounded by the four living creatures and the twenty-four elders. When Christ took the seven-sealed scroll from the hand of God, they worship Christ with a "new song" (5:9), proclaiming his worthiness. They are then joined by thousands of angels (5:12). Then every creature in heaven and earth join in the worship by ascribing Christ "praise and honor and glory and power for every and ever" (5:13) to which the four living creatures respond "Amen" and the elders fall down and worship.

Such intense worship breaks out at other key points in the book of Revelation (e.g. 7:9–11; 11:16–18; 19:1–10), thus permeating the book and showing that God's appearance as judge should elicit not fear but worship. Indeed, the call to and actual worship of God, the Father, and Christ reverberates throughout Revelation more than any other place in the New Testament.

But what exactly is worship? Throughout the Bible, we see that worship involves directing reverence and adoration toward God:

> Ascribe to the LORD, all you families of nations,
>> ascribe to the LORD glory and strength.
> Ascribe to the LORD the glory due his name;
>> bring an offering and come before him.
> Worship the LORD in the splendor of his holiness.
>> Tremble before him, all the earth! (1 Ch 16:28–30)

The book of Psalms is a book of worship, and we can see how God's magnificence is lauded particularly in the hymns:

> Ascribe to the LORD the glory due his name;
>   worship the LORD in the splendor of his holiness. (Ps 29:2)

As in Revelation, psalmic praise is often directed toward God as he sits on his throne as king (Ps 45:6; 47:8; 89:14; 93:2; 97:2; 103:19).

Worship delights God, not because it feeds his ego, but because it allows worshippers to orient their minds and hearts in the right direction that allows them to flourish as well. Proper worship includes an awareness that God is the Creator, and we are his creatures. Such awareness is signaled by gestures of humility in the context of worship, including falling down and bowing to God:

> Come, let us down in worship,
>   let us kneel before the LORD our Maker. (Ps 95:6, see also Ge
> 24:26, 48; Ex 4:31; 12:27; 34:8).

In the present passage, we see signs of submission when the twenty-four elders fall down before God and then lay their crowns before him (4:10).

Ultimately, though, worship involves more than proclaiming God's greatness. It includes our loyalty and obedience. Paul puts it well when he urges his readers to "offer your bodies as a living sacrifice, holy and pleasing to God—this is your true and proper worship" (Ro 12:1).

By describing such worship, the book of Revelation intends to stir its readers to such worship. As we will later observe ("Going Deeper into Idolatry: Revelation 13"), the difference between God's people and those who resist him is not a matter of whether one worships or not but rather where one's worship is directed. To read the book of Revelation as John intended it to be read should move us to full-orbed worship of God.

The Lamb of God Takes the Scroll (5:6–7)

5:6 *Then I saw a Lamb, looking as if it has been slain.* John then sees a lamb near the center of the throne on which God sits (v. 7). This Lamb is Jesus and so the Lamb looks as if it has been slain, a reference to the crucifixion, but this Lamb is very much alive (the resurrection) and able and worthy to open the seven seals that will open the scroll that contains judgments against the sinful world.

Seven horns and seven eyes, which are the seven spirits of God. The symbolic number seven, denoting completion and totality reverberate throughout the book. Horns denote power, and the description that the lamb has seven horns communicates that the slain lamb has complete, total power. The horn image comes from that of an ox or bull. In Daniel 7, the final beast, representing an evil human kingdom, had ten horns, each representing a separate political power. Seven eyes represent the Lamb's far-reaching sight. In one of his night visions, Zechariah asks "who dares despise the day of small things, since the seven eyes of the LORD will range throughout the earth will rejoice when they see the chosen capstone in the hand of Zerubbabel?" (4:10). This description of the Lamb highlights his omnipotence (seven horns), omniscience (seven eyes), and omnipresence (seven spirits throughout the world). (For the seven spirits of God, see note at 1:4.)

Revelation 5:6 Through Old Testament Eyes: The Lamb Who Was Slain

We first hear about a sacrificial lamb in Genesis 22, when God demands that Abraham take his beloved, only son Isaac to Mount Moriah to sacrifice him there. As they ascend the mountain, Isaac asks his father, "The fire and the wood are here . . . but where is the lamb for the burnt offering?" (22:7). While Abraham shows himself willing to be obedient to God's incredible demand, he expresses hope when he responds, "God himself will provide the lamb for the burnt offering, my son" (22:8). And at the last minute, God stays Abraham's hand, and provides the substitute ram.

In the later Mosaic law, lambs play a central role in the sacrificial system. The priests were to offer two lambs a day, one in the morning and one in the evening (Ex 29:40–41; Nu 28:4). Lambs were also sacrificed as part of the fellowship offering (Lev 3:6–7) and the sin offering (Lev 4:32–35).

Even so, the most immediate background to the picture of Jesus as the Lamb is surely the Passover sacrifice, instituted at the time when God freed Israel from Egyptian bondage. On the evening of the final plague, God instructed "the whole community of Israel that on the tenth day of this month each man is to take a lamb for his family, one for each household. If any household is too small for a whole lamb, they must share one with their nearest neighbor, having taken into account the number of people there are" (Ex 12:3–4). The Israelites were to take the blood of the slaughtered lamb and put it "on the sides and tops of the door frames of the houses where they eat the lambs" (12:7). That evening when God would strike down the firstborn of Egypt, he would pass over the houses that had the blood on the sides and tops of their door, so that "no destructive plague will touch you when I strike Egypt" (12:13). At this time, God instituted the Passover, an annual commemoration of this great day of deliverance from their slavery.

The Exodus was the paradigmatic salvation event of the Old Testament and became a template for future divine rescue. Thus, when the prophets spoke of the restoration of the people of God after the judgment that was coming due to their sin, they would frequently use exodus language. The exodus was not just a past, but a future event (see Isaiah 40:1–8 and Hosea 2:14–20 for just two examples of God's promise to lead his people in the wilderness).

The authors of the New Testament understood in the light of resurrection that Jesus' death and resurrection were the ultimate realization of the expectation of a second exodus. Indeed, Mark announces the connection between Jesus and the exodus by citing Isaiah 40 at the beginning of his Gospel (1:1–3). Then we can see how the outline of Jesus ministry follows the story of the exodus event:

- Jesus' baptism in the Jordan mirrors the Israelites' crossing through the Sea.[1]

- Jesus' forty days and nights of temptation mirrors Israel's forty years in the wilderness.[2]

- Jesus speaking about the law on a mountain (the Sermon on the Mount) mirrors God giving Israel the law on Mount Sinai.

- Jesus feeding the crowds in the wilderness mirrors God providing manna for Israel in the wilderness.

These parallels just scratch the surface of the connections that can be drawn between the exodus event and Jesus' life and ministry. In the light of these parallels, we should not be surprised that the crucifixion of Jesus takes place on the eve of the Passover, that annual commemoration of Israel's rescue from Egypt (Mt 26:17–30; Jn 19:14).

John the Baptist exclaimed at the beginning of Jesus' earthly ministry, "Look, the Lamb of God, who takes away the sin of the world!" (Jn 1:29). In the light of the crucifixion and resurrection, Paul more pointedly announced, "for Christ, our Passover lamb, has been sacrificed" (1 Co 5:7).

Besides this important background for the idea of the slain lamb in the exodus tradition, we might also cite Isaiah 53:7 as background to John's picture of Jesus as the lamb that was slain: "He was oppressed and afflicted, yet he did not open his mouth; he was led like a lamb to the slaughter, and as a sheep before its shearers is silent, so he did not open his mouth."

The Four Living Creatures and the Twenty-Four Elders Sing a New Song (5:8–10)

5:8 *Each one had a harp.* When the Lamb takes the seven-sealed scroll from the right hand of God who sat on the throne, the twenty-four elders worship him. The harp was an instrument that accompanied the worship of the Old Testament believers and is often mentioned in the psalms (Ps 33:2; 43:4; 49:4; 57:8–9, etc.).

Holding golden bowls full of incense, which are the prayers of God's people. In the Old Testament the priests would present incense to God, the sweet smell reminding those in the holy precincts that they were out of ordinary space and in holy space. The smell was thought to ascend to heaven into the very presence of God. In the same way, the elders offer the prayers of God's people as a sweet savor to their Lord. As the psalmist stated, "may my prayer be set before you like incense" (Ps 141:2a).

5:9 *They sang a new song.* The twenty-four elders then sing a "new song." The significance of this song being called "new" is not simply that this song had never been song before. "New song" is used in the book of Psalms (33:3; 40:3; 96:1; 98:1; 144:9; 149:1) and Isaiah (42:10) in the context of warfare as well as here in Revelation (as well as in 14:3). A new song is a hymn of victory sung after God has made all things new by his defeat of the forces of evil.[3] (See "Revelation Through Old Testament Eyes: Psalms" at Rev 12:5.)

Jesus, the Lamb that looks as if it had been slain, won a victory over the forces of evil by dying on the cross, being raised from the dead, and ascending into heaven. For this reason, Jesus' redemptive work is occasionally described using military language. Paul writes to the Colossians:

> When you were dead in your sins and in the uncircumcision of your flesh, God made you alive with Christ. He forgave us all our sins, having

canceled the charge of our legal indebtedness, which stood against us and condemned us; he has taken it away, nailing it to the cross. And having disarmed the powers and authorities, he made a public spectacle of them, triumphing over them by the cross. (Col 2:13–15)

Or regarding the ascension, he writes:

But to each one of us grace has been given as Christ apportioned it. This is why it says:
"When he ascended on high,
   he took many captives
   and gave gifts to his people." (Eph 4:7–8)

In the Ephesians passage, Paul cites Psalm 68, a hymn celebrating Yahweh's victory over Israel's enemies, and applies it to Christ. The new song is a victory hymn, celebrating the Lamb's victory over evil that was secured by his death and resurrection and that will be finalized in the judgment to come, that the book of Revelation ultimately anticipates.

You are worthy. The twenty-four elders worship the Lamb who is worthy of their praise and worthy to open the scroll by breaking open the seals. The Lamb's worthiness is mentioned throughout this section, beginning at 4:11; 5:4, 12. In the Old Testament, only Yahweh is worthy of praise (2 Sa 22:4; 1 Ch 16:25; Ps 18:3; 48:1; 96:4; 145:3). The Lamb's worthiness is centered in his death by crucifixion ("you were slain, and with your blood") which is the foundation for the reconciliation of many people of many different races and ethnicities.

Persons from every tribe and language and people and nation. God created all people in the world and loves them. Due to their sin, all people have been separated from God (Ro 3:23; 5:12). But right from the start God has pursued reconciliation with his sinful people. Indeed, God chose Abraham, not for special privilege, but for a special role in bringing a blessing not just to his descendants, the Israelites, but to "all peoples on earth" (Ge 12:3). This way of referring to all the people of the world echoes language from Genesis 10 (see note at 11:9). See also note at 7:9.

5:10 *You have made them to be a kingdom and priests. . . and they will reign on the earth.* Through his death and resurrection, Jesus has made his redeemed people into a kingdom and priests, or we can say a kingdom of priests. They will reign on the earth, meaning that they are kings as well as priests. Of course, at the time Revelation was written Christians were far from kings reigning on the earth. Many, including John himself, were persecuted and marginalized by their society. But John knew that their future was not continued subservience to the powers of this world, but rather they would reign in the future as priest-kings. This is the encouraging message of the book of Revelation.

Revelation 5:10 Through Old Testament Eyes: Kingdom and Priests

The language of "kingdom and priests" is most memorable of Yahweh's words to Moses when the Israelites were gathered at Mount Sinai and about to receive the law:

> This is what you are to say to the descendants of Jacob and what you are to tell the people of Israel: "You yourselves have seen what I did to Egypt, and how I carried you on eagles' wings and brought you to myself. Now if you obey me fully and keep my covenant, then out of all nations you will be my treasured possession. Although the whole earth is mine, you will be for me a kingdom of priests and a holy nation." (Ex 19:3–6)

God is king of all creation; his kingdom encompasses everything and everyone. The so-called enthronement psalms make this clear as they proclaim that "the LORD reigns" (Ps 97:1) and the Lord is "the King" (Ps 98:6, see Psalms 47, 93, 95, 96, 97, 99). In Psalm 103:19, we read: "The LORD has established his throne in heaven, and his kingdom rules over all." The Lord's "kingdom is an everlasting kingdom" and his "dominion endures through all generations" (Ps 145:13).

While Yahweh was king over the whole creation, most did not acknowledge his sovereignty. Psalm 2 captures this spirit of resistance:

> Why do the nations conspire
>   and the peoples plot in vain?
> The kings of the earth rise up
>   and the rulers band together
>   against the LORD and against his anointed, saying:
> "Let us break their chains
>   and throw away their shackles" (Ps 2:1–3)

It is in the light of Yahweh's universal kingship that God tells Moses to tell them that Israel is a "treasured possession" and, more to the point, a "kingdom of priests and a holy nation." Israel, in other words, had been chosen for a special purpose to being blessing to the nations (Ge 12:3).

They performed a priestly service to the rest of the world in mediating Yahweh's presence to others.

Much of the story of the Old Testament, unhappily, is the story of failure of God's people. Many resisted God's rule themselves and God judged them by sending them into exile in Babylon. But the exile was not the end of the story for God's people. The Babylonian exile would come to an end, but the oppression would continue. The story of continued oppression but ultimate rescue was a major theme of the book of Daniel. We see this theme expressed in dreams and visions that look forward to the future.

As Nebuchadnezzar, the Babylonian king, himself expressed that God's kingdom was present and will be eternal (Da 4:3); but in another sense, the perception was that evil human kingdoms were in charge, not God. In Daniel 2, though, Daniel interprets Nebuchadnezzar's dream of a multi-metaled statue in a way that indicates that perception is not reality. The different metals of the statue represented a succession of evil human kingdoms, but the feet of that statue were made of a fragile combination of clay and iron. The climax of the vision comes when "the God of heaven will set up a kingdom that will never be destroyed, nor will it be left to another people. It will crush all those kingdoms and bring them to an end, but it will itself endure forever" (Da 2:44).

When we turn to the New Testament, we hear John the Baptist proclaiming, "Repent, for the kingdom of heaven has come near" (Mt 3:2).[4] Thus, the Gospels announce one of the most prolific themes of the New Testament, namely the kingdom of God.

This commentary is not the place to do a detailed and exhaustive presentation of the theme in the New Testament, but we do want to address the question whether and in what way the kingdom of God arrived with the coming of Jesus, the messiah ("anointed king"). A fair reading of the New Testament material leads us to see that Jesus' coming, particularly his death and resurrection, inaugurates the advent of the kingdom, but that its full realization comes with his second coming. In other words, the kingdom is both present in an important sense, but also future in its full sense. The kingdom is "already" here, but "not yet" fully realized.

That the kingdom is present even at the time of Jesus is made clear in a passage like Luke 18:16–17: "But Jesus called the children and said, 'Let the little children come to me, and do not hinder them, for the kingdom of God belongs to such as these. Truly I tell you, anyone who will not receive the kingdom of God like a little child will never enter it" (see also Lk 4:43; 6:20; 7:28; 8:1, 10; 9:2, 11, 27, 60; 10:9, 11; 11:20; 13:18, 20; 16:16; 17:20–21; 18:24–25, 29; Ac 28:31). The teaching that the kingdom is coming in the future may be seen in the picture of the coming banquet that will celebrate the full realization of the kingdom: "When one of those at the table with him heard this, he said to Jesus, 'Blessed is the one who will eat at the feast in the kingdom of God'" (Lk 14:15).

In an important sense, God rules all creation despite the resistance of some of his creaturely subjects. To say that his kingdom is "not yet" refers to the fact that, because of that resistance, his rule is not completely manifest. The realization at the time of Christ's second coming will eradicate the resistance. The "already" nature of the kingdom is expressed in our present verse (Rev 5:10) in the statement that he has "made them to be a kingdom and priests to serve our God." The "not-yet," future nature of the kingdom is expressed by the statement "and they will reign on earth."

Thousands of Angels and Every Creature Join in the Worship (5:11–13)

5:11 *The voice of many angels, numbering thousands upon thousands, and ten thousand times ten thousand.* This picture of God on the throne accompanied by multitudes of angels mirrors the descriptions found in Isaiah 6, when the prophet in the temple has a vision of the heavenly throne room, and Daniel 7 (see v. 10), when the Ancient of Days sits on the throne to render judgment against the beasts that symbolize evil human kingdoms. (See "Revelation 4 Through Old Testament Eyes: God on His Throne.")

5:12 *Worthy is the Lamb.* See note at 5:3. Christ is worthy to open the seals of the scroll. He is worthy to receive the worship of the angels as well as the twenty-four elders, representing the tribes of Israel and the disciples, thus the Old and New Testament people of God. They are joined by everyone of God's creatures in heaven and earth (v. 13).

Four Living Creatures and the Elders Say "Amen" (5:14)

5:14 *Amen!* From the Hebrew which means "so be it!" The pronouncement signals that since the worthy one has been found and acclaimed by all in heaven and earth, the slain Lamb may commence unsealing the scroll.

REVELATION 6

The Seven Seals (Revelation 6:1–8:5)

The First Seal (6:1–2)

6:1 *The Lamb.* See note at 5:6.

The first of the seven seals. See note at 5:1.

The four living creatures. See note at 4:6–8.

Say in a voice like thunder, "Come!" (For "like thunder," see note at 4:5 and note on "A loud voice like a trumpet" at 1:10.) John now watches as the Lamb, the glorified Christ, opens the first four of the seven seals. As the Lamb opens each of these first four seals, one of the living creatures announces "Come!" (vv. 1, 3, 5, 7). Jesus opens the seals, and as he does so the living creature, a powerful heavenly being, calls forth the first of four horses and their riders. God is in control and the glorified Christ initiates the action, while a powerful heavenly being calls forth the judgments represented by the four horsemen.

6:2 *There before me was a white horse!* As mentioned, the opening of the first four seals will set loose four horses of different colors with their riders. The symbolism of these different colored horses is reminiscent of two brief visions in the book of Zechariah. The first is found in Zechariah 1:7–17. After the narrator introduces and dates the vision, we are told that "in a vision during the night, I saw a man sitting on a red horse that was standing among some myrtle trees in a small valley. Behind him were riders on red, brown, and white horses" (1:8 NLT). These four horsemen "are the ones the LORD has sent out to patrol the earth" (1:10 NLT). The report they bring back is positive: "We have been patrolling the earth, and the whole earth is at peace" (1:11 NLT).

Though the earth is at peace, God's people, who have experienced the exile, are still not made whole. God expresses anger at the nations who "went too far with the punishment" (1:15). God then determines to "return to Jerusalem with mercy, and there my house will be rebuilt. And the measuring line will be stretched out over Jerusalem" (1:16).

The second oracle of Zechariah that features multicolored horses is found in 6:1–8:

> I looked up again, and there before me were four chariots coming out from between two mountains—mountains of bronze. The first chariot had red horses, the second black, the third white, and the fourth dappled—all of them powerful. I asked the angel who was speaking to me, "What are these, my lord?" The angel answered me, "These are the four spirits of heaven, going out from standing in the presence of the Lord of the whole world. The one with the black horses is going toward the north country, the one with the white horses toward the west, and the one with the dappled horses toward the south." When the powerful horses went out, they were straining to go throughout the earth. And he said, "Go throughout the earth." Then he called me, "Look, those going toward the north country have given my Spirit rest in the land of the north."

As in the earlier vision in Zechariah, these horses, while powering chariots rather than carrying riders, patrol the earth. These chariots and their horses represent the "four spirits of heaven," again powerful heavenly beings closely associated with God. They spread out in different directions, but at the end the focus is on those "going toward the north country," pointing to the city of Babylon. The NIV translation of the final verse of the quoted passage (v. 8) can be improved with reference to Boda's translation "Then he cried to me and spoke to me, saying, 'Take note, the ones going out to the land of the north have exhausted my wrath on the land of the north.'"[1]

The idea here, relevant to our understanding of the four horsemen in Revelation, is that these patrolling chariots with their multicolored horses represent God's judgment against those who harm his people. According to Osborne, these "four horsemen of the Apocalypse" represent "conquest to civil unrest, famine and death,"[2] and according to Koester, "the horsemen represent conquest, violence, economic hardship, and death."[3] As in the Old Testament, judgment comes in more than one form. In speaking of the coming judgment of Jerusalem, Ezekiel reports: "For this is what the Sovereign LORD says: How much worse will it be when I send against Jerusalem my four dreadful judgments—sword and famine and wild bests and plague—to kill its men and animals" (14:21). Or in Jeremiah, "I will destroy them with the sword, famine, and plague" (14:12).[4]

Though multifaceted, they are all related. War brings unrest, famine, violence, and death. The sending forth of the four horsemen, in short, brings devastation on those who are God's enemies.

The first horseman rides a white horse. The color white is often associated with "biblical scenes of heavenly or transcendent reality."[5] This connection is particularly true in apocalyptic literature. Daniel 7 presents the prophet's first vision, which begins with a depiction of terrifying beasts that arise out of a chaotic sea. These beasts represent evil human kingdoms that oppress the people of God (7:17). The second half of the vision (7:9–14) turns attention first to God, the Ancient of Days, whose "clothing was as white as snow; the hair of his head was white like wool."

Elsewhere in the book of Revelation, it is the glorified Christ who rides a white horse (19:11), which leads some commentators to believe that it is Jesus who rides out on the first horse.[6] This understanding, however, is unlikely, considering that Jesus is the one who is opening the seals.

The rider on the white horse "held a bow, and he was given a crown, and he rode out as a conqueror bent on conquest" (6:2). This picture probably played on the contemporary fears of Rome, since one of their most formidable foes was the nation of Parthia, known for its calvary that used the bow.[7] In any case, there is no doubt that the first horseman represents the onslaught of war in the interest of expanding empire.

Revelation Through Old Testament Eyes: The Ten Commandments

With the seven seals we have the first of three major sets of seven judgments, this set being followed by the seven trumpets (Rev 8:6–11:19) and the seven bowls (Rev 15–16). But what is judgment based on? When it comes to the Old Testament, judgment results from disobedience to God's law. God had entered a relationship with his people, not because of anything that they did, but out of his grace. In Exodus, Israel's rescue from Egypt precedes God giving them his law, as we can see in the preamble to the Ten Commandments (Ex 20:2).

But God's continuing relationship with his people did depend on their following his law, as primarily expressed through the Ten Commandments (Ex 20:2–17; Dt 5:6–21). God warned his people that if they did not obey his law, they would suffer the consequences as expressed in the curses of the covenant (e.g., Dt 27–28). The Old Testament prophets can be understood as lawyers of the covenant. They came to bring charges of disobedience to God's people with the threat of punishment.

To be sure, the focus in the Old Testament is on Israel, God's chosen people, while the focus in Revelation is judgment on the whole world. As a matter of fact, as is typical of apocalyptic, John's message is a message of hope that his readers, Christians, would be rescued as their oppressors were judged. In other words, the message of judgment will come on those outside the circle of God's people. Still, even in the Old Testament, there is the understanding that those outside of Israel who resist God and act sinfully were subject to God's judgment (Amos 1–2).

All this to say, if we ask why the world outside the church will experience God's judgment, the answer—according to the book of Revelation—may be that they have broken the law as primarily articulated through the Ten Commandments. As we read the book's descriptions of those who will receive God's judgment, we can see that their evil attitudes and actions are infringements of many, though not all, of the commandments. The following gives examples:

First commandment. The first commandment insists that the God of Israel be one's only God. In the book of Revelation, that one God is known in three persons (the Father, the Son, and the Holy Spirit). In the seven letters, the glorified Christ warns believers not to join those who would worship other deities, as he also commends those who resist such worship.

Second commandment. The second commandment follows from the first when it forbids the worship of any human-made image (or idol). In the book of Revelation, the triune God is the only one deserving of worship. One can break the first two commandments by refusing to worship the true God, by worshipping anything other than the true God, or by worshipping the true God or any other thing in the form of an image.

The church in Pergamum, for instance, is commended for remaining true to Christ but even in this church there were some who "ate food sacrificed to idols" (2:14, see similar charge to church at Thyatira, 2:20). Later in the description of the sixth trumpet judgment, we hear that those who survived did not "stop worshipping demons, and their idols of gold, silver, bronze, stone and wood—idols that cannot see or hear or walk" (9:20). We also find mention of worshipping the dragon representing Satan (13:8) along with the beast and its image (13:4, 12–15).

Third Commandment. The third commandment prohibits "bearing" or "carrying" God's name in vain,[8] a law that would be flagrantly broken by blaspheming God's name. The sea beast, who was the emissary of the devil represented by the dragon, "opened its mouth to blaspheme God, and to slander his name and his dwelling place and those who live in heaven" (13:6). See also references to violations of the third commandment in 16:9, 11.

Sixth Commandment. The sixth commandment prohibits murder, the illegitimate taking of human life. The voices of the martyrs call out to God to "judge the inhabitants of the earth and avenge our blood" (6:10). Also, an angel sings out that God is just in his judgments because the objects of God's anger "have shed the blood of your holy people and your prophets" (16:6). For other references to murder as the reason for judgment, see 9:21.

Seventh Commandment: The seventh commandment prohibits adultery, sexual relationships outside the bounds of marriage. The glorified Christ censured some in the church of Pergamum for committing "sexual immorality" (2:14, see similar charge against the church at Thyatira, 2:20; see also 9:21). Later in the book, Babylon the Great, representing Rome and all worldly powers, is said to make the nations drink "the maddening wine of her adulteries" (14:8; 18:3, 9), which as explained in the commentary not only represents marital but also spiritual infidelity (and thus violation of the first commandment). For other references, see 17:1–2.

Eighth commandment: The eighth command prohibits theft, the taking of property that belongs to another. So, along with a list of other sins, mankind did not repent of "their thefts" (9:21) in the aftermath of the sixth trumpet judgment.

Ninth commandment: The ninth commandment prohibits "bearing false witness," which includes lying and deception. The faithful are described as those in whose mouths "no lie was found" (14:5).

The primary reason that judgment comes on the unbelieving world is that they refuse a relationship with God (commandments 1, 2, and 3). Still, this lack of a relationship with God manifests itself in the violation of other commandments that define the relationship between human beings (murder, adultery, theft, lying).

The Second Seal (6:3–4)

6:3 *The Lamb.* See note at 5:6 and "Revelation 5:6 Through Old Testament Eyes: The Lamb Who Was Slain."
> *The second seal.* See note at 5:1
> *The second living creature.* See note at 4:6–8.

6:4 *Another horse came out, a fiery red one.* See note at 6:2, where we mention that Zechariah's vision also includes a red horse (Zec 1:8; 6:2). With the opening of the second of the seven seals, the second of living creatures announces, "Come!" In response, the second of the horsemen appears, this time riding a red horse. The previous horsemen brought violence to the earth through conquest, using the bow as a weapon. Here, armed with a sword, the second horsemen robs the world of peace by turning people against each with lethal violence. Rather than conquest, this horseman brings internal conflict. In such a context, the red horse suggests blood.

The Third Seal (6:5–6)

6:5 *The Lamb.* See note at 5:6 and "Revelation 5:6 Through Old Testament Eyes: The Lamb Who Was Slain."
> *The third seal.* See note at 5:1.
> *The third living creature.* See note at 4:6–8.
> *There before me was a black horse!* The third horseman is on a black horse (see comments on Zec 6:1–8 at the note on Rev 6:2). Black is rarely used in a symbolic sense in the Bible but is on occasion associated with the appearance of God. If we move beyond the word *black* to the more general concept of darkness, which connotes a black color, we observe even more relevant passages that connect black with God's appearance specifically to judge or to implicitly threaten to judge. In Deuteronomy 4:10–11 Moses reminds the Israelites, the children of those who left Egypt, before they went into the promised land that "the day you stood before the Lord your God at Horeb . . . you came near and stood at the foot of the mountain while it blazed with fire to the very heavens, with black clouds and deep darkness." The prophet Joel describes the coming day of the Lord's judgment as "a day of darkness and gloom, a day of clouds and blackness" (Joel 2:2). Zephaniah too pictures the coming day of divine judgment as "a day of wrath—a day of distress and anguish, a day of trouble and ruin, a day of darkness and gloom, a day of clouds and blackness" (Zep 1:15). In the New Testament, Jude castigates false teachers as "shepherds who feed only themselves" (v. 12) and then chillingly announces that for them "blackest darkness has been reserved forever" (v. 13).

Rather than a weapon like a bow or a sword, this horseman carries a "pair of scales," a measuring device that weighs commodities for sale. When scales are mentioned in the Old Testament, there is an emphasis on using honest ones (Lev 19:36; Pr 11:1; 16:11; 20:23). Here scales are mentioned because the scarcity of food is leading to exorbitant prices. As the rider carries the scale, a voice coming from the four living creatures announces that two pounds of wheat will cost a whole day's wages (how the NIV understands the Greek *denarius*, though some believe that it really represents the average wage for two days' labor) as will six pounds of barley. Then the voice expresses caution over the oil and the wine.

The first two riders presage external and internal conflict, and such wars often lead to lack of food and famine. An Old Testament example may be seen in the Elisha narrative after Ben-hadad of Aram besieged the city of Samaria. According to 2 Kings 6:25: "there was a great famine in the city; the siege lasted so long that a donkey's head sold for eighty shekels of silver, and a quarter of a cab of seed pods for five shekels."

Going Deeper into God's Judgment: Revelation 6

John's divine throne vision (Rev 4–5) is the introduction to the description of the unsealing of the seven seals of the scroll that contains God's judgment against evil spiritual powers and humans who side with them against God. God's future judgment permeates the book of Revelation, starting with the description of Christ returning on a cloud that is his war chariot (see commentary at 1:7). The seven letters contain threats of judgment against those who do not persevere in their faith, but with the opening of the scrolls we have the first of several highly symbolic descriptions of God's judgment. These symbolic visions are filled with violent imagery that intends to comfort the oppressed people of God who live under the thumb of evil people. They communicate to them that, though it looks like evil people are in control, God is in control, and he will have the final victory, a victory which will be shared by his faithful followers.

The idea of a violent judgment against evil has sometimes been met with distaste even by Christ's faithful followers. This reaction is becoming even more common today, prompting reading strategies that try to minimize or even do away with the idea that God plans to judge evil people. Such reading strategies often marginalize or even do away with the book of Revelation.

One such strategy is to rightly point out, as I just admitted, that Revelation's picture of the end is described by means of figurative language. While this observation is true, we must also understand that a metaphor's vehicle (the figurative language) coheres with its tenor (the reality to which the figurative language points). As Robert Miller puts it, quoting Susan Hylen,[9] "metaphors do not make the violent imagery (of the Bible) 'transmuted into something nonviolent.'" In other words, violent metaphors, though not giving us literal picture, are telling us about a violent judgment.

Another strategy, proposed in a recent book by Gregory Boyd, suggests that everything in the Bible needs to be evaluated by the standard of Jesus on the cross. After all, he reasons, Jesus is the perfect expression of the nature of God (as we explored in "Going Deeper into the Glorified Christ: Revelation 1:12–16"). By that standard, Boyd believes that all the pictures of God's violent judgment against spiritual powers and human beings must be either the result of the human author's cultural context or his depraved nature,[10] and, while he mostly focuses on the picture of God as a warrior in the Old Testament, he also analyses the book of Revelation using this prism.[11]

In response, though, we would have to ask Boyd why he restricts our understanding of Jesus to Jesus on the cross. Why not also the glorified post-resurrected Christ? Why not Christ ascending into heaven, leading captivity captive (Eph 4:8)? Why not Christ in the book of Revelation, which Jesus himself anticipated in his speech to the disciples at the temple (Mk 13 and parallels)?

I think the reason might be that it does not fit in with Boyd's desire to find a nonviolent God in the Bible. The problem with this, however, is that the Bible, from Genesis 3 to Revelation 20, pictures God consistently as a God of judgment. The psalmist expresses well what the historical narratives, prophets, and law tell us about God:

> The LORD reigns forever;
>   he has established his throne for judgment.
> He rules the world in righteousness
>   and judges the people with equity. (Ps 9:7–8)

And this is good news! God is a God of justice. He judges fairly. God does not minimize evil, saying, "Boys will be boys," and pat them on their heads like a well-meaning but slightly out-of-touch grandfather. When we see the innocent imprisoned, the poor taken advantage of, the powerless abused, we all want to know that the perpetrators will be punished. When David was told the story of the rich man who stole and killed the poor man's lamb, it was this God-given sense of justice that roused David to say, "As surely as the LORD lives, the man who did this must die!" (2 Sa 12:5). Rather than critiquing the picture of God and Christ in the Bible and specifically in the book of Revelation, we should celebrate it along with the four living creatures, the twenty-four elders, and angels, and all God's people as we see throughout the book of Revelation (see "Going Deeper into Worship: Revelation 4–5").

The Fourth Seal (6:7–8)

6:7 *The Lamb.* See note at 5:6 and "Revelation 5:6 Through Old Testament Eyes: The Lamb Who Was Slain."
   The fourth seal. See note at 5:1.
   The fourth living creature. See note at 4:6–8.

6:8 *There before me was a pale horse!* The last of the riders comes forth upon the opening of the fourth seal. The horse is pale according to the NIV translation, but many other translations suggest something like "pale green" (NLT, see also NRSV; NAB). In the Old Testament the faces of those stricken with deep fear, particularly fear of death, turn pale. After receiving a deeply disturbing vision, Daniel reports "my face turned deathly pale and I was helpless" (10:8). As the prophet Nahum anticipates the fall of the great Assyrian city of Nineveh, he imagines the reaction of the population of the city: "Hearts melt, knees give way, bodies tremble, every face grows pale" (2:10). A pale or greenish pale horse itself suggests illness and perhaps a corpse.

The suggestion of death is confirmed by the name of the rider. The previous three riders were only described by what they held in their hands. This fourth rider is Death itself. Death is personified in the Old Testament as well. In a short prophetic judgment oracle, Jeremiah announces that "Death has climbed in through our windows and has entered our fortresses; it has removed the children from the streets and the young men from the public squares" (Jer 9:21; see also Job 18:13; 28:22; Pr 15:11; 27:20; Hos 13:14). In the Old Testament, personified Death evoked an association with the Canaanite god, Mot, also death. We will see in Revelation 13 and its picture of evil as a seven-headed sea monster that such mythological allusions were still current at the time Revelation was written.

Not only is the fourth rider, Death, named, he also has a companion on his heels, namely Hades. Hades is a Greco-Roman term used to refer to the underworld. In other words, the New Testament equivalent to Old Testament concept of Sheol. Sheol may sometimes only mean the grave, but in some contexts refers to the realm that the dead go to in at least a semiconscious, shadowy form. Sheol, like both Death and Hades in this passage, is personified. For instance, Isaiah 5:14: "Therefore Death [Sheol[12]] expands its jaws, opening wide its mouth; into it will descend their nobles and masses with all their brawlers and revelers."

Death and his companion Hades will gain power over a quarter of the earth's population. They will kill by multiple means: war, famine, plague, and even through wild beasts. Since apocalyptic uses numbers symbolically rather than literally, we should not press the idea that twenty-five percent of the population of the earth would be killed. Rather a substantial amount, but not even half, will be taken.

The Fifth Seal (6:9–11)

6:9–11 *When he opened the fifth seal.* For he (the Lamb), see note at 5:6. For seal, see note at 5:1. When the Lamb opened the first four seals, the four living creatures (see note at 4:6–8) announced "Come!" with the result that first a white, then a red, then a black, and finally a pale horse and rider came forth to bring God's judgment on the earth.

The opening of the fifth seal shifts to what appears to be a heavenly scene where those who have been martyred, killed because of their testimony, have gathered under the altar. This altar is in the heavenly temple (11:19; 14:17; 15:5) of which the tabernacle and the temple in Jerusalem were only an earthly replica.

In the earthly tabernacle/temple, there were two altars, the bronze altar for sacrifice (Ex 27:1–8) and the golden altar on which incense was burned (Ex 30:1–10). There is some question as to under which of these two altars the souls of the martyrs were gathered, the bronze sacrificial altar or the golden incense altar. The heavenly altar is mentioned later in Revelation and sometimes it is clearly the incense altar (8:3, 5) and sometimes it is unclear which altar is meant (11:1; 14:18; 16:7). Perhaps it is best to think that the sacrificial altar is meant here. The sacrifices performed on the bronze altar of the tabernacle/temple foreshadowed Christ's sacrifice on the cross (Heb 10:1–18). These martyred saints, then, are in heaven thanks to the redemptive work of Christ in his crucifixion, resurrection, and ascension.

To think of the souls of these saints as disembodied beings is to ignore the immediate context and read the passage in the light of Neo-Platonic philosophy with its body-soul dichotomy. Such a reading pervaded the Middle Ages when Neo-Platonic philosophy had a large influence on the church and its teachers. The Old Testament does not imagine at any point that God's human creatures exist without a body. Christian theology should speak not of the immortality of the soul but of the resurrection of the body. That these "souls" under the altar are embodied is confirmed by verse 10, in which each of the martyrs is given a white robe to wear. Throughout Revelation, angels and believers who have gone to heaven are pictured as wearing white robes, for as we said concerning the "white horse" of 6:2 (see also 3:18), the color white often is associated with "heavenly or transcendent reality."[13]

The martyred saints shout out to God, "How long before you judge the people who belong to this world and avenge our blood for what they have done for us?" (v. 10 NLT). They are anxious to see that those who brutalized them experience the judgment that is due them. They don't doubt that such judgment is coming. After all, God is "holy and true" as well as "Sovereign," but with their question "how long . . . ?," they express their impatience. In the Old Testament too, God's people would express their impatience to God, by asking God "how long?" (see Ps 6:3; 13:1–2; 35:17; 62:3, etc.).

The answer comes: "a little longer" (6:11). It's not quite time for the reckoning of God's judgment against those who persecuted them. Indeed, there will be more martyrs before that time. This message seems directed to those who read or heard the book of Revelation, to warn them to prepare to possibly meet the same fate as those who are now gathered under the altar. Yet even as they wait, they are to be reassured that "a little longer" will not last forever. What Revelation tells us here and throughout is that God, who remains in control despite what appears to be unrestrained evil, will ultimately have the final say, the final judgment, and the final victory.

The Sixth Seal (6:12–17)

6:12 *He (The Lamb).* See note at 5:6 and "Revelation 5:6 Through Old Testament Eyes: The Lamb Who Was Slain."

The sixth seal. See note at 5:1. With the opening of the sixth seal, we move back to a description of God's future judgment. This time judgment comes on a cosmic scale. Not only the earth ("there was a great earthquake"), but the very cosmos itself convulses in response to the breaking of the sixth seal.

In the Old Testament, earthly and cosmic convulsions often accompany God's appearance as a warrior who comes to judge the guilty. We might think of the opening of what is sometimes called "Isaiah's apocalypse" (chaps 24–27) where we hear, "See, the LORD is going to lay waste the earth and devastate it; he will ruin its face and scatter its inhabitants . . . the earth will be completely laid waste and totally plundered" (24:1, 3). Or the opening of the prophecy of Nahum, which describes God's coming judgment on the Assyrian city of Nineveh:

> His way is in the whirlwind and the storm,
>   and clouds are the dust of his feet.
> He rebukes the sea and dries it up;
>   he makes all the rivers run dry.
> Bashan and Carmel wither
>   and the blossoms of Lebanon fade.
> The mountains quake before him
>   and the hills melt away. (Na 1:3–5)

A great earthquake. At God's coming and in response to God's judgment the earth is shaken (see also Rev 8:5; 11:13, 19; 16:18). The people of God in Old Testament Israel and New Testament Judah were well acquainted with earthquakes, since the Jordan Rift Valley is a seismically fragile area.[14] Thus it is not surprising that earthquakes and the destruction associated with them connote God's judgment in the Old Testament (Isa 13:13; 29:6; Eze 38:19; Hag. 2:6, as well as Na 1:5 quoted above). When Jesus spoke of the end-time judgment, he described earthquakes as part of the final earthly and cosmic convulsion (Mt 24:7; Mk 13:8; Lk 21:11). The earthquake that occurred at the time of Jesus' crucifixion is likely to be seen as a harbinger of this judgment (Mt 27:54; see also 28:2).

The sun turned black like sackcloth made of goat hair. God created the sun to bring light and life to the world (Ge 1:14–18). But God's coming judgment undoes creation by making the sun as dark as sackcloth made from goat hair, which was deep black. Sackcloth in the Old Testament was associated with death and mourning (Ge 37:34; 1 Ki 21:27; La 2:10).

At the time of the ninth plague that came on Egypt (Ex 10:21–29), the sun went temporarily dark. In the context of the coming Day of the Lord, Isaiah describes how the "rising sun will be darkened" (13:10). Joel too describes the day of coming judgment as a time when "the earth shakes and the heavens tremble, the sun and moon are darkened, and the stars no longer shine" (2:10, see also 2:31; 3:15; Amos 8:9). Again, as Jesus describes the final judgment to his disciples, he also describes the darkening of the sun, specifically quoting Isaiah 13:10 (see Mk 13:24). The symbolic language used by apocalyptic means that it is unlikely that we should press this language literally any more than when we say that an event is earth-shattering.

6:13 *The stars in the sky fell to earth, as figs drop from a fig tree when shaken by a strong wind.* Continuing the theme of cosmic upheaval that accompanies God's judgment, we hear that the stars fell to the earth. God had made the stars, along with the sun and the moon, and set them in the heavens to demarcate time, the evening and morning (Ge 1:14–19; Ps 8:3). In the Old Testament, God's judgment most often is signaled by the darkening of the stars (as we just saw with the darkening of the sun; Isa 13:10; Eze 32:7; Joel 2:10; 3:15), but in Isaiah 34:4, we read in conjunction with his judgment against all the nations (34:1–2): "all the starry host will fall like withered leaves from the vine, like shriveled figs from the fig tree." Jesus cites this passage in part (along with Isa 13:10) in reference to the events of the end time in Matthew 24:29 (see also Mk 13:25). In Luke's account, Jesus speaks more generally that "there will be signs in the sun, moon and stars" (21:25). Jesus uses such language as the prophets do, employing cosmic imagery not to predict astronomical events but to convey the "galactic" significance of the acts of God in human affairs.

The connection between Revelation 6:13 and Isaiah 34:4 is confirmed by the analogy drawn between the stars falling and figs falling from the branches to the ground. Figs, along with olives and grapes, were staples of Israelite horticulture. The production of figs was thus a sign of prosperity and fruitfulness (Nu 13:23). However, ripe figs falling to the ground as they are blown by a sharp wind would represent the opposite, as do fig trees that do not produce fruit (Jer 8:13; Mic 7:1; Lk 13:6–9).

6:14 *The heavens receded like a scroll being rolled up.* In this depiction of judgment at the end of time, we have heard of the sun growing dark and the stars falling to the earth. Now John uses the image of the heavens being rolled up like a scroll. In ancient times, particularly during the Old Testament period, scribes wrote on scrolls, rolled-up writing surfaces of parchment, leather, or papyrus (see note at 5:1). To be read, they were unrolled and when finished, they were rolled up. Nowhere is the creation of the heavens likened to the unrolling of a scroll,[15] but we return to Isaiah 34:4 where we read in the context of God's judgment against the nations: "all the stars in the sky will be dissolved and the heavens rolled up like a scroll." It appears that the figurative description of the events following the opening of the sixth seal has a connection to Isaiah's oracle against the nations, but here the judgment expands beyond that of foreign nations to the entirety of the cosmos.

And every mountain and island was removed from its place. The events associated with the opening of the sixth seal began with a great earthquake before moving to a description of the convulsions of the heavens. We now return to the earth where mountains and islands are removed from their place. This removal may be associated with the earthquake, but again signifies the type of cosmic, heavenly and earthly, disruptions that are associated with what is God's final judgment against a sinful humanity.

In the Old Testament, mountains are the apex of grandeur and stability, often associated with the divine realm (Ps 46, 48). When God appears, these symbols of grandeur and stability are said to move, shake, or even melt in the Old Testament (Ps 18:7; 97:5; Isa 5:25; Jer 4:24; Eze 38:20; Na 1:5), signifying God's ultimate control over the nations and human history.

While mountains represent what appears to be immovable stability, the islands represent distant realms (Isa 66:19). Nowhere on earth is so far away that it will not be affected by God's coming judgment.

6:15 *Hid in caves.* In response to this coming cosmic debacle, people seek refuge or perhaps even a quick death in a futile attempt to avoid God's coming judgment. Whether powerful (king, general, rich, mighty) or not ("and everyone else"), whether slave or free, they will seek refuge because nothing can prevent them from the Lamb's wrath. Israel was and is a land with many caves that served as hiding places for people (1 Sa 22:1–2; 1 Ki 18:4; 19:9), so it was natural for people who feared harm to seek such protection. Our passage may be alluding specifically to Hosea, where in response to the announced judgment because of their idolatry people "will say to the mountains, 'Cover us!' And to the hills, 'Fall on us!'" (10:8). Isaiah 2:19 also envisions people fleeing to caves as they face the judgment of God.

6:17 *For the great day of their wrath has come.* In the previous verse, the "wrath of the Lamb" is mentioned specifically, which may be why some manuscripts have "the great day of his wrath has come." But if "their" is correct, then it surely refers to the wrath of the God, the Father, and of the Lamb, his son.

This day of wrath is referred to in the Old Testament as the "Day of the Lord" (or variant such as "in that day"), which is the day that God the warrior comes to bring his judgment against those who have resisted him and at the same time to save his people. Indeed, it was Von Rad who demonstrated the connection between the day of the Lord and Israel's holy war traditions. He succinctly stated the "Day of Yahweh encompassed a pure event of war."[16] In some references in the Old Testament, the Day of the Lord anticipates historical judgments on Israel and Judah (Isa 3:18–4:1; Amos 5:18–20) or the nations (Isa 13:1–22; Ob 15). But in other references (Zec 14), the day of the Lord looks to the final intervention of God against his enemies and in support of his people. The New Testament also anticipates this final day of judgment (1 Co 1:8; 5:5; 1 Th 5:2; 2 Th 2:2; 2 Pe 3:10, 12). In many of these passages we see a similar connection between this day of final judgment and cosmic upheaval.

And who can withstand it? The obvious answer is that no one can withstand the coming wrath of God and the Lamb. The prophet Nahum concludes his depiction of the future coming of God the warrior in a similar manner:

> Who can withstand his indignation?
>> Who can endure his fierce anger?
> His wrath is poured out like fire;
>> the rocks are shattered before him. (Na 1:6)

The prophet Joel also asks "who can endure it?" as he envisions the coming of the dreadful day of the Lord (Joel 2:11)

REVELATION 7

What the Structure Means:
Two Pictures of the People of God (Rev 7:1–17)

In chapter 7, an interlude between the opening of the sixth and seventh seals, we get two pictures of the people of God. The first is of 144,000 from the twelve tribes of Israel (7:1–8), and the second is "a great multitude that no one could count, from every nation, tribe, people and language" (7:9, see vv. 9–17). The former receive God's seal before the judgment on their forehead to mark them for preservation before the opening of the seventh seal, while the latter are dressed in white robes, praising God. The interpreting angel tells John that they are those "who have come out of the great tribulation; they have washed their robes and made them white in the blood of the lamb" (7:14). At first glance, we might think that the 144,000 and the "great multitude" are two different groups. After all, while 144,000 people are not insignificant, it does not seem to pair with a "great multitude that no one could count" (7:9). In addition, the first group is described as coming "from all the tribes of Israel" (7:4), while the "great multitude" comes "from every nation, tribe, people and language" (7:9). Koester, therefore, suggests that these two pictures of the people of God indicates that "the community of faith encompasses people from many tribes, nations, and languages (7:9–17), yet this same community represents the fulfillment of God's promises concerning the preservation of Israel (7:4–8)."[1]

Perhaps so, but there are also good reasons to think that the two groups are really different ways of referring to the same people, those who have remained faithful and are protected from the coming judgment and so worship God on his throne. The first indication that the 144,000 should not be understood to be a reference to God's Old Testament people alone is that they are the recipients of the seal on their forehead that will keep them from harm in the coming judgment (7:3). If we understand the 144,000 to refer to God's Old Testament followers, why would they need protection from a judgment that is in the future? If it refers to Jewish Christians, we might ask why no reference to the protection of Gentile Christians.

No, it is better to think of the 144,000 and the "great multitude" as the same people, God's faithful people. Interestingly, while John simply "heard the number of those who were sealed: 144,000" (7:4), he then "looked" and saw the "great multitude" (7:9), again suggesting they are one and the same. As Williamson summarizes it, "twelve times twelve, one hundred and forty-four seems to be a way of intensifying the meaning of twelve: the complete number of those who are truly God's people, his faithful followers."[2] For further support, that the 144,000 refer to all of God's people and not just those from the tribes of Israel, see 14:1–5 where the number is used again.

Interlude: The 144,000 and the Great Multitude (7:1–17)

7:1 *Four angels . . . four corners of the earth . . . four winds of the earth.* First, we hear that four angels stand at the four corners of the earth. From ancient times, the phrase "four corners of the earth" is a way of describing the entire world. Indeed, ancient Mesopotamian kings would on occasion take on the title "king of the four corners of the earth" (or variant) as a way of asserting their dominance. The first known king to use this title was Naram-Sin in the twenty-third century BC. In the Old Testament, especially when comparing the Greek version, we have a similar, expression in Ezekiel 7:2 in a similar context of worldwide judgment: "Son of man, this is what the Sovereign LORD says to the land of Israel: 'The end! The end has come upon the four corners of the land!'"

Such an expression may indeed have originated from the concept that the earth was flat and had four corners, but it is unclear and unimportant whether the author of Revelation thought the world was round or flat. After all, the Bible does not concern itself with teaching cosmology. The point of the expression is clear: the four corners encompass the earth in its entirety.

Since there are four corners of the earth, there are four angels at each of them and they are holding back the four winds (one from each direction) so that they don't blow on the land. They are protecting the land from disturbance for a purpose, as we will see in the following verses.

The idea that there are four dominant winds coming from the four cardinal directions also goes back to ancient times. We can find references to the "four winds" in Mesopotamian and Egyptian sources.[3] In the Old Testament, we see references to the "four winds" in Daniel 7:2; 8:8; 11:4. In Daniel 7:2 the four winds are whipping up a chaotic sea, a symbol of chaos and threat. In our passage, the angels are holding back the winds for the opposite effect.

What the Structure Means:
The Number Four in Revelation

Revelation 7:1 speaks of four angels, four corners of the earth, and four winds. The number four occurs elsewhere in the book. In Revelation 9:13 we read of the four horns of the altar, and in 9:14 in the context of the blowing of the sixth trumpet, we hear that four angels were released who had been bound at the Euphrates River. Throughout the book we also read about four living creatures (starting at 4:6) and twenty-four (a multiple of four) elders (starting at 4:4). The number four denotes universality or totality, probably deriving from the idea that the world had four corners.

7:2 *Another angel coming up from the east.* A fifth angel, who seems in charge of the first four, comes from the east. Eden, the place where God dwelt in harmony with humanity, was in the east (Ge 2:8), though it is a unclear what Eden is east of.[4] Estrangement from God is pictured as an expulsion from the east of Eden further east.[5] When Adam and Eve were expelled from the garden of Eden, they went to the east (Ge 3:24). After God judged Cain for killing of his brother Abel, he lived east of Eden (Ge 4:16). God told Abraham to move west to the land that he would show him (Ge 12:1), and from that place, they looked back eastward. We can see this in the orientation of both the tabernacle and the temple, which faced east (Ex 27:13; 38:13; Eze 47:1[6]). The angel coming from the east means that he is moving westward, perhaps back toward Eden and harmony.

Power to harm the land and the sea. These angels are harbingers of God's judgment on the world. They are holding back the four winds, but once released those four winds will cause devastation.

Going Deeper into "a Great Multitude": Revelation 7:9

Revelation 7 presents an interlude between the unsealing of the sixth and seventh seals. Before the judgment that accompanies the seventh seal, God sends out four angels to put a seal on 144,000 people[7] "from all the tribes of Israel" and then the scene shifts to "a great multitude that no one could count, from every nation, tribe, people and language, standing before the throne and before the Lamb" (7:9), and they offer worship to God and to the Lamb. Later we hear that this latter group, whose relationship to the 144,000 remain debated (see discussion in "What the Structure Means: Two Pictures of the People of God [Rev 7:1–17]"), "are they who have come out of the great tribulation" (7:14). This picture reminds us that God's people are not and never have been limited to one ethnic or national or racial group but is drawn from all peoples.

After all, the Bible consistently teaches that everyone is created in God's image (Ge 1:26–27) and descend from "one man" (Ac 17:24–28).[8] The Bible also makes it clear that all people "have sinned and fall short of the glory of God" (Ro 3:23). And most significantly, the Bible makes it clear that God, from the start, pursues all people regardless of race, ethnicity, or nationality to restore their broken relationship with him.

Yes, God chose Abraham and his descendants for special service to him. But notice that their election, which entailed no privilege but led often to suffering, was for the purpose that "all peoples on earth will be blessed through you" (Ge 12:3). And right from the start Gentiles could join themselves with the covenant people if they so chose (think Rahab, Shamgar, Ruth, Uriah the Hittite, and Naaman). Indeed, as Esau McCauley in his excellent book *Reading While Black* points out, Joseph, Abraham's great-grandson, has two biracial children with his Egyptian wife. So in the fourth generation after Abraham, the chosen "seed" is already diverse racially.[9]

But with the coming of Jesus the inclusion of the Gentiles becomes even more obvious and it soon becomes clear (see Ac 9–10, 15 for instance) that Gentiles who accept Christ do not have to take on distinctively Jewish practices like circumcision or keeping kosher. After all, as Paul tells the Galatians, "There is neither Jew nor Gentile. . . . If you belong to Christ, then you are Abraham's seed, and heirs according to the promise" (Gal 3:28–29). The "dividing wall of hostility" (Eph 2:14) has come down once and for all in Christ.

For this reason, Jesus commissioned his followers "to go and make disciples of all nations" (Mt 28:19). The picture that we have in Revelation 7 is a reminder of the fact that God is the God of all peoples and Jesus is the Savior of all who turn to him. It is also a reminder that thinking that one race, ethnicity, or nation is better in the eyes of God than another is a sin.[10]

This picture of the diverse people of God should not only motivate us to "go out" in the sense of mission to diverse people. We should also strive to represent the diversity of the people of God in our local churches. If our churches are not places where people of different races and ethnicities feel comfortable and accepted, then there is something deeply flawed in our communities.

7:3 *Put a seal on the foreheads of the servants of our God.* The presiding angel from the east tells them to hold back the devastation until the servants of God are marked with the seal of the living God, which he has brought with him (see v. 2). We have already, of course, encountered seals, but here the seal functions differently. The seals on the scroll that the Lamb now opens have the function of keeping the scroll closed and not able to be read until they are broken. Here the seal serves the function of identification of ownership. During the Old Testament period, people had seals that would leave an impression on soft material like clay to mark an object as one's own. We have many examples recovered through archaeological excavations of both stamp seals and cylinder seals. As the name implies the former would leave an impression by stamping the clay, whereas with the latter a person would roll it across the clay. The impression would be unique to the person and in this way would identify the owner. For an Old Testament example of the seal used for ownership, see Song of Songs 8:6.[11]

Thus, the idea here is that the servants of God would be identified as belonging to God, providing a contrast to the mark of the beast that the reader will later hear about (13:16; 14:9). The implication is that they will not experience the harm about to come on the land and the sea, because they belong to God. This identification also asserts that "authentication and protection rests on those who participate in his kingdom work."[12]

An Old Testament background may be seen first in the "mark" that God put on Cain when God punished him by making him wander even further from Eden. In response to Cain's fear that he would become the object of violence, God placed a mark on him that would protect him (Ge 4:15). In Ezekiel the prophet describes the heavenly command to those who would execute judgment against idolatrous Judah. Before the judgment is executed, they are told to first "go throughout the city of Jerusalem and put a mark on the foreheads of those who grieve and lament over all the detestable things that are done in it" (Eze 9:4) and are further told "do not touch anyone who has the mark" (9:6).

7:4 *144,000 from all the tribes of Israel.* As we read on, we will see that this number is the sum that results from adding up 12,000 people from each of the twelve tribes of Israel. The symbolic function of the number twelve begins with the constitution of the Old Testament people of God, Israel, as composed of twelve tribes who are the descendants of the twelve sons of Jacob, whose name was changed to Israel.

This number is obviously symbolic and not to be taken in a straightforward fashion as if there will be only and exactly 12,000 people from each of the twelve tribes of Israel. That said, the next unit (7:9–17) will turn attention to "a great multitude . . . from every nation, tribe, people and language." While some believe that the 144,000 represents Old Testament followers of God or specifically Jewish Christians, it is much more likely that the 144,000 is the same group, all followers of God, as the "great multitude" in 7:9–17 (see discussion in "What the Structure Means: Two Pictures of the People of God [Rev 7:1–17]"). Williamson suggests that this number has military overtones because "one thousand, besides symbolizing a large number, was also the largest military unit under a single commander in biblical Israel's army (e.g., Num 31:14, 48, 52, 54)."[13]

7:5–8 *From the tribe of.* As we examine the sequence of the names of Israelite tribes in this list, we can make some observations based on its Old Testament background. We cannot present every tribal list in the Old Testament, but we will list some of the most significant in Table 7.1.

Table 7.1 Old Testament Lists of the Tribes of Israel

Birth Order (Ge 29:31— 30:24; 35:16–29)	Jacob's Final Blessing and Curses (Ge 49)	Tribal Censuses in the Wilderness (Nu 1 and 26)	Moses' Final Blessings and Curses (Dt 33)	Revelation's List (Rev 7:5–8)
Reuben	Reuben	Reuben	Reuben	Judah
Simeon	Levi and	Simeon	Judah	Reuben
Levi	Simeon	Gad	Levi	Gad
Judah	Judah	Judah	Benjamin	Asher
Dan	Zebulun	Issachar	Joseph	Naphtali
Naphtali	Issachar	Zebulun	(Ephraim and	Manasseh
Gad	Dan	Ephraim	Manasseh)	Simeon
Asher	Gad	Manasseh	Zebulun	Levi
Issachar	Asher	Benjamin	Gad	Issachar
Zebulun	Naphtali	Dan	Dan	Zebulun
Joseph	Joseph	Asher	Naphtali and	Joseph
Benjamin	Benjamin	Naphtali	Issachar	Benjamin
			Asher	

Apparently, there is no stereotyped list of tribes in the Old Testament. While none of these representative lists are in the exact same order, each recognizes twelve tribes, though they are counted in different ways for various reasons.

The flexibility in the names in the lists are the result of two primary factors. First, Joseph, one of the twelve sons of Jacob/Israel, is granted a double portion of tribal allotments through his sons Ephraim and Manasseh (see Ge 48). The other factor results from Jacob's curse on Levi and Simeon that their descendants will not get a tribal allotment (Ge 49:5–7). Indeed, at the tribal allotment of land, both Simeon and Levi received cities within the boundaries of other tribes (Jos 13:14; 19:1–23; 21). We might notice that Simeon is missing from the list in Deuteronomy 33 because already that tribe is losing its distinctive identity.[14] It is also interesting that Levi is missing from the two tribal census accounts in the book of Numbers, but this can be explained in that these are really military registrations and the Levites, though considered bodyguards of God's holiness,[15] are not considered part of the army marching through the wilderness.

The second observation is that these lists follow a rough, but not precise birth order. This is true particularly at the beginning of the list since Reuben is listed first in our representative lists and Levi, Simeon, and Judah are usually toward the top. But in the final analysis these lists are quite fluid except in number. There are always twelve tribes, even though the tribes are numbered in different ways.

Regarding the list of tribes in Revelation (the last column in Table 7.1), we first note that twelve tribes are also listed. This number is achieved by treating Joseph as one tribe rather than two (Ephraim and Manasseh, though interestingly including the latter but not the former, see below), and naming both Simeon and Levi, the tribes that did not get a land allotment. In other words, this is a list of the tribes named for eleven of the sons of Jacob/Israel (swapping out the name of Dan [see suggested reason below] with Manasseh).

The second striking feature of this list is that Judah comes first, even though he was the fourth-born son. Judah's preeminence in the list is almost certainly the result of the fact that the tribe of Judah is the one David belongs to. The promise to David that "your house and your kingdom will endure forever before me; your throne will be established forever" (2 Sa 7:16) is ultimately realized in his descendant Jesus the Christ (Messiah, "anointed king").

The third interesting feature concerns the absence of Dan from the list, but still maintaining the number twelve by including Manasseh, but not Ephraim. We can only speculate as to why this is the case, but Tabb notes that Dan was particularly associated with idolatry because of a calf shrine built there by King Jeroboam (1 Ki 13, but see also the earlier story in Judges 17–18).[16]

7:9 *After this I looked.* The scene shifts from the 144,000 from the tribes of Israel, who were sealed by God before the destruction to be brought on the earth, to a heavenly scene of multitudes of people singing praises to God and the Lamb. For the argument that these are two ways of describing the same group, see "What the Structure Means: Two Pictures of the People of God (Rev 7:1–17)."

From every nation, tribe, people, and language. The previous scene depicted people specifically from the "tribes of Israel" (7:4), we now have a "great multitude" of people from every nation, tribe, people, and language" who will worship God.[17] See note at 5:9 and "Revelation 7:9 Through Old Testament Eyes: Every Nation, Tribe, People, and Language."

Throne. See notes at 3:21 4:2; 5:11. and "Revelation 4 Through Old Testament Eyes: God on His Throne."

Lamb. See note at 5:6.

Wearing white robes. See notes at 3:4, 18.

Holding palm branches in their hands. Palm trees were common in the Israel of the Old Testament, associated with oases (Ex 15:27), and thus a symbol of fertility and flourishing. The psalmist compares the righteous person to a palm tree: "The righteous will flourish like a palm tree, they will grow like a cedar of Lebanon; planted in the house of the LORD, they will flourish in the courts of our God" (Ps 92:12–13). The Solomonic temple (1 Ki 6:29, 32, 35; 7:36) as well as Ezekiel's eschatological temple (Eze 40:16, 22, 26, 31, 34, etc.) are ornamented extensively with depictions of palm trees. At the triumphal entry, Jesus is greeted by cheering crowds bearing palm branches (Jn 12:13). This event takes place on the eve of the Passover, but palm branches are not associated with the Passover celebration in the Old Testament.[18] Carson finds the precursor to the use of palm branches during the triumphal entry in references to moments of celebration during the Second Temple period (1 Macc. 13:52; 2 Macc. 10:7). He also references the citation of the palm in an apocalyptic vision of the end found in Testament of Naphtali 5:4. He believes that by the time of Jesus the palm "had already become a national (not to say nationalist) symbol" and that "it may well have signaled nationalist hope that a messianic liberator was arriving on the scene."[19]

Revelation 7:9 Through Old Testament Eyes: Every Nation, Tribe, People, and Language

The picture of this vast multitude in 7:9 flows ultimately from the promise given to Abraham that "all peoples on earth will be blessed through you" (Ge 12:3). During the Old Testament period, those who came from other nations (Ruth, Rahab, Uriah the Hittite, and others), could come and join Israel to participate in the covenant community, but there was a sharp division between the nations and the people of God. The latter were to stay separate from the former, though as they were faithful to God and God prospered them that would lead to the nations flowing to them (Isa 2:1–4; Mic 4:1–3). Israel's repeated rebellion did not allow that to happen on a large scale.

As Paul would later reflect, speaking to Gentiles about the past, "at that time you were separate from Christ, excluded from citizenship in Israel and foreigners to the covenants of promise, without hope and without God in the world" (Eph 2:12). But with the coming of Jesus the situation has radically been transformed. Paul, still speaking to the Gentiles, goes on to say, "But now in Christ Jesus you who once were far away have been brought near by the blood of Christ. For he himself is our peace, who has made the two groups one and has destroyed the barrier, the dividing wall of hostility. . . . For through him, we both have access to the Father by one Spirit" (Eph 2:13–14, 18).

The terminology of "nation, tribe, people, and language" is not the same but is reminiscent of the refrain that is repeated with some variation throughout Genesis 10, which describes in essence the theological origins of different languages and nations. The chapter describes the division of humanity after the Tower of Babel incident in Genesis 11:1–9.[20] The chapter depicts the division of humanity into three groups, each associated with one of the sons of Noah: Japheth, Ham, and Shem. Their descendants together constitute the seventy nations listed according to "their clans within their nations, each with its own language" (Ge 10:5, see also 10:20, 31). According to the concluding verse of the chapter, "from these the nations spread out over the earth after the flood" (Ge 10:32).

Nations may be seen as a token of God's grace over against the brokenness that results from human sin. Sin divides and fragments, and in judgment against the sinful attempt to build a tower "that reaches to the heavens" (Ge 11:4), God fragments what until then was their "common speech" (Ge 11:1). He could have eradicated any possibility of speech between humans, but he divides them into different language groups and in the picture given in Genesis 10 into different nations. While a token of grace, the division into different languages and nations is still the consequence of sin.

What is interesting is to read the account of Pentecost (Ac 2) with a background on the story of the confusion of languages at the tower. Pentecost has brought people from many nations speaking different languages to Jerusalem. But on that day all Jesus' followers "were filled with the Holy Spirit and began to speak in other tongues as the Spirit enabled them" (Ac 2:4). And the foreigners gathered there could understand them. In short, we have here a temporary reversal of the punishment that followed the rebellion at the tower, anticipating the healing of the fissure between the nations that now expresses itself in the present picture of God's people drawn from many different nations speaking different languages together, praising God.

7:10 *They cried out in a loud voice.* The great multitude waving palm branches praise God. They attribute salvation to God. This salvation, or victory, is still to take place in the future as God and the Lamb, the glorified Christ, will win victory over the forces of evil. Old Testament victory hymns also celebrated God's salvation from evil enemies that sought to harm the people of God (Ex 15:2; 2 Sa 22:3; Ps 18:2; Ps 98:1–3, etc.).

7:11 *All the angels.* The circle of praise expands from the white-robed multitude to include the angels. They stand around the throne of God near the elders (presumably the twenty-four elders, see 4:4, 9–10) and the four living creatures (see 4:6–8). Even the angels bow before the throne of God in worship.

7:12 *Amen!* The angels begin and end their short hymn of praise with "Amen," a Hebrew phrase best rendered, "So be it!" Thus, they affirm the prayer of the multitude. In between Amens, the angels ascribe praise, glory, wisdom, thanks, honor, power, and strength. One thinks of Daniel's prayer after God reveals Nebuchadnezzar's dream to him:

> Praise be to the name of God for ever and ever;
>   wisdom and power are his. (Da 2:20)

7:13–14 *These in white robes—who are they and where did they come from?* One of the elders here addresses John, the one experiencing the vision, about the identity of the multitude who were wearing the white robes (7:9; see 3:4, 18). But John does not know, so he throws the question back to the elder who does know.

The great tribulation. The elder tells John that the white-robed multitude are people who have experienced and come out of the great tribulation. The tribulation here refers to the persecution that the people of God were experiencing at the time John wrote the book of Revelation, not some future tribulation during the last days just before Christ returns. They are martyrs in other words (see 6:9–10). Their white robes were washed in the blood of the Lamb, a reference to Christ's crucifixion. As we have seen, white associates them with heavenly reality and here may also indicate purity or righteousness (see note at 3:4, 18), so the point would be that their heavenly association as well as their purity is the result of Christ's work.

They have washed their robes. The elder now explains to John how those who experienced the great tribulation came to wear white robes. They were washed, but not with water but with blood, specifically the blood of the Lamb, the glorified Christ who died on the cross.

Physical washing is frequently used as a symbol of spiritual transformation in Scripture. Cleansing the body or clothes often, as here, represents a spiritual cleansing. But, as opposed to the present context, dirty bodies and clothes were washed with water. The Old Testament uses dirty hands or clothes to represent a sinful heart (Job 9:30–31; Isa 4:3–4; Zec 3:1–10, see note at 3:4). For this reason, the repentant sinner calls on God to "wash away all my iniquity and cleanse me from my sin" (Ps 51:2). The Israelites were also given a divine command to wash their clothes in anticipation of their meeting with God as he made his presence known on Mount Sinai (Ex 19:10). Turning to the New Testament, we see a near-sacramental use of washing when Jesus washes the feet of the disciples (Jn 13:1–15) and the sacramental use of washing in baptism. As Ananias told Paul on the day of his conversion: "And now what are you waiting for? Get up, be baptized and wash your sins away, calling on his name" (Ac 22:16).

It is Jesus' work that leads to the type of spiritual transformation that the metaphor of washing (though different Greek terms are used for this concept) points to, a transformation from sinner to righteous. "But if we walk in the light, as he is in the light, we have fellowship with one another, and the blood of Jesus, his Son, purifies [NLT, "cleanses"] us from all sin" (1 Jn 1:7, see also 1 Co 6:11; Tit 3:5). Jesus' cleansing work results from an application of his death and resurrection, and thus derives the idea of washing the robes in his blood to turn them white.

7:15 *Before the throne of God.* See notes at 3:21; 4:2 and "Revelation 4 Through Old Testament Eyes: God on His Throne."

Serve him day and night in his temple. From the time of Solomon, the temple represented God's presence on earth. It replaced the tabernacle, which was a mobile symbol of God's presence and thus was appropriate during the time before the people of God were firmly established in the land.[21] The tabernacle/temple was the place where heaven met earth, and the idea was that the earthly temple represented the heavenly temple. In our present passage, the white-robed saints are seen as serving God before his throne in his heavenly temple. That they serve him in his temple day and night evokes a connection with the priests of the Old Testament who served day and night in the holy sanctuary (Ps 134:1; 1 Ch 9:33; 23:30).

7:16 *Never again will they hunger.* In Isaiah 49 we learn about the restoration of Israel after the judgment that was yet to come. The agent of this restoration was the servant of the Lord, likely in its original context a reference to the faithful remnant within Israel who would be in the vanguard of the post-judgment restoration. Jesus, though, is the Israel of one; he is the epitome of faithful Israel and thus the ultimate realization of Isaiah's servant (see 1 Pe 2:22 citing Isa 53:9; Ac 8:32–33 citing Isa 53:7–8; Lk 22:35–37 citing Isa 53:12). Thus, as the servant in Isaiah, he will restore exiled Israel, so that they will "neither hunger nor thirst, nor will the desert heat or the sun beat down on them" (Isa 49:10), so the white-robed saints "never again will they hunger; never again will they thirst. The sun will not beat down on them nor any scorching heat" (Rev 7:16).

The sun will not beat down on them. While the primary Old Testament reference is found in Isaiah 49:10 (see previous paragraph), the promise that the sun will beat down on the faithful who have experienced tribulation also echoes the picture evoked by Psalm 121:

> The LORD watches over you—
>> the LORD is your shade by your right hand;
> the sun will not harm you by day,
>> nor the moon by night. (Ps 121:5–6)

7:17 *The Lamb . . . will be their shepherd.* For Lamb, see note at 5:6. We should take note of the irony that the Lamb will be a shepherd, but this Lamb is none other than the resurrected and glorified Christ. He is the shepherd of his suffering and persecuted people. "Jesus is not only the sacrificial shepherd but also the sacrificed sheep."[22] Psalm 23 famously begins, "The LORD is my shepherd," and then develops the theme to emphasize God's protection, guidance, and provision of his sheeplike people. The leaders, particularly the kings, of Israel were to lead God's people like a shepherd. This picture is most closely associated with David, who was an actual shepherd as he grew up in the household of his father Jesse. But God "took you [David] from the pasture, from tending the flock, and appointed you ruler over my people Israel" (2 Sa 7:8). God entered a covenant with David that was a promise of perpetual kingship in his line: "your house and your kingdom will ensure forever before me; your throne will be established forever" (2 Sa 7:16). But David's descendants were not faithful to God and thus the last Davidic king to rule from Jerusalem, Zedekiah, ended his rule with no successor in 586 BC.

But that was not the end of the story. God had promised that a descendant of David would be over his people. Thus, the faithful expected a Messiah, an anointed king, who would come in the future to shepherd his people. The word of the Lord came to Ezekiel; "My servant David will be king over them, and they will all have one shepherd" (37:24). The Gospels proclaim that Jesus is the Messiah, the shepherd of God's people (Mt 2:6; 9:36; 15:24; cf. John 10:1–19; Heb 13:20; 1 Pe 2:25).

There may also be a Moses/Exodus reference here in this picture of the Lamb as shepherd. In Psalm 77, the psalmist proclaims to God "you led your people like a flock by the hand of Moses and Aaron" (v. 20).

Will lead them to springs of living water. The description of the Lamb's beneficent actions toward his suffering people again (see 7:16) derives from the Servant's work as depicted in Isaiah 49:10. We perhaps also have an allusion, particularly with the reference to the shepherd in the previous verse, to Psalm 23 where the divine shepherd leads his sheep "beside quiet waters" (Ps 23:2). Living water refers to the freshness of the water that comes from a spring in contrast to the stagnant water one might find in a storage container or cistern.

God will wipe away every tear. The earthly lives of God's people are filled with suffering, loss, pain, and ultimately with death. But God's people can face such tribulation knowing that a time is coming when such suffering will end. This picture of God wiping away the tears of his people comes from Isaiah 25:8. The prophet looks to the future as a great banquet that will follow the end of death. In the first part of 25:8 we hear that God "will swallow up death forever." This description reverses the picture of the god Death swallowing the god Baal in Ugaritic mythological texts. The end of death brings the end of lament.

REVELATION 8

The Seventh Seal (8:1–5)

8:1 *The seventh seal.* After an interlude following the sixth seal (for the interlude, see the previous chapter), we finally have the opening of the seventh and climactic seal (see 5:1 where the breaking of the seals is announced and begin). Now the scroll containing God's judgment can be completely opened.

Silence in heaven for about half an hour. The opening of the scroll results in a relatively brief period of silence. When the first six seals were opened, there were immediate judgments. Here there is silence, what turns out to be a silence before the storm. This silence is eerily foreboding. The silence is in heaven, meaning that the heavenly beings and the saints under the altar who were calling for God's judgment (6:9–11) cease speaking. The silence raises the level of expectation and anticipation. It is the silence of an army before it attacks.

8:2 *Seven angels . . . seven trumpets.* From the silence emerges seven angels associated with the divine presence, who each have a trumpet. Perhaps these seven are the seven angels who earlier were called the "seven spirits before his throne" (see note at 1:4). Again, we have the number seven that signifies totality and completeness. The seventh seal will now lead to another cycle of seven. In this case the seven trumpets which will be sounded in turn (8:6–11:19).

One key feature we will see in the structure of Revelation is that it is often not linear. Rather it keeps circling back to previous events like flashbacks or slow-motion replays in a movie. We can see three cycles of seven judgments (seals in Rev 6–8, trumpets in 8–11 and bowls in 15–16) not as consecutive but like spirals of similar content that move us closer to the final climax. See "What the Structure Means: Seals, Trumpets, and Bowls (Rev 6:1–7:5; 8:7–11:19; 15:1–16:21)" at the end of Revelation 16.

As observed at 1:10, trumpets announced the coming of God (Ex 19:13, 16, 19; Jos 6:20–21; see also Nu 10:1–10; Lev 25:9; Zec 9:14). The trumpet sound mimics thunder that accompanies a fierce storm.

Going Deeper into Prayer: Revelation 8:3–5

At the beginning of Revelation 8, upon the opening of the seventh seal and after the introduction of seven trumpet-bearing angels who will feature in the next cycle of judgment, yet another angel approaches the altar with a golden censer. At the altar he is given "much incense" which he then fills with fire from the altar, throws it to earth and "there came peals of thunder, rumblings, flashes of lightning and an earthquake" (8:5). In an earlier chapter too, we have a picture of the four living creatures and the twenty-four elders with harps and golden bowls full of incense singing a "new song" before the throne of God (5:8–9).

In both these cases, the smoking incense inside the censers are said to be the "prayers of God's people" (5:8; 8:4), reflecting the psalmist's petition that his "prayer be set before you [God] like incense" (Ps 141:2). Like the incense offered in the Old Testament sanctuary, the smoke rises to God and brings God joy. Why? Because his people are speaking to him. And this, apparently, is true whether the prayers are ones of praise, as in Revelation 5, or a call for God's judgment, as in Revelation 8. The prayers of God's people please him.

What an encouraging picture for our own prayer life! When we pray to God, our words go before God where he hears them and responds as appropriate. He hears our praise; he takes account of our petitions. The book of Revelation reminds us that our prayers matter and are directed to God who is the one who is in control, and he is the one who will have the final victory.

While prayer is only specifically mentioned in these two contexts, the book of Revelation is filled with prayers directed to God. They are the songs that are sung to God throughout the book. Songs of praise and lament are simply sung prayers, which is why the book of Psalms can be considered either a hymn book or a book of prayers (see, for example, the specific self-reference to prayer in Ps 4:1; 5:2; 17:1 [and title]; 39:12; 55:1; 61:1, and the colophon at the end of Psalm 72, "this concludes the prayers of David son of Jesse" (v. 20).

8:3 *Another angel.* Before the blowing of even the first trumpet, an eighth angel appears before the heavenly altar to offer incense, which is explained to be the prayers of the people. The prayers go to God while the angel takes the censer, fills it with fire, and hurls it to earth.

A golden censer. A censer is a container in which incense is burned by a priest in the presence of God. The first time a censer is explicitly mentioned in the Bible is when Nadab and Abihu the sons of Aaron used them to offer unauthorized incense before God. God responded by sending fire to burn them up (see below in 8:5). The first legitimate use of a censer is found in Leviticus 16:12 where Aaron is told to offer up incense before the Lord on the Day of Atonement.

Stood at the altar. This is the heavenly altar. The altar at the tabernacle/temple was an earthly representation of this altar. At 6:8–11 we also have a reference to this heavenly altar (see also 9:13; 11:1; 14:18; 16:7), and we questioned there whether the altar was the sacrificial altar (see Ex 27:1–8) or the incense altar (Ex 30:1–10). Here it is clearly the latter, since the angel is offering incense from a censer.

8:4 *The smoke of the incense, together with the prayers of God's people.* We read about the precious incense which the priests offered at the tabernacle and later temple in Exodus 30:34–38. In Psalm 141:2, the psalmist speaks of his prayer as incense that is offered up to God: "May my prayer be set before you like incense." The offering of incense intends to present a sweet fragrance before the Lord, and so the psalmist wants his prayer to similarly please God. He wants his prayer to be acceptable. Here in our present passage, the picture is of judgment against the wicked of the world. God receives the prayers of his suffering people favorably as they call for help against the wicked. As Keener states, the saints "have been crying out for vindication (Rev 6:10), and though the final judgment is not yet (6:11), some of their vindication occurs within history."[1]

8:5 *Filled it with fire from the altar, and hurled it on the earth.* God's judgment in the Old Testament sometimes came in the form of fire from heaven. By no means a strict parallel, the combination of censers, incense, and fire from heaven may be seen in the tragic story found in Leviticus 10 mentioned above. In that story, Aaron's sons took censers and added incense to offer what the narrative calls "unauthorized fire before the Lord" (10:1). In response, "fire came out from the presence of the Lord and consumed them, and they died before the Lord" (10:2).

There came peals of thunder, rumblings, flashes of lightning and an earthquake. We have already seen God's judgment associated both by storm and earthquake, powerful natural forces which are often disruptive. The imagery of thunder, rumblings, and lightning are associated with storm god (Baal, Hadad) imagery in the ancient Near Eastern world, applied to

Yahweh in the Old Testament (Ex 19:16; 20:18; 2 Sa 22:14; Ps 18:12, 14; 29:7, etc, see Rev 1:7; 4:5). God's judgment was also often associated with earthquakes that ripped the earth's crust causing great damage and often death. Old Testament passages such as Isaiah 13:13, Nahum 1:5, and Haggai 2:6 associated judgment and earthquakes. As here, other New Testament texts describe earthquakes accompanying the judgment at the return of Christ (Mt 24:7; Mk 13:8; Lk 21:11; Rev 6:12–14; 11:19; 16:18). Similar descriptions of God's judgment by storm and earthquake are also found in the description of the seventh trumpet (11:19) and the seventh bowl (16:18).

What the Structure Means: The Seven Trumpets (Rev 8:6–11:19)

John now moves from describing the opening of the seven seals to a new cycle of judgment represented by angels blowing seven trumpets.[2] The two cycles of seven are linked by the introduction of the seven angels with their trumpets at 8:2 (see note that explains that the trumpet sound mimics thunder and announces the appearance of God).

All seven angels are present with their trumpets, ready to blow them in succession (8:6). The first angel blows his trumpet (8:7), followed by the second (8:8–9), third (8:10–11), and fourth (8:12–13). These four trumpet blasts announce judgments that form a group, being briefly narrated and united by being echoes of the plagues that God brought on Egypt at the time of the Exodus (Ex 7–12). The first four judgments bring harm to different parts of God's creation. The first trumpet harms earth, trees, and grass; the second harms the sea, sea creatures, and ships; the third harms rivers and springs of water; the fourth the sun, moon, and stars, with an effect on the night. In each case, one third of the judgment's target is harmed. One third is a significant amount to be sure; but the number, rather than taken literally, communicates that, even though these are significant, the final judgment has not yet arrived.

A brief interlude follows these four when John reports hearing an eagle pronouncing a threefold woe, presaging the remaining three trumpet blasts (8:13).

We might see here a similarity with the first four seals opening, which brought forth a judgment connected to riders on four different-colored horses (6:1–8). They too are briefly narrated and form a unit by virtue of the four horses. However, no break occurs after the fourth horse; the action moves immediately on to the opening of the fifth seal.

While the narration of the first four trumpets is brief, the fifth seal (the first woe; 9:12) has a long description (9:1–12) providing more detail than the previous four. It begins with a star falling from the sky to earth. The star is a heavenly being who has the key to the Abyss, a fiery location deep in the earth. When the heavenly being opens the Abyss, the smoke that belches forth obscures the sky, and it is out of this smoke that demonic locusts emerge. These locusts have the sting of a scorpion but only had permission to torture, not kill, humans who do not have the "seal of God" on their foreheads (see note at 7:3). Even the torture they inflict has a time limit, five months (9:10). The lengthy description of these locusts underlines their destructive power and serves to evoke fear in those who would be the objects of their attacks.

Like the fifth, John provides lengthy narration of the sixth trumpet (9:13–21). After blowing the trumpet, a heavenly command goes out to release four angels who had been bound by the Euphrates. They apparently head up an invasion followed by "twice ten thousand times ten thousand" (9:16) horses with their riders. Like the locusts, the horses are hybrids, having the head of lions and tails like snakes. They also breath fire, smoke, and sulfur, which kills one third of humanity. The description ends with the note that the remaining two thirds of humanity did not repent of their horrific sins (9:20–21). This first mention of repentance outside the letters (see 2:5, 16, 21–22; 3:3, 19) alerts us to the possibility and hope that those outside the church might themselves wake up and turn their lives toward God. But by commenting on their lack of response, John tells us that these sinners are hardened to the point that not even these horrible judgments will elicit repentance from them.

As we observed with the seals, there is a sizable hiatus or interlude between the sixth and seventh trumpets. The first interlude focuses on a "little scroll" held in the hand of an angel who descends from heaven. While the descriptor "little" may differentiate it from the earlier scroll that the glorified Christ unsealed (5:1), there is no doubt but, like the earlier scroll, this one contains judgments. In what may be considered a second prophetic commissioning, the angel tells John to swallow the scroll (see notes at 10:9–11; see earlier at 1:11, 19) and to "prophecy again."

The second interlude between the sixth and seventh trumpet tells a story about two witnesses. As we explain in the notes to the chapter, these two witnesses represent the church who give testimony in the context of Gentiles, representing those who reject the gospel, who are trampling holy space. When people try to harm them, they have prophetic abilities to avoid injury and death, but then we are introduced for the first time to "the beast that comes up from the Abyss," who can kill them (11:7). This does not come until the chapter after the trumpet cycle, but John so casually introducing him into the story means that his readers had a previous understanding of what the beast stands for, namely the devil himself (12:9).

At first it looks as if the beast has once and for all defeated the two witnesses, but the victory is only apparent, since God raises them from the dead and brings them up to heaven (11:11–12). Afterward, an earthquake occurs that destroys a tenth of the city and kills seven thousand people.

At this point (11:14), we learn that the second of the three woes announced by the eagle (8:13) have passed, with one to go. Though separated by the interlude, this second woe is the sixth seal, and the announcement at this point prepares us for the seventh, climactic trumpet.

When the seventh trumpet is sounded, there is a heavenly announcement that the kingdom of the world has become the kingdom of the Lord and his Messiah (11:15) at which point the twenty-four elders break out in a song of praise (11:17–18). The heavenly temple was opened so that the ark of the covenant could be seen and then we hear that "there came flashes of lightning, rumblings, peals of thunder, an earthquake and a severe hailstorm" (11:19), reminding us of a similar occurrence with the seventh seal (8:5) and anticipating the pouring out of the seventh bowl (16:18).

The Seven Trumpets (8:6–11:19)

The First Trumpet (8:6–7)

8:6 *The seven trumpets.* See note at 8:2.

8:7 *The first angel.* The first angel blows his trumpet announcing judgment and it comes with "hail and fire mixed with blood." This judgment is reminiscent of the plague of hail sent against Egypt before the exodus (Ex 9:13–35; see also Ps 78:47–48; 105:32). The fire that accompanies the hail that comes with the blowing of the first trumpet likely recalls the lightning that came with the hail on Egypt ("When Moses stretched out his staff toward the sky, the LORD sent thunder and hail, and lightning flashed down to the ground. So the LORD rained hail on the land of Egypt; hail fell and lightning flashed back and forth," Ex 9:23–24a).

In the book of Job, God challenges Job by asking him, "Have you entered the storehouses of the snow or seen the storehouses of the hail, which I reserve for times of trouble, for days of war and battle?" (Job 38:22–23). The psalmist celebrates God's rescue, remembering that God "made darkness his covering, his canopy around him—the dark rain clouds of the sky. Out of the brightness of his presence clouds advanced with hailstones and bolts of lightning" (Ps 18:11–12; see also Isa 28:2). And of course, we might think of the battle against the southern Canaanite coalition at the time of the conquest. When Yahweh, "hurled large hailstones down on them, and more of them died from the hail than were killed by the swords of the Israelites" (Jos 10:11). The hail and fire are mixed with blood (perhaps an allusion to the Nile turning to blood; Ex 7:14–25) adding to the gory description and signaling the great harm and death that results from God's punishment.

A third of the earth . . . a third of the trees . . . all the green grass. The result of the hail, fire, and blood is an ecological disaster, as a third of the earth and its trees and all the green grass are burned up. We should not take the fraction a third to represent a precise quantity, but a way of saying a substantial part of the earth and its trees is destroyed, though the grass is depicted as totally burned up. In terms of a third of something being the object of God's judgment, we might think of Ezekiel's razor oracle (Eze 5), delivered in anticipation of the Babylonian defeat of the city of Jerusalem. God tells the prophet to shave his head with a sword and then weigh out the hair. Then he instructs him to burn a third of the hair inside the city of Jerusalem. He should take another third and strike it with a sword around the city, and then take the final third and throw it into the air. This presages that "a third of your people will die of the plague or perish by famine inside you; a third will fall by the sword outside your walls; and a third I will scatter to the winds and pursue with a drawn sword" (Eze 5:12).

The Second Trumpet (8:8–9)

8:8–9 *The second angel.* Following the sounding of the second trumpet by the second angel we have a second ecological catastrophe, but not on land like the preceding one. This judgment strikes the sea and its inhabitants. The disaster is caused by "something like a huge fiery mountain" being thrown into the sea. Perhaps we are to think of a meteorite plunging from the sky (though see comment on 8:10) into the sea. Again, this judgment affects a third (see note at 8:7) of its intended targets. A third of the sea turns to blood (again perhaps a reference to the plague of blood that struck the Nile). A third of the creatures in the sea die and a third of the ships that are at sea are decimated. We should take note that, though not made explicit, the destruction of ships would imply the death of those on board.

The Third Trumpet (8:10–11)

8:10 *The third angel.* The sounding of the second trumpet resulted in great harm to the waters of the sea and, implicitly, on those who sailed on seas. The sounding of the third trumpet announces great harm that targets the rivers and the springs of water, a source of drinking water with the resulting death of many people. While the fiery mountain that falls into the sea after the second trumpet may refer to a comet, there is no doubt that the "great star, blazing like a torch" that falls into the sea is describing a meteorite. We encounter a "falling star" in a taunt against an unnamed mighty king in one of Isaiah's oracles (14:12–15), but it does not seem to provide a background to the reference here since it is a story, probably based on a Canaanite tale,[3] of the defeat of a powerful king who challenged God's authority. Isaiah also records that "the starry host will fall" (34:4), a reference that stands behind Jesus' announcement at the end "the stars will fall from the sky" (Mt 24:29; Mk 13:25). While stars falling from the sky in all cases communicate cosmic upheaval (see note at 8:12), this is the only occasion where the falling star is an instrument of destruction (though see 9:1).

8:11 *Wormwood.* This star has a name. Wormwood is a plant that is bitter to the taste and, placed in water, can make its taste bitter. In one of his judgment oracles, Jeremiah proclaims, "I will make them eat bitter food ["bitter food" translates the Hebrew word for *wormwood*] and drink poisoned water" (23:15), and Amos (5:7) speaks of those who "turn justice into bitterness" (Hebrew "wormwood"). The Jeremiah reference is likely in the background of the name of the falling star since it combines wormwood with poisonous water in the context of judgment. Wormwood in water does not kill, so the name of the falling star derives from the bitter taste that results, but that the waters are poisonous becomes clear from the resulting casualties.

  A third. See note on 8:7 regarding "a third of the earth."

The Fourth Angel (8:12)

8:12 *The fourth angel.* The first trumpet signaled harm to a third of the land, the second to a third of the sea, and the third to a third of the rivers and springs. When the fourth angel sounds the trumpets a third of the celestial bodies are harmed, with the result that a third of a day was without light and a third of the night (apparently devoid of stars). Of course, we deal here with figurative language and a figurative use of numbers (see note at 8:7) because the actual loss of a third of the celestial bodies would result in diminished light not the loss of light for a third of the day and the night.

Such cosmic imagery is not intended to predict astronomical events but to convey the scope and significance of the acts of God in human affairs. The imagery of some type of celestial disruption (darkening light [Ex 10:21–29; Isa 13:10; Joel 2:10, 31; 3:15; Amos 8:9; Mk 13:24, see Rev 6:13], falling from the skies [Isa 34:4; Eze 32:7; Joel 2:10; 3:15; Mt 24:29; Mk 13:25, see Rev 6:13 and 9:1]) is common in anticipations and descriptions of judgment. Creation itself is described as going into tumult in expectation ultimately of a new heaven and a new earth that will emerge from the creation that had been "subjected to frustration, not by its own choice, but by the will of the one who subjected it, in hope that creation itself will be liberated from its bondage to decay and brought into the freedom and glory of the children of God" (Ro 8:20–21).

Interlude: An Eagle's Funeral Lament (8:13)

8:13 *An eagle.* Eagles are large with wing spans up to more than seven feet. They are powerful and fast birds of prey with deadly talons and beak. They can swoop down from the heights to kill and carry away their prey. They can tear their victims with their strong legs, talons, and hooked beaks. They are fearsome birds. That one of the four faces of the cherubim was that of an eagle indicates that they were considered the apex of their class. Thus, we can recognize why in the Bible they were associated with God's salvation of his people as well as his judgment on his enemies. When the Israelites journeyed from Egypt to the base of Mount Sinai, God told him to tell the Israelites "you yourselves have seen what I did to Egypt, and how I carried you on eagle's wings and brought you to myself" (Ex 19:4). More typically, the biblical writers associate the eagle with God's judgment. That judgment might be directed toward his own sinful people ("Put the trumpet to your lips! An eagle is over the house of the LORD because the people have broken my covenant and rebelled against my law," Hos 8:1), or toward other sinful nations like Moab ("Look! An eagle is swooping down, spreading it wings over Moab," Jer 48:40) or Edom ("Look! An eagle will soar and swoop down, spreading its wings over Bozrah," Jer 49:22). In our passage, the eagle serves the role of herald, announcing the judgment that will be initiated by the trumpet blasts of the next three angels.

Woe! Woe! Woe to the inhabitants of the earth. The eagle pronounces a series of three woes over the people of the earth. A woe is a calamity, and the announcement of woe anticipates the coming of great distress. The woe is repeated three times as a matter of emphasis and perhaps also because there are three more trumpets announcing judgment still to be blown (9:12). The background to the eagle's announcement is a type of oracle not infrequent in the Old Testament and given the name "woe-oracle" by scholars. They are particularly common in prophetic literature (Isa 5:18–19; Amos 5:18–20; 6:1–7; Mic 2:1–4; Na 3:1–3, for example). The Hebrew word translated "woe" (*hoy* or 'oy) and the Greek word used here (*ouai*) mimic the sound that grieving people make. Indeed, research indicates that this appears to be a form of speech commonly heard in funeral processions (1 Ki 13:30; Jer 22:18; 34:5; Amos 5:16).[4] Mourners would cry out this word in a funeral procession as they took the body to the gravesite. While mourners expressed grief at the death of the one whose funeral they were attending, the prophets both in the Old Testament and here used it with a different purpose. They were announcing that the object of the woe was "as good as dead"—and rather than mourning that fact, they celebrated it because the object of the woe, as here, was wicked people or nations who deserved what was coming to them. For Nahum, for instance, the woe was pronounced over oppressive and violent Nineveh, the capital of Assyria. For John, the eagle's woe was pronounced over all the wicked inhabitants of the world whose judgment was about to be introduced by the next three trumpet blasts.

REVELATION 9

The Fifth Trumpet (9:1–11)

9:1 *The fifth angel.* The previous four trumpet blasts announced judgments on the earth, the seas, the rivers, and the stars. Now the focus turns on the inhabitants of the earth.[1] The description of the consequences following from the fifth trumpet blast is longer than the previous four.

A star that had fallen from the sky. We have encountered and discussed stars falling from the heavens to the earth previously (see notes at 6:13 and 8:12), but this occasion is the first time that the star represents a heavenly being.

In the ancient Near East, the celestial bodies were thought to be gods. For instance, after his defeat of the sea monster Tiamat, the Babylonian god Marduk cut her body in two. He then made heaven with the upper half, and with the lower half he created the seas which he pushed back to form land. In the process of creation, Marduk places the gods in the skies as stars: "He made the position(s) for the great gods, He established (in) constellations the stars, their likenesses."[2] As often noted, in the first creation account the celestial bodies are created by God. They are not, nor do they represent, divinities (Ge 1:14–19; Neh. 9:6; Ps 33:6). Nonetheless, later Israelites sinned by worshiping the "starry hosts" (2 Ki 17:16; 21:3, 5; Jer 19:13; Zep 1:5). But there are also passages in which God's angels are associated with the stars. Here the scriptural authors re-mythologize the stars to figuratively depict the angels. They are never the object of worship (see Rev 19:10), but rather they are God's servants. In the Lord's first speech at the end of the book of Job, he challenges Job by asking him where he was when he created the foundations of the earth "while the morning stars sang together and all the angels shouted for joy?" (Job 38:7). The parallelism of this poetic line relates the "morning stars" and God's angels (Heb. "sons of God").

After the blowing of the fourth trumpet, John sees a star that falls from heaven. The star is clearly some type of angelic power since it was given a key to open the Abyss that initiates a horrific judgment. An argument can be made that this fallen star is a fallen angel of some sort (Isa 14:12–15). If so, we must understand that the means and ability to open the Abyss came from God. That is the best understanding of the passive of the verb ("was given," sometimes called the "divine passive," meaning "was given" by God). But the fallen star could also be understood to be one of God's heavenly servants, not a demon but an angel. Whether demon or angel, the fallen star's actions are accomplished by divine permission. But it is most likely, almost certain that the star should be seen as an angel not a demon, particularly in the light of Revelation 20:1 where it is clearly an angel coming from heaven that holds the key to the Abyss. This angel unleashes God's judgment on the earth.

The key to the shaft of the Abyss. The "star" has a key with which he opens the Abyss. Supporting our conclusion that the fallen star here is an angel rather than a demon is the fact that later we read of "an angel coming down out of heaven, having the key to the Abyss" (Rev 20:1). Abyss means "bottomless" (perhaps implying a "bottomless pit") and occurs seven times in Revelation (9:1–2, 11; 17:8; 20:1–3), clearly referring to an underworld place where demonic forces reside (see also Lk 8:31). In Romans, Paul uses the Greek term we translate "Abyss" in reference to the location of the dead (Ro 10:7). In the Septuagint, the Greek term is used to translate a number of different Hebrew terms, but perhaps the one context that most parallels its use in Revelation is found in Psalm 71 where it translates the Hebrew *tehom* ("depths") which in this context signifies the realm of the dead: "you will restore my life again; from the depths of the earth you will again bring me up" (v. 20). More immediately in the background, the book of Enoch uses Abyss to refer to a fiery place of torment.

9:2 *Like the smoke from a gigantic furnace.* The Abyss is a fiery place, so opening the shaft that leads to the Abyss results in the emission of smoke from the heat. To John, who witnesses the scene, it looked like the chimney of a huge furnace. Fire is often associated with God's powerful presence and his judgment in the Old Testament, and in particular in the fire of a furnace (Ge 19:28; Ex 19:18; Ps 21:8–9; Mal 4:1; Mt 13:42).

The sun and sky were darkened by the smoke. We have earlier seen that God's judgment is at times depicted by the darkening of the celestial bodies (see notes at 6:12–14 and 8:12), though the unique feature here is that it is smoke that obscures the light.

Revelation Through Old Testament Eyes: Exodus

With the mention of darkening skies (9:2) and a plague of locusts (9:3), the ten plagues from the book of Exodus come to mind. Indeed the theme of plagues is a prominent one in Revelation (see "Revelation Through Old Testament Eyes: The Ten Plagues" at 15:6). More than that, the whole book of Exodus plays a major role in the background to the book of Revelation, and no wonder.

The first part of the book of Exodus (Ex 1–15) recounts the salvation event *par excellence* in the Old Testament with the stirring story of God's rescue of his enslaved people from the clutches of mighty Egypt and its powerful ruler, the Pharaoh. Revelation was written during a time when another powerful nation, Rome, and its leader, the emperor, dominated God's people the church. The message of Revelation is that no worldly power can stop God from delivering his people and bringing them to himself. Allusions to the book of Exodus helps the book of Revelation teach this important truth.

The second part of Exodus (16–24) narrates the beginning of the wandering in the wilderness. After crossing the sea, Israel was now definitively freed from their bondage to Egypt, but their journey toward the promised land had just begun and would last longer than they would imagine. The apex of this part of the book describes the encounter between Israel, led by Moses, and God at Mount Sinai, which was the location of his encounter with God in the burning bush.

As Moses ascended Sinai, God reminded the people of the great act of deliverance out of the powerful nation of Israel, and "how I carried you on eagles' wings and brought you to myself" in safety from danger (Ex 19:4). This provides the background for the picture of the woman, who represents the New Testament people of God, being brought to safety out of reach of the dragon who represents Satan (Rev 12:14). Here the woman herself is given two eagle's wings to fly into the wilderness.

God then promised Israel in Exodus that if they obeyed him then "you will be my treasured possession. Although the whole earth is mine, you will be for me a kingdom of priests and a holy nation" (19:5-6). Priests are those who represent God in the world and function as a bodyguard of his holiness.[3]

This combination of kingdom and priestly status resonates in the picture of God's persevering people in the book of Revelation. At the very start of

Revelation, John opens with a doxology that praises God who has "made us to be a kingdom and priests" (1:6). This thought is repeated in the worship song of the four living creatures and twenty-four elders who proclaim that God had purchased the church by his blood and "made them to be a kingdom and priests to serve our God, and they will reign on the earth" (5:10).

Revelation also uses the language of God's appearance to Israel at this time to describe God's appearance to John. At Sinai and in Revelation, God appears accompanied by thunder and lightning (Ex 19:16; Rev. 4:5), smoke (Ex 19:18; Rev. 15:8), and with a cloud (Ex 19:9, 16; Rev 1:7; 14:14). At Sinai God revealed himself to his rescued people by giving Israel the law. In addition, the law, in particular the Ten Commandments, play a role in the book (see "Revelation Through Old Testament Eyes: The Ten Commandments" at 6:2).

The third part of Exodus (25–40) recounts the building of the tabernacle, the place where God made his abiding presence known to his people. God could appear anywhere, of course, and did when he chose, for instance to Moses at the burning bush (Ex 3:1–4:17). The tabernacle, though, was the place where God's presence dwelt with his people. The book of Revelation uses tabernacle/temple imagery to depict heavenly realities, because the tabernacle/temple was heaven on earth (see "Revelation 21 through Old Testament Eyes: The Heavenly Temple"). There may also be some echoes to the dress of the priests that are described in Exodus (see notes regarding "jasper and ruby" at Rev 4:3 and "shining linen" at 15:6).

9:3 *Locusts came down on the earth.* Locusts are a type of grasshopper that under certain conditions form thick swarms that devastate vegetation, causing great damage to food sources and therefore presenting significant threat to human well-being and life. A single locust swarm has tens of millions of individual locusts in a square mile and a single swarm can occupy a space of more than four hundred square miles. They can fly long distances. Thus, it is not shocking that locusts (and the famine they can create) are associated with God's judgment on sinful humanity.

Not surprisingly, since many of Revelation's depictions of judgment reflect the plagues against Egypt, we first hear of a devastating locust swarm associated with the eight plagues against Egypt. In announcing the coming plague, Moses told Pharaoh, "If you refuse to let them [the Israelites] go, I will bring locusts into your country tomorrow. They will cover the face of the ground so that it

cannot be seen. They will devour what little you have left after the hail, including every tree that is growing in your fields. They will fill your houses and those
of all your officials and all the Egyptians—something neither your parents nor
your ancestors have ever seen from the day they settled in this land till now"
(Ex 10:4–6; cf. Ps 105:34–35). The threat of locusts was terrifying, and in the
covenant renewal described in the book of Deuteronomy a locust swarm was
listed among the punishments that would follow disobedience (Dt 28:38, 42).

The prophet Joel presents the most striking use of the locust theme among
the prophets. The opening chapter is best interpreted as reflecting an actual
locust swarm that just struck the land of God's people:

> Tell it to your children,
>> and let your children tell it to their children,
>> and their children to the next generation.
> What the locust swarm has left
>> the great locusts have eaten;
> what the great locusts have left
>> the young locusts have eaten;
> what the young locusts have left
>> other locusts have eaten. (Joel 1:3–4)

This devastating locust swarm is likened to an invading army that has
plundered the land (Joel 1:6–7).

Then in Joel 2:1–2 we hear about a future locust invasion. Since God is at
the head of this army (Joel 2:11), locusts, which we just saw were used literally
in Joel 1, now are a figurative depiction of God's heavenly army[4] that brings
judgment. But eventually God will restore his repentant people:

> I will repay you for the years the locusts have eaten—
>> the great locust and the young locust,
>> the other locusts and the locust swarm—
> my great army that I sent among you. (Joel 2:25)

John's depiction of a locust swarm emerging from the smoking shaft of the
Abyss thus has a background in Old Testament scenes of judgment.

Given power like that of scorpions of the earth. Locust swarms destroyed
vegetation, but these locusts from the Abyss are given power like the scorpion, a feared arachnid, known for its venomous stinger. They were known in
ancient biblical times and lands. Indeed, a pass was named after the scorpion
(Akrabbim Pass; Nu 34:4; Jos 15:3; Judg. 1:36). In his final sermon to the
Israelites before they entered the promised land, Moses instructed them to

obey the Lord who had "led you through the vast and dreadful wilderness, that thirsty and waterless land, with its venomous snakes and scorpions" (Dt 8:15). God encourages the prophet Ezekiel not to be afraid of those to whom he is sending, "though briers and thorns are all around you and you live among scorpions" (Eze 2:6). While scorpions are to be feared by those who resist God, Ezekiel helps us see that they are not beyond the control of God, so his people do not need to be afraid.

9:4 *Not to harm the grass of the earth or any plant or tree.* The locusts with scorpion powers had orders not to harm the environment, but only human beings. Here we are reminded that these are picture images of destruction and not intended to be taken at face value. All the grass was destroyed as well as one-third of the trees after the blowing of the first trumpet (see note at 8:7). The instructions here are highlighting the fact that this judgment is on humans and humans alone. Of course, this is atypical of actual locusts who feed on vegetation and not humans. Even scorpions don't prey on humans but will only sting them if provoked.

   Those people who did not have the seal of God on their foreheads. The seal, a sign of ownership (see note at 7:3), marked the people who were not harmed as God's own people (anticipating a contrast with those who have the mark of the beast [13:16; 14:9]). Those who were not God's people were the object of the locusts' attention and thereby of God's judgment.

9:5 *Five months.* Though the locusts are demonic forces, God has put limits on the harm that the locusts can bring. First, they can only harm those without the seal of God; second, they can only torture, not kill; and there is a time limit on their torture, five months. While a limited time, it's a long time to suffer the sting of a locust with a scorpion tail. The five-month period reflects the average length that a locust lives.

   Like that of the sting of a scorpion when it strikes. We earlier (9:3) spoke of the scorpion's venomous stinger. There are hundreds of types of scorpions, but only a handful can kill a human with their sting. Even so the sting of any is extremely painful.

9:6 *Will long to die, but death will elude them.* The picture of enduring scorpion stings for a five-month period is horrific in and of itself. We can imagine that one might want to die rather than endure it. One thinks of Job after God gives the Accuser permission to afflict him, but not kill him (Job 2).

9:7 *Looked like horses prepared for battle.* A rather fantastical description of these locust-scorpions follows in the next few verses, first by commenting that they looked like horses prepared for battle. Indeed, the locust's head looks a bit horselike, or at least the suggestion of this picture image can evoke such a thought. The idea of locusts like a cavalry charge also is frightening to contemplate. The association between locusts and horses likely derives from Joel 2 (see 9:3), where we read concerning what turns out to be a metaphorical locust invasion:

> Before them fire devours,
>> behind them a flame blazes.
> Before them the land is like the garden of Eden,
>> behind them, a desert waste—
>> nothing escapes them.
> They have the appearance of horses;
>> they gallop along like cavalry.
> With a noise like that of chariots
>> they leap over the mountaintops,
> like a crackling fire consuming stubble,
>> like a mighty army drawn up for battle. (Joel 2:3–6)

They wore something like crowns of gold. There is no specific Old Testament background to this description of crown-wearing locusts. There are many different types of locusts and perhaps John has in mind a particular type that has a yellow-gold band at the top of its head. In any case, it communicates the sense of royalty. The fantastical description of these locusts suggest that they are not describing a literal locust plague.

9:8 *Their hair was like woman's hair.* Locusts have very fine antennae at the top of their head that may have suggested this description.

Their teeth were like lions' teeth. Lions are predator cats that tear their prey with their teeth. While locusts have serrated jaws rather than teeth, their chewing and consumption of vast swathes of vegetation suggests the type of ferocity of a lion. A lion in the Old Testament "evokes ferocity, destructive power and irresistible strength" and "is described as a valiant warrior (Pr 28:1; 30:30)"[5] in the Old Testament, thus the association ascribes similar traits to these locusts of God's judgment.

9:9 *Breastplates of iron.* Breastplates were part of ancient armor and thus further the picture of this locust swarm as an army on the march. This picture of a locust horde again is metaphorical, not of a literal locust swarm but standing for an army or, more likely, destruction and judgment.

The sound of their wings. The sound of a single flying locust would be barely perceptible, but the sound of the tens or hundreds of millions of locusts in a swarm would be reminiscent of a calvary or chariot charge. Again, we might draw attention to Joel 2:3–6, quoted above) that likens a locust swarm to a chariot charge.

9:10 *They had tails with stingers.* We have already heard that the locusts had "the sting of a scorpion when it strikes" (see note at 9:5) and that they would torment those who did not have the seal of God on their foreheads for five months, but this information is repeated as the strange locusts are described figuratively in their physical appearance.

9:11 *Whose name in Hebrew is Abaddon and in Greek is Apollyon (that is, Destroyer).* Though each of the locusts have a golden crown, they also have a king described as an angel of the Abyss. It is not clear, and actually doubtful, since the angel who opened the shaft of the Abyss fell from the sky, that this king is that same angel. One would think we are to imagine that king of the locust horde to emerge from the Abyss with his subjects and, after all, John tells us that he was an "angel of the Abyss." Thus, we realize that this being is a demon and that the names given to it are appropriate. Abaddon means "Destruction" in Hebrew. In the Old Testament the term is used in conjunction with Sheol, grave (Job 26:6; 28:22; 31:12; Ps 88:11; Pr 15:11; 27:20). Interestingly, Abaddon is often presented as a personification in the Old Testament, as in this case:

> Where then does wisdom come from?
>> Where does understanding dwell?
> It is hidden from the eyes of every living thing,
>> concealed even from the birds in the sky.
> Destruction [Heb. *Abaddon*] and Death say,
>> "Only a rumor of it has reached our ears." (Job 28:20–22)

Perhaps this personification suggested itself to John for use in reference to this demonic king from the underworld. The Greek equivalent to the Hebrew *Abaddon* is "Apollyon," and thus the association is made for John's Greek-speaking audience.

Interlude: One Woe Done; Two to Go (9:12)

9:12 *The first woe is past; two other woes are yet to come.* Three woes were announced in 8:13 (see there for the meaning of "woe"), anticipating the blowing of the last three trumpets. Just finishing the description of the first woe, we turn now to the second (the sixth trumpet) and eventually the third (the seventh trumpet).

The Sixth Trumpet (9:13–21)

9:13 *The sixth angel.* The trumpet blasts announce judgments that increase in intensity and focus on sinful humanity. While the first four were focused on the earth and the sky with some collateral human death, the fifth turned to humanity, the horrifying locust army under the leadership of the "Destroyer" (Abaddon/Apollyon) tortured but did not kill the objects of its terror. The results of the judgment presaged by the blowing of the sixth trumpet will lead to the death of one third of humanity.

A voice coming from the four horns of the golden altar that is before God. The Old Testament tabernacle/temple reflects heavenly realities. There was a golden incense altar with horns (Ex 30:1–10) situated right outside the curtain that separated the Holy of Holies, where God made his presence known above the ark of the covenant, so right "before God." The horns of the altar would refer to protuberances at the four corners of the top of the altar. Horns in the Old Testament symbolized strength (connected to the horns of a bull; Dt 33:17). Some people believe that the horns of the incense altar helped cradle a bowl of incense, but this is pure speculation. The implication of a voice coming from this location would be that it is divine. Whether in the present context it is God or Jesus is not clear.

9:14 *Release the four angels who are bound at the great river Euphrates.* The voice coming from the incense altar tells the sixth angel to perform a task, the first task beyond blowing the trumpet done by any of the previous five. This task was to release four other angels who were bound by the Euphrates River. That these angels were "bound" likely means they were fallen angels, in other words, demons. The Euphrates is one of the major rivers of the Near East. Along with the Tigris to its northeast they provide a rough border of Mesopotamia and so during the Old Testament period serve as a kind of border between the Israel and powers like Assyria and Babylon. During the time of Revelation the Euphrates was a border between the Roman Empire and their feared rivals the Parthians.

9:15 *For this very hour and day and month and year.* God's judgment is not impulsive or arbitrary. The timing is precise. The use of time references in apocalyptic literature are not intended to communicate to its readers a blueprint to determine when events happen, but rather to communicate that while evil seems to run amok, God is in control and will end it on his timetable.[6]

A third of mankind. A sizable portion of humanity, to be sure, but still less than half. The fact that the remnant does not repent may signal that the purpose of this judgment was to elicit repentance from the remainder of the population (9:20–21).

9:16 *The number of mounted troops was twice ten thousand times ten thousand.* Along with the released angels came a huge calvary, numbering some twenty million. John said he heard the number, since it would not be possible for him to calculate the number by sight.

9:17 *Fiery red, dark blue, and yellow as sulfur.* Fire (the red) and sulfur (the yellow; also known as brimstone) are often connected to God's judgment. God rained burning sulfur on Sodom and Gomorrah (Ge 19:24; see also Dt 29:23). The psalmist announces that "on the wicked he [God] will rain fiery coals and burning sulfur" (Ps 11:6). The connection between fire and sulfur and destruction may be related to volcanoes which emit both fire and sulfur. The colors may be related to the fire, smoke, and sulfur that comes out of the horses' mouths. The red fire and yellow sulfur may suggest that the smoke is represented by the dark blue of their breastplates.

The heads of lions. The demonic locusts of the fifth trumpet judgment had the teeth of lions; here the demonic army rides horses whose heads are like those of lions. Again (see note at 9:7), lions, unlike horses, are feared predators that were known for their speed, strength, and skill at killing their prey.

9:18 *A third of mankind was killed.* See note at 9:15.

By the three plagues of fire, smoke and sulfur. The judgments of fire, smoke, and sulfur pictured in 9:17 are here called plagues. Later, we will hear of seven additional plagues (see 15:6) bringing the total number of plagues in Revelation to ten, the same number that God sent against Egypt at the time of the exodus.

9:19 *The power of the horses was in their mouths and in their tails.* In 9:17, we heard that the horses' mouths breathed fire, smoke, and sulfur. Now we learn that their tails, like the tails of the locusts of the fifth trumpet judgment (see 9:5, 10), were also lethal. The horses' tails were like snakes, which could "inflict injury" by the bite of their heads.

9:20 *The rest of mankind . . . still did not repent.* The purpose, or perhaps hope, of the judgment of the sixth trumpet was to elicit the repentance of the rest of humanity from their idolatry and their evil behaviors. We might again think of the judgments against Pharaoh and Egypt during the time of the plagues. Each plague had as its purpose Pharaoh's repentance that would be signaled by his release of the Hebrew slaves, but none did until the climactic plague of the death of the firstborn, and even then Pharaoh had a change of mind that led to the climactic event at the Re(e)d Sea.

Worshipping demons . . . idols that cannot see or hear or walk. Idolatry is the worship of anything or anybody in the place of God. Here there is reference to "idols of gold, silver, bronze, stone and wood," representations of gods that would be placed in ancient temples.[7] During the Old Testament period, these represented gods of the surrounding nation, notably Canaanite Baal or Asherah. Indeed, Israel was the only nation that did not use idols in the worship of their gods. Jeremiah ridiculed such worship, and John seems to reflect Jeremiah's language in his diatribe against idolatry when he charges:

> Do not learn the ways of the nations
>> or be terrified by signs in the heavens,
>> though the nations are terrified by them.
> For the practices of the peoples are worthless;
>> they cut a tree out of the forest,
>> and a craftsman shapes it with his chisel.
> They adorn it with silver and gold;
>> they fasten it with hammer and nails
>> so it will not totter.
> Like a scarecrow in a cucumber field,
>> their idols cannot speak;
> they must be carried
>> because they cannot walk.
> Do not fear them;
>> they can do no harm
>> nor can they do any good. (Jer 10:1–5; see also Isa 40:18–20; 41:7,
>> 29; 44:6–23; 46:5–7).

There were also idol worshippers in John's time since Greco-Roman religion also utilized human-made statues in their religion, statues that were ornamented with precious metals and were thought to represent gods and goddesses.

Of course, idolatry, the worship of false gods and goddesses with physical images, is prohibited by the first two commandments (Ex 20:2–6; Dt 5:7–10), and indeed even the worship of the true God with images is prohibited by the second. But idolatry does not need to involve the worship of physical images. An idol can be anyone or anything that we put in the place of God as the most important thing in our lives.

John makes the interesting and frightening comment that correlates idols with demons. In one sense, as Jeremiah points out in the passage cited above, idols are nothing but lifeless blocks of wood covered with precious metals. But in another sense, the false gods they represent are actually demonic powers. We can see this connection in Psalms:

> They served their idols,
>   which became a snare to them.
> They sacrificed their sons
>   and their daughters to demons;
> they poured out innocent blood,
>   the blood of their sons and daughters,
> whom they sacrificed to the idols of Canaan;
>   and the land was polluted with blood. (Ps 106:36–38, NRSV; see also Dt 32:17)

9:21 *Nor did they repent of their murders, their magic arts, their sexual immorality or their thefts.* Idolatry often leads to, or at least is associated with, all kinds of moral failures. The prophets of the Old Testament not only pronounced judgment on God's people for worshipping other gods and goddesses but also for other serious moral violations. For one of many possible examples, Jeremiah castigates the people for murder, oppression of the vulnerable, lying, adultery, theft and more (Jer 7:4–11; 8:5–6, 19; 9:3–6, etc.). The mention of "magic arts" may be especially connected to idolatry since magic in general involved the inducing of spiritual powers to act on one's behalf. As Osborne points out, the Greek word used here (*pharmakon*) "can mean 'medicine' or even 'poison' in certain contexts but here refers to the use of 'magic potions' in religious rites in the Greco-Roman world."[8]

Going Deeper into Repentance: Revelation 9:20–21

Revelation is a book that pictures God's ultimate judgment on evil people and evil spiritual powers. The book's primary purpose is to encourage God's oppressed people who think that their oppressors have the upper hand. But that is not the book's only purpose; it also calls on evil people and wayward Christians to repent.

In the Bible, repentance is the route to forgiveness; there is no forgiveness without repentance. Jesus could not have been clearer when he told people "unless you repent, you too will all perish" (Lk 13:3, 5). At the core of his preaching ministry was the call to repent, "Repent, for the kingdom of heaven has come near" (Mt 4:17; also Mk 1:15). When his call to repent went unheeded in the towns he visited and in which he performed miracles, Jesus denounced them (Mt 11:20–21). After Jesus' death and resurrection, the disciples picked up his call to repentance: "Repent, then, and turn to God, so that your sins may be wiped out, that times of refreshing may come from the Lord" (Ac 3:19). Christ even told his followers that they should only forgive those who sin against them if they repent (Lk 17:3–4).

Repentance, after all, is a turning away from sin and idolatry and a turning toward Christ. Once that important transition occurs the groundwork is laid for forgiveness. Truth be told, though, repentance is not a one-time event for a Christian. Once we turn to Christ, we don't stop sinning. That is why Jack (C. John) Miller, founding pastor of New Life Church in Philadelphia where I was a ruling elder, constantly reminded us that we needed to "repent daily."[9]

In Revelation, we see that the call to repentance plays a major role in the letters to the seven churches. Christ called those churches and individuals that struggled in faith and obedience to repentance (2:5, 16, 21–22; 3:3, 19). We also take note that the judgments that are described in John's visions strongly imply that their hoped-for result was repentance. In the aftermath of the sixth trumpet judgment, we hear that "the rest of mankind who were not killed by these plagues still did not repent" (Rev 9:20–21). We hear of the same refusal to repent in the description of the fourth and fifth plague bowls (Rev 16:9, 11). In this, we are reminded of Pharaoh's refusal to repent in the face of the plagues. Both the exodus plagues and the judgments on sinful humans, though, still led to God's glorification.

REVELATION 10

Interlude: The Little Scroll (10:1–11)

What the Structure Means: The Seven-Sealed Scroll (Rev 5) and the Little Scroll (Rev 10)

In Revelation 5, God held a scroll with "writing on both sides and sealed with seven seals" (v. 1). In Revelation 10, we read about a "little scroll" (v. 2). What is the relationship between these two scrolls? Are they one and the same or are they two different scrolls? And what difference might it make to our understanding of the contents of the vision if they are the same or different?[1]

The feature that most strongly connects these two scenes is the role played by a "mighty angel" (5:2; 10:1). In the first, the mighty angel is the one who issues the challenge, "Who is worthy to break the seals and open the scroll?" (5:2). In the second, the mighty angel comes down from heaven holding a "little scroll."

Those who connect the two[2] believe that there is one scroll introduced in the divine throne room and whose seven seals are undone (6:1–8:5) so that it is now opened and brought down by the mighty angel in Revelation 10, ingested by John, who then speaks the prophecy of judgment contained therein. Koester does not believe that the judgments that accompany the opening of the seven seals are the content of the scroll.[3]

On the other hand, there are reasons to question this conclusion. In the first place, "mighty angel" is not a specific identifier, but refers to a class of angels. In other words, there can be more than one mighty angel.

Perhaps the fact that a "mighty angel" occurs in both places is because the connection with a scroll, whether one or two, that contains divine judgment, requires not an ordinary angel, but one of extraordinary status.

The other indicator that casts doubt on the connection between the two scroll references is that the second scroll is described as "little." In Revelation 5, the Greek has simply "scroll" (*biblion*), while the in Revelation 10, the Greek has the diminutive "little scroll" (*bibliardion*).[4]

Though this is a debatable issue, whether the scroll is the same or different does not significantly affect the interpretation of the judgments that follow the introduction of both scrolls, though it does question a strong structural link between Revelation 5 and 10.

10:1 *Another mighty angel.* See also 5:2 and 18:21. This mighty angel is pictured as robed in a cloud with a rainbow above his head, a face like the sun and legs like fiery pillars. While not God himself, this angel's description has elements associated with the appearance of God in the Old Testament. God's presence is often associated with a cloud, for instance in the pillar of cloud during the wilderness wandering (Ex 13:20–22; 14:19). Or we might think of the poet's complaint to God in the book of Lamentations: "You have covered yourself with a cloud so that no prayer can get through" (La 3:44).[5] For the association of God and a rainbow, see the note at 4:3 (with reference to Eze 1:28). The glorified Christ was said to have a face like the sun, which also has a background in the Old Testament (see note at 1:16). If the robing in a cloud reminds us of the pillar of cloud that led the Israelites during the day at the time of the wilderness wanderings, the mighty angel's legs like fiery pillars certainly recall the pillar of fire that appeared at night (Ex 13:21–22).

10:2 *A little scroll.* In biblical times, scribes wrote on scrolls, rolled up writing surfaces of parchment, leather, or papyrus. This little, or small, scroll lay open in the hand of the mighty angel, which may mean that this is the same scroll whose seven seals were undone in a previous scene (Rev 5:1–6:17; 8:1–5).[6] But perhaps the descriptor "little" differentiates it from this scroll. In any case, though not explicit, it seems reasonable to think that judgments are written on the little scroll just as they were on the earlier unsealed scroll.

His right foot on the sea and his left foot on the land. The mighty angel straddles both land and sea, the entirety of the earth, as he prepares to pronounce his oath which will have implications for all.

10:3 *A loud shout like the roar of a lion.* A lion's roar is both loudly resonant and fearsome because the lion is a powerful predator cat. In the Old Testament, God is often likened to a lion. Job complains to God that "if I hold my head high, you stalk me like a lion and again display your awesome power against me" (10:16). According to Hosea, God's people "will follow the LORD; he will roar like a lion. When he roars, his children will come trembling from the west" (11:10). In Amos 3:8, God's speech is likened to a lion's roar: "The lion has roared—who will not fear? The Sovereign LORD has spoken—who can but prophesy?" The mighty angel who here roars like a lion is not God but reflects God's fearsome power. See notes at 5:5 and 9:8.

The voices of seven thunders spoke. The mighty angel's roar elicits the speech of seven thunders. Seven is a symbolic number of completeness or totality. The sound of thunder is also associated with the presence of God (see note on "A loud voice like a trumpet" at 1:10). The psalmist associates God's voice with thunder in Psalm 29:

> The voice of the LORD is over the waters;
>> the God of glory thunders,
>> the LORD thunders over the mighty waters.
> The voice of the LORD is powerful;
>> the voice of the LORD is majestic.
> The voice of the LORD breaks the cedars;
>> the LORD breaks in pieces the cedars of Lebanon. (Ps 29:3–5)

10:4 *Seal up what the seven thunders have said.* Earlier, the Lamb unsealed a seven-sealed scroll of judgment (see 5:1). Seals were used to keep scrolls shut and unable to be read. In the previous verse the seven thunders spoke, and while John got ready to write down what they said, a voice from heaven (God's) prohibits him from doing so. The sealing probably indicates that it is not yet time for the judgments spoken by the seven thunders to commence. That seems to be the sense we find in the final chapter of Daniel, when he is told to "roll up and seal the words of the scroll until the time of the end" (Da 12:4) and an angel tells him, "Go your way, Daniel, because the words are rolled up and sealed until the time of the end" (Da 12:9).

Wold, citing Bauckham, intriguingly suggests, that though they are undeveloped, the fact that we have three other sevenfold judgment cycles (already seals and trumpets and soon bowls) means that there are four cycles. This, they believe, derives from Leviticus 26 which speaks of sevenfold punishment on four occasions.[7]

10:5 *Raised his right hand to heaven.* The mighty angel who had a foot on the sea and a foot on the land now raises his hand to swear an oath. The raising of the hand is likely a gesture toward God in whose name the oath is taken. In Genesis 14, after his defeat of the four eastern kings and after the king of Sodom offers him the plunder, Abraham responds with an oath that he will take nothing, beginning his oath by saying, "With raised hand I have sworn an oath to the LORD, God Most High, Creator of heaven and earth" (Ge 14:22; see also Dt 32:40). In a context closer to the present one, at the end of book of Daniel, an angel is described as a "man clothed in linen, who was above the waters of the river, lifted his right hand and his left hand toward heaven." Daniel goes on to say, "I heard him swear by him who lives forever, saying, 'It will be for a time, times and half a time. When the power of the holy people has been finally broken, all these things will be completed'" (Da 12:7). So in Daniel, like in Revelation, we have an angelic figure taking an oath, the oath having to do with the timing of the judgment. Interestingly, in the Daniel passage, a special emphasis is put on the oath by saying that the angel lifted both his right and his left hands to heaven.

10:6 *Swore by him who lives forever.* God is the only being who lives forever. An oath is made in the name of God, so if the oath is broken it is an offense against God himself. By taking an oath in God's name, the angel is affirming the certainty of the pronouncement that judgment will come without delay.

Who created. God is the one who lives forever, and he is also the one who created everything—the heavens, the earth, and the seas (Ge 1–2 and other frequent affirmations that God is the creator). Psalm 19, for example, begins "The heavens declare the glory of God; the skies proclaim the work of his hands" (v. 1). Psalm 24 also begins with an affirmation that God created everything: "The earth is the LORD's, and everything in it, the world, and all who live in it; for he founded it on the seas and established it on the waters" (vv. 1–2). These examples could be multiplied.

There will be no more delay! In the previously referenced passage in Daniel 12 when the angel made the double-handed gesture to emphasize his solemn oath, he was responding to the question, "How long?" (12:6). How long until God's rescue of his people and the concomitant judgment on the wicked. The answer was, "It will be for a time, times, and half a time" (12:7). While this enigmatic chronological reference cannot be used to determine a specific time in the future, it communicated that God was in control and that there was a set time. It was not now, but in the future. Here in our present passage, the swearing angel proclaims no more delay; the judgment is imminent.

10:7 *When the seventh angel is about to sound his trumpet.* See 11:15–19.

The mystery of God will be accomplished. A mystery is a truth or reality that is hidden from people. A mystery of God is something that he knows but of which humans are not aware at least until a moment of disclosure. God reveals mysteries to his servants as he sees fit. In Daniel 2 Nebuchadnezzar has a dream, but no one can interpret it. The king, in frustration, determines to kill all the wise men. When the executioner comes to Daniel and his three friends, they "plead for mercy from the God of heaven concerning this mystery, so that he and his friends might not be executed with the rest of the wise men of Babylon" with the result that "during the night the mystery was revealed to Daniel in a vision" (2:18–19; see also 4:9). Here the mystery which will be accomplished is God's judgment on the wicked and his rescue of his people.

As he announced to his servants the prophets. God had revealed to the Old Testament prophets that he would bring judgment upon the wicked and salvation for his people. Sometimes the judgment was long term, but there was always a sense that in the end God would bring evil to final judgment.

10:8 *The voice that I had heard from heaven.* While the mighty angel is on earth, the voice from heaven is that of God who had spoken earlier (10:4).

Take the scroll. That is the "little scroll" mentioned in 10:2, which is open and in the hand of the mighty angel whose feet span the sea and the land.

10:9 *Take it and eat it.* God instructs John to get the little scroll and eat it. This scene echoes the experience of Ezekiel at the time of his divine commission to be a prophet. God commands Ezekiel to go and speak his word to his people. Ezekiel reports in the first person: "I saw a hand stretched out to me. In it was a scroll, which he unrolled before me. On both sides of it were written words of lament and mourning and woe" (2:9–10). Then he heard God say to him: "Son of man, eat what is before you, eat this scroll; then go and speak to the people of Israel" (3:1). Ezekiel obeys and ate it and says "it tasted as sweet as honey in my mouth" (3:3). While these were bitter words ("words of lament and mourning and woe," 2:10), they tasted sweet in the prophet's mouth because they were God's word, and he was the one commissioned to deliver them to the people. See "2. The Scroll of Judgment" in "Revelation through Old Testament Eyes: Ezekiel" at 20:7.

10:10 *It tasted sweet as honey in my mouth, but when I had eaten it, my stomach turned sour.* Like Ezekiel, the ingested scroll tasted sweet in John's mouth, but unlike Ezekiel (though observe that later we hear Ezekiel say, "I went in bitterness and in anger of my spirit," Eze 3:14), it turns sour in John's stomach, likely due to the note of severe judgment that the scroll anticipated.

10:11 *You must prophesy again.* Eating the little scroll means that God's words to his people have become a part of John, the prophet, as it did for Ezekiel (see also Jer 15:16). He must now go out and speak those words to "many peoples, nations, languages and kings."

REVELATION 11

Interlude: The Two Witnesses (11:1–13)

11:1 *I was given a reed like a measuring rod.* A reed is a tall thin grass that grows in watery areas. Reeds were stiff yet breakable, but because of the former trait they could be used as measuring devices. So here John is given a reed so he can measure the temple and its altar. The scene echoes Ezekiel's vision of an angel who measures a temple and its courtyard in anticipation of a future temple after the destruction of the first temple (Eze 40:3–43:5). Ezekiel's vision anticipated the rebuilding of the physical temple in Jerusalem after the exile (Ezr 1–6), but eventually it anticipates Jesus himself who made God's presence known among us, thus rendering a physical temple unnecessary (Jn 1:14). This present passage is not a fulfillment of the prophecy in Ezekiel, but by the connection, reading it in the light of the fact that the church was said to be the temple of God in the New Testament (2 Cor 6:16; Eph 2:19–22), a signal that when John speaks of the temple here and the two witnesses he is figuratively depicting the church (see following note).

Revelation 11:1–2 Through Old Testament Eyes: The Temple

John is given instructions to "go and measure the temple of God and the altar, with its worshipers" (11:1). In the Old Testament, the temple was the building that represented God's presence on earth. In Genesis 2, God was present with humanity. There was harmony between humans and God, so no special place was needed for God to make his presence known to them. However, in Genesis 3 we have the story of humanity's rebellion against God. Adam and Eve asserted their moral autonomy (in essence saying, "We, not God, will decide what is right and wrong") and created separation with him. They could no longer come easily into the presence of a holy God.

Still, God would come to his people in special places surrounded by all kinds of restrictions and requirements, so that they could meet with him, offer sacrifices, and worship him. At first, these special places were marked by the construction of a simple altar. But in the aftermath of the exodus from Egypt, when the people of God had grown to be nation-sized, God commanded Moses to build a tabernacle, a mobile symbol of God's presence on earth (Ex 25–31; 35–40). The tabernacle was appropriate as long as Israel was not firmly established in the land. But by subduing the last of the internal enemies of Israel in the promised land and thus achieving "rest from all your enemies around you so that you will live in safety" (Dt 12:10), God through David, the conquest completer, created the conditions for the transition from the tabernacle to the temple. But it wasn't for David to build the temple, rather his son Solomon whose name means "Peaceful," to do so.

From the time of Solomon on, the temple played a central role in the worship of Yahweh in the Old Testament. Of course, God could appear to Israel or anyone at any place he so chose, but the temple was that place where God chose to make "a dwelling for his Name" (Dt 12:11; 2 Sa 7:13). When Israel wanted to come into the presence of God, they would go to the temple and there they would offer their worship and sacrifices.

In a word, the temple was heaven on earth. Isaiah's account of his divine commission takes place in the temple where he sees God and all his attending angels (Isa 6, see reference to temple in v. 1).

Due to God's judgment on his sinful people, the Solomonic temple was destroyed by the Babylonians in 586 BC, but it was rebuilt in the first generation after the exile (completed in 515 BC).

This was the temple, aggrandized by Herod the Great, that Jesus knew. But by the time of the book of Revelation and John's vision here, that temple too had been destroyed, this time by the Romans (AD 70). This situation leads to the question, "What temple was John supposed to measure?"

It is unlikely, nearly impossible, to think that this reference refers to some future physical temple. Some people refer to the end of Ezekiel, which bears comparison with our present passage, where the prophet sees a man "standing in the gateway with a linen cord and a measuring rod in his hand" (Eze 40:3), who goes on to measure and describe a vision of a future temple. Again, one school of thought takes this as a reference to a future third temple.

The idea of a third temple to be built in John's (or our) future is a strange one since the coming of Jesus and the sending of the Holy Spirit renders a temple unnecessary, even a perverse thought. After all, after Jesus came to earth there was no longer a need for a special place to be set aside for God to make his presence known as there was up to that moment. Jesus is the very presence of God, "The Word became flesh and made his dwelling among us" (Jn 1:14). The Greek verb here translated "made his dwelling" (*skenao*) derives from the Greek word for tabernacle (*skene*). Jesus himself expresses his awareness that he is the fulfillment of what is represented by the tabernacle/temple when he anticipates the destruction of the temple by saying "destroy this temple, and I will raise it again in three days" (Jn 2:19). When Jesus ascended to heaven, God sent the Holy Spirit, the third person of the Trinity, to make God's presence palpable throughout the world, again rendering a physical building that symbolically represents God's presence unnecessary. Because God is with us individually (1 Co 6:19–20) and corporately (1 Co 3:16–17; 2 Cor. 6:16; Eph 2:19–22), we are the temple of God.

And here is the key to interpreting the temple in the present context. The temple stands for the church.

In the first and second temple, the altar was placed right outside the temple itself. Priests would bring animal sacrifices to be burned on the altar to symbolize the restoration of relationship between a sinner and God (atonement). Of course, Christ's death is the "once for all" sacrifice rendering the need for animal sacrifices unnecessary (Heb 10:1–18). Like the temple, the altar that John measures is symbolic in this case for the fact that atonement is in the heart of the church.

John is also to use the reed measuring rod to measure the worshipers. How one would do that literally is a little unclear, but then again we are dealing with figurative language. Taken together, the temple, the altar, and the worshippers depict the church. (See also "Revelation 4 Through Old Testament Eyes: God on His Throne" and "Revelation 21 Through Old Testament Eyes: The Heavenly Temple.")

Going Deeper into the Perseverance of the Church: Revelation 11

The book of Revelation is addressed to seven churches in Asia Minor (1:4, 11, 20; 22:6), but its message is intended for all the churches at the time, and though not written directly to the church today, the church through the ages has recognized the continuing relevance of its message. That is what is behind the long-standing affirmation that the book of Revelation is part of the canon (the standard of faith and practice).

Revelation is written to a church at that time that was marginalized and perhaps persecuted by the broader culture of the day. Christians lived in a society that was toxic to their faith. While after the emperor Constantine converted to Christianity in the fourth century there have been times when Christians thought they were the broader culture, this belief was wrong-minded and dangerous, since it often led Christians to impose their values by political coercion on others.

So it is good to be reminded by the book of Revelation that the church is a marginalized group within society and must be wary of the danger of compromise or betrayal of the faith. In a word, the church knows that the broader culture is toxic to their faith and needs to expect marginalization and humiliation and even suffering. After all, the church is sent into the world, but is not "of the world" (Jn 17:14–19). And in the world, we are to be as "shrewd as snakes and as innocent as doves" (Mt 10:16).

The call in Revelation is for the church to maintain their faith in the face of oppression and persecution, not to take political power to impose its vision on others outside the church. While the church should seek to persuade the rest of the world that its biblical values result in human flourishing, what is important is to know that, as an eminent Welsh minister of the past generation put it, God wants Christians to stay faithful and for non-Christians to become Christians, not act like Christians.[1]

It's hard enough for the church to stay faithful, which is why the glorified Christ in the seven letters to the churches in Asia Minor both encouraged the churches that were faithful and called to faithfulness those that were wavering. That is why each letter promised reward at the end to "the one who is victorious," victorious over the temptations to wander (see 2:7, 11, 17, 26; 3:5–6, 12–13, 21–22).

And beyond the letters, John encourages perseverance through the presentation of his visions. A number of these visions depict the church under extreme duress, but thanks to God moving from present attack to future victory. The first of three examples comes from Revelation 11, where the two witnesses represent the church (see commentary). The two witnesses prophecy and give testimony with great power, but eventually the beast from the Abyss kills them. It looks like the church is done, but no, it is not done. God raised them from the dead and brought them up to heaven. The message is that, yes, the church will experience harm at the hands of evil people and spiritual powers, but God will preserve them.

The second example is in the next vision where a pregnant woman represents the church. She is attacked by a dragon, whom we find out is "the devil, or Satan" (12:9). After giving birth to the child (representing Christ), she escapes harm by fleeing to a divinely prepared place in the wilderness. Later we hear that the dragon threatens the woman again, but now she is given wings like an eagle and escapes again to the wilderness.

The third example comes by way of a vision of a heavenly celebration at "the wedding supper of the Lamb" that comes after the fall of Babylon, representing Rome and other worldly authorities (Rev 19:1–10). This encouraging picture of the ultimate vindication of the church as a wedding is picked up in the final vision of the New Jerusalem that comes "down out of heaven from God, prepared as a bride beautifully dressed for her husband" (21:2).

Revelation provides much needed encouragement for a besieged people of God. The message is, as Jesus said during his lifetime, that "the gates of Hades will not overcome it" (Mt 16:18). This message that encourages perseverance is as important today as it was at the time Revelation was written, and indeed down through the ages.

11:2 *Exclude the outer court . . . because it has been given to the Gentiles.* While the Old Testament temple and the second temple built by Zerubbabel had a courtyard surrounding the building, the reference to an outer court which allowed the entrance of Gentiles is likely modeled on Herod's aggrandized temple, which had a courtyard dedicated to Gentiles which was outside the boundaries where only Jews were allowed to go (Jn 12:20–22; Ac 21:27–29). Indeed, in the twentieth century archaeologists discovered an ancient "warning" sign from the second temple period: "No foreigner may enter within the balustrade around the sanctuary and the enclosure. Whoever is caught, on himself shall he put blame for the death which will ensue."

John is told to exclude this section from his measurements presumably because those who were there were not part of the covenant. Of course, by the time of Revelation, Gentile believers have been firmly integrated into the church (see Ac 15; Eph 2:11–21), so the reference to Gentiles must be used to represent nonbelievers.

They will trample on the holy city. Indeed, these Gentiles (pagans) are said to do harm to the holy city. The holy city is Jerusalem. Jerusalem was made holy (set apart) because God chose to make his presence known there in the temple. The act of trampling implies desecration as well as harm and destruction. This picture may hearken back to one or possibly two visions found in the book of Daniel. In Daniel 7, Daniel receives a vision of four horrific beasts rising out of a chaotic sea. The interpreting angel later tells Daniel that these beasts represent "four kings that will rise from the earth" (7:17). In the vision itself, the fourth beast, described as having iron teeth and iron claws was "terrifying and frightening and very powerful. It had large iron teeth; it crushed and devoured its victims and trampled underfoot whatever was left. It was different from all the former beasts, and it had ten horns" (Da 7:7, see also vv. 19 and 23). In the next vision (Daniel 8), Daniel sees a ram, representing Persia, and a goat, representing Greece, butting heads. The goat had a prominent horn (representing the Greek king and conqueror Alexander) and with it defeated the ram and trampled it (8:7, 10). The prominent horn had broken off (Alexander died soon after his victories) and was replaced by four horns (the four generals who ultimately inherited and divided Alexander's kingdom).

Revelation 11:2–3 Through Old Testament Eyes: The 42 Months

The Gentiles will trample on the holy city for a period of forty-two months, or three and a half years. In the commentary on 11:2, we saw a background to the Gentiles actions in both Daniel 7 and 8. There may be a further connection here between the vision in Daniel 7 and the forty-two months of our present passage. The fourth beast had ten horns (symbols of power) and after a while an eleventh little horn that uprooted three of the ten initial horns. The horns represent kings. The little horn "will speak against the Most High and oppress his holy people and try to change the set times and the laws. The holy people will be delivered into his hands for a time, times and half a time" (7:25). So, in answer to the question, how long will the little horn do its damage, the answer is an enigmatic statement about "a time, times, and half a time."

What is the meaning of this reference in the context of Daniel, and how might it relate to the forty-two months that the Gentiles trample the holy city?

Some understand the word "time" in Daniel to be a cipher for a year. They, in addition, understand "times" as two years. Thus, they understand the reference in Daniel to be equivalent to "a year, two years, and a half a year" which equals three and a half years (see for instance the NIV note to 7:25). We are focusing on Daniel 7 because the chronological reference here is connected to the theme of "trampling," which provides an interesting connection with our passage in Revelation. But we might also point out that there is a similar chronological reference in Daniel 12 when Daniel asks the angelic spokesperson how long it would be until the end and received the answer, "it will be for a time, times, and half a time" (12:7).

But should these two references be understood as three and a half years? Perhaps, but there are reasons to be hesitant. First, if this were a reference to years, why not use that term rather than an Aramaic (in the case of Daniel 7) or Hebrew (in the case of Daniel 12) word that references an unspecified length of time? Second, the second reference to "times" is plural, not dual. Goldingay suggests that the dual had passed out of use in Aramaic by this time, but that seems speculative for this context.[2]

Still there is another argument that might push us toward understanding these references as pointing to three and a half years. And these concern a reference at the end of the vision in Daniel 8 to a period of the desecration of the sanctuary that would last for "2,330 evenings and mornings" (v. 14), perhaps a reference to evening and morning sacrifices. Perhaps, and again we are dealing with a bit of uncertainty, this refers not to 2,300 days, but to 1,150 days, which is roughly three and a half years. We might say the same about the references at the end of the book to a period of desecration that lasts 1,290 days along with a pronouncement of blessing on "the one who waits for and reaches the end of 1,335 days" (Da 12:12).

Even if we are to take the Daniel references to "years" with a total of three and a half years, we are still likely dealing with a symbolic number. Perhaps it is best to see the progression from a "time" to "times" to "half a time" as communicating two important truths. First, the desecration has a definite end. This fits in with the major theme of the book of Daniel that "in spite of present troubles (evil looks to be in charge), God is in control and he will have the final victory."[3] The numbers we get in Daniel are not for the purpose of our knowing exactly when that time is, but to give us the assurance that evil will have a definite end. The other thing the progression teaches us as we move from a time, to times, to half a time is that it will look like evil will gain momentum (a time, times), but then be cut back (half a time) before coming to a complete stop.

How does our exploration of the book of Daniel illuminate or help us understand the reference to the 42 months of the desecration of the holy city in Revelation 11? It appears that John understood the reference in Daniel to be a reference to three and a half years (42 months). Indeed, in the next verse he will speak of the period that the two witnesses will prophesy as 1,260 days (which is the equivalent of 42 months; see also Rev 11:3).

As we will see in Revelation 12:6 and 14, it appears that the book of Revelation is taking the Daniel phrase and using it like the Old Testament book to describe the period of time that evil is in control before God's intervention. But it has turned the phrase into a more specific time indication by understanding time as a year (or a day in the case of Rev 11:9) and by understanding "times" as a dual or "two years." Thus, a time, times, and a half a time because a year, two years, and half a year (or a day, two days, and half a day). Rather than using Revelation though to read back to Daniel, we are on stronger grounds reading Revelation in the light of Daniel. That is, these time indications are not to be placed on a calendar, but are rather communicating that God is in control of evil, even though it looks like it is gaining power. God will slow it down and bring it to an ultimate end.

Again, as with Daniel, we are not to take this as a reference to a literal time period, but as communicating the same message as Daniel—that evil has a limit, and the desecration will not last forever.

11:3 *I will appoint my two witnesses.* Witnesses bear testimony to the truth. This language comes from the courtroom and may explain why there are two witnesses and not just one since "on the testimony of two or three witnesses a person is to be put to death, but no one is to be put to death on the testimony of only one witness" (Dt 17:6). These witnesses testify to the wickedness of those who desecrate the things of God (holy things), a crime deserving of death. By the time of Revelation the Greek term for "witness" (*martyr*) had taken on the additional meaning of bearing testimony that leads to one's death (thus the English word "martyr"). We will see that the testimony of the two witnesses does lead to their death (see also 2:13 where Antipas "my faithful witness" was put to death).

For 1,260 days. See "Revelation 11:2–3 Through Old Testament Eyes: The 42 Months."

Clothed in sackcloth. The two witnesses are clothed in sackcloth, referring to garments made of rough material (burlap) that one wears while in a period of mourning. The mourning might be brought about by sadness at death or a sense of one's sinful state. However, here the mourning is likely evoked by the desecration wrought by the Gentiles trampling of the holy city.

Revelation 11:4 Through Old Testament Eyes: The Two Witnesses

When John mentions "the two olive trees" and the two lampstands that "stand before the Lord of the earth," he is quoting from Zechariah 4. Thus he associates the two witnesses with one of Zechariah's night visions, the fifth that that Old Testament prophet received (found in that chapter). We will begin our exploration by a look at Zechariah's vision[4] and then consider in what way it informs John's description of the two witnesses.

Prodded by an angel to report what he saw, Zechariah says that he saw a solid gold lampstand with a bowl on top. The bowl had seven lamps on it with seven channels to the lamps and two olive trees by it, one on the right and one on the left of the lampstand. Zechariah knows what he sees but he has no idea what they are, that is what they represent.

First, we should say that while there is an association being drawn here with the gold lampstand that stood in the sanctuary, they are not identical in description. The tabernacle menorah (or "lampstand") had a central lampstand rather than a single bowl on top with seven lamps within it. The tabernacle lampstand had six branches, which along with the lamp on top of the lampstand had seven lamps (Ex 25:31–40). There is of course no mention of olive trees on both sides of the menorah in the tabernacle itself.

As the angel explains the significance of the vision of the lampstand to Zechariah, there are certain matters that seem clear and others that remain obscure. The interpretation focuses on Zerubbabel, the Jewish leader at the time. He was appointed governor by the Persian authorities and was a descendant of David. He was also charged with rebuilding the temple that had been destroyed at the time the Babylonians defeated Jerusalem (586 BC). Once the Persians had defeated the Babylonians, they allowed the Jewish exiles to return to the land and to rebuild the temple. However, for likely economic reasons, if not political ones, they had been distracted from the rebuilding effort. An important thrust of Zechariah's prophetic message was to urge the Jewish leaders like Zerubbabel to resume their efforts.

The word of the Lord to Zerubbabel begins by reminding him that his efforts will not come from his might or power, but rather from God's Spirit. The angel then triumphantly speaks to a "mighty mountain" that it will become a level plain before Zerubbabel, presumably because of the Spirit, not his own might or power. What the mighty mountain represents is not made specific, but probably refers to circumstances or people who stand in the way of temple rebuilding.

Boda explains the reference to Zerubbabel bringing out the capstone as a part of the ritual of temple building or rebuilding of ancient shrines known from the ancient Near East. The first step is to receive a mandate from the god to accomplish the task. After that, second, the building site needs to be prepared, accompanied by various rituals. After this, in the third step of the early stages of construction, the foundation was laid. Boda notes that a special brick played a role in the laying of the foundation. Boda believes that this capstone represents the special brick deposited at the time of foundation building.

In short, the intention of the oracle is clear: it is to encourage Zerubbabel that his efforts to rebuild the temple are divinely supported and will achieve success. What exactly the different parts of the vision represent is not quite as clear. But most likely the lampstand represents God himself. The two branches of the olive trees that stand to the right and the left of the lampstand are, according to the interpreting angel, "the two who are anointed to serve the Lord of all the earth" (Zec 4:14). Who are these two servants? Perhaps Zerubbabel and Joshua the High Priest (see Zec 3). Or perhaps they are the two prophets Haggai and Zechariah whom God uses to urge Zerubbabel back to the task of rebuilding.[5]

While it is important to be as clear as we can be on the meaning of Zechariah's fifth night vision in its Old Testament context, we can see that that passage is not a prophecy that looks forward to the moment being anticipated here in Revelation. In other words, while the lampstand in

Zechariah represents God and the two olive branches (connected to the two olive trees) represents either a royal figure like Zerubbabel and a priestly one like Joshua or two prophetic figures, Zechariah and Haggai, we are not to import that interpretation to the present text.

Williamson rightly comments on the connection between the two passages when he says, adopting the first identification above, "just as Zerubbabel and Joshua were the Lord's anointing instruments in building the second temple, the two anointed witnesses whom Christ has authorized prepare the way for the eschatological temple, the new Jerusalem."[6] But then who are these two witnesses who are the two olive trees? Notice too, that while in Zechariah, the lampstand is singular and represents the Lord, here there are two lampstands who are also associated with the two witnesses.

The two witnesses could be two real individuals who will arise at the end of time to represent the Lord over against the forces of evil. Or, according to Williamson, they could represent the church and its witness to the truth down through the ages, extending to the end of the ages. But if so, why two? Williamson believes that the answer comes when we remember that "the testimony of two witnesses indicates that adequate testimony has been rendered and those who have hear are responsible for their choices," noting that throughout Scripture two witnesses were the standard for compelling testimony (Nu 35:30; Dt 17:6; 19:15; 2 Cor. 13:1; 1 Ti 5:19).[7]

11:5 *Fire comes from their mouths.* God has given the witnesses the ability to protect themselves from evil people that is near-divine. God often sent fire to consume evildoers (e.g., against Nadab and Abihu who offered unauthorized fire before God; Lev 10:2). But at no time does the text say that fire came from God's mouth. Perhaps the closest parallel comes from an episode of the Elijah story. King Ahaziah sent a group of fifty soldiers to arrest the prophet, but Elijah said, "If I am a man of God, let fire come down from heaven and destroy you and your fifty men" (2 Ki 1:10 NLT). This happens a second time when the king sent a second contingent of soldiers out to arrest the prophet (1:12). Thus, fire came from heaven in response to the words of the prophet. We will see that this is not the only connection between the description of the two witnesses and Elijah, but we should also point to another text. In Jeremiah 5:14, God tells Jeremiah, "because the people are talking like this, my messages will flame out of your mouth and burn the people like kindling wood" (NLT).

The testimony of the two witnesses, like the prophecy of Jeremiah, will deal death to those who through their evildoing deserve it.[8]

11:6 *To shut up the heavens so that it will not rain.* Elijah through the words of his mouth called down fire from heaven, he also announced that no rain would fall from the sky (1 Ki 17:1). God kept it from raining because the people had turned their attention to Baal, a storm god, in the hopes of increased fertility. In essence God said that if you look to Baal to get rain, I, who am really in charge of the rain, will withhold it from you. The lack of rain sets up the epic confrontation on Mount Carmel between the prophets of Baal and Elijah (really a contest between Baal and Yahweh). The winner would be the prophet who could call on their god to send fire on the altar to burn the sacrifice. Fire from heaven refers to lightning. Of course, the prophets of Baal failed because Baal is a false god.[9] On the other hand, God immediately sent fire from heaven in response to the prophet's prayer. Right after this confrontation, Elijah informs King Ahab that rain would come again, and it does (1 Ki 18:41–46). The two witnesses have the same power to shut up the heavens, showing that they are in the prophetic line of Elijah. Interestingly, Malachi 4:5–6 anticipates that there will be prophets like Elijah in the future.

Power to turn the waters into blood and to strike the earth with every kind of plague. The two witnesses are not only in the line of the prophet Elijah, but also of Moses. Their power to turn waters into blood is clearly reminiscent of Moses who through his divinely given power was able to turn the waters of the Nile into blood (Ex 7:14–25). That they can strike the earth with every kind of plague alludes to the other plagues with which God through Moses struck Egypt with the final result of their exodus from bondage. Interestingly, Deuteronomy 18:15–18 anticipates that there will be prophets like Moses in the future.

11:7 *The beast that comes up from the Abyss.* The two witnesses bear testimony to the truth. They have tremendous power as we have seen in the previous two verses. However, now they meet a force that overwhelms them in the form of a beast that rises out of the Abyss. We assume that this beast is the same one that will be described in even more detail in Revelation 13 where the beast arises out of the sea.

We should note here and in chapter 13 a connection with Daniel 7 in which we find Daniel's first vision of four horrifying beasts arising out of a chaotic sea. The sea itself is a symbol of chaos and evil (see note at 4:6–8). The beasts represent different kingdoms that dominate and terrify the people of God (Da 7:17–25). The beast that comes from the Abyss here and from the sea in chapter 13 may be more specifically associated with the fourth and climactic beast and the single horn that "was waging war against the holy people and defeating them" (7:21). The interpreting angel informs Daniel about this final horn that it represents "another king . . . different from the earlier ones. . . . He will speak against the Most High and oppress his holy people and try to change the set times and the laws. The holy people will be delivered into his hands for a time, times and half a time" (7:24–25). This connection leads us to agree with Williamson that the connection between this scene and Daniel 7 "lends support to the interpretation that the two witnesses represent the people of God,"[10] since the two witnesses are the object of the beast from the Abyss' murderous rage just as the people of God were of the little horn that emanated from the fourth beast. See "Revelation 11:4 Through Old Testament Eyes: The Two Witnesses."

11:8 *Their bodies will lie in the public square.* After the beast killed the two witnesses, their bodies were displayed in a public area so that people could see them and wickedly celebrate their deaths (v. 10). The intention of public exposure would also be to shame them since respect would require their proper burial. According to the Mosaic law, even criminals were to be immediately buried after their execution (Dt 21:22–23). Not to be buried immediately or properly mourned was a fate dreaded in ancient Israel. Jeremiah announces the Lord's judgment on his people and says that "both high and low will die in this land. They will not be buried or mourned, and no one will cut themselves or shave their head for the dead" (Jer 16:6). While the exposure of the bodies of the two witnesses was not a sign of divine judgment, it was an attempt on the part of wicked people to shame them.

Which is figuratively called Sodom and Egypt—where also their Lord was crucified. The city where the Lord was crucified was, of course, Jerusalem. In Revelation, though, it is Rome that is usually vilified and compared to wicked cities like Babylon (see Rev 13), and (the New) Jerusalem is the city that represent the kingdom of God (Rev 21 and 22). However, in this context, Jerusalem is in the process of being desecrated by Gentiles trampling the outer courts of the temple (11:2); and also the crucifixion of Jesus, the most heinous crime of all, took place right outside that city.

For this reason, John associates Jerusalem with two of the most notoriously wicked locations from the Old Testament, first Sodom and then Egypt. Sodom first[11] appears in the Abraham narrative when Lot and Abraham must settle in different places due to their tremendous wealth. Lot chooses the area around Sodom and its sister city Gomorrah because it was "well, watered, like the garden of the Lord." But even here we get the foreboding anticipation of its destruction ("This was before the Lord destroyed Sodom and Gomorrah," Ge 13:10).

Genesis narrates the account of its destruction in chapters 18–19. God determines to judge Sodom (and Gomorrah) because "the outcry" against those cities "is so great and their sin so grievous" (18:20). God, though, warns Lot and his family to leave the city before he destroyed it. But once they left, though Lot's wife disobeyed the instructions and turned into a pillar of salt, God "rained down burning sulfur on Sodom and Gomorrah" (19:24).

Later Scripture looked back on these two cities as the epitome of evil that deserve divine judgment. In Deuteronomy, God warns his people if they disobey his covenant law that the judgment he will bring will "be like the destruction of Sodom and Gomorrah, Admah and Zeboyim, which the LORD overthrew in fierce anger" (29:23).

Thus, we should not be surprised that the prophets invoke comparisons between God's sinful people and Sodom, along with the threat that they will experience the same horrific judgment as that city unless they repent. Isaiah does this in 3:8–9 (see also 1:9–10; 13:19).

Similarly, Jeremiah reports God as accusing the false prophets of Jerusalem that "they are all like Sodom to me" (Jer 23:14, see also 49:18 [against Edom]; 50:40 [against Babylon]). Turning to Ezekiel, that prophet refers to Sodom amid a lengthy allegory that compares Jerusalem's idolatry to adultery (Eze 16:44–52).[12] Amos (4:11) and Zephaniah (2:9; in reference to Moab) also refer to Sodom in this way. When judgment did come on Judah and its capital Jerusalem, the book of Lamentations describes it as Sodomlike (La 4:6).

Even before Revelation, other New Testament authors use Sodom to describe human sin and the threat of punishment. Matthew tells us that Jesus instructed the disciples to go out to proclaim that the kingdom of God was near. If their listeners reject them, Jesus told them, then "it will be more bearable for Sodom and Gomorrah on the day of judgment than for that town" (Mt 10:15; see also Lk 10:12). Jesus makes similar comparisons in Matthew 11:23–24 and Luke 17:28–30. Paul (Ro 9:29, citing Isa 1:9), Peter (2 Pe 2:6), and Jude (v. 7) also refers to Sodom in contexts of judgment.

The equation of Egypt and wicked Jerusalem most obviously flows out of the story of the exodus (Ex 1–15). The Egyptians reduced the descendants of Abraham to slave status. And they were roughly treated. When God sent Moses to lead his people out of bondage, Pharaoh resisted and increased the burden of their slavery. In response God sent plagues of judgment against the Egyptians until Pharaoh finally acquiesced and allowed them to depart. But even after that decision, Pharaoh changed his mind and pursued the Israelites thinking that he had them pinned down at the R(e)ed Sea. But God had other things in mind as he opened the Sea, allowing the people of God to escape, and then closed it on the Egyptians.

11:9 *For three and a half days.* The exposure of the bodies of the two witnesses will last for three and a half days while people come and gloat over their death. The three and a half days is yet another echo from Daniel and most likely specifically chapter 7, which announces that the forces of evil will have sway for a "time, "times, and half a time" (Da 7:25). In 11:2, see note, we connected this reference to the 42 months (three and a half years) that the Gentiles would trample the holy city. We explained there that the Danielic expression was not clearly intended to be years but periods of time, nor were the "times" clearly intended to be understood as "two times"; rather, the idea was a gaining of momentum on the part of evil people (time, times) that suddenly and abruptly slows down (half a time) and then stops. The ambiguity, however, allows John to treat the number, which here also reflects the initial momentum and ultimate cessation of evil, as either three and a half years (42 months) or three and a half days.

Every people, tribe, language and nation. A way of referring to the inhabitants of the whole world. The language is like that found in reference to the descendants of the three sons of Noah after the flood, altogether pointing to the population of the world. Each of the three sections of the text, which has the form of an ancient genealogy, ended with a variant of "These are the sons of X by their clans and languages, in their territories and nations" (Ge 10:31, see also 10:5, 20). See "Revelation 7:9 Through Old Testament Eyes: Every Nation, Tribe, People, and Language."

Refuse them burial. An expression of contempt toward the two witnesses (see note at 11:8).

11:10 *Will celebrate by sending each other gifts.* The testimony of the two witnesses enraged people probably because, like the prophets before them (Jer 18:18–20; 36; Amos 7:10–17), their message exposed sin and called for repentance. Thus their death was greeted with celebration as if it were some kind of victory. The psalmist would ask God to prevent the gloating of their enemies (Ps 13:2; 35:24) or thank God for preventing their enemies' joy (Ps 30:1; 41:11), but here God does not appear to have prevented such gloating. But as we move on, we see it is not the end of the story.

11:11 *But after the three and a half days.* There is a short time limit to the gloating of wicked people over the death of the two witnesses. Their perverse joy is cut short when God gives life to the two witnesses, and they come to their feet again. The span of time between their death and their revivification is primarily symbolic in the sense spelled out in the note to 11:9, but the period is long enough to give certainty (since in that time decomposition would have started) that they had truly died and were being brought to life as opposed to simply passing out. Lazarus had spent four days in the tomb before Jesus brought him back to life (Jn 11:17). Jesus himself was in the tomb for three days after his crucifixion.

The breath of life from God. In Genesis 2:7 we read "then the LORD God formed a man from the dust of the ground and breathed into his nostrils the breath of life, and the man became a living being." Granted John here uses "spirit" (*pneuma*) rather than "breath,"[13] but the concepts are similar. Interestingly, in the Greek version of Ecclesiastes, Qohelet speaks of death by saying "the dust returns to the ground it came from, and the spirit (*pneuma*) returns to God who gave it" (Ecc 12:7).

The language here is also reminiscent of Ezekiel's vision of the valley of dry bones. In his vision, God took Ezekiel to a valley full of bones that "were very dry" (37:2), meaning that they were the bones of people long dead. But God told Ezekiel to prophecy to the bones and say, "I will make breath enter you, and you will come to life" (37:5). The word translated "breath" here (*ruah*) can also be translated "spirit" and indeed was so translated by the Greek version (*pneuma* again; see also 37:6). Ezekiel 37 speaks to the revival of the people of God after judgment that comes on them for their sins. It is not a prophecy of the events in Revelation per se, but the language used would likely evoke the memory of Ezekiel's vision of God's people, reinforcing our understanding of the two witnesses as also representing the people of God, the church.

11:12 *A loud voice from heaven.* Once again, a loud voice speaks from heaven (1:10). This voice could be an angelic one, but more likely God speaks from heaven.

They went up to heaven in a cloud. After coming back to life, the two witnesses were taken up into heaven by means of a cloud. At the end of his life, the prophet Elijah (with whom John as already made a connection in 11:5), was taken up to heaven in a whirlwind (2 Ki 2:11), but the two witnesses are the only ones besides God said to ride the cloud. Earlier in Revelation the exalted Christ is described as coming on the clouds (see note at 1:7 with related Old Testament texts).

11:13 *There was a severe earthquake.* Earthquakes and other cataclysmic terrestrial and celestial events accompany God's judgment (see notes at 6:12 on "a great earthquake" and at 6:14). This earthquake results in the deaths of seven thousand people. Those who were left were so frightened that they finally gave glory to God.

Interlude: Two Woes Done; One to Go (11:14)

11:14 *The second woe has passed; the third woe is coming soon.* "Woe" is a word associated with funerals. To pronounce a woe is to say that a person or people are "as good as dead" (see note at 8:13). The first woe ended with the blowing of the fifth trumpet, and the second began at 9:12. The second woe was completed with the blowing of the sixth trumpet, but the announcement of its completion awaited the telling of the interludes of the little scroll and two witnesses. With the seventh trumpet, we now begin the telling of the third and final woe.

The Seventh Trumpet (11:15–19)

11:15 *The seventh angel sounded his trumpet.* We left off the depiction of angels announcing judgment by blowing trumpets at the end of Revelation 9. Six angels have sounded their trumpets presaging increasing horrific punishment from 8:6–9:21. Revelation 10–11 presents several interludes, including an angel holding a little scroll followed by an account of the two witnesses. We have noted the symbolic nature of the number seven at various places in the preceding commentary (see 1:4, 11, 12; 5:1; 8:2). Indeed, the book of Revelation is built on cycles of seven. There are seven letters written to seven churches (1:19–3:22), seven seals that were undone 6:1–17; 8:1–5, now seven angels blowing trumpets, and there will be seven bowls of judgment (16:1–21). The use of the number seven is more extensive than these examples, but these examples relate to the structure of the book. Besides being the final of the series, the seventh sounding of the trumpet by the seventh angel is the climactic moment in the series of judgments.

There were loud voices in heaven. A loud voice is commanding, demands attention, and expresses authority. Here a chorus of voices are heard from heaven. The identities of the speakers are not specified and could be angelic or else those saints who were already in heaven (see 7:9–10). Whatever their exact identity, they break out in praise of God for what is about to happen.

The kingdom of the world has become the kingdom of our Lord and of his Messiah. Two times the book of Daniel anticipates this moment. Daniel 2 reports a time when king Nebuchadnezzar has a disturbing dream that none of his Babylonian wise men can interpret. Their interpretation depends on the king telling them the content of the dream. They tell him that what he asks "is too difficult. No one can reveal it to the king except the gods, and they do not live among humans" (Da 2:11).[14] Thanks to God's revelation of the dream and its interpretation, Daniel is able to tell the king his dream and what it means, thus showing God's superiority to the false gods of the Babylonians.

In his dream, Nebuchadnezzar saw a multi-metaled statue. The head was gold, the chest and arms were silver, the belly and thighs bronze, its legs iron, and its feet partly of iron and baked clay (2:32–33).

After describing the statue, Daniel tells Nebuchadnezzar that he watched as a "rock was cut out, but not by human hands. It struck the statue on its feet of iron and clay and smashed them" (2:34). The rest of the statue, no matter the metal, broke into pieces which were blown away by the wind. On the other hand, the rock "became a huge mountain and filled the whole earth" (2:35).

After the description, the prophet moved on to his divinely given interpretation. The different metals represented different kingdoms of this world that would succeed each other, one after another. The diminishing worth of the metals signify a weakening of power. There is only one specific identification made between the head of gold and Nebuchadnezzar who himself stands for the Babylonian kingdom. The identification of the other parts of the statue is debated[15] and is unimportant for our purposes.

When it comes to the rock that destroys the statues that represent kingdoms of this world, using the language of Revelation, Daniel proclaims "in the time of those kings, the God of heaven will set up a kingdom that will never be destroyed, nor will it be left to another people. It will crush all those kingdoms and bring them to an end, but it will itself endure forever. This is the meaning of the vision of the rock cut out of a mountain, but not by human hands" (2:44–45).

The second vision that communicates much the same point—that the human kingdoms that dominate the present will be destroyed and replaced by God's rule—is found in Daniel 7. Scholars have noted the similarity between the visions of Daniel 2 and 7 before. Completely different imagery is used, but both anticipate the rise of four oppressive world kingdoms, culminating with offshoots of the fourth (the clay-iron feet/ten horns). They both also anticipate the ultimate destruction of these kingdoms by God and the establishment of the kingdom of God that lasts forever.

The imagery used is that of four horrific beasts that arise out of a chaotic sea. The sea itself symbolizes chaos and even evil (see note at Rev 4:6–8). Though not specifically aquatic in description, the beasts are nonetheless creatures that emerge from the sea. The vision depicts the beasts' harmful actions. Two beasts are hybrids (the first and third), something considered unclean by the Israelites, and the final beast is described only as having "iron teeth" (7:7) and "bronze claws" (7:19).

The interpreting angel tells Daniel that these "four great beasts are four kings that will arise from the earth" (7:17). But they are not the end of the story. The second half of the vision pictures God as the Ancient of Days sitting on his throne in his courtroom about to render judgment (7:9–10). Into his presence rides "one like a son of man" riding a cloud (7:13) indicating his divine status (for which, see note at Rev 1:7). The "one like a son of man" is the divine warrior who will defeat the beasts with the result that "the holy people of the Most High will receive the kingdom and will possess it forever—yes, for ever and ever" (7:18). Or as the angel who interprets the vision for Daniel puts it:

But the court will sit, and his power will be taken away and completely destroyed forever. Then the sovereignty, power and greatness of all the kingdoms under heaven will be handed over to the holy people of the Most High. His kingdom will be an everlasting kingdom, and all rulers will worship and obey him (7:26–27).

And he will reign forever and ever. The loud voices in heaven join in with the psalmist in celebrating God's eternal reign. While scattered throughout the psalms, the praise of God's eternal kingship is repeated especially in the so-called kingship psalms such as in the following examples:

God reigns over the nations;
    God is seated on his holy throne.
The nobles of the nations assemble
    as the people of the God of Abraham,
For the kings of the earth belong to God;
    he is greatly exalted. (Ps 47:8–9)

The LORD reigns, he is robed in majesty;
    the LORD is robed in majesty and armed with strength;
    indeed, the world is established, firm and secure.
Your throne was established long ago;
    you are from all eternity. (Ps 93:1–2)

The LORD reigns, let the earth be glad;
    let the distant shores rejoice. (Ps 97:1)

11:16 *The twenty-four elders, who were seated on their thrones before God.* We first encountered the twenty-four elders on their thrones around the throne of God in Revelation 4 and 5 (see note at 4:4 for the significance of the number twenty-four). Here as there, they worship God by offering their thanks and praise.

11:17 *We give thanks to you.* The twenty-four elders offer their thanks to God for destroying the nations that have expressed their anger toward God and his people, and for rescuing his people as we will learn in the verses that follow. The form of this thanksgiving follows those that may be found in the book of Psalms (e.g. Ps 18, 30).

Lord God Almighty. The Lord God is the Almighty (*pantokrator*; see also 1:8), the Greek equivalent to the Hebrew *yahweh seba'ot*, the Lord of Hosts. The Hosts refer to God's heavenly army, and the use of *Almighty* contributes to the heavy emphasis on the triune God's role as warrior who comes to save his people.

The One who is and who was. In Revelation 1:4 John conferred grace and peace to the seven churches from "him who is, and who was, and who is to come." In 1:8 God himself announced that he was the one "who is, and who was, and who is to come." In the notes to these verses, we observed that this formula was associated with God's revelation of his covenant name, Yahweh, to Moses and asserts that God was an eternal being.

Here, though, the formula has been reduced to two parts, proclaiming God's past and present existence, omitting the reference that he is also the one who was to come. The likely reason is that he has now come. The future has become the present.

And have begun to reign. As Psalm 93 proclaims concerning God, "your throne was established long ago; you are from all eternity" (v. 2). But still God allowed evil human kingdoms to dominate. While God was always in control, he allowed the nations to rage until the moment he chose to intervene. The theme of the book of Daniel, after all, is "in spite of the fact that it looks like evil human kingdoms dominate, God is really in control and he will have the final victory."[16] Thus the twenty-four elders celebrate not the first time God reigns but the first time God's kingdom displaces the evil world kingdoms.

11:18 *The nations were angry, and your wrath has come.* As the psalmist asks:

> Why do the nations conspire
>> and the peoples plot in vain.
> The kings of the earth rise up
>> and the rulers band together
>> against the LORD and against his anointed, saying,
> "Let us break their chains
>> and throw off their shackles." (Ps 2:1–3)

God laughs at their futile anger and

> He rebukes them in his anger
>> and terrifies them in his wrath, saying,
> "I have installed my king
> on Zion, my holy mountain." (Ps 2:5–6)

And God proclaims his decree to his king:

> "You are my son;
>> today I have become your father.

Ask me,
> and I will make the nations your inheritance,
> the ends of the earth your possession.
You will break them with a rod of iron;
> you will dash them to pieces like pottery." (Ps 2:7–9)

While this psalm almost certainly functioned as an installation song for a new Davidic king (notice its citation of 2 Sa 7:14), the deeper eschatological meaning of the psalm as pointing to David's descendant Jesus who would fit the role as the one who would crush God's enemies at the final day of judgment was recognized in the New Testament.

For judging . . . and for rewarding. The twenty-four elders praise God for coming to render final judgment that will result in reward for "your servants the prophets" and "your people who revere your name" as well as "for destroying those who destroy the earth." Teaching about the afterlife was subtle at best in the Old Testament[17] except for Daniel 12:1–3:

> At that time Michael, the great prince who protects your people, will arise. There will be a time of distress such as has not happened from the beginning of nations until then. But at that time your people—everyone whose name is found written in the book—will be delivered. Multitudes who sleep in the dust of the earth will awake: some to everlasting life, others to shame and everlasting contempt. Those who are wise will shine like the brightness of the heavens, and those who lead many to righteousness, like the stars for ever and ever.

Though an outlier, this passage does show that, by at least the end of the Old Testament period, at least some Jews (remember the later split on this subject between Pharisees who affirmed the afterlife and the Sadducees who denied it) now believed there was an afterlife. Theologians call this the progress of revelation as God slowly and overtime revealed more and more about a topic.

11:19 *God's temple in heaven was opened.* With the blowing of the climactic seventh trumpet, the temple in heaven opened (see note at 4:1) to reveal the ark. The earthly temple (and the tabernacle before it) was the place where God made his special presence known to his people. In this sense, it was heaven on earth. One way the heaven-earth nexus was communicated in the architecture of the tabernacle was that its innermost curtain depicted the heavenly realm, being composed of "finely twisted linen and blue, purple and scarlet yarn, with cherubim woven into them" (Ex 26:1). In terms of the temple, we might think of Isaiah's vision at the time of prophetic calling where he saw "the Lord, high and exalted, seated on a throne; and the train of his robe filled the temple. Above him were seraphim, each with six wings" (6:1–2). As they sang, "Holy, holy, holy is the LORD Almighty; the whole earth is full of his glory," Isaiah reports that "the temple was filled with smoke" (6:3–4).

The tabernacle/temple, in other words, was heaven on earth, a reflection of heavenly realities. Thus, heaven itself can be described as a temple. See "Revelation 11:1–2 Through Old Testament Eyes: The Temple" and "Revelation 21 Through Old Testament Eyes: The Heavenly Temple."

The ark of his covenant. In the earthly tabernacle/temple, the ark of the covenant occupied the most holy space. While a simple box of modest dimensions (Ex 25:10–22), it was covered in pure gold, as befits such a holy object. Its holiness is due to its being the most potent symbol of God's presence. The ark was a mobile object, capable of being carried, but when it was stationary it was in the Holy of Holies. It was called the ark of the covenant because as a container it held, among other objects, the two tablets of the law which represented God's covenant relationship with his people. As part of the furniture of the sanctuary it was considered God's footstool (1 Ch 28:2; Ps 99:5; 132:7–8) with God enthroned above it. Thus, John's depiction of heaven being opened and the ark being revealed takes us to the heart of God's presence in heaven.

Flashes of lightning, rumblings, peals of thunder, an earthquake and a severe hailstorm. The description that follows the blowing of the seventh trumpet and preceded by the praise and thanks of the twenty-four elders seems relatively subdued compared to the descriptions of the previous six. But we should not be confused. As we have already seen, storms and earthquakes accompany God's devastating judgments (see notes at 4:5; 6:12–14; 8:3–5, 7; 11:13), so we should not consider these the judgments but the accompaniments of the arrival of the divine warrior who will judge the wicked and save the righteous. The details are left to our imagination. We should take special note of similar descriptions at the opening of the seventh seal (8:5) and the pouring out of the seventh bowl (16:18).

What the Structure Means: The Unholy Trinity Wars Against the Church (Rev 12–13)

After the cycle of seven trumpets and before the cycle of the seven bowls of God's wrath, John describes a series of visions, beginning with the picture of the war between the forces of heaven and the dragon followed by a battle between the dragon, joined by two beasts, on earth against the woman who represents the church (see notes on Rev 12:1, 2, 5 and 6). There are no explicit narrative signals linking or providing a transition between the description of the seven trumpets and the present vision.[1] We have moved from a section describing God's judgment on sinful humanity (the seven trumpets) to a vision that narrates the struggle between God and his people against Satan, his associates, and those who follow them. The dragon, the beast from the sea, and the beast from the earth represent an unholy trinity that mimics the Father, Son, and Spirit.

Revelation 12 opens with a "great sign . . . in heaven," namely "a woman clothed with the sun, with the moon under her feet and a crown of twelve stars on her head" (12:1). She is pregnant and gives birth to a son who "will rule all nations with an iron scepter" (12:5), namely Jesus. Since Mary was Jesus' mother, perhaps at this point we might be thinking that the pregnant woman represents her. But later in the chapter, she will be described as being taken into the wilderness for protection (like the Old Testament people of God, 12:6, 14). Indeed, the woman might represent Israel, which gives birth to the Messiah; and the twelve stars represent the twelve tribes. But then later (12:17), the woman's offspring are described as those "who keep God's commands and hold fast their testimony about Jesus," suggesting the church. Perhaps the woman represents Israel, Mary and the church, thinking of Mary as the mother of the church by virtue of her role as mother of Jesus.[2]

Before she gives birth, we read about a second sign that appears in heaven, namely a "red dragon with seven heads and ten horns and seven crowns on its heads" (12:3). Later we will be told explicitly that this dragon is none other than "that ancient serpent called the devil, or Satan" (12:9). The dragon desires to devour the child of the woman, but God intervenes and snatches him to heaven. The woman then flees to the wilderness for safety.

Then battle breaks out in heaven between the dragon and his angels and Michael, who leads an angelic army (12:7). The former is no match for the latter and the dragon is hurled to the earth.

Celebration breaks out in heaven since this victory signals that "now have come the salvation and the power and the kingdom of God and the authority of his Messiah" (12:10; for a similar statement, see the announcement at the time of the seventh seal, 11:15).

But still the battle rages on, not in heaven but on earth where the serpent has been hurled. The dragon again attacks the woman. But God gives the woman the wings of a great eagle to fly to a place of protection in the wilderness. The dragon continues his assault by trying to overcome her with a torrent of water from his mouth, but he is thwarted when the earth opens its mouth to divert its threat. The passage ends as the dragon turns from the woman to fight against "her offspring." These represent members of the church, for we are immediately told that they are "those who keep God's commands and hold fast their testimony about Jesus" (12:17).

In Revelation 13, the dragon receives two allies, both described as beasts, one from the sea (13:1–10) and one from the earth (13:11–18). This trio form a kind of unholy trinity. The first beast is a twisted parody of Christ, bearing a relationship to the dragon echoing that of the Son to the Father. The second beast shares traits with the Spirit as well as a relationship with the first (sea) beast like that of the Son and the Spirit.

The sea beast "seemed to have a fatal wound, but the fatal wound had been healed" leading to the veneration of the beast (13:3). Accordingly, those who worshiped the dragon also worshiped the sea beast (13:4) and the sea beast waged "war against God's holy people" (13:7).

The earth beast, on the other hand, was not the object of worship, but urged people to worship the sea beast. The earth beast placed a mark on the forehead or right hand of those who worshipped the sea beast. The chapter ends by citing the number of the earth beast which is 666.

But before we move on, we should observe that this picture of the dragon's fight with the woman echoes themes from the story of the two witnesses. Indeed, we should not think of this vision as anticipating events completely different than the vision of the two witnesses in 11:1–14. As we describe the present vision we will see that through the use of different imagery the two visions both describe the tremendous struggle between the powers of evil, Satan and his spiritual and human supporters, and God and his people, the church. In Revelation 11, the two witnesses represent the church and the "beast that comes up from the Abyss" (11:7) represents the devil. The beast wins a temporary victory over the two witnesses, but God rescues and protects them. At the end, judgment comes in the form of a severe earthquake (11:13). In Revelation 12–13, the celestially ornamented woman represents the church, harried by the red dragon, representing Satan. Again, God protects his church. We then learn about a heavenly war (12:7–9) where Satan is hurled to the earth where the battle continues between the church and Satan who is joined in the fight by two beasts, one from the sea and one from the earth, representing Rome and its propagandists respectively. Again God protects the church, but the final victory is not narrated in this vision but remains to be realized.

The Woman versus the Dragon, the Land Beast, and the Sea Beast (12–13)

The Dragon Pursues the Woman (12:1–17)

12:1 *A great sign appeared in heaven.* John tells us explicitly that he is not describing a literal woman but that the woman is a sign. A sign is something that can be seen that points toward something that cannot be seen. Or in this case the sign about to be described presents in figurative terms a spiritual reality that lies behind it.

There are various types of signs in the Old Testament. We might think of the "signs" of the covenant. The reality behind these signs points toward covenants and represent them, also serving as reminders of those covenants. Examples include the rainbow—the sign of the Noahic covenant (Ge 9:13), circumcision—the sign of the Abrahamic covenant (Ge 17:11), and the Sabbath—the sign of the Mosaic covenant (Ex 31:15–17). Signs are given to encourage faith. John speaks of Jesus' miracles as signs (Jn 4:54; 6:14; 12:18), and they intend to provoke faith in Jesus (Jn 20:30–31). This introduction of a great sign is followed by a description of a woman (see 12:2). As we will see, the woman is a sign that points toward the church.

A woman clothed with the sun, with the moon under her feet and a crown of twelve stars on her head. Sun, moon, and stars—celestial symbols adorn this woman. In the first creation story, the sun, moon, and stars, created on the fourth day, populate the heavens (or sky), created on the second day. The fact that there are twelve stars may intentionally remind us of Joseph's second dream in which Joseph saw the sun (representing his father), the moon (representing his mother), and eleven stars (representing his brothers) bowing down to him.[3] Perhaps so, but we must acknowledge that the connection depends on Joseph himself being a star, never mentioned in Genesis (37:9–11). But if correct, then this celestial imagery represents the people of God since Jacob's other name was Israel and the twelve sons would represent the twelve tribes of Israel, and thus the people of God. This connection between the sun, moon, and stars worn by the woman and the people of God in the Old Testament makes sense in the light of the fact that the woman represents the people of God, both Israel and the church, as the description of her continues in the chapter. Her crown of twelve stars represents her authority.

12:2 *She was pregnant.* This woman, representing the church, was pregnant and about to give birth, crying out in pain. The idea of the pain of childbirth giving way to the joy of the birth itself is found in Scripture in relationship to suffering giving way to salvation or joy. A negative example comes from Isaiah, though, where the people of God are to have said:

> As a pregnant woman about to give birth
>   writhes and cries out in her pain,
>   so were we in your presence, LORD.
> We were with child, we writhed in labor,
>   but we gave birth to winds.
> We have not brought salvation to the earth,
>   and the people of the world have not come to life. (Isa 26:17–18)

But thanks to God this negative example of childbirth gives way to rescue and joy:

But your dead will live, LORD;
    their bodies will rise—
let those who dwell in the dust
    wake up and shout for joy—
your dew is like the dew of the morning;
    the earth will give birth to her dead. (Isa 26:19)

In the verses to follow we will see that the woman's travails will indeed give birth to salvation.

12:3 *Then another sign appeared in heaven.* See 12:1.

An enormous red dragon with seven heads and ten horns and seven crowns on its heads. Multiheaded dragons represent forces of evil and chaos against whom God fights. The imagery goes back to the picture of Lothan, the seven-headed sea monster against whom the god Baal fought, according to Canaanite mythology. The Old Testament also uses the figure of Lothan (Heb., *Leviathan*) as symbolic of chaos that God controls (Job 41), defeats, and kills. In Psalm 74, Leviathan's many heads are mentioned though not specified as seven. Leviathan, representing chaos, is defeated by God:

It was you who split open the sea by your power;
    you broke the heads of the monster in the waters.
It was you who crushed the heads of Leviathan
    and gave it as food to the creatures of the desert.
It was you who opened up springs and streams;
    you dried up the ever-flowing rivers. (Ps 74:13–15)

The defeat of Leviathan (chaos) is the prelude to an account of creation in verses 16–17.

Isaiah 27, though not mentioning the many heads of Leviathan, may provide an even more relevant background to Revelation since it describes Yahweh's defeat future defeat of Leviathan. Here, in a verse widely thought to be virtually a direct quote of an Ugaritic text,[4] God's future defeat of evil is described symbolically as the divine killing of Leviathan:

In that day,
the LORD will punish with his sword—
    his fierce, great and powerful sword—
Leviathan the gliding serpent,
    Leviathan the coiling serpent;
he will slay the monster of the sea. (Isa 27:1)

The dragon is red, the color of blood and violence, underlining the danger of this beast. The creature has seven heads (like Lothan/Leviathan), and ten horns (like the final beast in the vision in Da 7:7) and seven crowns. The numbers ten and seven are frequently used symbolically for totality or completion. Horns are symbolic of power (see note at 5:6 on "seven horns") and having seven signifies that this creature is dangerously powerful. Like the woman, the dragon has a crown perhaps signifying its authority in its realm over against the realm of the woman. Later we hear of another beast and this one too will have seven heads and ten horns, but ten rather than seven crowns (13:1).

12:4 *Its tail.* Dragons are walking serpents (Ge 3; see comments at 12:9 on "that ancient serpent") and so his tail is serpentine, and with it this dragon swept away one third of the stars in heaven. The dragon, representing the devil, causes cosmic damage (symbolizing spiritual attacks). One third of the stars would be substantial but nowhere near complete damage.

Might devour her child. The dragon wants to devour or swallow up the child of the pregnant woman when she gives birth. The metaphor of death as devouring or swallowing goes back to ancient Canaanite ideas. The god Mot (Death), who is the rival of Baal is described as a god who had his upper lip in the heavens and lower lip on the earth, eventually swallowing everything in its wake (Mot even swallows the god Baal in the Ugaritic Baal myth). The motif of death as swallowing that we see in Canaanite literature is powerfully reversed in Isaiah:

> On this mountain the Lord Almighty will prepare
> 　　a feast of rich food for all peoples,
> a banquet of aged wine—
> 　　the best of meats and the finest of wines.
> On this mountain he will destroy
> 　　the shroud that enfolds all peoples,
> the sheet that covers all nations;
> 　　he will swallow up death forever. (Isa 25:6–7)

12:5 *A male child, who will "rule all the nations with an iron scepter."* John identifies the child as the one anticipated by an eschatological reading of Psalm 2, specifically verse 9 (see note at 11:18 and "Revelation through Old Testament Eyes: Psalms" below). Jesus is the child! He is the one who will bring judgment against the raging nations. No wonder the dragon wants to destroy the child.

We have earlier associated the woman with the church. We still think that is the best primary association. But there is some credence to the possibility that the woman stands for, or perhaps also stands for, Mary the mother of Jesus. After all, the church did not give birth to Jesus, but rather he gave birth to the church.

Her child was snatched up to God and to his throne. We likely here have the use of the so-called divine passive. In other words, though not explicitly mentioned it is God who took the child up to his presence. The verb "snatch" confers a note of urgency. Jesus was quickly taken to heaven to avoid being devoured by the dragon. Of course, Jesus did die on the cross and descended into hell, but after three days he rose and after forty more he ascended into heaven.

Revelation Through Old Testament Eyes: Psalms

The book of Psalms is widely quoted and alluded to throughout the New Testament. Revelation is no exception. In fact, the opening of Revelation immediately sounds a note suggesting that we should view the book in light of the whole psaltery. While most scholars recognize that Psalm 1 (along with Psalm 2) serves as an intentional introduction to the book as a whole, psalm expert Chee Wun Peter Ho has called my attention to an interesting connection. In a personal communication, he notes that Psalm 1 "begins with a beatitude for those who read, hear, and keep the prophetic word."[5] He then notes that John's opening blessing is also on "the one who reads aloud the words of this prophecy, and blessed are those who hear it and take to heart what is written in it" (Rev 1:3).

Following this, John uses Psalms in two main ways. First, he cites kingship psalms and applies them to Christ. Jesus, after all, is the Messiah, David's greater son, the fulfillment of the divine promise to David that "your house and your kingdom will endure forever before me; your throne will be established forever" (2 Sa 7:16). The second use of Psalms in Revelation connects to the pervasive worship that occurs through the book. Psalms are not the only hymns that are cited in celebration of the triune God in Revelation, but they strike a major chord. Let's look at each of these two major uses in turn.

Jesus, the Messiah

The New Testament authors recognized that Jesus was the fulfillment of the long-expected David-like king, or messiah, who would come to lead his people while vanquishing their enemies. After the demise of the monarchy in 586 BC, when the last Davidic descendant ruled from Jerusalem, the expectation that David's house would last forever took on an eschatological significance. A descendant of David would come and be their messiah in the future. Thus, royal hymns took on a future orientation.[6]

We see an example of this in Revelation right from the start in 1:5. John introduces Jesus in his opening benediction when he refers to Jesus as "the faithful witness" and the "ruler of the kings of the earth," both epithets referring to David in Psalm 89 (vv. 37 and 27 respectively).

Another royal psalm applied to Jesus in the book of Revelation is Psalm 2. Many scholars believe that this psalm was moved to its position in the book of Psalms to serve, along with Psalm 1, as an intentional introduction to the book. This likely happened during the post-monarchical period when psalms like this one were read with a future orientation. Psalm 2 can be divided into four stanzas:

Stanza 1 (vv. 1–3): The psalmist begins by questioning the reasons why the kings of the earth would rise up against "the LORD and his anointed" (v. 2).

Stanza 2 (vv. 4–6): The psalmist turns attention from the earth to heaven, who reacts in anger and dismisses the threat of these rebellious kings by proclaiming, "I have installed my king on Zion, my holy mountain" (v. 6).

Stanza 3 (vv. 7–9): In the third stanza, the focus turns back to earth, but now the anointed king speaks. He quotes 2 Samuel 7:14, "You are my son; today I have become your father." In Samuel, these words are directed to David, but apply also to his descendants, which explains why this psalm is sometimes thought to be a Davidic psalm, though there is no title designating authorship. God also informs the anointed king that he will be his agent in quelling the threat of the kings of the earth.

Stanza 4 (vv. 10–12): The psalmist concludes by exhorting the kings to "be wise" (v. 10) and to "serve the LORD with fear and celebrate his rule with trembling" (v. 11). Further, they should submit to his royal son, the anointed king (v. 12).

This psalm almost certainly functioned as some type of coronation psalm during the monarchical period, but later readers including the New Testament authors understood, the ultimate realization of this expectation was Jesus (before Revelation, for example, Ac 4:25–28; 13:33; Heb 1:5; 5:5).

John, in Revelation, understands that Jesus is the ultimate anointed king or Messiah who will win the final battle against the "kings of the earth" who seek to threaten God and his people. For this reason, he quotes

Psalm 2:9 (Christ "will break them with a rod of iron; you will dash them to pieces like pottery") three times in the book (Rev 2:27; 12:5; 19:15). Psalm 2 (vv. 1, 5) is also behind the proclamation given by the twenty-four elders that "the nations were angry and your wrath has come" (Rev 11:18). Psalm 2 also provides a background to the description of the final battle that Revelation locates at a place called Armageddon, where the kings of the earth gather to fight against the triune God.

Other psalms are also applied to Jesus in this way. He is said to be "just" in his judgments in Revelation 16:5, alluding to Psalm 9:7–8; 89:14; 97:2. As Jesus with a sword coming out of his mouth rides a white horse into the final climactic battle, we hear "with justice he judges and wages war" (Rev 19:11; Ps 98:7–9, also 96:11–13).

Praising the Triune God

While most casual readers of Revelation think of it as a dark book of judgment, a close reading finds it full of heavenly and earthly worship. Worship punctuates the book, particularly when the focus is on heaven and God's throne in heaven (as in Rev 5). The book of Psalms informs the shape of the worship in the book of Revelation.

Praise directed to God and to the glorified Christ on occasion even cites or alludes to specific psalms. For instance, we might cite the acclamation of Jesus as worthy to open the seals of the scroll ("you are worthy," Rev 5:9) as echoing the psalmist's affirmation that God is worthy (Ps 18:3; 48:1; 96:4; 145:3) or the assertion that God will "reign for ever and ever" (Rev 11:15, 17; 19:6; 22:5) and the similar praise directed to God in the Psalter (Ps 47:8–9; 93:1–2; 97:1). We also find that the worship hymns of the book of Revelation share similar calls to corporate praise. In Revelation 19:1 and elsewhere, for instance, worshippers call out "Hallelujah!" ("praise the LORD"; Ps 146:1, 10; 147:1, 20; 148:1, 7, 14; 149:1, 9; 150:1); and in Revelation 19:7, we hear the call "let us rejoice and be glad" (see Ps 40:16; 70:4).

But beyond specific citations, the worship songs in Revelation utilize the same hymnic poetry of the book of Psalms, which is not ultimately surprising because the latter is rightly thought of as the hymnbook of the Old Testament people of God.

Also reminiscent of the book of Psalms is the worship of God accompanied by a harp (Rev 5:8; 14:2, see Ps 33:2; 43:4; 57:8). We might also mention the picture of angels holding bowls of incense, said to represent the prayers of God's people (Rev 5:8; 8:3–5, see Ps 141:2). Or the description of a song of praise as a "new song" (Rev 5:9, see Ps 33:3; 40:3; 96:1; 98:1; 144:9; 149:1). A new song is a hymn of victory sung after God has made all things new by his defeat of the forces of evil.[7]

12:6 *The woman fled into the wilderness.* While entertaining the possibility that the woman refers to Mary the mother of Jesus in the previous verse, with this description, we are back to what appears to be a reference to the church. The book of Hebrews (3:7–19) describes the church as presently in the wilderness. The Old Testament background, of course, is Israel wandering in the wilderness (Exodus 16 through Deuteronomy). Having left slavery in Egypt, the Israelites travel to the promised land. The wilderness is a time of testing and refinement. So too the author of Hebrews exhorts his readers that, while they have been saved from the bondage of sin, they have not yet entered the promised land (heaven).

After the child (Jesus) was snatched up to God (the ascension), the woman (the church) went to a hiding place in the wilderness provided by God himself. God protects the church from utter destruction by evil spiritual forces (the dragon). Even in the Old Testament, the wilderness was sometimes pictured as a place of protection:

> My heart is in anguish within me;
>   the terrors of death have fallen on me.
> Fear and trembling have beset me;
>   horror has overwhelmed me.
> I said, "Oh, that I had the wings of a dove!
>   I would fly away and be at rest
> I would flee far away
>   and stay in the desert;
> I would hurry to my place of shelter,
>   far from the tempest and storm." (Ps 55:4–8)

For 1,260 days. This period of protection is equivalent to three and a half years. As explained earlier (see "Revelation 11:2–3 Through Old Testament Eyes: The 42 Months"), these time references have Daniel (7:25; 8:14; 12:7, 12) as an Old Testament background. The three-and-a-half-year reference is symbolic of the time that evil is in control and seems to gain in momentum, then slows down, and ceases. It is during this time that God protects the woman (the church).

12:7 *Michael and his angels fought against the dragon.* There is a battle going on in heaven between powerful spiritual forces. We get glimpses of this heavenly battle in the Old Testament as well. The most dramatic is found in Daniel 10.

Daniel had a disturbing vision that he did not understand. He struggled with it for three weeks before an angel came to interpret it for him. The angel is unnamed here, but most likely is Gabriel, whose role seems to be the delivery of heavenly messages (Da 8:16; 9:21; Lk 1:19, 26).

He then explains to Daniel why it took three whole weeks to come to him. "Since the first day that you set your mind to gain understanding and to humble yourself before your God, your words were heard, and I have come in response to them. But the prince of the Persian kingdom resisted me twenty-one days. Then Michael, one of the chief princes, came to help me, because I was detained there with the king of Persia" (Da 10:12–13).

Then later he tells Daniel, "Do you know why I have come to you? Soon I will return to fight against the prince of Persia, and when I go, the prince of Greece will come; but first I will tell you what is written in the Book of Truth. (No one supports me against them except Michael, your prince. And in the first year of Darius, I took my stand to support and protect him)" (Da 10:20–11:1).

Gabriel thus informs Daniel of a heavenly battle that mirrors earthly conflict. As background, we should note that God had assigned various angelic beings to specific nation states according to Deuteronomy 32:8–9: "When the Most High apportioned the nations, when he divided humankind, he fixed the boundaries of the peoples according to the number of the gods, the LORD's own portion was his people, Jacob his allotted share" (NRSV).[8]

Thus, the fight between Michael (referred to above as "your [Daniel's/Israel's] prince") and the prince of Persia and the prince of Greece are references to spiritual entities that are in conflict with one another.

Milton, in *Paradise Lost,* famously takes these passages from Daniel and Revelation as inspiration for a war in which Michael leads the forces of God against Satan and his followers who are finally cast out of heaven. For Milton, the war takes place before Satan tempts Adam and Eve. In Revelation, Satan's war against the church is currently taking place and will continue for a period.

12:8 *But he was not strong enough.* He (the dragon) and his angelic allies had tried to assault heaven, but they could not stand against the powers of heaven. While this victory is not the end of the story, it is the beginning of the end. As we will see, the battle will continue on earth in the next episode.

Going Deeper into the Devil: Revelation 12

John's visions help pull back the curtains to remind us, first, that Christians are engaged in a spiritual battle and, second, that the triune God will certainly defeat the spiritual powers of evil. At the head of the spiritual powers is the devil, also called Satan, and in Revelation 12:9 he is identified with the "ancient serpent" of Genesis 3. Interestingly, it is doubtful that the original author or readers of Genesis 3 would have known that the serpent was the devil, but they would be aware that walking serpents were representative of personified evil. Indeed, the teaching on the devil and demons is rare in the Old Testament. Those places where Satan is mentioned in the Old Testament (1 Ch 21:1; Job 1:6–9; 2:1–7; Zec 3:1–2) are extremely unlikely references to the devil of the New Testament, but rather to an angel in God's service who has taken on the role of an "accuser" or "adversary" or possibly "executioner,"[9] which is the meaning of the Hebrew name Satan.[10] We see an angel playing such a role in the speech of the prophet Micaiah to King Ahab (1 Ki 22:22–24).[11]

That said, the devil did not spring into existence in the New Testament. The New Testament makes it clear, as here in Revelation (12:9), that indeed the serpent that represented evil in Genesis 3 was indeed the devil. The progress of revelation allows New Testament readers to understand the nature of the spiritual powers and authorities more clearly than our Old Testament forebears.

As to the origin of the devil and his spiritual minions, we know nothing, or at least the Bible does not speak directly about it. The idea that some of God's angels rebelled against him even before the fall is an inference from the biblical teaching that God created everything good, so that, like human beings, it likely was that sentient spiritual creatures, angels, did turn against God and become evil. Probably so, but what is clear is that since Genesis 3 evil spiritual powers have sought to entice humans toward rebellion against God. That there is a spiritual battle is clear from the punishment levied on the serpent in Genesis 3:15: "And I will put enmity between you and the woman, and between your offspring and hers"; as is God's ultimate victory, "he will crush your head, and you will strike his heel." In the Old Testament, we get glimpses of a struggle between God's angels and evil spiritual powers in a place like Daniel 10:12–14, 20–21 as well as God's ultimate victory as in Isaiah when evil spiritual powers are represented by the serpentine Leviathan (Isa 27:1). In the New Testament, we learn that God's victory over the devil becomes assured by the crucifixion, resurrection, and ascension (Eph 4:8; Col 2:13–15; Heb 2:14).

While we get glimpses of a spiritual battle in the Old Testament, we learn more about it in the New Testament, where God's people are invited into the fray: "Put on the full armor of God, so that you can take your stand against the devil's schemes" (Eph 6:11, see 10–20).

The book of Revelation provides graphic statements and images that the devil is a real threat to the church and that there is an ongoing spiritual struggle. Christ warns the church at Smyrna that "the devil will put some of you in prison" (Rev 2:10) after telling them there was a "synagogue of Satan" in their midst (2:9). He commends the church in Pergamum for remaining faithful even though their city was a place "where Satan has his throne" (2:13). He expresses his concern that some in Thyatira have learned "Satan's so-called deep secrets" (2:24).

In Revelation 12 we hear about the devil's past and present attempts to subvert and destroy the church. A dragon, again a serpentine form, represents the devil which seeks to devour the child (Christ) to be born to the woman (the church); see note at 12:5 on "a male child." This leads to a war in heaven when the dragon is hurled to the earth by Michael and his angels. But there the conflict continues, though God preserves the woman throughout. Still the battle is fierce as we hear at the end of the chapter: "the dragon was enraged at the woman and went off to wage war against the rest of her offspring—those who keep God's commands and hold fast their testimony about Jesus" (12:17).

Interestingly in the next chapter, the reader encounters two beasts, one from the earth and one from the sea, who become the agents of the dragon in this battle, creating what most scholars see as a kind of unholy trinity. Wright helpfully explains that the presentation of these agents informs us that the devil works through other "dark forces."[12] He also rightly indicates that the sea beast represents the "dark power of pagan empire" and that the earth beast represents "the local power brokers" who facilitate the worship of that empire.[13]

Revelation not only reminds us about the ongoing battle, but it also assures us of the ultimate victory. We see this at the end of the vision in Revelation 19 when not only God's human enemies but also the sea beast and the beast from the earth are thrown into the lake of fire

(19:17–21). Then too the devil himself is judged and thrown into that fiery lake (20:7–10).

From the book of Revelation, then, Christians today should realize that they fight against spiritual powers and authorities, including the devil. We also learn that we should fight with the confidence that comes knowing that our God will win the final victory.

12:9 *The great dragon was hurled down.* In defeat at the hands of Michael and his angelic army, the great dragon was hurled down, thrown with tremendous force. Though he was thrown down from the heights of heaven to the earth where he will continue to inflict harm, the act of hurling shows that he was defeated by an overwhelming force. We might remember the way Moses described the defeat of the Egyptian army at the Re(e)d Sea similarly as a hurling down:

> I will sing to the LORD,
> > for he is highly exalted.
> Both horse and driver
> > he has hurled into the sea. . . .
>
> Pharaoh's chariots and his army
> > he has hurled into the sea. (Ex 15:1, 4; see also 21)

In the prophets too, we learn that God will hurl down those who rebel against him (Isa 22:17; Jer 10:18; 22:26)

That ancient serpent called the devil, or Satan, who leads the whole world astray. The dragon symbolically represents the devil. The first of the three identifications, though, is "ancient serpent," a reference back to Genesis 3:1, where we read "now the serpent was more crafty than any of the wild animals the LORD God had made." At the beginning of Genesis 3, which is the story of humanity's first sin, the serpent was walking, an implication that God's later punishment includes the announcement that "you will crawl on your belly and you will eat dust all the days of your life" (3:14). Reading this text in its ancient Near Eastern context, we understand that the original readers of the story would have taken the serpent as a figurative representation of evil.[14] Another Old Testament serpentine representation of evil is the figure of Leviathan particularly in Isaiah 27 (as discussed in 12:3). A dragon itself is a large walking serpentine creature that serves as a symbol of chaos and evil not only here, in the Old Testament, and the ancient Near East, but in many cultures around the world at many different times.[15]

Thus, the original author and reader of Genesis would have understood the serpent to represent personal evil, but not specifically the devil or Satan (see note at 2:9 where the Old Testament references to Satan in 1 Chronicles 21, Job 1–2, and Zechariah are not equivalent to the devil but rather are references to an angel in God's heavenly court).

That said, the reference here and in Romans 16:20 allows the New Testament reader of the Old Testament to have a more precise understanding of the Genesis reference to know that that personal agent of evil is indeed the one whom the New Testament identifies as the devil.

12:10 *I heard a loud voice in heaven.* A loud voice is commanding, demands attention, and expresses authority. The speaker is ambiguous. A single loud voice from heaven might be Jesus (1:10), God, or an angel (5:2; 11:12). Most likely, this is an angelic speaker because the voice praises God and his Messiah in the third person. Old Testament victory hymns also celebrated God's salvation from evil enemies that sought to harm the people of God (Ex 15:2; 2 Sa 22:3; Ps 18:2; Ps 98:1–3, etc.).

The kingdom of our God, and the authority of his Messiah. Earlier, after the seventh angel blew his trumpet, loud voices in heaven celebrated the victory of the kings of the Lord over the kingdom of the world (see note at 11:15 on "loud voices in heaven"). The arrival of the kingdom of God and the beginning of his Messiah's, the Christ's, authority now begins with Satan being hurled to the earth.

For the accuser of our brothers and sisters. As discussed in the note in 12:9, the name Satan comes from the Hebrew root that can mean "to accuse." The devil is the epitome of accusation. He constantly accuses people before the presence of God. The picture does remind the reader of the opening scene of Job and may have suggested this description to John, though it is very unlikely that the author or original readers of Job would have equated "the accuser" with the devil.[16]

12:11 *They triumphed over him.* God and his Messiah have defeated Satan by hurling him down from heaven to earth.

By the blood of the Lamb. This triumph was accomplished by the crucifixion of Jesus, the blood of the Lamb (see "Revelation 5:6 Through Old Testament Eyes: The Lamb Who Was Slain").

By the word of their testimony. Jesus died and his people bore witness to the significance of that death. As they spread the word, the dragon was defeated. But they did more than talk. Many bore witness by following their Lord's example of dying rather than holding on to their lives. They were unwilling to give up their life-changing testimony even when faced with death.

12:12 *Therefore rejoice, you heavens and you who dwell in them!* At the crucifixion and resurrection of Christ, Satan was hurled from heaven. Thus the loud heavenly voice calls on all the inhabitants of heaven to rejoice.

But woe to the earth and the sea. While Satan has been defeated in heaven, he is now on the earth. The work of Christ in his crucifixion, resurrection, and ascension accomplished redemption, but that redemption has not yet fully been realized and won't be until the second coming of Christ. The devil remains active and dangerous on earth. Thus a woe is pronounced on the earth, land, and sea, that warns of the threat that remains and the harm that is still to come. For woe and its connection to funeral rites, see note at 8:13.

He knows that his time is short. Christ's work on the cross may not have led to immediate and total victory over evil, but it assures that outcome. Jesus defeated sin and death on the cross, but that victory will not be secured until his return. Oscar Cullmann helpfully made an analogy between D-Day, the battle that broke the back of the Nazi power during World War II, and V-Day, when Berlin fell to the Allied Forces.[17] After D-Day there was no doubt about the fall of the Nazis, though there was plenty of fighting and dying yet to happen. Satan is defeated, but the final battle is yet to come. According to John, Satan is aware of this and knows that it is just a matter of time, and that time will be short. However, rather than giving up, this knowledge only increases his fury.

12:13 *He pursued the woman who had given birth to the male child.* After the divine victory in heaven accomplished by the work of Christ, Satan, represented as a dragon, continues his attacks on the woman (the church) who had given birth to the male child (Jesus). See note at 12:5 on "a male child."

12:14 *The woman was given the two wings of a great eagle.* The use of the so-called divine passive as well as the context suggests that it is God who gives the persecuted woman (representing the church) the wings of an eagle to escape the dragon. In this context, it is the speed of this most noble of birds that is emphasized (see notes at 4:6–8 on "four living creatures" and at 8:13 on "eagle"). In terms of Old Testament background, we hear echoes of God's words to Israel after the exodus from Egypt and at the beginning of the wilderness wandering. The Israelites are at the foot of Mount Sinai when we read:

> This is what you are to say to the descendants of Jacob and what you are to tell the people of Israel: "You yourselves have seen what I did to Egypt, and how I carried you on eagles' wings and brought you to myself. Now if you obey me fully and keep my covenant, then out of all nations you will be my treasured possession. Although the whole earth is mine, you will be for me a kingdom of priests and a holy nation." (Ex 19:3–6)

To the place prepared for her in the wilderness. See note at 12:6.

For a time, times and half a time. See "Revelation 11:2–3 Through Old Testament Eyes: The 42 Months" and note at 12:6 on "1,260 days." The purpose of these time references is not to provide information that can be placed on an actual calendar, but to signal that even though evil's control seems to ramp up, it will slow down, and has an abrupt and definite end.

12:15 *The serpent spewed water like a river.* The serpent, the dragon, who represents the devil tries to overwhelm the woman by spewing water. The volume and force of the water is communicated by the comparison with a river. Here too we again see mythological allusion at work. In the Old Testament, the sea, a symbol of chaos and evil which is ultimately controlled and ruled over by God (Ge 1:2; Job 7:12; 26:12; 38:8–11; Ps 74:12–14; 89:9–10; Isa 27:1; Jer 5:22; Da 7:2–3), is often seen in parallel with the image of a river (Ps 72:8; 89:23–25; Zec 9:10).

The broader ancient Near Eastern background may be seen in Ugaritic literature which reflects the thought of those who worship Baal. In one story, the Baal Myth, Baal fights and conquers the god Yammu (Sea). Many scholars believe that this story was a prelude to a creation account which has been lost.[18] Yammu (Sea) represents the forces of chaos and evil that needs to be quelled for creation to happen. For our purposes it is significant that Yammu has another name, Naharu (river), as in the following text where the craftsman-god Kotharu instructs Baal:

> Strike Prince Yammu on the head,
>   Ruler Naharu on the forehead.[19]

The parallel "sea" and "rivers" may also be seen in the Old Testament in contexts where they too represent powerful forces of chaos and evil that need to be controlled. God can control the chaos as can his appointed agents like the Davidic king as in the divine oracle cited in Psalm 89. God says of David:

> I will crush his foes before him
>   and strike down his adversaries. . . .
> I will set his hand over the sea,
>   his right hand over the rivers. (Ps 89:23, 25)

12:16 *Swallowing the river.* The serpent's plan to sweep away the woman with a torrent is thwarted when the earth opens up its mouth to swallow the river.

12:17 *To wage war against the rest of her offspring.* Foiled at its attempt to sweep away the woman (the church), the serpent (Satan) goes after the woman's offspring. The offspring are described as "those who keep God's commands and hold fast their testimony about Jesus." They are faithful Christians who through faith and obedience have a deep relationship with Jesus. The war that is waged has its background in the physical battles of God's people against their enemies, particularly during the conquest. But with the coming of Jesus, the battle transforms into a spiritual battle as Paul tells us: "Finally, be strong in the Lord and in his mighty power. Put on the full armor of God, so that you can take your stand against the devil's schemes. For our struggle is not against flesh and blood, but against the rulers, against the authorities, against the powers of this dark world and against the spiritual forces of evil in the heavenly realms" (Eph 6:10–12).

This battle is not won with conventional weapons Paul goes on to say, but rather with truth, righteousness, the gospel of peace, faith, salvation, and "the Spirit, which is the word of God" (Eph 6:17).

REVELATION 13

The Sea Beast (13:1–10)

13:1 *The dragon stood on the shore of the sea.* At the end of the previous chapter, the dragon was unable to overwhelm the woman, who represents the church, but he continues to attack the woman's offspring, individual Christians. Now the dragon stands on the shore of the sea. We might remember Daniel's first vision, already referenced several times as background to John's own visions, where he describes his vantage point as on the shore of the sea: "In my vision at night I looked and there before me were the four winds of heaven churning up the great sea. Four great beasts, each different from the others, came up out of the sea" (Da 7:2–3). We have already shown (see especially note at Rev 4:6–8; also at 1:7; 11:7; 12:15) that the sea and its monsters symbolize chaos and evil.

And I saw a beast coming out of the sea. Even without further description we know that this beast represents evil because of its origins from the sea (see previous note).

It had ten horns and seven heads, with ten crowns on its horns. The dragon (see note at 12:3) had seven heads, ten horns, and seven crowns. Likewise here seven and ten are both numbers that denote completion and totality, and horns indicate power (see note at 5:6). Crowns obviously point to royal authority and power. This beast has the same number of heads and horns as the dragon, but even more crowns. Like the dragon, the Old Testament background to this beast is the fourth and final beast in Daniel's vision, which also had ten horns (Da 7:7, 19, 23).

On each head a blasphemous name. We don't know the specific names; all that is important is that those seven heads each bore a name that was blasphemous, that is an expression of contempt toward God. To blaspheme God's name carried the death penalty in the Old Testament. In Leviticus 24 we have the story of a man who blasphemed God's name with a curse. When they made an inquiry as to the penalty required, God announced "anyone who curses their God will be held responsible; anyone who blasphemes the name of the LORD must be put to death" (Lev 24:15–16). While Old Testament penalties were no longer observed after the coming of Christ,[1] this law shows what a serious offense blasphemy involved.

As Williamson points out, the beast refers to the antichrist (see 1 Jn 2:18, 22, which should also be associated with Paul's "the lawless one," 2 Th 2:8–9), but at the time the Roman emperor would have been considered an embodiment of evil. He goes on to say then that the blasphemous names might refer to the titles that the emperor took on himself or were conferred on him by the Roman senate, names like "'Lord,' 'Savior,' and 'Son of God.'"[2]

13:2 *Resembled a leopard, but had feet like those of a bear and a mouth like that of a lion.* The beast is a hybrid, a mixture of animals, not just one type. Typically, animals of mixed essence (what the Germans call *Mischwesen*) are considered unclean by virtue of being hybrids. Mixtures in general were considered repulsive in the Old Testament (see Lev 19:19). David Bryan puts it this way as he discusses the hybrid nature of the beasts in Daniel 7: "Unclean animals such as the lion, the bear and the leopard embody the powers of chaos in the world. The *Mischwesen* are best seen as an intensified unclean creature, that is an increase of the presence of chaos in the world."[3] The beast that has just emerged from the sea has features associated with the third (leopard, Da 7:6), the second (bear, Da 7:5), and the first (lion, Da 7:4) of the four beasts in Daniel's vision. We have already seen that the horns connect this beast with the fourth and final beast. Thus, the beast may be seen as an embodiment of all the evil human kingdoms represented in the four beasts of Daniel 7.

The dragon gave the beast his power and his throne and great authority. Williamson says, "alert readers will be stuck by an odd parallel between the dragon's delegation of authority to the beast and God's delegation to Christ (Jn 3:35; 5:21–23; Php 2:9–11)."[4]

13:3 *One of the heads of the beast seemed to have had a fatal wound.* The analogy between the beast and Christ continues, but it is an apparent similarity. Christ died, spent three days in the grave, and was resurrected. The beast also received a fatal wound, but then he was healed from it in a way that resulted in the whole world being amazed and then becoming the beast's followers.

13:4 *People worshiped the dragon . . . and they also worshipped the beast.* People treated the dragon (Satan) and the beast, its agent, as if they were God, offering their submission and proclaiming their power. By so doing, they act like unfaithful, idolatrous people of God in the Old Testament. In the wilderness they bowed the knee to the golden calf rather than to Yahweh (Ex 32). They worshiped other idols as well. As found in the note to 9:20, Psalm 106 tells us that the false gods represented by idols are in actuality demonic powers. This worship of the dragon and the beast, false gods, stands in contrast to the worship offered to God on his throne in Revelation 4–5.

Who is like the beast? Who can wage war against it? In their adoration of the beast, the people ask two rhetorical questions to assert their affirmation of the beast's uniqueness and their belief that the beast is not able to be defeated.

But God is the only one who is unique and unparalleled as Moses sang after the crossing of the Sea:

> Who among the gods
> is like you, Lord?
> Who is like you—
> majestic in holiness,
> awesome in glory,
> working wonders?
> (Ex 15:11; see also Dt 33:26; 1 Ki 8:23; 2 Ch 6:14; Ps 113:5; Jer 10:6)

As God showed his overwhelming power against Pharaoh, so God will defeat the beast and all the powers of evil.

13:5 *Was given a mouth to utter proud words and blasphemies.* The first half of Daniel's initial vision in Daniel 7 imagines evil in the form of four successive beasts that arise out of the sea. The fourth beast had ten horns, like the beast here, but then a little horn emerges and uproots three of the first horns. This little horn seems to be the culmination and apex of evil that challenges God and his people at the end of time. This little horn had eyes like "a human being and a mouth that spoke boastfully" (Da 7:8, see also v. 20), thus providing a connection with the beast. Later the interpreting angel will inform Daniel that this little horn represented a king who will "speak against the Most High and oppress his holy people and try to change the set times and the laws" (7:25). In Daniel's fourth and final vision, a succession of kings of the north and kings of the south culminates in a particularly aggressive final king who, while perhaps pointing initially to the Seleucid king Antiochus Epiphanies IV who persecuted the Jews so viciously in the mid-second century BC, looks forward to the end of time and evil forces that will emerge to threaten the people of God and challenge the authority of God. In other words, the forces that the beast represents. Thus, we should not be surprised that the interpreting angel tells Daniel that this final king, like the little horn in Daniel 7 is proud and blasphemous: "The king will do as he pleases. He will exalt and magnify himself above every god and will say unheard-of things against the God of gods" (11:36). That this vision in Revelation uses imagery and descriptions that echo these visions in Daniel indicate that the evil anticipated in the distant future in Daniel is close at hand.

We should take note of the passive here "was given," which does not explicitly identify the one who gives the beast a mouth. While we have seen examples of the divine passive, it is doubtful that it would be God who gave the beast this power. Thus in the context, we conclude that it is Satan (the dragon) who is the unnamed giver (see also Rev 13:7, 15).

And to exercise its authority for forty-two months. In Daniel 7, the little horn that speaks proud words and blasphemies will dominant the people of God for "a time, times and half a time" (Da 7:25). This formula indicates that, while it looks like evil will gain momentum, it will be cut short and then brought to an abrupt end. For how this formula is understood by the book of Revelation as a period of three and a half years, which equals forty-two months, see "Revelation 11:2–3 Through Old Testament Eyes: The 42 Months."

13:6 *To slander his name and his dwelling place and those who live in heaven.* In the ten commandments, God says, "You shall not misuse the name of the LORD your God, for the LORD will not hold anyone guiltless who misuses his name" (Ex 20:7). God's name is holy because God's name reflects his reputation and who he is. Wherever God makes his presence known is also holy, and for that reason the sanctuary was considered sacrosanct during the Old Testament period. After all, the sanctuary was the place he chose as a "dwelling for his Name" (Dt 12:11). But when Revelation was written, the temple was no more and no longer needed. Jesus "made his dwelling among us" (Jn 1:14). When he ascended into heaven, he sent the Spirit to be with us and dwell in us. Here, God's dwelling place is heaven itself. The beast slandered God's name, his heavenly dwelling place and those angels and saints who dwelt with him in heaven.

13:7 *It was given power to wage war against God's holy people.* Evil spiritual powers have been in conflict with God's people since the introduction of sin into the human experience. In his judgment speech to the serpent (see note at 12:9 for the association with Satan), God announced "And I will put enmity between you and the woman, and between your offspring and hers; he will crush your head, and you will strike his heel" (Ge 3:15). For the use of what I am calling the satanic passive, see notes at 13:5 on "was given a mouth" and at 13:15 on "was given power."

Authority over every tribe, people, language and nation. No group escaped the attempted control of the beast. But that not everyone came under the sway of the beast may be seen in the appearance of this phrase in 7:9 (see note) as well as the next verse.

13:8 *All whose names have not been written in the Lamb's book of life.* In Psalm 69, the composer ends his imprecation on his enemies by saying "may they be blotted out of the book of life and not be listed with the righteous" (vs. 28). In the psalm, the book of life is a list of everyone who is alive. In Revelation (see also note at 3:5), the book of life is the list of those who will enjoy eternal life with God. In this way, John makes it clear that though the beast's authority and control is widespread, it is not universal. God's people will remain true to him.

The Lamb who was slain from the creation of the world. The translation of this sentence has been questioned. The NIV rendering, given here, raises interesting theological questions since, of course, Jesus' crucifixion took place at a specific historical time long after creation. In addition, the question might arise why Christ's death took place, or was even contemplated, before sin entered the human experience. Theologians might raise questions about God's relationship to time as it relates to human experience of time, but there might be a better solution provided by an equally possible translation that would follow the lines of the NRSV: "everyone whose name has not been written from the foundation of the world in the book of life of the Lamb that was slaughtered." While this expression is not without its own questions, the thought is in conformity with Paul's statement that God "chose us in him before the creation of the world to be holy and blameless in his sight" (Eph 1:4). See also "Revelation 5:6 Through Old Testament Eyes: The Lamb Who Was Slain."

13:9 *Whoever has ears, let them hear.* The call is not simply to hear sounds, but to hear them and to understand and respond in obedience to the words that follow. See note at 2:7.

13:10 *If anyone is to go into captivity.* The first part of this verse is a quote, or at least an allusion, to Jeremiah 15:2. Jeremiah 14:17–22 provides the context where Jeremiah seeks to intercede on behalf of the sinful inhabitants of Judah that God not bring his fearsome judgment against them. God responds to the prophet very bluntly: "Even if Moses and Samuel were to stand before me, my heart would not go out to this people. Send them away from my presence! Let them go!" (Jer 15:1). Moses and Samuel were two prophets who successfully interceded on behalf of the people (Ex 32:11–14, 30–34; Nu 14:13–19 and 1 Sa 7:5–11; 12:17–23, respectively) He goes on, in the passage quoted in Revelation 13:10 by stating that their judgment is fixed:

And if they ask you, "Where shall we go?" Tell them, "This is what the
LORD says:

> 'Those destined for death, to death;
> those for the sword, to the sword;
> those for starvation, to starvation;
> those for captivity, to captivity." (Jer 15:1–2)[5]

John thus uses this passage from Jeremiah to assure God's people that those
who were persecuting them would receive their due punishment. They will
get what they deserve.

This calls for patient endurance and faithfulness. However, this assurance
comes at a time when God's people suffer persecution at the hands of their
enemies. Reality seems to suggest that the wicked are in control and will get
away with their evil. That is why God's people need to exercise patient endurance and remain faithful despite the harm that comes their way. They can do
so knowing that their persecutors and those who exploit them will definitely
get the punishment they deserve.

The Second Beast from the Earth (13:11–18)

13:11 *A second beast, coming out of the earth.* The dragon, representing Satan
(12:3–17), now has a second agent, also described as a beast. The first emerged
from the sea (13:1–10), but this second beast emerges from the earth.

One might be reminded of the end of Job where Yahweh, in his second
speech to Job speaks of two incredibly powerful creatures, Behemoth (40:15–
24) and Leviathan (41:1–34). Despite efforts to identify these two creatures
with actual animals (like the elephant and the crocodile), they are not actual creatures but rather the most powerful animals imaginable.[6] Behemoth's
name is the plural of *behema*, the plural sometimes being used as a superla-
tive. Leviathan, as already discussed (see note at 12:3), was a mythical sea
monster. In Job, they both represent the forces of chaos, which God controls
but does not remove. Here the sea beast and the land beast are agents of the
dragon, which God will indeed defeat and remove. But now they are a threat
to the people of God.

Two horns like a lamb, but it spoke like a dragon. We have seen that the sea
beast bore some similarities to Jesus and perhaps the lamblike horns suggest
that the land beast too bore a superficial resemblance to Jesus, though we
will see the earth beast has more similarities with the Holy Spirit. But when it
spoke, its dragonlike voice showed its true alliance with its master the dragon,
representing Satan.

13:12 *It exercised all the authority of the first beast on its behalf.* While bearing Christlike features, the fact that it exercised authority on its (the first beast's) behalf may suggest another superficial relationship, this time to the Holy Spirit. Jesus said to his disciples that after he ascended to heaven, the Father will send the Holy Spirit in Jesus' name, and will remind them "of everything I have said to you" (Jn 14:26). Later Jesus will say that the Spirit "will not speak on his own; he will speak only what he hears, and he will tell you what is yet to come. He will glorify me because it is from me that he will receive what he will make known to you. All that belongs to the Father is mine. That is why I said the Spirit will receive from me what he will make known to you" (Jn 16:13–15). Thus, the relationship among the dragon, the sea beast and the land beast is a type of unholy trinity.

Made the earth and its inhabitants worship the first beast. In the gospel of John we also read, "When the Advocate comes, whom I will send to you from the Father—the Spirit of truth who goes out from the Father—he will testify about me" (Jn 15:26). Just as the Spirit testifies to the Son, so the land beast, the third member of the unholy trinity, testifies to the sea beast and causes people to worship him. The role of the land beast may also be seen to have the function of a prophet, who bears witness to another. He points to the sea beast to elicit worship. Indeed, later (16:13; 19:20; 20:10) this beast is called "the false prophet."

13:13 *And it performed great signs.* The land beast's message is accompanied by signs. In the Old Testament, the prophets' message was accompanied by signs that would authenticate their role as a true prophet. Since the prophet's message typically would only come to realization in the future, whether a year or far into the future, the prophet needed a sign to show that they were truly God's servants. We might think of the storm that God sent when Samuel led Israel in a covenant renewal (1 Sa 12:16–18), the freezing of Jeroboam's arm and crack in his altar as an unnamed prophet spoke of the future destruction of the altar (1 Ki 13:4–5), or the birth of a child to a young woman when Isaiah told Ahaz that his fears of a Syrian-Ephraimite coalition would not materialize (Isa 7:13–17). Thus, the signs that accompany the speech of the land beast mimic the signs that accompany the true prophets of the Old Testament, but see the next note.

Even causing fire to come down from heaven. Elijah's role as a true prophet of Yahweh was attested by God throwing fire down from heaven to consume those who were trying to arrest him (2 Ki 1:10, 12). And the truth is that even false prophets have a limited ability to provide signs. We see this when the Egyptian wise men can turn their staffs into serpents (Ex 7:8–13) and later water into blood (Ex 7:14–24). That is why there is a second test to determine whether a prophet is true or false in the Old Testament: Do they speak in the name of the true God (Dt 13:1–4; see next note)?

13:14 *It deceived the inhabitants of the earth.* Again, the signs performed by the land beast intend to communicate that the beast is a true prophet, and they apparently convince many that he was. However, they should never have been fooled by the signs. In Deuteronomy, we read:

> If a prophet, or one who foretells by dreams, appears among you and announces to you a sign or wonder, and if the sign or wonder spoken of takes place, and the prophet says, "Let us follow other gods" (gods you have not known) "and let us worship them," you must not listen to the words of that prophet or dreamer. The LORD your God is testing you to find out whether you love him with all your heart and with all your soul. It is the LORD your God you must follow, and him you must revere. Keep his commands and obey him; serve him and hold fast to him. (Dt 13:1–4)

An image in honor of the beast. The land beast functioning as a prophet violates the law found in Deuteronomy 13 by directing worship of an image or idol of the sea beast, who is an agent of the dragon (Satan) rather than toward God. Thus, although his words are accompanied by signs, he deserves the fate of a false prophet, which according to Deuteronomy is death ("that prophet or dreamer must be put to death for inciting rebellion against the LORD your God," Dt 13:5).

13:15 *The second beast was given power.* We have seen instances of the divine passive where God is implied by the passive as the agent of an action (see notes regarding "was snatched" at 12:5 and "was given" at 12:14); here we have what we might consider the satanic passive, since it is most likely that it was the dragon who is implied here (see note at 13:7)

To give breath to the image of the first beast. Here the land beast mimics the power of God. In Genesis 2:7 "God formed a man from the dust of the ground and breathed into his nostrils the breath of life, and the man became a living being." Here the land beast gives breath to an inanimate object that then not only can speak but also kill those who refuse to worship the image of the beast.

And cause all who refused to worship the image to be killed. In Daniel 3, Nebuchadnezzar erected a ninety-foot-tall golden statue and demanded that all his subjects worship it on pain of death. We are not certain whether this was a statue of a false god or of Nebuchadnezzar himself, but in either case, the king demanded worship and the three friends of Daniel refuse. They were thrown into a furnace, but God saved them, causing Nebuchadnezzar himself to praise the true God.[7]

Going Deeper into Idolatry: Revelation 13

The second commandment prohibits idolatry: "You shall not make for yourself an image in the form of anything in heaven above or on the earth beneath or in the waters below. You shall not bow down to them or worship them; for I, the LORD your God, am a jealous God" (Ex 20:4–6; cf. Dt 5:8–10).

But what exactly is idolatry? In the Old Testament, idolatry in the first place took the form of the worship of false gods, which is expressly forbidden in the first commandment: "You shall have no other gods before me" (Ex 20:3; cf. Dt 5:7), gods who were worshipped utilizing physical representations. Baal, the Canaanite storm god, was the most commonly worshipped foreign god through the history of the people of God in the Old Testament, though there were others. But it is true that idolatry could also take the form of the worship of Yahweh using physical objects. Indeed, there is a question whether the golden calf in the wilderness is a false god or Yahweh himself. After all, after making the idol Aaron calls for a "festival to the LORD" (Ex 32:5). At heart, idolatry is treating a creature or some created thing as if it were the Creator (Ro 1:23).

Idolatry of this sort, forbidden in the strictest manner, is the cause of God's judgment on his people, and is the source of ridicule of the prophets:

> With whom, then, will you compare God?
>   To what image will you liken him?
> As for an idol, a metalworker casts it,
>   and a goldsmith overlays it with gold
>   and fashions silver chains for it.
> A person too poor to present such an offering
>   selects wood that will not rot;
> they look for a skilled worker
>   to set up an idol that will not topple. (Isa 40:18–20; cf. Jer
>   10:1–5; Isa 41:7, 29; 44:6–23; 46:5–7)

And this type of idolatry was current during the time of Christ and after in the Greco-Roman world that birthed Christianity. We might remember the time when Paul was in Athens, "he was greatly distressed to see that the city was full of idols" (Ac 17:16). The Jerusalem Council warned Gentile converts to "abstain from food polluted by idols" (Ac 15:20; cf. 15:29; 21:25). The apostle Paul, while saying that food sacrificed to idols is sacrificed to no god at all, still advises Christians to avoid eating such food for fear that it would make the weaker brother or sister stumble (1 Co 8).

The book of Revelation recognizes that idolatrous practices were occurring both in and outside of the church. The letters to the seven churches confront those who flirt with idolatry and eat food sacrificed to idols (2:14–15, 20). The visions describe how the devil's minion, the earth beast, created an idolatrous worship of the sea beast, representing the cultic worship of the power of Rome itself (13:15; 14:9; 19:20). Those who persist in their idolatry will receive judgment, being thrown into the lake of fire (21:8; see also 22:15).

This type of false worship of idols is not foreign to the twenty-first century but will be outside the experience of many who read this commentary. But still, idolatry is a common temptation to everyone because at the heart of it an idol is anything or anyone who occupies the place of God in our hearts and our minds. For readers of Revelation, unless the triune God is the center of their lives, then they are idolaters.

This is not a modern concept. We might think of the book of Ecclesiastes as a kind of idol-buster as the main character, the Teacher, tries to find the meaning of life in things like wisdom, wealth, pleasure, work, relationships, even religion, but each time he comes up empty: "Meaningless! Meaningless! . . . Everything is meaningless" (Ecc 1:2; 12:8). At the end of the book, though, a second wise man using the Teacher's thought as a background directs his son away from idolatry to the worship of the true God: "Fear God and keep his commandments, for this is the duty of all mankind. For God will bring every deed into judgment, including every hidden thing, whether it is good or evil" (Ecc 12:13–14).[8]

Idolatry is easy to define but hard to detect. Every human being worships someone, something, or some cause. By definition, non-Christians are idol worshipers. But as James K. A. Smith puts, channeling the thought of Augustine, such "idolatry is a persistent witness to the ineradicable religious impulse to worship that is constitutive of human being."[9] But even Christians are prone to such false worship. John Calvin rightly said that the human mind was a factory of idols. Due to sin, our lives are easily disordered but hard to see.

The book of Revelation is a reminder to guard constantly against the danger of idolatry. In his first letter, John puts it concisely, "Dear children, keep yourselves from idols" (1 Jn 5:21).

13:16 *Great and small, rich and poor, free and slave.* Every social strata must show allegiance to the image that represents the sea beast.

Receive a mark on their right hands or on their foreheads. The mark turns out to be the name of the beast, given in 13:18, thus publicly identifying the person so marked as under the control of the beast. Williamson points out that "the 'mark' (NIV) of the beast mimics the 'seal of the living God' (7:2–4) and the names of God and the Lamb written on the foreheads of the one hundred and forty-four thousand (14:1) and of the redeemed (22:4)."[10]

13:17 *They could not buy or sell unless they had the mark.* The faithful, who are not given the mark of the beast, will be excluded from economic activity. Williamson puts forward the suggestion that "it is likely that the requirement of participation in pagan rites excluded Christians from guilds."[11]

13:18 *This calls for wisdom.* In the Bible, wisdom is different than intelligence.[12] Typically, as in the book of Proverbs, wisdom has three dimensions. The first is a practical wisdom, the ability to navigate life, something like a skill of living. But then there is the ethical level. The wise person is righteous, the opposite of wicked, following the law of God. And then there is the most fundamental, and essential, theological level. "The fear of the LORD is the beginning of wisdom" (Pr 9:10). The preface to the book of Proverbs invites people to read to grow in this type of multifaceted wisdom. Among the many positive effects of growing in wisdom, we learn that wisdom will also help people "understand proverbs and parables, the sayings and riddles of the wise" (Pr 1:6). In this verse, the reader is presented with an enigma.

That number is 666. The beast, and this reference is to the sea beast not the beast from the earth (see also 15:2), is human, or a man. The number given is six repeated three times. While seven is the number to totality and completeness and often associated with God and people and things associated with God, seen throughout Revelation, six falls short of seven and thus is associated with imperfection, chaos, evil. To repeat six three times is to suggest gross imperfection or evil. The number 666 may also be a cipher for a person's name since letters carried numerical values. After mentioning that some ancient Greek manuscripts have the number 616 instead of 666, Metzger and deSilva helpfully explain:

> Among the names and titles that have been proposed to solve the cryptogram, the most probably candidate is the emperor Nero. If we add the numerical values in the Hebrew spelling of the name Neron Caesar, we obtain 666; on the other hand, since his name can equally well be spelled without the last N, if we omit the final N, the total will be 616. There does not appear to be any other name, or a name with a title, that satisfies, both 666 and 616.[13]

REVELATION 14

What the Structure Means:
Three More Visions (Rev 14)

John reports three more visions in succession, each introduced by the Greek *kai eidon*, which the NLT translates as "then I saw" in 14:1, 14 and simply as "and I saw" in 14:6. This phrase could also be translated "and I saw." In other words, the connection is marked by the simple conjunction "and."

Even so, there are connections between these three new visions and the preceding. For instance, the first vision features 144,000 "who had his [Christ's] name and his Father's name written on their foreheads" (14:1). We remember this group, who were given the seal of God on their foreheads in Revelation 7:1–8. Here, they are presented as the blameless, redeemed people of God who were with Jesus on Mount Zion, praising God with a new song.

After, the second "I saw" (14:6) we hear three angels making three pronouncements as they flew in midair. The first proclaimed the "eternal gospel" and called on everyone to worship God. The second angel announced the downfall of "Babylon the Great," a cipher for Rome and for all worldly power that resists God (14:8). The use of "Babylon the Great" or "Babylon" in this way is the first of six (see also 16:19; 17:5; 18, 2, 10, 21) and links this chapter with the visions to come. (That Babylon equals Rome becomes clear at 17:9 where Babylon the Great is said to sit on seven hills, something Rome was famous for.) The third angel warns of the horrific judgment that will come on those who "worship the beast and its image, or for anyone who received the mark of its name" (14:11). In the previous chapter, we heard that it was the land beast who encouraged the worship of the sea beast and its image, and that those who did received a mark with the name of the sea beast or the number of its name (13:16–17). This section ends with an exhortation that the faithful persevere until judgment comes on these evil forces and a blessing on those who "die in the Lord" (14:13).

The third vision, again introduced by John saying, "I saw" (14:14 NLT), has two parts involving agricultural implements, both a sickle. In the first (14:14–16), an angel sitting on a cloud swings his sickle and harvests the earth, a metaphor of gathering the faithful. The second angel swings his sickle and gathers the grape, places them in a winepress, and crushes them so that the "blood flowed out of the press" (14:20), an obvious picture of judgment.

Thus, these three additional visions with their intratextual links to what comes before and after further the picture of the rescue of the faithful and judgment on the wicked. Their purpose is primarily to provide comfort for the former and to encourage them toward faithfulness despite their present difficult situation.

The 144,000 (Again), Three Angels, Harvesting and Trampling (Revelation 14)

The 144,000 Sing a New Song (14:1–5)

14:1 *There before me was the Lamb, standing on Mount Zion.* For Jesus as the Lamb, see "Revelation 5:6 Through Old Testament Eyes: The Lamb Who Was Slain." Here John sees the Lamb standing on Mount Zion, the only explicit mention of this sacred mountain in the book of Revelation. Mount Zion, of course, was the place where God chose to make his special presence known to his people, thus making it holy ground. Solomon built the first temple there, and people flocked to it to offer worship and sacrifices. In Psalm 48, the composer calls on Israel to praise God by celebrating Zion itself:

> Great is the LORD, and most worthy of praise,
>> in the city of our God, his holy mountain.
> Beautiful in its loftiness,
>> the joy of the whole earth,
> like the heights of Zaphon is Mount Zion,
>> the city of the Great King.

God is in her citadels;
  he has shown himself to be her fortress. (Ps 48:1–3)

Thus, John sees Jesus in this most holy place, a place where his people go to offer their praises.

And with him 144,000 who had his name and his Father's name written on their foreheads. See note at 7:4, where 144,000 people from the tribes of Israel are also described as marked by a seal on their forehead as belonging to God. There we explained the number as being the result of multiplying the twelve tribes of Israel by the number 12,000. In other words, 144,000 is a figurative number not the actual number of people in the group. But here there is no indication that this group is the same as the one in Revelation 7, as we will see in verse 4. While many had the mark of the beast on their right hands or their foreheads (13:16), God's people have their foreheads marked by the name of Jesus and the Father.

14:2 *Like the roar of rushing waters and like a loud peal of thunder.* These similes describe the sound of harp and singing found in the text to follow. Of course, harps and singing don't sound like this literally. This description is figurative. Rushing waters (see note at 1:13–15 and notice its occurrence at 19:6) as well as thunder (see notes at 4:5 and 8:5) often accompany God's appearance.

Like that of harpists playing their harps. Harps accompanied songs sung in the temple as attested by the psalms (Ps 33:2; 43:4; 71:22, etc.).

14:3 *And they sang a new song before the throne.* See note at 5:9 and "Revelation 4 Through Old Testament Eyes: God on His Throne."

Before the four living creatures and the elders. See notes at 4:4 and 4:6–8.

14:4 *For they remained virgins.* At first blush, this passage seems to suggest that those who remain celibate (and are male) are closest to God. Indeed, the passage has been used to support the monastic movement. But that would be to treat this figurative passage as if it were not figurative. The point is that they are not spiritually profligate but put their attention on the Lord alone and not any rival deities. Marriage is never denigrated in the Bible, Old or New. Indeed, Genesis 2:23–25 shows that marriage was part of God's creation ideal. These spiritual virgins follow God wherever he goes.

While the Bible never disparages marriage, there are passages that may be behind this text. These texts suggest that refraining from sexual relations, even for a brief time, allows one to focus on one's relationship with God. At Mount Sinai, for instance, before God makes his presence known at the top of the mountain, Moses tells the people, "Prepare yourselves for the third day. Abstain from sexual relations" (Ex 19:15). Or we might think of David's words to the High Priest when he asked that his men be allowed to partake of the consecrated bread. The priest had said, "I don't have any ordinary broad on hand; however, there is some consecrated bread here—provided the men have kept themselves from women." To which David replied, "Indeed women have been kept from us, as usual whenever I set out. The men's bodies are holy even on missions that are not holy. How much more so today!" (1 Sa 21:4–5). This latter reference is of particular interest because it is in a military context, and in the book of Revelation there is a spiritual battle going on.

In 1 Corinthians, Paul expresses the idea, particularly since he believes it will be a brief time before Christ would come again, that, if one is able, he or she should not marry. This is not because there is anything wrong with marriage. Paul knows it was established by God at creation and believes that it reflects the relationship between Christ and the church (Eph 5:21–33). Rather, the purpose is so people can keep their undivided attention on Jesus (1 Co 7:32–35).

They were purchased from among mankind. The 144,000 devoted followers of the Lamb were purchased, that is redeemed, from among the rest of humanity. In other words, they were bought with a price and that price was Christ's crucifixion. In the Old Testament redemption as a purchase is mentioned in Psalm 74, a lament asking God to help them after a disaster, almost certainly the destruction of the temple by the Babylonians. The psalmist calls on God to "remember the nation you purchased long ago, the people of your inheritance, whom you redeemed—Mount Zion, where you dwelt" (Ps 74:2). The purchase of the nation of Israel was at the exodus when God brought them out from slavery and brought them to Mount Sinai where he gave them the law and took them to the promised land, where the temple was eventually built at Mount Zion.

Offered as firstfruits to God and the Lamb. The Festival of the Harvest (or Weeks) was also known as Pentecost since it took place fifty days after Passover. At this celebration the people of God were to bring the firstfruits of the harvest (Ex 23:16). These firstfruits were harbingers of the crops to come. Paul uses "firstfruits" metaphorically as he asserts that Christ's followers "have the first-fruits of the Spirit" (Ro 8:23). He also speaks of Christ as "the firstfruits of those who have fallen asleep" (1 Co 15:20, 23), referring to Christ who has first been raised from the dead to be joined by those who follow him. Here the 144,000 virgins who have been redeemed are the first of those offered to God with the implication that they would be followed by many others.

Warnings from Three Angels (14:6–13)

14:6 *I saw another angel.* The first of three angels who will make pronouncements as they fly "in midair." The first angel speaks the "eternal gospel," the good news that Jesus has come, died, and was raised.

To every tribe, language and people. See "Revelation 7:9 Through Old Testament Eyes: Every Nation, Tribe, People, and Language."

14:7 *Fear God and give him glory.* The admonition to "fear God" is best known from Proverbs (1:7 and throughout), but can be found throughout the Old Testament not only in the wisdom books (see Job 1:1; Ecc 12:13), but in many books.[1] As in those Old Testament passages, this fear is not one that makes one run away, but does indicate that people understand their creaturely status before their awesome Creator. Thus, this fear, which in other contexts leads to obedience, here leads to awe and worship.

The hour of his judgment has come. The message of Daniel was that, although it looked like the forces of evil were in control, in actuality God was in control and he would come in the future to secure his victory.[2] The expectation of the period of time between the Old and New Testament was that the divine warrior would come and beat their enemies, led by God's anointed one, typically thought to be a human leader in the line of David. When Jesus came into the wilderness, John the Baptist immediately recognized him as the one, but John received disturbing reports while he was in jail and Jesus began his ministry. John expected Jesus to bring immediate judgment: "I baptize you with water for repentance. But after me comes one who is more powerful than I, whose sandals I am not worthy to carry. He will baptize you with the Holy Spirit and fire. His winnowing fork is in his hand, and he will clear his threshing floor, gathering his wheat into the barn and burning up the chaff with unquenchable fire." (Mt 3:11–12).

But the report John received was that Jesus was healing the sick and infirm, raising the dead and preaching the good news to the poor (Mt 11:4–6). Where was the judgment? What John did not understand was that Jesus was coming not once but twice. In the first coming, he defeats Satan by his death, resurrection, and ascension (Eph 4:8; Col 2:13–15). But Jesus himself announced that he would come again and win the final victory over all evil (Mk 13 and parallels). This is the judgment that the first angel announces is coming soon. See "Going Deeper into Jesus the Divine Warrior Who Defeats Evil" after Revelation 22.

Worship him who made the heavens, the earth, the sea and the springs of water. As mentioned above, fear of God rises from the awareness that God is the Creator of all things (Ge 1–2), and people are his creatures.

14:8 *Fallen! Fallen is Babylon the Great.* The first angel called on all the people of the world to respond to the eternal gospel before God's judgment fell on those who do not worship him. The second angel proleptically announces the fall of Babylon. The words echo a passage from Isaiah (21:1–10), an oracle announcing the future fall of Babylon. Isaiah imagines a lookout who sees a chariot whose rider comes and tells him: "Babylon has fallen, has fallen! All the images of its gods lie shattered on the ground!" (Isa 21:9). Isaiah's vision looks forward to a fall of Babylon in his near future. We cannot be sure whether this oracle anticipates one of several Assyrian defeats of that city (710, 700, 689 BC), thus underlining the prophet's message to Judean kings like Hezekiah (Isa 39) not to ally with Babylon. Or whether it anticipates the ultimate fall of Babylon to the Persians in 539 BC. In any case, Babylon in the book of Revelation is not a reference to the city in Mesopotamia which no longer exists, but to Rome. This is made clear at 17:9 where Babylon the Great is said to sit on seven hills, for which Rome was famous. At the time of John's writing, Rome dominates the world of the Mediterranean and looks invincible, but, as the second angel announces, it will fall.

The maddening wine of her adulteries. As wine is intoxicating, so is sexual pleasure. Here adultery is figurative for idolatry. After all, there are only two relationships that are exclusive. God's people in this figure are in the position of a wife and God is the husband. A wife can have only one husband, and if she sleeps with another man then she has violated that relationship. People can have only one God, the triune God, and to have a relationship with a false god is a form of spiritual adultery as powerfully presented by Ezekiel 16, 23, and Hosea 1. The picture of Babylon the Great as a whore will be more fully developed in Revelation 17 (vv. 2, 4), 18 (v. 3), and 19 (v. 2)

14:9 *If anyone worships the beast and its image and receives its mark.* The first angel presented the eternal gospel and warned of imminent judgment. The second angel announced the fall of Babylon, figuratively representing Rome, indeed representing all those who chose to worship the beast, the agent of the dragon (Satan) rather than the true God. The third angel now issues another warning by describing the horrific judgment that will come on those who resist. For the beast's image, see note at 13:15 and for the mark placed on the head or hands of the followers of the beast, see note at 13:16.

14:10 *Will drink the wine of God's fury, which has been poured full strength into the cup of his wrath.* The cup metaphor appears frequently in the Old Testament and has two sides depending on what fills the cup. The psalmist, for instance, says to God, "You anoint my head with oil; my cup overflows" (23:5) as well as, "I will lift up the cup of salvation and call on the name of the LORD" (116:13). But obviously here in Revelation the background is found in the second use of the cup image, "the cup of God's wrath," which is filled with the "wine of God's fury." Perhaps the most sustained use of this metaphor is found in Jeremiah 25.[3] Here God calls on Jeremiah to go to several foreign courts and pronounce judgment on them. God says to the prophet: "Take from my hand this cup filled with the wine of my wrath and make all the nations to whom I send you drink it. When they drink it, they will stagger and go mad because of the sword I will send among them" (Jer 25:15–16). The idea behind the cup metaphor is that, rather than the refreshing and life-giving liquid in the cup of salvation, the cup of wrath is filled with potent brew that leads to staggering and an inability to protect oneself.

Jesus himself utilizes the cup image when he is in the garden of Gethsemane and asks God to take "this cup" away from him, but also says "if it is not possible for this cup to be taken away unless I drink it, may your will be done" (Mt 26:42). Jesus on the cross experiences the judgment that we deserve, and he does it on our behalf. Because of Jesus' death and resurrection, his people can drink the cup of God's salvation (1 Co 11:23–26). But those who refuse relationship with Christ will drink from the cup of God's wrath.

They will be tormented with burning sulfur. By this time in the commentary, we don't need to be reminded that we are dealing with figurative language. That said, the metaphor points to a reality of excruciating pain, though what is not clear is whether the pain is psychological, spiritual, physical, or a combination of all the above. As Robert Miller puts it, quoting Susan Hylen, "metaphors do not make the violent imagery (of the Bible) 'transmuted into something nonviolent.'"[4] In other words, violent metaphors, though not giving us a literal picture, are telling us about a violent judgment. The origin of the metaphor likely comes from the judgment that God brought on the sinful cites of Sodom and Gomorrah (Ge 19:24) on which he rained burning sulfur. Later God warned the Israelites that if they violate the covenant that they had just reaffirmed before Moses' death that "the whole land will be a burning waste of salt and sulfur" (Dt 29:23). The psalmist too threatens "on the wicked he will rain fiery coals and burning sulfur; a scorching wind will be their lot" (Ps 11:6).

14:11 *The smoke of their torment will rise forever and ever.* Just as at Sodom after God rained burning sulfur on them, Abraham looked toward the destroyed city and "saw dense smoke rising from the land, like smoke from a furnace" (Ge 19:28). In an oracle against the nations, Isaiah speaks of the Lord's day of vengeance, where Edom's streams will turn into pitch and "its smoke will rise forever" (34:10).

14:12 *This calls for patient endurance.* We have already seen a similar call for patient endurance in 13:10 (see note). John knows that at the present the forces of evil are seemingly in control, but he has just heard the angels announce certain judgment against that evil. But it is a future judgment, meaning that

God's people will have to continue exercising patience in the face of suffering. As they do, they need to continue to obey ("keep his commands") and remain faithful to Jesus.

14:13 *Write this.* The instruction to write something down is to make a permanent record and allowing for better memory of it (see note at 1:19). When God issued a judgment against the Amalekites, for instance, he told Moses, "write this on a scroll as something to be remembered" (Ex 17:14). In this way God's people will be able to give thanks and praise to God for what he has done and how he keeps his promises.

Blessed are the dead. That the judgment is in the future means that God's faithful people may yet die because of their faith. The voice from heaven, probably God's but maybe an angel's, confers a blessing and command that it be written down, showing its permanency and authority, that those who die will be blessed. The Spirit affirms this heavenly pronouncement and adds that death will bring them rest from their labors, and that their continuing faithfulness and good acts will follow them. There are seven such blessings conferred through the book of Revelation (see note at 1:3, and occurrences at 16:15; 19:9; 20:6; 22:7, 14).

Reaping the Harvest (Salvation) and Trampling the Grapes (Judgment) (14:14–20)

14:14 *A white cloud, and seated on the cloud was one like a son of man.* Revelation opened with a picture of Christ riding a cloud, also alluding to Daniel 7:13–14 (see note at 1:7 and "Revelation Through Old Testament Eyes: Daniel" at 1:7). Interestingly, this passage is the only one which pictures the cloud that God or Jesus rides as white, since the imagery comes ultimately from ancient Near Eastern storm god imagery where the clouds would be dark (note also Ps 18:9). In those other contexts, God comes to judge the wicked. Here, the image of harvesting grain may rather point to God bringing history to an end and gathering everyone together (judgment of the wicked will be executed by the angel who follows; see next note).

With a crown of gold on his head and a sharp sickle in his hand. The golden crown indicates authority, and the sharp sickle the tool of his judgment, figuratively speaking. The background to the use of the sickle here may be found in the parable of the weeds in Matthew 13:24–30. Here the kingdom of heaven is compared to a man who sows a field with good seed, but then his enemy comes and sows weeds along with the good seed. The owner tells his servants to let both grow together until the end for fear that the plants produced by the good seed might be harmed. The parable ends with the owner saying, "Let both grow together until the harvest. At that time I will tell the harvesters: First collect the weeds and tie them in bundles to be burned; then gather the wheat and bring it into my barn." We might also note the positive use of the harvesting theme in "the parable of the growing seed" (Mk 4:26–29).

14:17 *Another angel came out of the temple in heaven.* For temple in heaven, see note at 11:19.

He too had a sharp sickle. Since this angel comes out of the heavenly temple, we understand that he is God's agent, doing God's will as he judges the wicked. The background to the sickle image here may be found in an oracle of judgment in the prophet Joel:

> Let the nations be roused;
>> let them advance into the Valley of Jehoshaphat,
> for there I will sit
>> to judge all nations on every side.
> Swing the sickle,
>> for the harvest is ripe.
> Come, trample the grapes,
>> for the winepress is full
>> and the vats overflow—
> so great is their wickedness! (Joel 3:12–13)

14:18 *Still another angel, who had charge of the fire.* Fire is an image of judgment in various places in the Old Testament (Dt 32:22; Amos 7:4; Zep 3:8) and the New Testament (2 Th 1:7; Heb 10:27; 2 Pe 3:7).

14:19 *The great winepress of God's wrath.* A winepress is a vat, perhaps carved in rock and covered in plaster where ripe grapes were thrown in and crushed perhaps by the feet of workers, so that grape juice might flow out. The grape juice might be reminiscent of blood and thus suggested the winepress as an image of judgment. We can see this in the oracle from Joel cited in the note to 14:17. We also see the use of this image in the first poem of Lamentations where the weeping widow (a personification of defeated Jerusalem) laments:

> The Lord has rejected
>> all the warriors in my midst;
> he has summoned an army against me
>> to crush my young men.
> In his winepress the Lord has trampled
>> Virgin Daughter Judah. (La 1:15)

Lastly, in a passage that has particular relevance for Revelation 19:15 (see note), God proclaims:

> I have trodden the winepress alone;
>> from the nations no one was with me.
> I trampled them in my anger
>> and trod them down in my wrath;
> Their blood spattered my garments,
>> and I stained all my clothing. (Isa 63:3)

14:20 *Rising as high as the horses' bridles for a distance of 1,600 stadia.* Sixteen hundred stadia is about 180 miles (see NIV note). That is, needless to say, a lot of blood—indicating that the judgment at the end of time is both violent and extensive. But Williamson helpfully points out the figurative sense: "The number sixteen hundred, whether calculated as forty squared or four squared times ten squared, indicates that this judgment is complete and worldwide in scope."[5]

REVELATION 15

What the Structure Means: Seven Bowls (Rev 15–16)

Next John moves to "another great and marvelous sign," the previous sign being that associated with the pregnant woman (12:1) and the red dragon (12:3). There is no explicit link or transitional statement, beyond the simple connection "and" (Greek *kai*, which could also be translated "then,") at the beginning of Revelation 15–16, giving the impression of the presentation of a succession of visions.

The vision itself encompasses Revelation 15–16 and is a third cycle of seven judgments. For how these three cycles (seals, trumpets, and bowls) relate to each other, see "What the Structure Means: Seals, Trumpets, and Bowls (Rev 6:1–7:5; 8:7–11:19; 15:1–16:21)" at the end of Revelation 16. There we will point out that these three cycles are not a description of twenty-one sequential judgments, but circle back to again prophetically describe the judgment coming on evil people. That said, we will also observe that this cycle comes with a sense of finality. When the seven angels appear, they are said to have "the last seven plagues—last because with them God's wrath is completed" (15:1).

But before the seven angels are commissioned to their judgment task, John directs our attention to "those who had been victorious," specifically those who have resisted the worship of the beast and its image (13:14–15; 14:9–11) and "over the number of its name," which we learned is 666 (13:17–18). These saints are standing by "a sea of glass glowing with fire" (15:2), "sea" being symbolic of chaos but here under control.

These victorious ones then worship God. They praise him for his powerful deeds and holiness, as well as the justice of his ways. They imagine all the nations coming to worship this great God. Beginning in Revelation 4 and 5 we have seen how God and the glorified Christ elicit praise for his heavenly and human followers. These portrayals of worship also intend to lead the reader to worship God.

Then "after this" (15:5), John sees the heavenly temple, also called the "tabernacle of the covenant law" (15:5). Out of the temple proceed the seven angels who have the seven plagues. At this point one of the living creatures gives each of them a bowl filled with the wrath of God that they will pour out in judgment. Smoke fills the heavenly temple which will remain until the seven plagues are completed.

Continuing, the seven angels pour out the contents of their bowls one at a time. The seven bowls are poured in succession with no interludes as we observed with the seals and the trumpets. While the interludes in the previous cycles delayed the conclusion and thus generated excited anticipation, the lack of interludes communicates a sense of urgency.

A heavenly voice commands the angels to pour out "the seven bowls of God's wrath on the earth" (16:1). The contents of the bowls each is an act of God's judgment on evil.

In the seal cycle and the trumpet cycle we saw that the first four of each had brief narrations that also bound them together. The first four seals described the four horsemen who brought war, internal conflict, economic devastation, and death (6:1–7). The first four trumpets caused devastation in four different sectors of creation—earth, sea, springs of water, and then celestial bodies.

The first four bowls are also given relatively brief narration, though the third is the longest of the four. Like the first four trumpets, the first four bowls bring devastation on the earth, the sea, the rivers and springs of water, and the celestial bodies in succession. The third trumpet narration is the longest because after the bowl is poured out on the waters, the angel in charge of the waters responds by saying that the judgment is just because the evil people who killed the prophets will now themselves drink blood. Still people refused to repent.

The fifth angel pours out his bowl on the throne of the beast itself (16:10–11) with the result that darkness covers its kingdom and those who worshiped the beast "gnawed their tongues in agony" (16:10). Again, despite the judgment, people refused to repent.

With the sixth bowl, the mighty Euphrates River that separated the Roman Empire from the Parthian kingdom dried up. Then three frogs emerge from the mouths of the dragon, the sea beast, and the land beast. They go out and gather the kings of the earth to a place called Armageddon, presumably to prepare for war. In the midst of the description of the consequences of the pouring out of the sixth bowl, a voice, almost certainly that of Christ, warns that he would come "as a thief" (that is, suddenly and quietly), along with the exhortation to stay awake and clothed (that is, to be prepared at all times for Christ's coming). The implication is that there will not be obvious warning signs that will signal that Christ is about to make his return.

At the beginning of this section, we saw statements that asserted the finality of the judgments accompanying the pouring out of the seven bowls. Thus with the seventh, we hear a loud voice from the throne where God sits, announcing "It is done!" (16:17). As with the seventh seal and the seventh trumpet we then learn that meteorological and seismic convulsions occur. But there is a more intense note to these occurrences here. This earthquake will be like no earthquake before it (16:18) and the hailstones will be huge, "each weighing about a hundred pounds" (16:21). But again, rather than repenting, people "cursed God on account of the plague of hail, because the place was so terrible" (16:21).

The Seven Bowls of God's Wrath (Revelation 15–16)

Presentation of the Bowls and Angelic Commission (15:1–16:1)

15:1 *Another great and marvelous sign.* As we saw in 12:1 [see note] and 12:3, a sign points toward something that cannot presently be seen and often speaks of realities in the spiritual realm. In this way, the sign functions like a metaphor. In the following verses, we get a picture of a future punishment in the form of seven angels who bring seven plagues. Like a metaphor, the sign participates in and represents the reality that it points to. Thus, signs/metaphors of suffering point toward real suffering, though the suffering may not come in the straightforward way depicted by the sign/metaphor.

Seven angels with the seven last plagues. Seven is a number that pervades Revelation. It is a symbolic number of completeness. Of most relevance, since they are similar cycles of judgment, to the seven angels who carry seven plagues in seven bowls to pour out God's wrath (see 15:7) are the seven seals whose unsealing brought punishment (see note at 5:1) and the seven trumpets when sounded initiated punishment (see note at 8:2).

Because with them God's wrath is completed. The judgments symbolized by the three cycles of seals, trumpets, and plague-bearing bowls are not sequential to each other as if the bowls follow the trumpets that follow the seals. Rather each points beyond the previous toward the end. Here in the third cycle, we reach the apex of God's judgment. See "What the Structure Means: Seals, Trumpets, and Bowls (Rev 6:1–7:5; 8:7–11:19; 15:1–16:21)" at the end of Revelation 16.

15:2 *I saw what looked like a sea of glass glowing with fire.* For "sea of glass" and its association with God's throne and his appearance, see note at 4:6–8. Here, the sea of glass is said to be glowing with fire, perhaps indicative of God's appearance to bring judgment since fire is often associated with God's punishment (see note at 8:5). Bauckham, however, seems to suggest that this sea glowing with fire is suggestive of the Red Sea.[1] Perhaps so, but it is hard to be dogmatic. The people so standing have been redeemed and are about to sing "the Song of God's servant Moses and of the Lamb" (15:3).

Standing beside the sea. This refers to the sea of glass, but as explained in the note at 4:6–8 (and elsewhere), the sea represents the power of chaos and evil.

Those who had been victorious. See note at 2:7. This phrase refers to those who had not succumbed to the worship of the beast, the agent of the dragon (Satan, see notes at 12:3 and 9). That they stand by the sea shows that they have subdued the forces of chaos and evil.

Over the beast and its image. See notes at 13:1, 15, 18.

They held harps. See note at 5:8.

15:3–4 *Sang the song of God's servant Moses and of the Lamb.* Those who were victorious over the beast and who are now in heaven sing a song that is described as the song of both Moses and the Lamb (Christ). That song will be quoted in these verses and derives from several psalms but also from the "song of Moses" in Deuteronomy 32 (see below). The song of Moses may also recall the song Moses led after the crossing of the Sea in Exodus 15 which would reinforce the themes of victory and liberation here in Revelation; notice especially Exodus 15:11, which expresses that God alone is "awesome in glory" as those who are victorious proclaim that God alone is holy (Rev 15:4).[2] This psalm is also the song of the Lamb whose work provides redemption for the people. The thesis of the song is that God acts with justice and with power. He is holy and he is righteous and therefore all the nations will fear him and worship him.

The song sung is a montage of the following from the Old Testament:

Great are the works of the LORD;
    they are pondered by all who delight in them.
Glorious and majestic are his deeds,
    and his righteousness endures forever. (Ps 111:2–3)

He is the Rock, his works are perfect,
    and all his ways are just.
A Faithful God who does no wrong,
    upright and just is he. (Dt 32:4)

Who should not fear you, LORD;
    King of the nations?
This is your due. (Jer 10:7)

All the nations you have made
    will come and worship before you, Lord;
    they will bring glory to your name. (Ps 86:9)

The LORD has made his salvation known
    and revealed his righteousness to the nations. (Ps 98:2)

Lord God Almighty. Finally, he is the Almighty (*pantokrator*), the Greek equivalent to the Hebrew *yahweh seba'ot*, the Lord of Hosts. The Hosts refer to God's heavenly army, so that the use of the title Almighty in this context contributes to the heavy emphasis on the triune God's role as warrior who comes to save his people. See also 1:8; 11:17; and "Going Deeper into Jesus the Divine Warrior Who Defeats Evil" after Revelation 22.

Going Deeper into the Fear of God: Revelation 15:4

At the beginning of Revelation 15, John reports seeing seven angels appear who bring "seven last plagues—last, because with them God's wrath is completed" (15:1). At the end of the chapter, we will hear that these angels emerge from the heavenly temple with the plagues and the bowls "filled with the wrath of God" (15:7), which they will pour out in judgment one by one (Rev 16).

But before they do, God's victorious saints sing a song that celebrates the "Lord God Almighty," asking the question, "Who will not fear you, Lord, and bring glory to your name?" (15:4). Considering the intensity of the judgments described thus far and the ones to be pictured in the following chapters, we might readily understand why God evokes fear in the hearts of his human creatures. Still, Christians today might balk at the idea that our God is the type of God who wants people to fear him. Isn't that an Old Testament thing to talk about the "fear of God"? Doesn't God want our love, not our fear? After all, we know "perfect love drives out fear" (1 Jn 4:18).

The type of fear about which the departed saints sing is the type that leads to worship and glory for the name of God (Rev 15:4). This fear does not make one run away and hide but leads to proper praise of God. This fear derives from the recognition that God is sovereign over all and we are his creatures. This type of fear is not in conflict with love but complements love.

This fear is the fear that is the beginning of wisdom (Pr 1:7; see also Job 28:28; Ecc 12:13–14). Christians, according to Paul, are to "work out your salvation with fear and trembling" (Php 2:12). Reading the book of Revelation should remind us how great our God is and move us toward this kind of worshipful fear that both leads us to obedience as well as to worship.[3]

15:5 *I saw in heaven the temple.* For heaven as temple, see note at 11:19 and see "Revelation 11:1–2 Through Old Testament Eyes: The Temple" and "Revelation 21 Through Old Testament Eyes: The Heavenly Temple." For the opening of heaven, see note at 4:1.

The tabernacle of the covenant law. The law of the covenant, as represented by the two tablets of the ten commandments, were placed in the ark of the covenant (Ex 25:21) and located in the Holy of Holies, which is why the ark is sometimes called "the ark of the covenant" or "ark of testimony."

15:6 *Out of the temple came the seven angels with the seven plagues.* The seven angels with their seven plagues were introduced in 15:1 (see note), but now they depart the heavenly temple to bring punishment on the earth. Three plagues occurred earlier (see note at 9:18), which added to the seven here brings the total to ten, the same number as the plagues God sent on Egypt at the time of the exodus. In this way John suggests that judgment on the enemies of God will lead to the liberation of and victory of his people as it did at the time of the exodus.

Dressed in clean, shining linen and wore golden sashes around their chests.
Linen could be worn by anyone (Pr 31:24), but priests could only wear linen
and no other fabric (Ex 28:42; Lev 16:4). Priests were the only ones allowed to
dwell in the temple precincts as a normal part of their lives, and these angels
dwell in the heavenly temple (see also Da 12:6–7 for angels wearing linen).
Clean clothes reflect a blameless life. In Zechariah 3, Joshua the High Priest's
dirty clothes were changed into new clean clothes by God to reflect the fact
that God had forgiven him his sins and was preparing him for service in the
second temple under construction at the time. Linen is white material and
the fact that it is described as shining accentuates the garment's brightness.
In the book of Acts, Cornelius described an angel of God who appeared to
him as "a man in shining clothes" (10:30). A sash serves no practical purpose, but is rather ornamental and shows status. In the Old Testament, priests
wore sashes, along with tunic and capes, "to give them dignity and honor"
(Ex 28:40).[4] Golden sashes indicate a particular high status due to its association with the expensive metal. Earlier in Revelation, the one "like the son of
man" (the glorified Christ) was pictured as wearing a golden sash (Rev 1:13).
Later, the people of God will be pictured as God's bride dressed in "fine linen,
bright and clean" with the explicit explanation that "fine linen stands for the
righteous acts of God's holy people" (19:8, see also 19:14).

Revelation Through Old Testament Eyes:
The Ten Plagues

The biggest imprint of the book of Exodus on Revelation comes from the
ten plagues that God sent on Egypt to induce Pharaoh to let the Israelites
leave their bondage. Pharaoh was reluctant so God had to send a series
of ever more intensive plagues against him until he finally relented.
Revelation has ten plagues, as does Exodus (see note at 15:6). Below I
mention just the plagues from Exodus that inform pictures of judgment
in Revelation:

First Plague: Blood (Ex 7:14–24). In the first plague, God told Moses to
stretch his staff over the Nile with the result that the water would turn
into blood, rendering it undrinkable. This first plague is perhaps the most
frequently used picture of judgment in the book of Revelation. The first
three occur in descriptions of judgments (8:7; 16:3 and 4). The fourth use
is a description of the power of the "two witnesses" who I argue represent
the church (see commentary). They have the "power to turn the waters
into blood and to strike the earth with every kind of plague" (11:6). In
other words, they have the same God-given power as Moses.

Second Plague: Frogs (Ex 7:25–8:15). Seven days after God turned the waters of the Nile into blood, he sent a plague of frogs. This may have been thought to be an assault on the frog-headed Egyptian goddess of fertility, Heqet.

Outside of the book of Exodus, frogs only appear twice in the Old Testament, both times in rehearsals of the plagues of Egypt (Ps 78:45; 105:30). In the New Testament, frogs are mentioned only once, in the book of Revelation.

When the sixth angel poured out the contents of his bowl, the Euphrates river dried up to allow for easy access for an invasion by the kings of the East. At that moment, three "impure spirits that looked like frogs" came out of the mouth of the dragon, who represents Satan (16:13). These frogs that are "demonic spirits that perform signs" go out to gather kings to fight against God.

Sixth Plague: Boils (Ex 9:8–12). In the sixth plague, God commands Moses to take some soot from the ground and throw it into the air. The soot then became fine dust, and as the fine dust settled over the land of Egypt, the skin of people and animals alike broke out into boils. In Revelation, an angel poured out the contents of the second bowl with the result that "ugly festering sores broke out on the people who had the mark of the beast and worshiped its image" (16:2).

Seventh Plague: Fiery Hail (Ex 9:13–35). Pharaoh continued to remain deaf and blind to God's repeated attempts to get him to relent and let his people leave their bondage. God then sent the hail with great force. Two times Revelation alludes to this plague. The first occurs in 8:7 which combines hail with turning water into blood (the first plague). The second allusion to the seventh plague of the exodus is found in connection with the pouring out of the seventh plague bowl (Rev 16:21).

Eighth Plague: Locusts (Ex 10:1–20). After his failure to respond to the plague of hail, God tells Moses to threaten Pharaoh with a plague of locusts (10:5). Though only used once, the book of Revelation's allusion to the eighth plague comes during the dramatic aftermath of the blowing of the fifth trumpet (Rev 9:1–11). The hybrid locusts inflicted much harm yet were not allowed to touch the earth, but only people, and they could not kill the people, but only torture them. Their leader was known as "the angel of the Abyss, whose name in Hebrew is Abaddon and in Greek is Apollyon (that is, Destroyer)" (9:11).

Ninth Plague: Darkness (Ex 10:21–29). God instructed Moses to stretch out his hand toward and sky and when he did, darkness descended on Egypt, but not on Goshen where the Israelites lived. To understand the full psychological impact of this plague of darkness on the Egyptians, we need to remember that the most important god in their pantheon was the god of the sun. Such a plague would have been perceived as an assault on the god of the sun, but still Pharaoh could not bring himself to repent.

Revelation alludes to the ninth plague of darkness at least two times: first, in the aftermath of the opening of the sixth seal (6:12–13a); second, after the pouring out of the fifth plague bowl on the throne of the beast (16:10).

Tenth Plague: Death of the Firstborn (Ex 11:1–12:30). It is true that there is nothing comparable to the death of the firstborn in the book of Revelation. However, in the picture of the "Lamb, looking as if it had been slain" we hear echoes of the Passover Lamb who was sacrificed on behalf of the Israelite children who were spared. As explained in the commentary at 5:6, this fits in with the expansive theme of Jesus being the fulfillment of the expectation of the second exodus theme of the prophets.

Conclusion. Just as the Egyptian plagues overtook a recalcitrant leader, Pharaoh, who represented a kingdom that exploited God's people, so the plagues described by Revelation come on those who resist God and persecute his people. Just as the Egyptian plagues did not elicit the hoped-for repentance of Egypt, so the plagues of Revelation only led to further resistance to God.

15:7 *Seven golden bowls.* The four living creatures, the ones closest to the throne of God (see note at 4:6–8), now give bowls to the seven angels whose contents they will pour out over humanity to bring divine judgment upon them. Since the angels are said to bring the plagues with them out of the temple, we may presume that they now place the plagues in the provided bowls. The interaction of the four living creatures and the angels, all agents of God, allows no question but that this punishment comes from God himself, which is confirmed by the fact that the bowls are said to be "filled with the wrath of God." Attempts to minimize or remove God's active involvement in this description of violent judgment ring hollow.[5] Metzger and DeSilva explain, "The Greek word for 'bowls' denotes vessels that are broad and shallow, shaped like a saucer, so that their contents can be poured out completely and suddenly. They ironically resemble the very bowls used by Greek, and Roman priests to pour out offerings over the fires on the altars of their rival gods."[6]

15:8 *The temple was filled with smoke.* When Moses led the Israelites to Mount Sinai to meet God and receive his commandments, we read that "Mount Sinai was covered with smoke, because the Lord descended on it in fire. The smoke billowed up from it like smoke from a furnace, and the whole trembled violently" (Ex 19:18). Isaiah has a vision of God in his temple at the time of his commission. It is a picture of incredible intensity in its description of God's power. He is surrounded by all the heavenly creatures, including the seraphim, who call out "Holy, holy, holy is the Lord Almighty; the whole earth is full of his glory" (Isa 6:3). In response, "the doorposts and thresholds shook and the temple was filled with smoke" (Isa 6:4). God is so great that he cannot be seen, and smoke obscures vision and hides the full force of God's glory from human perception. Thus, smoke (and often the fire that produces it) frequently accompanies a description of God's appearance. On the Day of Atonement, as the High Priest enters the holy place in the tabernacle, "he is to put incense on the fire before the Lord, and the smoke of the incense will conceal the atonement cover above the tablets of the covenant law, so that he will not die" (Lev 16:13). It is precisely above the atonement cover of the ark that God was imagined to be enthroned.

REVELATION 16

16:1 *I heard a loud voice from the temple.* John hears a loud voice from the heavenly temple where God dwells. The statement from the temple speaks of God in the third person, so it may be an angel uttering the command on behalf of God or it could still be God himself. In any case, there is no question from what follows that the punishments represented by the pouring out of the seven bowls comes from God himself.

The seven bowls of God's wrath. See note at 15:7.

The First Bowl (16:2)

16:2 *Ugly, festering sores broke out.* When the first angel poured out the contents of his bowl, people who had the mark of the beast (see note at 13:16–17) and worshiped its image (see note at 13:15) broke out in festering sores. At the time of the exodus God had brought a plague of festering boils on the Egyptians (Ex 9:8–12). Moses threw soot from a furnace up in the air in the presence of Pharaoh, which became fine dust and "festering boils broke out on people and animals" (Ex 9:10). Despite this horrible calamity, Pharaoh did not repent or let the people go.

Just before Moses died, he led Israel in a renewal of the covenant commitment that they had made at Mount Sinai. His speech is reported in the book of Deuteronomy and announces punishments if the people violate their covenant commitments, including that "the LORD will afflict you with boils of Egypt and with tumors, festering sores and the itch, from which you cannot be cured" (Dt 28:27).

No wonder then that the three friends of Job thought that he had sinned, since God allowed the accuser to afflict "Job with painful sores from the soles of his feet to the crown of his head" (Job 2:7) and he himself attested "my body is clothed with worms and scabs, my skin is broken and festering" (Job 7:5). But the case of Job is told to debunk the idea that all suffering is the result and only the result of sin. But still open sores are often the consequence of sin as Isaiah says, "Therefore the Lord will bring sores on the heads of the women of Zion; the LORD will make their scalps bald" (Isa 3:17, see also Hos 5:13).

The Second Bowl (16:3)

16:3 *It turned into blood like that of a dead person.* When the second angel pours out the contents of his bowl, the sea turns into blood and every living thing in the sea dies. Clearly, the shape of this plague intends to recall the turning of the Nile water into blood early in Moses's confrontation of Pharaoh at the time of the exodus (Ex 7:14–24). To understand this moment at the time of the Exodus, we must realize that the Nile is the source of all fertility, life, and flourishing in ancient Egypt. Every year the Nile would flood, and as the waters receded, arable soil would be deposited that could then be planted. A further dimension to our understanding of the assault on the Nile is that there was an Egyptian god named Hapi associated with the Nile. Hapi was a god of fertility and, when the Nile waters turned into blood, it would have been thought to be an attack on this god. We have already seen that the sea in Revelation represents chaos and evil (4:6; 13:1; 15:2; 17:1; 22:1) which God controls or even defeats.

The Third Bowl (16:4–7)

16:4 *The third angel poured out his bowl.* The judgment represented by the third angel and his bowl appears to be an extension of the second bowl and thus also reflective of the plague that turned the Nile into blood at the time of the Exodus. The second bowl turned the sea to blood; here the rivers and the springs. Water, of course, brings life, particularly the fresh waters from rivers and springs; but now, turned to blood, they only represent death.

16:5 *The angel in charge of the waters.* We only get glimpses of the roles of the angels, but at times Scripture talks about how God puts his angels in charge of certain places or assigns them certain roles. For instance, Moses says "When the Most High apportioned the nations, when he divided humankind, he fixed the boundaries of the peoples according to the number of the gods, the LORD's own portion was his people" (Dt 32:8–9 NRSV).[1] Here "gods" stands for the angels, to whom God assigned specific nations. In Daniel 10, we learn from Gabriel (whose responsibility appears to be that of God's messenger) that Michael, who is said to be the angel assigned to Israel, had to fight the angel (or perhaps demon) associated with Persia and will fight the one assigned to Greece. In this passage, we learn that there is an angel assigned to the waters.

You are just in these judgments, O Holy One. The angel in charge of the waters confirms that God's punishments on the waters are deserved. As Abraham said to God, as he was negotiating with him about the judgment coming on Sodom, "Far be it from you to do such a thing—to kill the righteous with the wicked, treating the righteous and the wicked alike. Far be it from you! Will not the judge of the world do right?" (Ge 18:25). And indeed God responds as Abraham knew he would and only brought judgment on the wicked, allowing Lot and his family to leave the city. In several psalms, the composer extols God for his just judgments (Ps 9:7–8; 89:14; 97:2).

God is here called the "Holy One," because he is set apart from sinful humanity, which allows him to render just judgment. The name Holy One is the favorite of the prophet Isaiah, occurring over twenty-five times (1:4; 5:19, 24; 10:17, 20; 12:6, etc.). The quintessential threefold "Holy" of Isaiah 6:3 contrasts with the sinfulness of the prophet and the people (6:5). In the whole book of Isaiah God's holiness is the ground on which Israel is condemned for her sins.

You who are and who were. Compare Revelation 1:4, 8; 4:8, all of which add "and is to come." The future element is probably omitted here because the God of judgment has now come.

16:6 *For they have shed the blood of your holy people and your prophets.* The people of God, and in particular God's prophetic spokespersons, have been persecuted through history up to the time of John, thus they deserve death themselves. As God told Noah,

> Whoever sheds human blood,
>   by humans shall their blood be shed;
> for in the image of God
>   has God made mankind. (Ge 9:6)

As for the prophets, they were consistently rejected and persecuted during the Old Testament time period (1 Ki 18:4; 2 Ch 24:20–21; Neh 9:26; Isa 50:6; Jer 20:1–2; 26:20–23), and some even killed in the pages of the Old Testament. That said, when Jesus pronounces his woes over the Pharisees, he says that "this generation will be held responsible for the blood of all the prophets that has been shed since the beginning of the world, from the blood of Abel to the blood of Zechariah, who was killed between the altar and the sanctuary. Yes, I tell you, this generation will be held responsible for it all" (Lk 11:50–51). Even closer in time, John the Baptist was put to death by Herod (Mt 14:1–12).

16:7 *I heard the altar respond.* This vision concerns the heavenly temple (16:1), so now the altar speaks by way of personification and reiterates the pronouncement of the angel in charge of the waters (16:5) that the judgment that has come in the form of the bowls of God's wrath is just and true, that is, the punishment is proportional to the crime. The altar in the earthly tabernacle/temple was where sacrifices were offered on behalf of repentant sinners. That the altar speaks may imply that where there is no repentance there is just and true punishment.

Lord God Almighty. See note at 11:17.

True and just are your judgments. God is bringing judgment against evil doers and here those judgments are called "true and just," meaning that the punishment fits the crime. While this is not an allusion to Psalm 119, the giant psalm that extols God's word, it certainly imbibes of the same ethos. (See also Rev 19:2.)

The Fourth Bowl (16:8–9)

16:8 *The fourth angel poured out his bowl on the sun.* The first bowl brought punishment to the people who worshipped the beast and bore his mark. The second and third bowls turned the waters of the earth into blood; now the fourth bowl affects the heavens, specifically the sun. In the first three bowl-judgments we observed parallels with the plagues against Egypt. We also know that there was a plague of darkness, the penultimate plague, that extinguished the light of the sun (Ex 10:21–29). However with the fourth bowl, this plague does not lead to darkness but to an intensification of the heat of the sun so that it scorches people with fire.

16:9 *They cursed the name of God.* A gross violation of the third commandment ("you shall not misuse the name of the LORD your God," Ex 20:7). God's name reflects who he is and to curse his name is to slander his reputation. See note on "a blasphemous name" at 13:1.

Who had control over these plagues. Though God uses angelic agents to execute his judgments, John knows who is ultimately in control of them. We see the same dynamic in the prose preface to the book of Job where he uses an angel known as "the accuser" (or "executioner") to bring suffering into the life of Job.[2] We also see God using an angel to bring judgment on King Ahab. The prophet Micaiah tells the king that he had a vision of God on his heavenly throne, commissioning an angel (called "a spirit") to put a lying spirit into the mouth of the king's prophets so they will go out and will convince Ahab that he will defeat the city of Ramoth Gilead, even though he will not and will actually die in the attempt (1 Ki 22:19–23).

But they refused to repent and glorify him. Again, we think of the plagues that were sent against Egypt, which intended to elicit repentance and the release of the Israelite slaves. But Pharaoh remained adamant until the very end, and so those who worship the beast also resist the call to repentance and worship.

The Fifth Bowl (16:10–11)

16:10 *The fifth angel poured out his bowl on the throne of the beast.* The beast set itself up as a rival to Christ (see notes at 13:2 and 3), who is seated on a heavenly throne. The first four bowls of God's wrath brought punishment on those who worshipped the beast, now the fifth strikes at the beast itself.

And its kingdom was plunged into darkness. While there is no mention of the darkening of the sun here, we again (see note at 16:8) may have an echo of the plague of darkness at the time of the exodus.

People gnawed their tongues in agony. The assault on the throne of the beast plunged its kingdom into darkness with the result that his followers chewed their tongues in pain. It is unclear whether the pain is because of the tongue gnashing or that they gnash their tongue because of the pain. But this can also be a response to fear and anxiety.

16:11 *Cursed the God of heaven . . . they refused to repent of what they had done.* As we saw in the aftermath of the pouring out of the fourth bowl (16:9), those who felt the effects of the punishment represented by the fifth bowl also did not repent, but rather cursed God.

The Sixth Bowl (16:12–16)

16:12 *The sixth angel poured out his bowl on the great river Euphrates.* The sixth bowl results in the drying up of the Euphrates, the river that during the Old Testament time separated Syria-Palestine from the great Mesopotamian empires, including Babylon, which represents Rome, and indeed the worldly kingdoms that try to dominate God's kingdom.

To prepare the way for the kings from the East. During the Old Testament period, God used the kings of Assyria and later Babylon as tools of his judgment. During the time when the book of Revelation was written, the great threat to the Roman Empire came from east of the Euphrates, namely the Parthians. The divine drying up of the waters of a river allowed easier crossing for God's people to enter the promised land and then conquer the Canaanites (Jos 3:1–4:24). Likewise here, judgment will come on those who oppress God's people, and they will receive the victory promised by God.

Going Deeper into Judgment and the Environment: Revelation 16

Today, we are sensitive to issues concerning the environment and rightly so. The threat of global warming already is having an adverse effect on our world and threatens to grow even more dangerous in the coming decades. Throughout my lifetime there has been an increasing concern about pollution of our seas and land, but also on the part of some a resistance to acknowledging the full extent of the threat—and on the part of some Christians, even something of an attitude of indifference. After all, some reason, why should we care about issues like climate change or pollution if this world is going to just be destroyed at the end and we are all going to go to heaven? While it is hard to know how pervasive this view is among Christians, there is little doubt that people outside the church believe that Christians hold that view. Some also believe that the Bible supports that view.

Some believe Genesis 1 encourages the exploitation of the environment. After all, God declares the first humans to be created in his image of God and commissioned to "subdue" the earth and "rule over" all the other creatures (Ge 1:28). Further, when God judges humans for their sin, he not only punishes them but also harms the environment, the flood being an early example (Ge 6–9).

In the book of Revelation too, God's judgment includes damage on the environment. Even restricting ourselves to Revelation 16, we see several examples. After the second angel poured out his bowl on the sea, the sea turned into blood and everything that lived in the sea died. When the third angel poured out his bowl, "the rivers and springs of water . . . became blood" (16:4). Pouring out the sixth bowl resulted in the Euphrates River drying up (16:12). Again, similar examples may be drawn from other descriptions of God's judgment in the book of Revelation.

Does this indicate to us that God does not care about the environment? Does it mean that his intention is to destroy the world as we know it and replace the earth with heaven? Does it mean that when we die we will go to a nonmaterial spiritual realm and so we should not care about this present earth?

Absolutely not! Such a view results from a faulty understanding of key texts, starting with Genesis 1.[3] The key to understand God's commission to subdue and rule creation is that we are to reflect the one whose image we bear. God is not an exploitative king, but a benevolent king of the creation that he created "good." Thus, rather than an excuse to violate, our commission is a mandate to steward creation.

According to Genesis 2–3, God's good creation experiences problems not because God created it that way, but because sin disrupted the harmony between God and humans and thus between humans and creation. We see a glimpse of this in the punishment directed at Adam that now his work on the land will be marred by "thorns and thistles" (Ge 3:18). We also hear of sin's impact on the created order when Paul, reflecting on Genesis 3, tells his readers that "the creation was subjected to frustration" and is in "bondage to decay" (Ro 8:20–21).

However, sin does not eradicate our responsibility as God's image-bearers. After all, the story of God's creation is not one doomed to decay and then eradication. Rather, the future does not see the destruction of creation as we know it but transformation, and this transformation comes via God's judgment. The book of Revelation itself does not speak of a transition from earth to heaven, but rather, as we will see in Revelation 21–22, to a new heaven and a new earth.

That is why the psalms picture creation rejoicing at the coming of God to judge the earth (Ps 98:7–9). And Paul himself speaks of the creation waiting "in eager expectation" because "the creation itself will be liberated from its bondage to decay and brought into the freedom and glory of the children of God" (Ro 8:19, 21).

In the interim, God's people do not simply sit back and wait for God to transform his creation any more than we should simply ignore the health of our bodies. Yes, creation will struggle to the end and our bodies will ultimately give out when we die.[4] But just we will be transformed into a resurrected body, so the creation will not be discarded, but rather transformed. In the meantime, we work for the health of our environment.

16:13 *I saw three impure spirits that looked like frogs.* Three frogs emerge from the mouths of the dragon (Satan; see note at 12:9) and his two agents, the sea beast and the land beast. The only other place where frogs are mentioned in the Bible is in connection with the plague of frogs that came right after

God brought the plague of blood on the Nile (Ex 8:1–5, see also Ps 78:45; 105:30). Here after the plague that struck the Euphrates and dried up its waters, three frogs representing impure spirits emerge from the mouths of the unholy trinity of dragon, sea beast, and land beast. It is possible that the plague of frogs at the time of the exodus was thought to be an assault on the frog-headed goddess of fertility, Heqet.

The mouth of the false prophet. In earlier descriptions of the land beast, we noted that he functioned as a false prophet, bearing witness to the sea beast (see notes at 13:12 and 14), but this is the first time that this beast is explicitly called a false prophet (see also 19:20; 20:10). False prophets in the Old Testament are whose who either bear witness to another god or whose message is misleading and not from the true God. Such prophets deserve death (Dt 13:1–5; 18:14–22).

16:14 *They are demonic spirits that perform signs.* Impure is here further qualified as demonic. As demonic forces, they do have the ability to perform signs, but since their signs point away from the true God and toward a false god, they should be ignored and not followed. At the time of the exodus, the Egyptian wise men were able to mimic the divinely given signs performed by Moses and Aaron (turning their staffs into serpents and water into blood). They apparently got the ability to do so from their gods, whom God ultimately defeats (Ex 12:12). Their gods are really demonic powers.

To gather them for the battle on the great day of God Almighty. See note at 6:17.

God Almighty. See note at 11:17.

16:15 *I come like a thief!* The first-person speaker is Jesus, who will come quietly and with surprise on the day of God's judgment. The point is that there will not be signs that will indicate that he will appear; he will appear suddenly. Thieves can only do their work if they come quietly and without announcement. The roots of this simile are found in Jesus' own words when he told his disciples that the time of his return is not known and will not be made known. Because of that, he tells them, "keep watch, because you do not know on what day your Lord will come. But understand this: If the owner of the house had known at what time of night the thief was coming, he would have kept watch and would not have let his house be broken into. So you also must be ready, because the Son of Man will come at an hour when you do not expect him" (Mt 24:42–44). Paul too informed the church in Thessalonica that they knew "very well that the day of the Lord will come like a thief in the night" (1 Th 5:2, see also 2 Pe 3:10).

Blessed is the one. This is the third of seven blessings in the book (see note at 1:3).

So as not to go naked and be shamefully exposed. In the garden of Eden, Adam and Eve were "both naked, and they felt no shame" (Ge 2:25). Because they lived in harmony with God, they lived in harmony with each other and therefore could be completely open to each other. In the aftermath of their sin recorded in Genesis 3, their relationship with God was broken and they could no longer stand naked without shame in each other's presence. There was too much to hide. As a sign of his grace, God gave them clothes to wear (Ge 3:21). Thus, while the Song of Songs attests to the possibility of the redemption of sexual relationship,[5] nakedness and shame are intertwined with each other. Shameful exposure as a metaphor for sin may be seen, among others, in a judgment oracle in the prophet Nahum. He taunts the Assyrian city of Nineveh by saying:

> "I am against you," declares the LORD Almighty.
>   "I will lift your skirts over your face.
> I will show the nations your nakedness
>   and the kingdoms your shame.
> I will pelt you with filth,
>   I will treat you with contempt
>   and make you a spectacle.
> All who see you will flee from you and say,
>   'Nineveh is in ruins—who will mourn for her?'
>   Where can I find anyone to comfort you?"
> (Na 3:5–7; see also Isa 47:3; Eze 16:37; Hos 2:3)[6]

16:16 *Gathered the kings together to the place that in Hebrew is called Armageddon.*[7] The froglike demonic spirits gather the kings at a place called Armageddon. The name means "mountain of Megiddo," but there is no mountain known by that name. That said, the city of Megiddo was near mountains, so it may not be a specific place name, but just a geographical reference. Indeed, Megiddo may have suggested itself because it was a place of strategic importance where many battles have been fought through the years going back to biblical times and up to the present day. In Deborah's song, celebrating Israel's victory over the Canaanites led by Jabin, we read:

> Kings came, they fought,
>   the kings of Canaan fought.
> At Taanach, by the waters of Megiddo,
>   they took no plunder of silver. (Jdg 5:19)

Perhaps the most famous Old Testament battle at Megiddo took place in 609 BC during the reign of King Josiah. At that time, Necho king of Egypt marched his army up the coast through Israel in an attempt to bolster Assyrian forces against the Babylonians. The coast highway jogs inland at Megiddo, and Israel under Josiah attacked the Egyptians at that place. The Israelites were unsuccessful and Josiah himself was killed (2 Ki 23:29–30; 2 Ch 35:20–27).

The highly figurative nature of the description of the end in the book of Revelation means that we should not understand this reference as pointing to an actual battle in the vicinity of Megiddo. The idea of the massing of angry kings for battle also reminds us yet again (see "Revelation 5:10 Through Old Testament Eyes: Kingdom and Priests" and note at 11:8) of Psalm 2:

> Why do the nations conspire
> > and the peoples plot in vain?
> The kings of the earth rise up
> > and rulers band together
> > against the LORD and against his anointed, saying,
> "Let us break their chains
> > and throw off their shackles." (Ps 2:1–3)

There may also be a connection with Ezekiel's vision of a great final battle and God's victory over the nations in Ezekiel 38 and 39. Here the final victory over the nations will take place on the "mountains of Israel" (39:2, 4, 17).

The Seventh Bowl (16:17–21)

16:17 *The seventh angel poured out his bowl . . . "It is done!"* The final and climactic angel pours out the contents of his bowl on the air and this brings, as the number seven symbolically suggests, the cycle of judgments to an end.

16:18 *Flashes of lightning, rumblings, peals of thunder.* God's appearance in judgment is often accompanied by fierce storms (see notes at 4:5; 8:5; 14:2). We should take special notice of similar description at the unsealing of the seventh seal (8:5) and the blowing of the seventh trumpet (16:18).

No earthquake like it has ever occurred since mankind has been on earth. God's coming in judgment was often accompanied by terrestrial convulsions, particularly earthquakes (Isa 29:6; Eze 38:19; Zec 14:5). Earlier in Revelation, they resulted from the opening of the sixth seal (see notes at 6:12, 14), the seventh seal (see note at 8:5), at the time the two witnesses were taken to heaven (see note at 11:13), and with the sounding of the seventh trumpet (see note at

11:19). That the earthquake that follows the pouring out of the contents of the seventh bowl is described as unprecedented in intensity indicates its climatic place among the descriptions of judgment.

16:19 *The great city . . . Babylon the Great.* Old Testament Babylon represented the evil human kingdoms that oppressed God's people. The use of Babylon as a symbolic reference to Rome will become even more obvious in Revelation 17. But as Tabb points out, Rome itself points beyond itself: "Babylon is not simply a cipher for Rome but is a rich biblical-theological symbol for the world's idolatrous, seductive political economy—the archetypal godless city."[8]

The cup filled with the wine of the fury of his wrath. See note at 14:10.

16:20 *Every island fled away and the mountains.* The islands represent the far reaches of the earth and the mountains represent grandeur and permanence (Ps 46), but they both flee away (by way of poetic personification) because of their fear of God's judgment. In Psalm 114, the sea and the mountains were described as fleeing from the presence of God:

> When Israel came out of Egypt,
> > Jacob from a people of foreign tongue,
> Judah became God's sanctuary,
> > Israel his dominion.
> The sea looked and fled,
> > the Jordan turned back;
> the mountains leaped like rams,
> > the hills like lambs. (Ps 114:1–4)

16:21 *Hailstones, each weighing about a hundred pounds.* Here we have yet another similarity with the Egyptian plagues, since God brought hail down on the Egyptians because they would not let the Israelites depart Egypt (Ex 9:13–35). But this is not the only time that God used hail as an instrument of his judgment. As the southern coalition of Canaanite kings fled before Joshua, God extended the day and rained hailstones on their head. The result was that "more of them [Canaanites] died from the hail than were killed by the swords of the Israelites" (Jos 10:11). The prophets also spoke of future judgment coming in the form of a devastating hailstorm (Isa 28:17; 30:30; 32:19; Eze 13:11, 13; 38:22). Here the hailstones are of immense size, thus indicating the climactic and unprecedented nature of his judgment.

They cursed God. Rather than repenting in the light of God's judgment, they curse him (see also 16:9, 11).

What the Structure Means: Seals, Trumpets, and Bowls (Rev 6:1–7:5; 8:7–11:19; 15:1–16:21)

Reading through the book of Revelation, one is struck by three series, or cycles, of seven judgments. The first series follows the opening of the seven seals of a scroll (6:1–7:5), the second follows the blowing of seven trumpets (8:7–11:19), and then finally there are seven judgments that follow the pouring out of seven bowls of wrath (15:1–16:21). Though not following each other immediately in the narrative of the book, they are bound together not only by being cycles of seven judgments, but, according to Bauckham, because "the seventh-seal opening includes the seven trumpets and the seventh trumpet includes the seven bowls."[9]

How are these series related to each other? Are they sequential, so that the seven bowls follow the seven trumpets after the seven seals, with a total of twenty-one judgments? This view is unlikely because the devastation in each of the cycles is such, even understood figuratively, that there would not be much left for the following cycle. Or are they giving three versions of the same seven plagues? This view also seems unlikely, since if you compare the three cycles with each other, they don't line up in that way: the unsealing of the first seal leads to war; the blowing of the first trumpet results in one third of the earth, trees, and grass being burned up by hail and fire mixed with blood; when an angel pours out the contents of the first bowl, boils break out on people who have the "mark of the beast" (16:2).

The best way to view the relationship is to see them in a spiral fashion, with each cycle moving further and further toward the end. This perspective is supported by the way that the third cycle, the bowls, are described. In the introduction to the seven bowls, we read that John "saw in heaven another great and marvelous sign: seven angels with the seven last plagues—last, because with them God's wrath is completed" (15:1). Notice the emphasis on these being the last plagues and that with them God's wrath against sin is completed, in the sense of "finished." In addition, with the pouring out of the seventh bowl, we hear a loud voice from the throne in the heavenly temple, meaning that it is the voice of God himself, saying, "It is done!" Thus, it is best to see the relationship between these three cycles of seven as recapitulating each other and carrying the picture further each time.

Even though we believe that is the best understanding of the relationship between the three cycles of seven, the climactic role of the bowls does not mean that John will receive no further visions of the final climactic battle between God and his heavenly forces and evil spiritual and human forces. More is yet to come before the concluding vision that will take us beyond the end of evil to the final establishment of God's kingdom described as a new heavens and a new earth, a New Jerusalem, and a restored, yet better, Eden (Rev 21–22).

But before we leave the subject of the three cycles of seven, we want to make a few more observations on the similarities and differences between them. In particular, consider the role of interludes in the telling of the cycles as well as the similarity between the seventh seal, the seventh trumpet, and the seventh bowl.

The description of the opening of the seals is interrupted after the sixth seal (6:9–11) with an interlude that calls out to the four angels who were "given the power to harm the land and the sea" (7:2) to hold off until they put the seal on "the foreheads of the servants of our God" (7:3) followed by a picture of a white-robed multitude of people praising God who are then joined by the twenty-four elders and the four living creatures (7:9–17).

The description of the blowing of the seven trumpets follows the same pattern as the seals where the first six trumpets are described consecutively (8:7–9:21), but then there is a lengthy interlude before the telling of the seventh trumpet (11:15–19). There are two episodes in the interlude here, the first giving the account of a little scroll ingested by John the prophet (10:1–11) and the second telling the story of the "two witnesses" (11:1–14).

The function of the delay between the sixth and seventh seals and trumpets serves to heighten the dramatic tension. At first we might be surprised that there is no interlude in the bowl cycle; the seventh bowl (16:17–21) immediately follows the telling of the pouring out of the sixth bowl (16:12–16). Perhaps this results from this cycle being the climactic last one.

Finally, we take note of the similar nature of the seventh seal, trumpet, and bowl. After a half-hour silence, when an angel throws a censer of fire to the earth, followed by "peals of thunder, rumblings, flashes of lightning and an earthquake" (8:5). Likewise, after the blowing of the seventh trumpet, we peer into God's heavenly temple and see the ark of the covenant, and then "there came flashes of lightning, rumblings, peals of thunder, an earthquake and a severe hailstorm" (11:19). Then finally when the angel pours out the contents of the seventh bowl, "there came flashes of lightning, rumblings, peals of thunder and a severe earthquake" (16:18).

Similar, yes, and in the commentary we describe how these terrestrial and meteorological convulsions relate to the appearance of God as warrior. But there is once again an intensity to the description that follows the pouring out of the final bowl that is not paralleled by the seventh seal or the seventh trumpet. All three describe an earthquake, but the earthquake connected to the seventh bowl was like no earthquake that ever occurred before and resulted in the great city being split into three parts and other cities of the world collapsing. And while the seventh trumpet mentions hail, the hailstones which accompanied the final bowl were a hundred pounds each. Thus, even with the similarity there is a sense of climax to the final cycle.

REVELATION 17

The Demise of the Great Prostitute (17:1–19:10)

The Great Prostitute Riding the Beast (17:1–6)

17:1 *Come, I will show you the punishment of the great prostitute.* One of the angels who carried a bowl of God's wrath beckons John to come see the punishment of a figure referred to as "the great prostitute." By having one of the angels from the previous episode become John's guide provides a transition to the next episode and links it with the previous episode. The identity of the great prostitute—that is, what she represents—will be revealed in what follows, but for now we should note that a prostitute was often a symbol of idolatry. Just as a prostitute violates the exclusive covenant bond of marriage, so an idolater worships a false god in the place of the true God. In the Old Testament there is a pervasive metaphor of God's relationship with his people being like that of a husband with a wife. Just as a wife can have one and only one husband through that intimate bond created by covenant commitment, so a person can have one and only one God, namely Yahweh. Thus, in the Old Testament, Hosea's marriage to a prostitute named Gomer was illustrative of God's relationship with Israel at the time (see Hos 1; see also Eze 16 and 23). We see this analogy in the Torah as well, where false worship is considered a form of spiritual prostitution: "They must no longer offer any of their sacrifices to the goat idols to whom they prostitute themselves" (Lev 17:7, see also Ex 34:15; Lev 20:5–6; Nu 15:39; Dt 31:16). In the prophets, foreign nations too are likened to prostitutes (Isa 23:15–17; Na 3:4).

Who sits by many waters. Waters in many forms (especially the sea, rivers, the deep) often connote chaos and evil. We have already witnessed this in several earlier places in Revelation (4:6; 12:15; 13:1; 16:3). In the ancient Near

East, Baal fought Yamm, the sea, while in Babylon Marduk defeated Tiamat, the sea. The phrase "many waters" shares the connotation of chaos and evil in the Old Testament. The Hebrew phrase is *mayim rabbim* and occurs several times in the Old Testament.[1] Since the NIV translates the phrase *mayim rabbim* in different ways, italics will mark the phrase in the following examples:

> The voice of the LORD is over the waters;
>   the God of glory thunders,
>   the LORD thunders over the *mighty waters*. (Ps 29:3)

> Mightier than the thunder of the *great waters*,
>   mightier than the breakers of the sea—
>   the LORD on high is mighty. (Ps 93:4)

> Although the peoples roar like the roar of *surging waters*,
>   when he [God] rebukes them they flee far away. (Isa 17:13)

> The LORD will destroy Babylon;
>   he will silence her noisy din.
> Waves of enemies will rage like *great waters*;
>   the roar of their voices will resound. (Jer 51:55)

The fact that the prostitute sits by the many waters indicates that she is a force of chaos and evil. In the Old Testament God controls and ultimately defeats the many waters. The same fate awaits the prostitute. The reference to the people of Babylon raging like "many waters" is especially important in the light of the fact that below we will learn that this prostitute represents Babylon the Great which itself is a cipher for Rome (and all godless worldly powers).

Going Deeper into the Intersection of Idolatry and Adultery: Revelation 17

In Revelation 17 we meet the "great prostitute," with whom the "kings of the earth committed adultery, and the inhabitants of the earth were intoxicated with the wine of her adulteries" (17:1–2). The prostitute is later called Babylon the Great (17:5), which is clearly a cipher for the Roman Empire and ultimately all worldly power that resists the true God.

The original readers of John's reported vision would have understood immediately that adultery signified idolatry, the worship of a false god.

Here in the book of Revelation the charge is that people worshiped not the triune God, but rather the power of Rome. They put Rome first.

The metaphor that compares idolatry to adultery is a longstanding one in the Bible and, as all powerful metaphors do, throws important light on the nature of idolatry. Behind this expression is the root metaphor of God's relationship to his people being a marriage. Since in the Old Testament the marriage has gone awry, we only get glimpses of a positive use of the root metaphor, and then typically the perspective is backward-looking. In Jeremiah, for instance, we hear God say, "I remember the devotion of your youth, how as a bride you loved me and followed me through the wilderness, through a land not sown" (2:2; see also Hos 2:14–15). More typically God's disobedient people are pictured as promiscuously seeking other lovers like a prostitute (Eze 16, 23; Hos 1, 3; and numerous places throughout the Old Testament).

The New Testament, though, uses the metaphor more positively, as we see in Ephesians 5:21–33. Here Paul likens the church's relationship to Christ to a marriage, calling for husbands and wives to submit to each other (5:21–22) and love and respect each other (5:25). After citing the Genesis text that establishes marriage ("That is why a man leaves his father and mother and is united to his wife, and they become one flesh." 2:24), he explains "this is a profound mystery—but I am talking about Christ and the church" (Eph 5:32).

Every metaphor of our relationship with God that we encounter in Scripture (king, shepherd, warrior, rock, and countless others) illumines some aspect of his nature and of our relationship with him. In this case, we have a metaphor used predominantly on the negative side, showing a broken relationship, but we understand this better if we also see the positive side.

How is our relationship with God like a marriage? Marriage as divinely intended is an exclusive relationship between a man and a woman.[2] Indeed, it is the only human-to-human relationship which is mutually exclusive. God's people are likened to a wife who can only have one husband. If the wife enters an intimate relationship with another man, then she has broken that exclusive relationship and committed adultery.

The marriage metaphor stands behind those texts that speak of God's jealousy (e.g., Ex 20:4–6), which in human relationships is often abused,

> but can be a redemptive energy to restore a broken relationship. God
> demands our exclusive loyalty. After all if we make anything or anyone
> other than God the most important thing in our life, it will let us down
> and harm us.

17:2 *Committed adultery.* She is a prostitute, and it turns out that earthly kings committed adultery with her. Since adultery often represents idolatry (see note at 17:1), the point is that they too betrayed their exclusive relationship with God. The prophet Nahum described the Assyrian capital city Nineveh using similar language: "the wanton lust of a prostitute, alluring, the mistress of sorceries, who enslaved nations by her prostitution and peoples by her witchcraft" (Na 3:4).

Intoxicated with the wine of her adulteries. See note at 14:8 which celebrates the fall of Babylon, "which made all the nations drink the maddening wine of her adulteries." The similarity of reference here hints already that the prostitute stands for Babylon, which itself stands for the Roman Empire.

17:3 *In the Spirit.* This is the third (see 1:10 and 4:2) of four (see also 21:10) occurrences of this phrase that highlights John's prophetic role. He speaks in the Spirit, that is, under divine inspiration. This phrase also occurs at the beginning of important structural divisions, here at the beginning of the description of a prostitute riding a beast, representing Babylon, while the next occurrence at 21:10 will introduce the contrasting vision of the New Jerusalem.

Into a wilderness. In Revelation 12:14, we saw that the woman who represented the church fled to the wilderness and was pursued by the dragon (Satan). There the wilderness was a place of sanctuary. The wilderness location of the prostitute, though, may recall the Old Testament wilderness as a place of temptation for the Israelites as they traveled toward the promised land. As we have seen in the previous verse, many have fallen prey to her seductions. Since the woman represents Babylon the Great (see 17:5), there may also be a connection with an oracle against Babylon found in the book of Isaiah:

A prophecy against the Desert [or Wilderness] by the Sea:

Like whirlwinds sweeping through the southland,
> an invader comes from the desert,
> from a land of terror. (Isa 21:1; see v. 9)

A woman sitting on a scarlet beast that was covered with blasphemous names. The prostitute rides a beast the color of blood, suggesting that she deals in death.

For blasphemous names, see note at 13:1 where we learn that the dragon that stands for Satan has seven heads that each had a blasphemous name.

Seven heads and ten horns. See note at 13:1. Like the dragon (12:3) and the sea beast (13:1–10), the beast that carries the woman has seven heads and ten horns, both numbers that convey completeness. Indeed, this beast is likely to be connected to the beast first introduced in Revelation 13. The seven heads of the beast mimic the many-headed Leviathan in the Old Testament which has as its background the seven-headed Lothan of Ugaritic mythology (see note at 12:3).

17:4 *The woman was dressed in purple and scarlet.* The colors of royalty and blood respectively.

Glittering with gold, precious stones and pearls. Here jewel and precious metal ornamented clothing emphasize her incredible wealth. Imperial Rome was indeed wealthy beyond imagination.

A golden cup in her hand, filled with abominable things and the filth of her adulteries. We would expect a wealthy person, or perhaps royalty, to drink from an expensive cup, but the beautiful exterior has something vile in it, the "wine of her adulteries" (see note at 17:2).

17:5 *The name written on her forehead was a mystery.* For "mystery," see notes at 1:20; 10:7; 17:7.

BABYLON THE GREAT THE MOTHER OF PROSTITUTES AND OF THE ABOMINATIONS OF THE EARTH. While the beast she rode bore blasphemous names, the woman herself had a name prominently displayed on her forehead. She is identified as Babylon the Great, the nation that under their king Nebuchadnezzar had defeated Jerusalem, destroyed its temple, and exiled its leading citizens in the year 586 BC. However, Babylon was no more. Here she represents another, more contemporary foe to the people of God (see 17:9). We have already been introduced to her as a "great prostitute" (see note on 17:1). Here she is called the mother of prostitutes. She not only is a prostitute, but she has produced many others like her. As a prostitute who violates marriage covenants, she is an abomination, something deeply wrong which evokes revulsion.

17:6 *The woman was drunk with the blood of God's holy people.* Drunkenness leaves one uninhibited, disoriented, and often out of control. One can imagine that the woman's drunkenness might lead to wanton destruction and death. But at a certain point the drunk staggers and collapses. The prophets used the picture of drunkenness to highlight the ultimate demise of the wicked (Isa 51:17, 21–23; 63:6; Jer 25:27–29; Na 3:11). But then there are also pictures in the Old Testament of people being drunk on blood. In Isaiah 49:26, we read that God will bring judgment on Israel's oppressors. God announces, "I will make your oppressors eat their own flesh; they will be drunk on their own blood, as with wine." Then in Ezekiel 39, we read in the oracle against Gog, the chief prince of Meshek and Tubal (see note at 20:8), whom God has used to punish his sinful people, that he will himself become the object of judgment. Rather than animals being sacrificed, Gog's army will be sacrificed and consumed by the animals in a big gory banquet. God tells Ezekiel (the "son of man" in 39:17) to announce to the animals, "'You will eat the flesh of mighty men and drink the blood of the princes of the earth as if they were rams and lambs, goats and bulls—all of them fattened animals from Bashan. At the sacrifice I am preparing for you, you will eat fat till you are glutted and drink blood till you are drunk. At my table you will eat your fill of horses and riders, mighty men and soldiers of every kind,' declare the Sovereign LORD" (Eze 39:18–20). See note at 19:17–18 for a similar gory banquet.

The Mystery Explained (17:7–18)

17:7 *The mystery of the woman and of the beast she rides.* A mystery is something veiled from understanding at least until there is a further disclosure about its meaning. In apocalyptic literature, interpreting angels have the role of assigning meaning to the highly symbolic language of the visions given to the seer, in this case John, and in the Old Testament God reveals the mystery to Daniel (2:17–23, 30, 47). See also notes at Rev 1:20 and 10:7.

17:8 *The beast . . . once was, now is not, and yet will come out of the Abyss.* The Lord Almighty has been described earlier in Revelation as "him who is, and who was, and who is to come" (see note at 1:4, with variants at 1:8; 4:8; 11:17). God is a being with a past, present, and future. The beast, however, was in the past, but is not now present, but will come out of the Abyss (see notes at 9:1 and 11:7). This beast was in the past (13:1–10). We might remember that the beast was described as having "a fatal wound," but that "the fatal wound had been healed" (13:3). Also, we might remember that in the previous chapter, the fifth angel poured out his bowl of God's wrath on the throne of the beast "and its kingdom was plunged into darkness" (16:10). Perhaps this explains the "is not," but whatever the scenario there is a future for the beast in that he will again come again out of the Abyss.

Whose names have not been written in the book of life from the creation of the world. According to Revelation 13:8, "All inhabitants of the earth will worship the beast—all whose names have not been written in the Lamb's book of life, the Lamb who was slain from the creation of the world" (see note at

13:8 for the background in Ps 69). So here it is those who worship the beast who are astonished that he has come back to life again.

17:9 *This calls for a mind with wisdom.* See note at 13:18. This mystery (17:7) takes wisdom to unravel. On the one hand, wisdom is acquired by study and observation and experience, but wisdom is also a gift of God. Here, as the next verses demonstrate, the mind of wisdom is informed by the angel's explanation of the significance of the vision that John sees. We see this type of divine gift of wisdom in Daniel 2 where Daniel can tell Nebuchadnezzar the king's dream as well as its interpretation. Daniel can only get that type of information if God chooses to disclose it to him through revelation. He does and Daniel proclaims:

> Praise be to the name of God for ever and ever;
>   wisdom and power are his. . . .
> He gives wisdom to the wise
>   and knowledge to the discerning.
> He reveals deep and hidden things;
>   he knows what lies in darkness,
>   and light dwells in him. (Da 2:20–22)

The seven heads are seven hills on which the woman sits. Here it becomes obvious that the woman ("Babylon the Great") and the beast represent Rome, the city which was famously situated on seven hills. Referring to Rome as "Babylon the Great" is not so much to have a code that people outside the church would not understand, but to draw connections between Rome and that horrific enemy of Israel in the past.

17:10 *They are also seven kings. Five have fallen, one is, the other has not yet come.* While the seven heads represent the seven hills of the city of Rome, they also represent seven kings, presumably of Rome, showing the polyvalent nature of symbolism. Five of these kings have fallen, presumably meaning they have reigned and died. One is, presumably meaning that he presently reigns. And one is to come, presumably a successor to the one who is presently ruling. But this seventh king will only have a short reign. The question of the identity of these kings (or perhaps, some believe, they are kingdoms) is much debated.[3] Hoskins persuasively suggests that we are not to look for seven kings (or kingdoms) here, but that seven is a symbolic number which reaches back to the past and stand for "the rulers in history who have shown by their rule that they are followers of the beast and the dragon rather than followers of God and of the Lamb."[4]

He must remain for only a little while. The final, seventh, king (see next verse) will be climactic, but will only last for a brief period.

17:11 *An eighth king.* The beast's seven heads stand for the seven hills of Rome as well as seven kings, but now we hear of an eighth king who is the beast himself, the one who once was, and now is not, but will come. How is he the eighth king and yet belongs to the seven? This question is difficult and not amenable to a dogmatic answer, but Hoskins, in my opinion, gets it right, when he says, "the beast is more than the seventh king, he is also an eighth king, because he is and has always been the power behind the seven kings, his seven heads (17:11). As the second member of the dragon's unholy trinity,[5] he is greater than merely the sum of his heads. He will reveal the fullness of his power when he ascends from the Abyss to wage war with the Lamb in the final battle (17:14). His defeat will mean the end of his rule and the end of his story."[6]

17:12 *The ten horns you saw are ten kings.* For "horn" as symbolic of power, see note at 5:6. In the previous paragraph, we observed that the seven heads of the beast represented both the seven hills of Rome, which is itself representative of evil human kingdoms through the centuries, and seven kings. We noted that the number seven was not to be taken to indicate seven specific kings, but rather godless rulers who oppressed the people of God through the ages. The picture of them as the heads of the beast means that they derive their power from the beast.

Now we hear that the ten horns of the beast are ten kings who will come ("who have not yet received a kingdom") who will rule at the same time as the beast (the final king in v. 11). Just as the final king is to "remain for only a little while" (v. 10), so these ten kings will have authority along with the beast for a short period of time ("for one hour"). Like seven, ten should be taken as a symbolic number representing all the world powers of the time and not specifically ten.

17:13 *They have one purpose.* The picture the vision draws is of all the world powers ranged against Jesus, here called the Lamb, who are supporting the beast's efforts to defeat the Lamb. See "Revelation 5:6 Through Old Testament Eyes: The Lamb Who Was Slain."

17:14 *They will wage war against the Lamb.* Ever since the fall, there has been a conflict between those who follow God and those who follow the serpent (understood by New Testament times to stand for the devil, Ge 3:15). During the Old Testament period, God the warrior would fight on behalf of his faithful people (and against them when they themselves turned against God).

Jesus revealed himself as the divine warrior and heightened and intensified the battle so that it was directed not against "flesh and blood," but toward the spiritual powers and authorities (Eph 6:10–20). Throughout the book of Revelation, and pointedly here, we read about the denouement of this battle, which will lead to the destruction of both God's spiritual and physical enemies.[7] See "Going Deeper into Jesus the Divine Warrior Who Defeats Evil" after Revelation 22.

But the Lamb will triumph over them. The beast and his ten kings are no match for the power of the Lamb. The battle here is not described at all, just an announcement of the Lamb's victory, giving the impression of an easy victory.

He is Lord of lords and King of kings. In the Old Testament, the title "king of kings" is given to the most powerful king alive and is applied to Nebuchadnezzar the king of the Babylonian empire (Eze 26:7; Da 2:37) and Artaxerxes the later king of the extensive Persian empire (Ezr 7:12). God, of course, is the ultimate King of kings, though that title is not used of God until the New Testament (1 Ti 6:15). The title "Lord of lords," though, is used exclusively in reference to God in the Old Testament (Dt 10:17; Ps 136:3; see also 1 Ti 6:15 which is the only place where the two titles are used together outside of Rev 17:14 and 19:16). Here the titles are used to refer to the Lamb, Jesus, whom we know as the second person of the Trinity.

With him will be his called, chosen and faithful followers. At the time of the writing of Revelation, the people of God were oppressed, but this vision places before them the sure hope of victory over their persecutors. These are the people who have responded to the divine call to relationship with him. They are God's chosen and they have responded with faith and obedience.

17:15 *The waters you saw . . . are peoples, multitudes, nations, and languages.* In the note at 17:1 we saw that the great prostitute sat on "many waters," a term that has mythological connotations connected to chaos and evil. Here we learn that chaos comes in the form of people from many different countries, speaking many different languages on whom the prostitute sits, a metaphor of domination.

17:16 *The beast and the ten horns you saw will hate the prostitute.* Surprisingly, the beast on which the woman rides turns against her. Surprising too because all parties represent evil forces, but they apparently turn on each other.

Leave her naked; they will eat her flesh and burn her with fire. The prostitute will be annihilated by the beast and its accompanying ten kings. They will leave her naked (a shameful exposure that was a punishment experienced by prostitutes during the Old Testament time and that was utilized by the prophets in judgment oracles; Eze 16:39; Hos 2:3; Na 3:5). But the beast will do more than simply shame her; he will destroy her, eating her flesh and finally annihilating her by burning her corpse with fire.

17:17 *For God has put it into their hearts to accomplish his purpose.* Now we know the real reason why the beast and its associated kings turn against the woman: God has made it so. God is in control, and he will have the final victory. He will even use evil powers to accomplish his judgment. We see this in the Old Testament in how God used Babylon to punish sinful Israel, but then turned against Babylon itself (Jer 51; Hab 1–2).

17:18 *The woman you saw is the great city.* The vision ends with a reminder of the identity of the woman. She represents the great city of Babylon (see note at 17:5), which represents the great city of Rome (see note at 17:9), which itself represents all worldly power that stands against God and his kingdom.

REVELATION 18

What the Structure Means:
The Fall of "Babylon the Great" (17:1–19:10)

This major section (17:1–19:10) presents a vision of the fall of "Babylon the Great," meaning Rome (see note on the "seven hills" at 17:9) along with the consequences for all those who support it. Again, the transition from the cycle of seven bowls to this one is marked by a simple connective conjunction, the Greek *kai* (untranslated in the NIV, though it could be either "and" or "then"). But a more substantial linkage comes when "one of the seven angels who had the seven bowls" (17:1) takes the lead and directs John to come so he could show him "the punishment of the great prostitute" (17:1). Indeed, we should think of this as a closer look at the fall of Babylon that was the focus of the seventh bowl (16:17–21). The chapter then is like other apocalyptic visions (see for instance Daniel 7) where the prophet sees a vision 17:3–6), and then an angel follows it up with an interpretation of the vision (17:7–18).

John is shocked by all God's people who are killed by the great prostitute of Babylon in his vision; the angel is surprised by John's reaction and proceeds to explain the vision, the details of which can be found in the running commentary.

The chapter ends with a surprising twist. After their defeat by the Lamb, the beast and the ten horns will turn on the prostitute and will destroy her. Why? We wouldn't be wrong to point out that evil is destructive by nature, bringing harm to the good, the true, and the beautiful. But evil's character can also become self-destructive, turning on itself. Rivalries among those who oppose God lead to just the scenario portrayed here.

But according to the angel there is a deeper reason behind this turn of events: "God has put it into their hearts to accomplish his purpose by agreeing to hand over to the beast their royal authority, until God's words are fulfilled" (17:17).

The transition from Revelation 17 to 18 is signaled by the phrase "after this" (18:1). After the vision and angelic interpretation of Babylon the Great's fall in chapter 17, we now hear the reaction to the news. First, "another angel" (18:1), then by another voice in heaven calling on God's people to depart the city both so they don't participate in the city's sin or share in its punishment. After this we get a reaction from three groups of people who benefitted from the city's corruption, riches, and power: kings (18:9–10), merchants (18:11–17), and sea captains (18:17–19). A counterpoint is then provided by heavenly and human followers of God. Rather than mourning, they rejoice that judgment has come on the city (18:20).

The chapter ends with an account of that judgment and a hymnic reaction. The destruction of the city here comes as a mighty angel picks up a boulder the size of a large millstone and throws it in into the sea.

Revelation 19 begins similarly to 18 with the simple connecting phrase "after this." So after the vision of the fall of Babylon the Great and its interpretation (Rev 17), followed by the mournful responses of those who benefitted from that city, a brief reaction of joy from heavenly and human voices that suffered at the hands of the city, and finally a depiction of its destruction, we now get pure celebration. Worship rises from several different quarters. First, from "a great multitude in heaven" (19:1–4), and then from a voice "from the throne" (presumably Christ, see note at 19:5) In response, the "great multitude" sings again their hallelujah and introduce the theme of the "wedding of the Lamb" (19:7, see also 21:2).

After this celebration, the angel turns to John and tells him to write down a blessing on those invited to the wedding supper of the Lamb.

Lament over the Destruction of Babylon (18:1–3)

18:1 *I saw another angel coming down from heaven.* Yet another angelic intermediary enters the scene. Though of great authority and splendor, the angel is not further identified.

The earth was illuminated by his splendor. See also the note at 21:11. In the Old Testament, there are various words that can be translated as "splendor," including *kabod* (most often translated "glory," as it is in 21:11). The Greek word translated "splendor" in this verse (*doxa*) is often used to translate *kabod* in the Old Testament (of many examples see Hab 2:14). In the Old Testament, glory is most often associated with God himself.[1] Light is associated with glory in the Old Testament:

> The moon will be dismayed,
> > the sun ashamed;
> for the LORD Almighty will reign
> > on Mount Zion and in Jerusalem,
> > and before its elders—with great glory. (Isa 24:23)

> Arise, shine, for your light has come,
> > and the glory of the LORD rises upon you.
> See, darkness covers the earth
> > and thick darkness is over the peoples,
> but the LORD rises upon you
> > and his glory appears over you.
> Nations will come to your light,
> > and kings to the brightness of your dawn. (Isa 60:1–3)

Here enough light to illuminate the earth accompanies the angel's splendor, his *doxa*.

18:2 *Fallen! Fallen is Babylon the Great!* This angel comes with a dire pronouncement of the end of Babylon the Great, beginning by quoting Isaiah where in an oracle against historical Babylon the prophet imagines an announcement given by a man in a chariot presumably coming from the city, saying, "Babylon has fallen, has fallen!" (Isa 21:9, see also note at Rev 14:8).

Demons . . . every impure spirit . . . every unclean bird . . . every unclean and detestable animal. Once the great city is destroyed and depopulated, vile creatures fill the void. Demons and ghosts and unclean birds and other animals roam about. Demons are rarely mentioned in the Old Testament. Most translations render the Hebrew terms *shedim* as "demons" (Dt 32:17; Ps 106:37) with the exception of the NIV 2011 which renders the word "false gods."[2] Evil spiritual forces are mentioned in Daniel 10 where the "prince of the Persian kingdom" (v. 13) and the "prince of Greece" (v. 20) are understood to be evil spiritual beings, which could also be understood as demons. Impure spirits are also not mentioned in the Old Testament but may refer to the ghosts of the wicked dead. The Old Testament does know of the *rephaim*, which is a word that in certain contexts refer to shades of the departed who are in Sheol (the grave typically, but sometimes with overtones of the underworld; Job 26:5; Ps 88:10; Pr 2:18; 9:18; Isa 14:9; 26:14, 19).[3] Still, we learn much more about the dark spiritual realm in the New Testament than in the Old.

In the Old Testament, though, the idea of unclean birds and other animals is well known (for instance, see Leviticus 11). We should also mention that the Old Testament often depicts destroyed cities as becoming the haunts of birds and animals, often those considered to be unclean (Jer 9:11 [Jerusalem]; Isa 13:21–22 [Babylon]; 34:13–15 [Edom]). Thus these creatures are associated with judgment.

18:3 *The maddening wine of her adulteries.* See note at 14:8 as well as at 17:2.
  The kings of the earth committed adultery with her. See note at 17:2.
  The merchants of the earth grew rich. One of the attractions of the prostitute who represents Babylon the Great, symbolic for Rome and all worldly power, is that people can grow rich, so they are willing to pay obeisance to her.

Going Deeper into the Danger of Wealth: Revelation 18

In Revelation 18 John sees an angel come down from heaven announcing the demise of Babylon the Great, a symbol of the Roman Empire and all godless human powers. The vision pictures Babylon the Great as a prostitute. Among those who have committed adultery with her (see "Going Deeper into the Intersection of Idolatry and Adultery: Revelation 17") are the "merchants of the earth" who "grew rich from her excessive luxuries" (18:3b). When the prostitute falls, "the merchants of the earth will weep and mourn over her because no one buys their cargoes anymore" (18:11). Later we read that their "luxury and splendor have vanished, never to be recovered" (18:14). In addition, sea captains will join in the lament:

> Woe! Woe to you, great city,
>   where all who had ships on the sea
>   became rich through her wealth!
> In one hour she has been brought to ruin! (18:19)

This vision warns of the seduction of riches and the horrible fate of those who are sucked into its pursuit as it involves entanglements with dark political and economic forces. In a word, the pursuit of wealth can easily entail idolatrous relationships or can become an idol itself.

In the letters to the seven churches, the glorified Christ warns and condemns those who would compromise their faith to enter the economic system of Rome. This would include those who would eat meat offered to idols so they could engage in a public ritual that would gain them access to the economic life of the city (Rev 2:14–15, 20).[4] In Revelation 13 John sees a beast emerge from the earth after witnessing a first beast come out of the sea. These both are agents of the dragon or Satan. This beast from the earth sets up a cult of worship for the sea beast and forces people to "receive a mark on their right hands or on their foreheads, so that they could not buy or sell unless they had the mark" (13:16–17). Those who had the mark were thus those who sold their faith in return for access to the pagan-infused economy of the day. They will suffer God's judgment (14:9–10).

The book of Revelation recognizes the seductive power of wealth and the human propensity to seek meaning in its accumulation at the cost of relationship with God. But wealth, like any idol, will always be inadequate to bring meaning to life. At this point we might think of the book of Ecclesiastes, where Qohelet, variously translated Teacher or Preacher, tried to find the meaning of life in wealth only to be let down (5:10–6:9). Put God first, the final speaker in the book says (12:13–14), to find the true meaning of life and then everything else will find its proper place.[5]

Indeed, it would be wrong to suggest that the Bible was antimoney or even antiwealth. Money is not the root of all evil, but as Paul told Timothy, "the love of money is the root of all kinds of evil. Some people, eager for money, have wandered from the faith and pierced themselves with many griefs" (1 Tim 6:10). Some of the Bible's most storied characters were wealthy— Abraham, Jacob, Joseph, David, Solomon, and Joseph of Arimathea come to mind. They were not perfect, but they were not criticized for their wealth as such. Indeed, at times material success is seen as a sign of God's provision and blessing. We might think of the book of Proverbs as it encourages people toward wisdom, righteousness, and godliness by suggesting that it is the best route toward material security (Pr 3:9–10; 10:15, 22; 14:24). It's important to know that the book of Proverbs was not in the business of promising material rewards. Job is the prime biblical example of a person who feared God yet suffered, though even Job at the beginning and end of the book illustrates that the wise could indeed be godly and wealthy.

Again, the issue is not wealth as such, but whether the desire for and accumulation of wealth undermines one's fundamental loyalty to God. If it does, then a person will seek wealth at the expense of others and use it to oppress others, which was the case with those condemned in the book of Revelation.

While money and wealth are not inherently idolatrous, they are extremely seductive. Like many other good things (sexual pleasure being an obvious example), one can never have enough, which means that there is this constant temptation to want and work for more. After all, we were made for Eden and no amount of money will fulfill all our desires. We need to remember that we are bound for the new, even better Eden, and be content whatever our circumstances (Php 4:10–11). Thus, we must keep our priorities straight: "Do not work for food that spoils, but for food that endures to eternal life, which the Son of Man will give you. For on him God the Father has placed his seal of approval" (Jn 6:27).

God's People Warned to Leave (18:4–8)

18:4 *Come out of her, my people.* Another, presumably angelic voice, then speaks, and calls to God's people to get out of the city about to be destroyed. If they don't get out, they might participate in the wicked city's sins and suffer the plagues that God will send on the city.

As the NIV note points out, the voice echoes Jeremiah 51:45, a judgment oracle against historical Babylon, calling on God's people to get out before God destroys it:

> "Come out of her, my people!
>> Run for your lives!
>> Run from the fierce anger of the LORD."

We might think also of the story of the destruction of the wicked city of Sodom, where God's angels escort Lot and his family out of the city before the destruction comes (Ge 19).

18:5-6 *Her sins are piled up to heaven.* Perhaps an echo of Jeremiah 51:9, which in reference to historical Babylon says:

> We would have healed Babylon,
>> but she cannot be healed;
> let us leave her and each go to our own land,
>> for her judgment reaches to the skies,
>> it rises as high as the heavens.

Give back to her as she has given. The sins of the prostitute are so great that if they could be put on top of each other they would reach the very heavens. That God remembers these crimes means that he will act to judge them. They will now receive the treatment that she has given others. In other words, she deserves the punishment that she is about to receive.

Pay her back double. The call is for a severe punishment that goes beyond the simple idea that the punishment fits the crime. No, the angel asks for double the punishment. This principle of paying double for a crime may be seen in the punishment of someone who steals from another: "Anyone who steals must certainly make restitution, but if they have nothing, they must be sold to pay for their theft. If the stolen animal is found alive in their possession—whether ox or donkey or sheep—they must pay back double" (Ex 22:3–4).

The idea of a double punishment may be seen in the prophets as well. Jeremiah anticipated a judgment against Israel where they would receive a punishment that would be double the sin: "I will repay them double for their wickedness and their sin, because they have defiled my land with the lifeless forms of their vile images and have filled my inheritance with their detestable idols" (Jer 16:18, see also 17:18). As Isaiah contemplated Israel's future restoration after her divine punishment, he also notes how she has received double for her sins (Isa 40:1–2).

A double portion from her own cup. According to 17:4 (see note), the prostitute "held a golden cup in her hand, filled with abominable things and the filth of her adulteries." There might also be an allusion here back to 16:19 (see note) where we read that "God remembered Babylon the Great and gave her the cup filled with the wine of the fury of his wrath."

18:7 *I sit enthroned as queen, I am not a widow; I will never mourn.* The angel quotes the prostitute as asserting her royal status and denying that at any point she might be a widow. Of course, the difference between a queen, who has status and power, and a widow, who in ancient society was considered among the most vulnerable and wretched (witness Naomi in the book of Ruth), was substantial. The book of Lamentations pictures Jerusalem, in the aftermath of its destruction by the Babylonians, as a one-time queen, now widow:

> How deserted lies the city,
>   once so full of people!
> How like a widow is she,
>   who once was great among the nations!
> She who was queen among the provinces
>   has now become a slave. (La 1:1)

But, as the footnote to the NIV tells us, the most direct connection is to be drawn from the prophet Isaiah. After all, the prostitute stands for Babylon the Great, who in turn stands for Rome and all worldly powers. In Isaiah 47, we have an oracle anticipating the fall of the city of Babylon. Like the prostitute in Revelation she claims to be a queen who will never be a widow:

> You said, "I am forever—
>   the eternal queen!"
> But you did not consider these things
>   or reflect on what might happen.
> Now then, listen, you lover of pleasure,
>   lounging in your security
> and saying to yourself,
>   "I am, and there is none besides me.
> I will never be a widow
>   or suffer the loss of children." (Isa 47:7–8)

In the case of historical Babylon (Isaiah) as well as symbolic Babylon (Revelation), these claims will prove to be so much false hubris.

18:8 *In one day her plagues will overtake her.* In Isaiah (see note on previous verse), historical Babylon claimed to be a queen and denied she would ever be a widow or childless, but Isaiah goes on to say:

> Both of these will overtake you
>   in a moment, on a single day:
> loss of children and widowhood. (Isa 47:9)

In the same way, quickly ("in one day"), her destruction will come in the form of death, mourning, and famine. She might be a powerful nation, but "mighty is the Lord God who judges her."

Three Woes over Destroyed Babylon (18:9–19)

The Kings of the Earth (18:9–10)

18:10 *Woe! Woe to you, great city, you mighty city of Babylon!* Thus begins the first of three woes (see also 18:16, 19) over burning Babylon, a symbol of Rome and all worldly powers that experience God's judgment. For woe as associated with funeral rites and a prophetic way of saying, "You are as good as dead," see the note at 8:13 where we also have a threefold woe over all the inhabitants of the earth. This first woe comes from the kings of the earth. More are to come.

In one hour your doom has come! In 18:8 the suddenness of the city's demise was expressed by it happening in the period of "one day," the same point is here intensified by saying it will happen in "one hour" (see also 18:17a, 19).

The Merchants (18:11–17a)

18:11 *Because no one buys their cargoes anymore.* The kings of the earth who were associated with the prostitute mourn because they know her demise means an end to their economic boon. These verses go on to describe luxury merchandise including precious metals and jewels (gold, silver, precious stones and pearls), fine textile materials (fine linen, purple, silk and scarlet cloth), rare and expensive articles (made of ivory, costly wood, bronze, iron and marble), exotic spices and oils (cinnamon and spice, of incense, myrrh and frankincense), agricultural products ("wine and olive oil, of fine flour and wheat"), livestock and their accouterments (cattle and sheep; horses and carriages) as well as slaves.

In Ezekiel 27 there is a mocking lament of Tyre that similarly bemoans the destruction of an economic behemoth. Tyre was an important commercial port on the Mediterranean that did business with the nations of the world. The lament lists all the items that the various countries used to trade with Tyre. At one point, Tyre "satisfied many nations; with your great wealth and your wares you enriched the kings of the earth," but "now you are shattered by the sea in the depths of the waters; your wares and all your company have gone down with you" (Eze 27:33–34).

18:14–15 *The fruit you longed for is gone from you.* The merchants continue their mourning at the demise of the prostitute and express their horror that she is no more. The fruit she longed for was presumably wealth and decadent luxury. Though they are shocked by the demise of the prostitute, their sorrow is self-interested since their own wealth depended on the prostitute.

18:16–17 *Woe! Woe to you, great city.* Here the merchants of the world reiterate the lament expressed by the kings of the earth over the end of the prostitute, using a funeral dirge to announce that she is as good as dead (see note at 18:9–10).

Dressed in fine linen, purple and scarlet. The prostitute's ornate clothing and accompanying jewelry represents the wealth and luxury of the great city of Babylon, which symbolically represents Roman and other worldly powers (see note at 17:4).

18:17a *In one hour such great wealth has been brought to ruin.* Though rich, the prostitute is quickly ("one hour," see also 18:10 and 18:19) reduced to nothing.

Sea Captains and Sailors (18:17b-19)

18:17b–19 *Every sea captain, and all who travel by ship, the sailors.* The third woe is spoken by those who "earn their living by the sea," joining those expressed by the kings of the earth (18:9–10), the merchants of the earth (18:11–17a).

They will throw dust on their heads. Throwing dust on one's head is an ancient gesture of mourning and death (Jos 7:6; 1 Sa 4:12; Job 2:12). Perhaps the custom stems from the fact that, according to Genesis 2:7, the first human was created from the dust of the earth and the breath of God, so at death all that is left is dust (Ge 3:19; Ecc 12:7). Dust represents death well because it is dry and lifeless.

Woe! Woe to you great city. See note at 18:9–10 as well as 18:16–17.

In one hour she has been brought to ruin! See note at 18:9–10 as well as 18:17a.

Rejoice! (18:20)

18:20 *Rejoice.* The kings of the earth, as well as the merchants and sea captains bemoan the destruction of the prostitute, who represents the worldly powers that feed their wealth. But others rejoice. Thus, the angelic voice calls on the heavens (spiritual powers like the angels), the people of God, and the apostles and prophets to celebrate her demise. After all, the prostitute represents those who oppress and persecute the people of God.

God has judged her with the judgment she imposed on you. The prostitute oppressed and persecuted the people of God, now God will judge the woman so that she will experience the pain and suffering long endured by the church.

The End of Babylon the Great (18:21–24)

18:21 *Picked up a boulder the size of a large millstone.* A millstone is a rock shaped with a flat surface that would be used to grind grain. A boulder the size of even a large millstone would not really be sizable enough to destroy a city, but then again this description is not a literal depiction of an event, but a metaphorical one ("with such violence").

In the Bible millstones, even when they are actual objects, are sometimes mentioned in connection with their regular purpose of grinding grain (see Dt 24:6; Isa 47:2; La 5:13; see also Rev 18:22), but also in the context of a punishment or judgment. So in the context of Abimelek's abortive and wicked attempt to assert himself as king, he besieged the city of Thebez where "a woman dropped an upper millstone on his head and cracked his skull" (Jdg 9:53).[6] But being crushed is not the only way death might be imagined by means of a millstone. Jesus warned, "If anyone causes one of these little ones—those who believe in me—to stumble, it would be better for them if a large millstone were hung around their neck and they were thrown into the sea" (Mk 9:42; see also Lk 17:2). The mighty angel suggests the millstone-like boulder will be thrown into the sea and presumably the waters (perhaps with overtones of the waters of chaos, see note at 4:6–8) will overwhelm the city so that it will disappear forever ("never to be found again").

Williamson draws our attention to a background in Jeremiah 51:63–64, which ends a judgment oracle again Babylon: "When you finish reading this scroll, tie a stone to it and throw it into the Euphrates. Then say, 'So will Babylon sink to rise no more because of the disaster I will bring on her. And her people will fall.'" He comments, "In John's vision, however, the stone is much larger, like a huge millstone weighing hundreds of pounds, and it is thrown into the sea rather than a river."[7]

18:22 *The music . . . will never be heard in you again.* The silencing of music signals the city's demise. As Isaiah, in his so-called Apocalypse, notes, when the Lord destroys the earth and devastates it, then "all the merrymakers groan. The joyful timbrels are stilled, the noise of the revelers has stopped, the joyful harp is silent" (Isa 24:7–8).[8]

No worker of any trade. The city will be destroyed, and no building or restoration will ever happen again.

The sound of a millstone will never be heard in you again. Grinding grain, a regular part of a city's activity, will cease.

18:23 *The light of a lamp.* The lights of the city will go out with its demise. Darkness will descend on it.

The voice of bridegroom and bride. Weddings are celebratory events at which there is much joy. They also represent the continuance of life since they imply the potential of children. The lack of a voice of bridegroom and bride means the end of joy and life. As Jeremiah anticipates the judgment that would come on Jerusalem and Judah, he says, "I will bring an end to the sounds of joy and gladness and to the voices of bride and bridegroom in the towns of Judah and the streets of Jerusalem, for the land will become desolate" (7:34; 16:9). He also describes the restoration after the judgment as a time when "there will be heard once more the sounds of joy and gladness, the voices of bride and bridegroom" (Jer 33:10–11).

By your magic spell. Here the prostitute is likened to a sorceress casting spells over the nations. Perhaps they are spells that cause a person to fall in love or be sexually attracted to another person. The prophet Nahum, for instance likens the Assyrian city of Nineveh to a sorceress casting spells over the nations. He says of Nineveh, "All because of the wanton lust of a prostitute, alluring, the mistress of sorceries, who enslaved nations by her prostitution and peoples by her witchcraft" (Na 3:4). Thus, Nahum, like Revelation, pictures a world power to both a prostitute and a sorceress, each of which encounter the judgment of God.

18:24 *The blood of prophets.* See note at 16:6.

REVELATION 19

Hallelujahs over the Destruction of Babylon (19:1–10)

19:1 *What sounded like the roar of a great multitude in heaven.* We have a bit of initial ambiguity as to who is speaking here with a voice that "sounded like the roar of a great multitude." After all in Daniel, it was God himself[1] who spoke with a "voice like the sound of a multitude" (Da 10:6). However, the words themselves praise God and are certainly spoken by a group about God. Perhaps we have here the same "great multitude" mentioned in Revelation 7:9.

Hallelujah. Hallelujah is simply a transliteration (in English based on the Greek transliteration) of the Hebrew phrase *hallelu yah*, or "praise the Lord." This expression is found frequently particularly in the Psalms (for examples, see Ps 146:1, 10; 147:1, 20; 148:1, 7, 14; 149:1, 9; 150:1, 6).

19:2 *For true and just are his judgments.* See note at 16:7. The judgment has come against the great prostitute, and her judgment fits the crime since she corrupted the earth by her adulteries (see note at 17:2, with background in 14:8; 18:3) and persecuted and killed those who followed God (see note at 16:6; also 18:24).

19:3 *Hallelujah!* See note at 19:1. The multitude "praise the Lord" because of the destruction of the prostitute.

19:4 *The twenty-four elders and the four living creatures.* The picture of God on his throne surrounded by these figures is reminiscent of the scene in Revelation 4. See notes at 4:4 and 4:6–8.

Amen, Hallelujah! The twenty-four elders and the four living creatures affirm the proclamation of the multitude with an Amen (Hebrew for "so be it") and Hallelujah (Hebrew for "praise the Lord," see note at 19:1).

19:5 *Then a voice came from the throne.* This is the throne on which God sits, but the glorified Christ also stands by it (see note at 3:21). Since the voice calls for the praise of God referred to in the third person, it may seem awkward that the voice comes from the throne (as we mentioned in reference to the voice in 19:1), but not impossible. Perhaps we are to imagine Christ calling for praise of the Father. (See "Revelation 4 Through Old Testament Eyes: God on His Throne.")

Praise our God. As we find in many hymns in the book of Psalms (Ps 113:1; 134:1, etc.), the voice from the throne issues an exhortation to praise God.

All you servants, you who fear him, both great and small! Those who follow God have a relationship with him like a servant to a master. They, accordingly, fear him. This is not the type of fear that makes one run away, but one that acknowledges God's vast superiority (see note at 14:7). These include people of much influence (great) as well as little (small). Great and small constitute a merism, which is the citation of two poles that means everything in between.

19:6 *What sounded like a great multitude, like the roar of rushing waters and like loud peals of thunder.* Such a voice could refer to God's speech, but in this case is more likely an angel (see 19:9). For "great multitude," see note at 19:1. For rushing waters, see notes at 1:13–15 and 14:2. For loud peals of thunder, see note at 4:5.

Hallelujah! See note at 19:1.

For our Lord God Almighty reigns. For "Lord God Almighty," see note at 11:17. This language reflects the praise of God as king found especially in the so-called "kingship hymns" of the Psalms (see especially Ps 93:1; 97:1; 99:1).

19:7 *Let us rejoice and be glad.* This encouragement is also something that we see in a few hymns in the Old Testament, particularly to celebrate God's salvation (Ps 40:16; 70:4; Isa 25:9).

For the wedding of the Lamb has come, and his bride has made herself ready. The reference to the wedding of the Lamb brings to culmination a long biblical-theological trajectory that pictures the relationship between God and his people as a marriage. God is the groom/husband, and his people are his bride/wife. The marriage metaphor for the divine-human relationship is an apt one because marriage involves an exclusive relationship between a wife and her husband that can be likened to the exclusive relationship between God and his people. Most of the time the marriage analogy is used in the negative sense when people are unfaithful to God (Eze 23:5–8, 20; Hos 2:2; see note at Rev 17:1 and "Going Deeper into the Intersection of Idolatry and Adultery: Revelation 17"), but behind this negative use stands the positive idea of God and his people in an intimate, exclusive, faithful relationship. In Jeremiah, God says:

I remember the devotion of your youth,
 how as a bride you loved me
And followed me through the wilderness,
 through a land not sown. (Jer 2:2; see also Hos 2:14–15)

And of course in the New Testament, Paul likens the church's relationship to Christ as a marriage: "For the husband is the head of the wife as Christ is the head of the church, his body, of which he is the Savior. . . . 'For this reason a man will leave his father and mother and be united to his wife, and the two will become one flesh.' This is a profound mystery—but I am talking about Christ and the church" (Eph 5:23, 31–32).

With the defeat of evil as represented here by the prostitute, the moment has come for the realization of the intimate and exclusive relationship between God and his faithful people. This realization or culmination is pictured as a wedding between the Lamb, Jesus, and the bride, the church. The latter, through its endurance and faithfulness, has shown herself ready.

19:8 *Fine linen, bright and clean.* The bride, standing for the people of God, will be dressed in clean white linen. Here we get a rare explicit explanation of the meaning of the image when the verse goes on to say that "fine linen stands for the righteous acts of God's holy people"; see note at 15:6.

19:9 *Write this.* See notes at 1:19 and 14:13.

Blessed are those who are invited. This blessing is the fourth of seven (see note at 1:3) in the book of Revelation. Here the recipients are the guests at the wedding of the Lamb, Jesus, and his bride, the church. The guests must stand for individual Christians.

19:10 *I fell at his feet to worship him.* The angelic messenger is a being of such majesty and speaks so authoritatively that John fell at his feet prostrate in an act of worship. The angel, though, refuses worship and instructs John to worship God alone.

The Spirit of prophecy. The Spirit of prophecy is the Holy Spirit, the third person of the Trinity, that bears testimony to Jesus (Jn 15:26–27). As Peter states, "Above all, you must understand that no prophecy of Scripture came about by the prophet's own interpretation of things. For prophecy never had its origin in the human will, but prophets, though human, spoke from God as they were carried along by the Holy Spirit" (2 Pe 1:20–21).

What the Structure Means: The Final Telling of God's Ultimate Victory (19:11–20:15)

John continues to report on the visions that he experienced. Each vision, or part thereof, is introduced by the simple connector "and I saw" (*kai eidon*, though the NIV does not always translate the copulative *kai*; 19:11, 17, 19; 20:1, 4, 11). The conceptual connection between 19:11–20:11 and what has preceded is not made explicit, but in that John tells us a vision of Christ's ultimate victory over the dragon and the two beasts (Rev 12–13), we might think of this as the final telling of the conclusion of the great battle between God and the forces of evil. We observed that in the telling of the climactic (seventh) seal, trumpet, and bowl that God's appearance in the final judgment is suggested by seismic and meteorological convulsions (see 8:1–5; 11:15–19; 16:17–21). Here we get a further developed picture, of course filled with figurative language, of the battle with the glorified Christ at the head of his heavenly army marching into battle.

John does not narrate the details of the battle itself, rather the results. First, an angel calls out to the birds to come together for a great feast, a feast of the bodies of the vanquished. Then the beast and the kings of the earth gather their armies together (echoing earlier passages where the kings of the earth gather [as at Armageddon; 16:16]). In this battle, Christ vanquishes all his spiritual and human enemies. In terms of the former, the beast (from the sea) and the false prophet (also known as the beast from the land) are defeated and thrown into the lake of burning sulphur. Two of the three members of the unholy trinity are thus vanquished, only leaving the final and most powerful enemy of all left, the dragon. It is to the story of the fall of the dragon, Satan himself, that John now turns.

With the vision of Revelation 20, we scroll back time to before the final victory which had been depicted in 19:11–21. Indeed, as Williamson points out 20:1–10 "recapitulates the vision of Rev 12:7–17 but changes the imagery and completes the story."[2] In the earlier story, there is a war between God's angels, led by Michael, the dragon and his angels (demons). The latter were not strong enough to resist the forces of heaven and the great dragon, representing Satan, is thrown down on the ground along with his evil associates. On earth, the dragon kept up his campaign of evil and pursues a woman, who represented the church, who was giving birth to a child (Jesus). The woman was given wings by God (indicated by the divine passive, see note at 12:14), so she could give birth. The dragon persists by spewing water out of his mouth to try to overwhelm her, but the earth opened and engulfed the water before it could harm her. Even so, the dragon continued its pursuit of the woman, and that is the end of the first story. In Revelation 20, we learn of God's final victory over the dragon.

At the beginning of Revelation 20, once again (see 9:1) we read about an angel who comes down with a key to the Abyss. He seizes the dragon who is Satan, throws him into the Abyss, and seals it up for one thousand years. The binding specifically is so that the dragon can no longer deceive the nations (see note at 20:3). But for reasons not given, at the end of the thousand years, the dragon "must be set free for a short time" (20:3). Even though no reason for this release is given here, perhaps we should think it is so that he will reach his end as described in 20:7–10.

Before describing the end of the dragon, John then tells us that he saw thrones on which the martyrs were seated (20:4). They have been given authority to judge along with God himself. They had died and were now raised to rule along with Christ during this thousand-year period. Since they will not die again, they will not experience the second resurrection.

In 20:7–10, we learn that once released, the dragon does again what he did before—deceive the nations. He gathers the nations to fight against God, but they are quickly and efficiently dispatched when fire comes down from heaven after which the dragon is thrown into the lake of burning sulfur into which the two beasts had earlier been thrown.

Then comes what we would call the final judgment. Everyone appears before the throne, where they are judged "according to what they had done as recorded in the books" (20:12). And then all who were not found in the book of life were thrown into the lake of fire.

Judgment now completed, the final visions turn to the glorious picture of what awaits those whose names are in the book of life. We now read about the new heavens and the new earth, the new Jerusalem, and restored Eden (Rev 21:1–22:8).

The Final Telling of God's Ultimate Victory (19:11–20:15)

Jesus the Warrior Wins the Final Battle (19:11–21)

19:11 *I saw heaven standing open.* See note at 4:1.

There before me was a white horse. After the glorified Christ opened the first seal (see 6:1–2), a white horse emerged bringing war on the face of the earth. While the rider there was not to be identified with Christ as here, we noted there that white associated the rider with heavenly and transcendent realities and indicated the rider's righteousness.

Whose rider is called Faithful and True. See note at 3:14, where Jesus is called "the faithful and true witness."

With justice he judges and wages war. Psalm 98 is a divine warrior hymn,[3] a new song, which we earlier observed celebrated God's victory that made all things new (see note at 5:9). The first two stanzas of the psalm praises God for winning a victory over their enemies in the past (vv. 1–3) and for being their king in the present (vv. 4–6). The third stanza completes the song:

> Let the sea resound and everything in it,
>   the world, and all who live in it.
> Let the rivers clap their hands,
>   let the mountains sing together for joy;
> let them sing before the LORD,
>   for he comes to judge the earth.
> He will judge the world in righteousness
>   and the peoples with equity. (Ps 98:7–9; see also Ps 96:11–13)

The psalmist looks to the future in this final stanza and observes that God would come as a future just/righteous judge, who would set creation right. Here this hope is applied to Jesus, who leads the heavenly army into the final battle.

19:12 *His eyes are like blazing fire.* See note at 1:13–15; also 2:18.

On his head are many crowns. Crowns are a symbol of royal authority.

A name written on him that no one knows but he himself. While today, names seem arbitrary and without much special significance, in the biblical world names have real meaning, and in a context like this points to the essence of a person. The glorified Christ has many names that we know—Jesus, Lamb, Christ, Morning Star, and many more. Indeed, in 19:13 we will learn that his name is the Word of God and in 19:16 we will hear that he has a name written on his robe and on his thigh—KING OF KINGS AND LORD OF LORDS. But this name is known only to himself, and presumably indicates that this name reveals his nature even more fully. Some believe that name is Yahweh, but then Osborne points out that the "I am" statements of Jesus make that name known.[4] The idea may well be that this name that points to an even deeper revelation of Jesus' nature may be ultimately unknowable or perhaps something that will be revealed at the end. In this regard, we might remember the promise given to those who are victorious in the church of Thyatira that they would receive a white stone with a new name written on it, "known only to the one who receives it" (2:17). Though possibly referring to a new name for an individual, it may be that this refers to the name of Christ that will be revealed at the end.

19:13 *A robe dipped in blood.* Jesus' robe is blood-splattered. While some interpreters[5] argue that this is his own blood, the fact that he is described in martial terms riding into battle suggests otherwise. The description derives from the picture of Yahweh the divine warrior found in Isaiah:

> I have trodden the winepress alone;
>> from the nations no one was with me.
> I trampled them in my anger
>> and trod them down in my wrath;
> their blood spattered my garments,
>> and I stained all my clothing. (Isa 63:3)

Jesus is the divine warrior who has come to complete God's victory over his human and spiritual enemies.

His name is the Word of God. He is the logos, the Word of God, as expressed at the beginning of the Gospel of John: "In the beginning was the Word, and the Word was with God, and the Word was God" (Jn 1:1). But as Osborne insightfully points out, while in the gospel the title means "living revealer," here it means more like "authoritative Word" attesting to the "gospel message."[6]

19:14 *The armies of heaven were following him.* Jesus is here pictured at the head of an angelic army, again assuming the position that Yahweh occupied in the Old Testament and showing that Jesus himself has divine status. Yahweh in the Old Testament was called "Lord of Hosts" (*yahweh sebaʾot*), the hosts being an army of angels. Zechariah 14 describes an initial victory of the nations against the city of Jerusalem, but then "the LORD my God will come, and all the holy ones with him" (Zec 14:5) to defeat them.

19:15 *Coming out of his mouth is a sharp sword.* Psalm 59 is a lament that calls on God to help against threatening dangerous enemies. They snarl like dogs, and he calls on God to "see what they spew from their mouths—the words from their lips are sharp as swords" (Ps 59:7). Words can hurt; indeed they can kill. A more positive use of the metaphor is found in the mouth of the suffering servant in Isaiah, who proclaims that God "made my mouth like a sharpened sword" (Isa 49:2). While the immediate referent of the servant in Isaiah is the remnant of Israel, Jesus is seen as the "Israel of one" in the New Testament. Here in Revelation Jesus has a sword coming out of his mouth as he rides into battle. That the sword comes from his mouth indicates that he kills by the power of his word (see 19:21; also 1:16; 2:12). The object of his violence is the "nations," here representing those who have refused to repent. In Isaiah, the Messiah will also bring judgment with his mouth, but here rather than a sword, his mouth is likened to a rod (Isa 11:4).

He will rule them with an iron scepter. The quote is from Psalm 2:9, a psalm that ridicules the efforts of the nations that rage against God and speaks of God's anointed king whom God will use to defeat and then rule over the nations. A scepter is a symbol of royal rule and is here applied to Jesus who is the anointed (Messiah), the descendant of David. This verse is earlier quoted at 2:27 (see note) and 12:5 (there also see "Revelation Through Old Testament Eyes: Psalms").

Treads the winepress of the fury of the wrath of God Almighty. See notes at 14:10 and 19:13. For "God Almighty," see note at 11:17.

19:16 On his robe and on his thigh. According to Osborne, this should be more accurately rendered, "on his robe, namely his thigh," meaning that the name was written once on the part of his robe that covered his thigh, "where it would be conspicuous on a mounted warrior."[7]

KING OF KINGS AND LORD OF LORDS. See note at 17:14.

19:17-18 Gather together for the great supper of God. Celebratory meals were common after victories in the ancient Near East. This particularly gruesome celebration is enjoyed by the birds. This scene is reminiscent of the banquet enjoyed by carrion birds and wild animals in the aftermath of the destruction of the forces of Gog of the land of Magog and chief prince of Meshek and Tubal (Eze 39:17-20; see note at 20:8). God tells Ezekiel to call on the birds and the wild animals to gather to gorge on the slain bodies of the army of Gog. To the birds and animals he says, "You will eat the flesh of mighty men and drink the blood of the princes of the earth as if they were rams and lambs, goats and bulls—all of them fattened animals from Bashan" (39:18).

19:19 The beast and the kings of the earth and their armies. The beast (see note at 13:1), representing Rome, and his allied kings, representing other worldly authorities, here enter the final battle against Jesus, the rider on the horse, and his angelic army.

19:20 The false prophet who had performed signs on its behalf. The false prophet was the beast that emerged from the land (see notes at 13:11-18).

Received the mark of the beast and worshipped its image. See note at 13:16-17.

Into the fiery lake of burning sulfur. This lake is to be equated with the "lake of fire" to be mentioned in 20:14. This lake is not mentioned elsewhere in Scripture but seems to be the place of final judgment. Here we learn that all of the unholy trinity (see note at 13:12), namely the dragon (devil), the beast and the false prophet (the land beast) reach an end. Even so, they seem to maintain consciousness even after in that they are said to experience perpetual and eternal torment.

19:21 *The sword coming out of the mouth of the rider on the horse.* See note at 19:15.

All the birds gorged themselves on their flesh. See note at 19:17–18.

REVELATION 20

The Dragon Bound a Thousand Years (20:1–6)

20:1–3 *Having the key to the Abyss.* In Revelation 9, a star, whom we understand to represent an angel (see note at 9:1) took a key and opened the Abyss, an underworld place where demonic forces reside (see note at 9:2), loosing them on the world. The beast also emerges from the Abyss (see 11:7; 17:8). But now an angel comes with the key and a chain with which he will bind the dragon, who represents Satan (see note at 12:9), and then throw him into the Abyss and lock it shut.

From deceiving the nations anymore. The act of removing Satan from the earth has as its purpose to prevent the nations from being deceived, most likely regarding the truth of the testimony about Jesus.

Until the thousand years were ended. Apocalyptic literature is notorious for its use of symbolic numbers, so this number should not be pressed literally as it if represents a thousand years of actual time. As Williamson points out, "The Old Testament also often uses the number 'thousand' to indicate a very large number rather than a precise quantity (e.g., Deut 7:9; Ps 90:4)."[1] That is why many theologians believe that this number which extends from the time that Satan is bound until the time he is loosed for a little while before his destruction (20:7–10) refers to the time between the resurrection, which was a victory over Satan (see, for instance, Col 2:13–15), and the second coming when Jesus will win the final victory. When accused of being an agent of the devil, named Beelzebul in the context, Jesus responded by saying, "How can anyone enter a strong man's house and carry off his possessions unless he first ties up the strong man? Then he can plunder his house" (Mt 12:29), claiming that his ability to exorcise demons was the result of the devil being bound up.

The thousand-year period mentioned in Revelation 20:1–7, known as the Millennium, has been a contested concept throughout church history. While I do not have the time to discuss the various views, interested readers have several good books to consult which give overviews and analyses of the options, including *The Meaning of the Millennium*, edited by Robert G. Clouse and *Three Views of the Millennium and Beyond*, edited by Darrell Bock.

He must be set free for a short time. If the thousand years refers to the time between the resurrection and the second coming of Christ, then the idea that Satan will be released from his captivity must refer to an intensification of evil toward the end of time. The idea that this final flourish is brief is a theme found earlier in the book (see 11:11; 12:12; 17:10).

20:4 *They . . . reigned with Christ for a thousand years.* During this thousand-year period the martyrs are said to reign with Christ, presumably from heaven. They are given thrones as symbols of their rule. These thrones may reflect Daniel's first vision where the picture of heaven begins with the placing of multiple thrones among which God (the Ancient of Days) sat: "As I looked, thrones were set in place, and the Ancient of Days took his seat" (Da 7:9). Those who reign with Christ will participate in the coming judgment. They did not worship the beast and so they did to receive the mark on their foreheads or hands to indicate their allegiance to the beast (see note at 13:16–17).

20:5 *The rest of the dead.* Since the dead who were brought back to life in the previous verse were martyrs, the rest of the dead would refer to the rest of humanity who died before the final judgment. The resurrection of the martyrs is here called the first resurrection.

20:6 *Blessed and holy are those who share in the first resurrection.* This blessing is the fifth of seven (see note at 1:3) in the book of Revelation. Here the blessing is conferred on the martyrs who were the first brought back to life from death. They are also holy or set apart by their fidelity to the point of their martyrdom.

The second death has no power over them. At the end of the chapter, we will learn about the final judgment of all the dead. All the dead will be raised at that time, and those who are evil will be thrown into the lake of fire, which is "the second death" (see 20:14). The martyrs brought to life at the first resurrection will not experience this second death.

They will be priests of God and of Christ and will reign with him for a thousand years. Great reward follows the faithfulness of the martyrs who are in heaven. They are given both priestly and royal roles during the period between the first and second coming ("for a thousand years"). In Genesis 1 and

2, Adam and Eve are pictured as having both priestly (as guardian and atten-
dant of the garden of Eden the place where God met his human creatures) and
royal roles (being created in his image, they are God's royal representatives
who will "subdue it" [the earth] and "rule over the fish in the sea and the birds
in the sky and over every living creature that moves on the ground," Ge 1:28).
Thus, the martyrs fill the role intended for humanity from the start. See also
notes at 1:6 and 5:10.

The End of the Devil (20:7–10)

20:7 *Satan will be released from his prison.* At the end of the thousand years,
understood to be the period between the first and second comings of Christ,
Satan will be released from the prison into which the angel threw him in the
Abyss. This release was anticipated above ("he must be set free for a short
time," 20:3).

Revelation Through Old Testament Eyes: Ezekiel

John clearly situates himself in the apocalyptic prophetic tradition of
Ezekiel. In the opening of the book that bears his name, Ezekiel shares
his prophetic commissioning which included a dramatic vision of God
surrounded by his heavenly servants, including the cherubim. He reports
that in his thirtieth year while he was near the Kebar River (in Babylon)
among the exiles "the heavens were opened and I saw visions of God"
(Eze 1:1). While not necessarily an allusion to Ezekiel, John on several
occasions tells us that the heavens were also opened to him with the result
that he too experienced visions of God (Rev 4:1; 11:19; 15:1; 19:11). Along
with this, we may see a similarity with Ezekiel in John's fourfold assertion
that "I was in the Spirit" when he experienced his heavenly visions (Rev
1:10; 4:2; 17:3; 21:10, compare Eze 3:12–15; 11:24; 37:1).

Besides other incidental echoes, Ezekiel's unique influence on the book
of Revelation concentrates in four areas: the depiction of the glorified
Christ, the scroll of judgment, the vision of Gog and Magog, and the
measuring of the temple. We will look at each in turn.

1. The Depiction of the Glorified Christ
Ezekiel describes his encounters with God in the following ways:

> High above on the throne was a figure like that of a man. I saw
> that from what appeared to be his waist up he looked like glowing

metal, as if full of fire, and that from there down he looked like fire; and brilliant light surrounded him. Like the appearance of a rainbow in the clouds on a rainy day, so was the radiance around him. (Eze 1:26–28)

I saw a figure like that of a man. From what appeared to be his waist down he was like fire, and from there up his appearance was as bright as glowing metal. (Eze 8:2)

His voice was like the roar of rushing waters. (Eze 43:2)

John's description of God's appearance as well as of the glorified Christ show connections to Ezekiel. Here, in John's first encounter with Christ, he says the Lord was

dressed in a robe reaching down to his feet and with a golden sash around his chest. The hair on his head was white like wool, as white as snow, and his eyes were like blazing fire. His feet were like bronze glowing in a furnace, and his voice was like the sound of rushing waters. (Rev 1:13–15)

John also describes God on his throne in the following terms:

A rainbow that shone like an emerald encircled the throne. . . . Also in front of the throne there was what looked like a sea of glass, clear as crystal. In the center, around the throne, were four living creatures, and they were covered with eyes, in front and in back. (Rev 4:3, 6)

While the two sets are not verbatim, we hear similarities. We acknowledge also that these pictures from Revelation are also informed by Daniel's experience (see "Revelation Through Old Testament Eyes: Daniel" at 1:7).

In addition, surrounding the throne on which God sits with Jesus in the center of it in Revelation stood four living creatures (Rev 4:6), the same number that were with God in Ezekiel's vision (Eze 1:5 and throughout the opening vision). These living creatures were also called cherubim in Ezekiel (10:5) and their description in Revelation (4:7) resembles their description in Ezekiel.

Whether in Ezekiel or Revelation, this imaginative depiction of God's presence shows that the writer was not interested in what we would call photographic description. The light, the fire, the roar of his voice all emphasize not only that he is ineffable, but all-powerful, magnificent, and awe-inspiring.

2. The Scroll of Judgment

Scrolls also play roles in both books. While the image of the scroll is much more prominent in Revelation, there is a clear link back to Ezekiel.

After God made his awesome presence known to the prophet as recorded in Ezekiel 1, we hear that God commissions Ezekiel to bring his prophetic message. The people have sinned, and God wants Ezekiel to call them to repentance. God's message will be one of judgment and is represented as contained on a scroll: "Then I looked, and I saw a hand stretched out to me. In it was a scroll, which he unrolled before me. On both sides of it were written words of lament and mourning and woe" (Eze 2:9–10).

In Revelation, God's message of judgment is also written on a scroll, this one with seven seals. As with Ezekiel's scroll, the writing is on both sides, not a typical technique, and both scrolls containing judgments. Also similar is the picture of God holding the scroll in his hand. In Revelation, we read, "Then I saw in the right hand of him who sat on the throne a scroll with writing on both sides and sealed with seven seals" (Rev 5:1).

God then commissions Ezekiel, saying to the prophet: "Son of man, eat what is before you, eat this scroll; then go and speak to the people of Israel," and the prophet responds by doing just that (Eze 3:1–2). He reports that "it tasted as sweet as honey in my mouth" (3:3). That sounds odd for a scroll that contains "words of lament and mourning and woe" (2:10), but it probably reflects the idea that the message is right for the moment.

This commission echoes in a second scroll scene in Revelation, this one more directly commissioning John as message-bearer (Rev 10:8–11). There is a debate over the connection between this scroll, called a "little scroll" (10:9) and the seven-sealed scroll, but there is no question that Ezekiel's commission lies behind both scenes. The angel with the little scroll says to John, "Take it and eat it. It will turn your stomach sour, but 'in your mouth it will be as sweet as honey,'" which is precisely what happens (10:9–10). Ingesting the scroll symbolizes how the message becomes an integral part of the prophet. That it was sweet to the taste again represents how the message was fit for the occasion, but here that the scroll turned sour in the stomach suits the message that presages horrific judgment on God's enemies.

3. Gog and Magog

In certainly the most well-known allusion to Ezekiel in the book of Revelation, we hear of a great final battle between God and Satan who is supported by the nations at Gog and Magog. Satan had just been bound in prison for a thousand years, but now was released. He once again deceived the nations so that they "marched across the breadth of the earth and surrounded the camp of God's people, the city he loves" (Rev 20:9). This reference to Gog and Magog comes from Ezekiel 38–39, but not only is the reference to Gog and Magog in Revelation enigmatic to a contemporary reader, but so is the role they play in Ezekiel.

In Ezekiel, Gog is a person and Magog is a place. God instructs Ezekiel to "set your face against Gog, of the land of Magog, the chief prince of Meshek and Tubal; prophesy against him" (Eze 38:2–3). In Revelation both Gog and Magog are place names (Rev 20:8). This apparent discrepancy could be disturbing if we thought of Ezekiel 38 and 39 strictly as a prophecy of the final judgment against Satan, but that is not the best way to think about the relationship between the two passages. As explained in the commentary at 20:8, Magog in Ezekiel either represents Babylon or what Cook calls a "mythic-realistic entity"[2] that represents those forces that are hostile toward God and his people. By alluding back to Ezekiel 38–39 in this way the book of Revelation uses the imagery of the book to communicate the certainty and the definitiveness of this final battle against Satan and his minions.

4. Measuring the Temple

In the year 597 BC Ezekiel was among the early exiles taken to Babylon along with King Jehoiachin. He prophesied from there. Jerusalem would again rebel against Babylonian dominance, and when Nebuchadnezzar marched his armies to Jerusalem, he destroyed the city, removed the king, and tore down the temple. The latter was perhaps the worst part of the disaster that befell Jerusalem.

After the temple was destroyed, indeed in the fourteenth year after Jerusalem fell to the Babylonians (Eze 40:1), God gave Ezekiel a vision of a future temple. The vision begins when he sees "a man whose appearance was like bronze . . . standing in a gateway with a linen cord and a measuring rod in his hand" (Eze 40:3). The next section (extending to 43:27) has this figure, probably representing an angel, measuring the temple courtyard and the temple itself. The vision looks into the future and communicates to the people that though the temple has been destroyed that is not the end of the story.

Indeed, the temple would be rebuilt after the exile (completed in 515 BC) and that temple would last through the time of Jesus' earthly ministry until the Romans destroyed it in AD 70 as they put down a Jewish insurrection. Even though this second temple probably was in the purview of Ezekiel's vision, it likely did not exhaust its significance. For one thing, Ezekiel envisioned God's glory entering the temple in a dramatic way, something that seems to be missing from the second temple.

For that reason, we might think of the coming of Jesus as also anticipated by this vision of a restored temple. The temple was a place where God made his glory manifest on earth, and according to John in Jesus "the Word became flesh and made his dwelling among us. We have seen his glory, the glory of the one and only Son, who came from the Father, full of grace and truth" (Jn 1:14). With the coming of Jesus and the sending of the Holy Spirit, God's presence is with us in an intimate way. So intimate that it seems odd to think that the future would bring a future physical temple.

With this background, we note that on two occasions in the book of Revelation a person is given a measuring stick to measure in the first instance (11:1) the temple and its altar and in the second the heavenly city, the New Jerusalem (21:15). As explained in the commentary, in Revelation 11 the temple and its altar along with the two witnesses represent the church, while in the second episode an angel measures the New Jerusalem with the announcement that there was no temple in the city "because the Lord God Almighty and the Lamb are its temple" (21:22). Thus, with this vision of the New Jerusalem we have the fulfillment of the expectation of the picture of the eschatological temple given to Ezekiel. Indeed, the ultimate reality far exceeds that of a physical temple because the divine presence permeates the whole city.

We find one final allusion back to Ezekiel in the picture of this New Jerusalem without a temple and that is "the river of the water of life, as clear as crystal, flowing from the throne of God and of the Lamb down the middle of the great street of the city" (Rev 22:1–2). Here the connection may be seen with Ezekiel 47 where the man with the measuring rod brought the prophet back to the temple where he saw "water coming out from under the threshold of the temple toward the east" (47:1). As the water flowed from the temple to the Dead Sea, vegetation flourished and life abounded. In Revelation, we hear that there are two trees of life on each side of the river. The New Jerusalem is also restored, but as an even better Eden.

20:8 *Deceive the nations in the four corners of the earth.* "Four corners" was an ancient way of referring to the whole earth (see note at 7:1). As we saw above (20:3), the thousand-year binding of Satan hindered him from deceiving the nations so that the gospel might go out into the world.

Gog and Magog—and to gather them for battle. We have seen various ways in which the book pictures the combined worldly powers that rage against Christ and the church. In Revelation 17 and 18 we encountered the prostitute, called Babylon the Great, which was a cipher for Rome and other worldly powers, in alliance with other earthly kings. Here the vision draws on Ezekiel 38 and 39, which speaks of Gog as a ruler and Magog as a place.[3] God addresses Ezekiel, "Son of man, set your face against Gog, of the land of Magog, the chief prince of Meshek and Tubal" (Eze 38:1). The next two chapters describe how God is going to destroy Gog and the forces that follow him for their mistreatment of the people of Israel.

But who is Gog and where is Magog? Whom is God going to destroy? Of course, the answers through the centuries have varied, but we should begin to answer that question by asking how these chapters would be understood by Ezekiel himself and his audience.

The first clue is to remember that Israel's main antagonist at the time was Babylon. Indeed, Babylon was God's tool to bring judgment against sinful Judah and Jerusalem. But Babylon was God's unwitting tool, and so, according to the prophets (Jer 51:20–26) were themselves subject to God's judgment. Isaiah (13:1–14:27) and Jeremiah (Jeremiah 51–52) both have lengthy oracles against Babylon among others. Interestingly, Ezekiel's oracles against the foreign nations (chaps 25–32) do not have one against Babylon as one would expect, considering Babylon at the time was Israel's main enemy. Thus, Magog may well be a slightly veiled reference to Babylon.

If correct, it is indeed slightly veiled because Magog can be seen as a code (similar to a technique called atbash) for Babel. In such a cipher, the name Babel is written backward and with the letter that follows the normal letter in the alphabet. In Hebrew, *b* (beth) is followed by *g* (gimel) and *l* (lamed) is followed by *m* (mem). Thus reversing the order of the letters and replacing them with the following letter in the alphabet turns B(a)b(e)l into M(a)g(o)g.

Alternatively, in the book of Ezekiel, Gog may not be an actual person nor Magog an actual place. As Cook sees it, "Gog is not a mundane figure of history but a 'mythic-realistic entity,' physically real but mythological, that is, fantastic and archetypal, proportions."[4] Or as Duguid puts it, "The biblical Gog is no mere historical figure, then, but rather a fear-inducing figure of cosmic proportions."[5] And Magog would not be an actual place but also a kind of mythical place that could be seen to represent the horrific forces that were ranged against God and his people, but whom God defeats.

The book of Revelation marshals this ancient prophetic oracle to describe a future final battle between God and evil. Just like the prophetic picture in Revelation 17 and 18 used ancient Babylon (the Great) to stand for Rome and all worldly power, so this reference to Gog and Magog uses a judgment oracle that in the past concerned historical Babylon (or possibly a mythic representation of ungodly enemies) to stand for the forces that side with the devil. It's not that Ezekiel 38–39 is a prophecy of the final event. Rather it is a prophecy of the demise of historical Babylon or a mythic representation of God's enemies, but the book of Revelation sees it as a template that will be played out in the final confrontation between God and the forces of evil.[6]

Like the sand on the seashore. The sand on the seashore of course is impossible to count and therefore a hyperbolic statement that means a great number. The expression comes from the Old Testament where it is on occasion used to refer to an immense army (Jos 11:4; 1 Sa 13:5; 2 Sa 17:11).

20:9 *Surrounded the camp of God's people, the city he loves.* The final battle describes an attack on the people of God who are camped in Jerusalem, the city that God loves. The figurative nature of this description keeps us from thinking that this must be an actual battle that takes place at Jerusalem (after all, earlier visions picture the final battle at other locations; see for instance Armageddon in 16:16). This picture of the final battle finds a background in Zechariah's vision at the end of the book. Zechariah opens by saying, "A day of the LORD is coming, Jerusalem, when your possessions will be plundered and divided up within your very walls. I will gather all the nations to Jerusalem to fight against it" (14:1–2). The battle initially goes in favor of the attacking army, but then God intervenes ("then the LORD my God will come, and all the holy ones with him," 14:5) and destroys the invading army.

But fire came down from heaven and devoured them. At various times in the past, God sent fire from heaven to bring judgment on those who were his enemies (see notes at 8:3–5; 11:5).

20:10 *Lake of burning sulphur.* See note at 19:20.

Going Deeper into the Issue of Hell:
Revelation 19:20; 20:10, 14

The word *hell* never occurs in the main English translations of the book of Revelation, though what is referred to as hell (*geennan* [*gehenna*]; *tartessos* in 2 Pe 2:4) elsewhere, is prominent under other names in the book of Revelation. The "Abyss" is a fiery place, the abode of demons (Rev 9:1, 2, 11; 11:7; 17:8; 20:1; 20:3). At the end of Revelation we read that the wicked, the two beasts, Satan himself, and even Death and Hades are thrown into the fiery lake of burning sulfur (with variants).

Hell, the final destination of those who resist God, is often associated with fire even before the book of Revelation. In the Sermon on the Mount, Jesus warns that "anyone who says, 'You fool!' will be in danger of the fire of hell" (Mt 5:22). James teaches that the tongue can corrupt "the whole body" and set "the whole course of one's life on fire, and is itself set on fire by hell" (Jas 3:6).

We should be quick to point out that the fire of hell is metaphorical language; but if anything, that only underlines the idea that it nonetheless points to an undesirable destination, whether speaking spatially or psychologically. In other words, to turn hell exclusively into a state of oblivion or annihilation violates the integrity of the metaphor which denotes some kind of torment, though one could conceivably debate the length of time.[7]

Why does the New Testament and Jesus in particular (Mt 5:29–30; 10:28; 18:9; 23:15, 33; Mk 9:43, 45, 47; Lk 12:5) speak frequently of hell? Not because he wants anyone to experience it, but rather so that people will turn to him. I say this as a person who took the gospel seriously in high school more than fifty years ago after thinking about hell and the fate that would await if I persisted in resisting God. In other words, the Bible's teaching on hell has a redemptive purpose. We do well to heed its message and not try to explain it away.

The Final Judgment (20:11–15)

20:11 *A great white throne.* (See "Revelation 4 Through Old Testament Eyes: God on His Throne.") This is the only place in Scripture that speaks of a white throne. Throughout Revelation, white stands for blamelessness and righteousness as well as association with heavenly realities (see notes at 3:4, 18), so it seems reasonable to think that white here carries the same connotation. In the Old Testament, sin was often compared to filth or dirtiness and the removal of sin meant that a person would be "whiter than snow" (Ps 51:7). In Isaiah the contrast is between scarlet and white: "Though your sins be as scarlet, they shall be as white as snow" (Isa 1:18). In Revelation, the saints wear white clothes (3:3–4; 4:4; 6:11; 7:9, 13–14; 19:14).

The earth and the heavens fled from his presence. God on his white throne is so majestic that the very earth and heavens flee. In Old Testament theophanies we read about the earth going into upheavals at the appearance of the Lord (Na 1:4–5). And Psalm 114 uses personification of mountains and rivers fleeing to express God's awesome power at the time of the crossing of the Sea:

> When Israel came out of Egypt,
>   Jacob from a people of foreign tongue,
> Judah became God's sanctuary,
>   Israel his dominion.
> The sea looked and fled,
>   the Jordan turned back;
> the mountains leaped like rams,
>   the hills like lambs. (Ps 114:1–4)

20:12 *Which is the book of life.* See notes at 3:5; 13:8; 17:8. Here we have the picture of the final judgment. In the Old Testament there are just glimmers of this moment, the most explicit being in Daniel 12:1–3:

> But at that time your people—everyone whose name is found written in the book—will be delivered. Multitudes who sleep in the dust of the earth will awake: some to everlasting life, others to shame and everlasting contempt. Those who are wise will shine like the brightness of the heavens, and those who lead many to righteousness, like the stars for ever and ever.

The fuller description of the final judgment comes from the New Testament, especially in a passage like the one we have here in Revelation.

What they had done as recorded in the books. The book of life as used in Revelation, as we have seen, is a book that contains the names of those who will live forever in God's presence. But there are also other books mentioned here that record the deeds of peoples' lives. The next verse will also mention that people will be "judged according to what they have done." The emphasis on deeds would have served as an encouragement for those who follow Christ to live lives of faithfulness and obedience. For the relationship between the role of faith and grace on the one hand and deeds on the other, see "Going Deeper into 'I Know Your Deeds': Rev. 2:2, 19; 3:1, 8, 15."

20:13 *The sea . . . death and Hades.* Here the sea, death, and Hades are all personified and spoken of as if they had control of the dead. We have seen already that the sea, especially when personified, represents the forces of chaos derived from the Old Testament with an ancient Near Eastern background (Baal versus Yam [Sea], see note at 4:6–8). Personified death also has mythical connotations going back to ancient Ugaritic stories about the conflict between Baal and the god Mot ("Death," see note at 6:8). Hades is the Greek equivalent to *sheol* which typically simply means the grave but sometimes has connotations of the underworld. Another word for *sheol* in the Old Testament is Abaddon ("Destruction," see also note at 9:11), and it is interesting to see the personified sea, death, and Abandon play a role in Job 28. In this chapter, Job reflects on how wisdom is difficult to find. At one point, he makes this point by even saying that the powerful forces of the sea, death, and Abaddon cannot find it (Job 28:14, 22).[8]

20:14 *Then death and Hades were thrown into the lake of fire.* Now that we have come to the final judgment there is no longer a need for these holding places for dead humans.

Second death. See note at 20:6. The dead experience their first death at the end of their earthly lives. Now those who are not in the book of life (see notes at 3:5; 13:8; 17:8) will suffer a second and final death.

REVELATION 21

The Future World (21:1–22:5)

A New Heaven and a New Earth (21:1–8)

What the Structure Means:
The New Heavens and the New Earth, the New Jerusalem,
and Restored—Yet Better—Eden (Rev 21:1–22:5)

We have seen how John has been connecting visions in this latter part of his book with the simple phrase *kai eidon*, which the NIV translates as "and/ then I saw" or simply "I saw." For the last time, John uses that phrase at the head of the vision of the post-judgment world, though we can divide this final vision into three interconnected parts: (1) the new heavens and the new earth (21:1–8), (2) the New Jerusalem (21:9–27), and (3) Eden restored—yet better (22:1–5). These are three picture images all describing the same future, wonderful reality for those who faithfully follow God in Christ.

In the first picture image John reports that he saw "a new heaven and a new earth" (21:1), linking to the last vision of judgment before the judgment of the dead where "the earth and the heavens fled from his (God's) presence" (20:11). This new heavens and new earth are remarkable because there is no longer any sea, a symbol in the previous parts of Revelation and throughout the Bible for the forces of chaos and evil. Linking to the next major section (21:9–27), John then tells us that he saw "the Holy City, the new Jerusalem, coming down from heaven from God" (21:2). What makes the New Jerusalem special is that God's presence permeates the city ("God's dwelling place is now among the people, and he will dwell with them . . . and be their God," 21:3). As a result, all pain and suffering will disappear (21:4).

God, who sits on the throne, is the one who is making these things happen and so he proclaims, "I am making everything new!" (21:5). After commanding John to write everything down again (see also 1:19; 14:13), he then proclaims that "those who are victorious will inherit all this" (21:7), designating those who persevere in their faith in a similar way to that found in the seven letters to the churches (2:7, 11, 17, 26; 3:5, 12, 21; see also 15:2). On the other hand, evil people will be thrown into the lake of burning sulfur (21:8), as we have already heard in 20:15, along with the two beasts (19:20) and the dragon himself (20:10).

As we move from the depiction of the post-judgment period as the new heavens and the new earth to the New Jerusalem, we note some links to previous material. First, John tells us he is now escorted in his vision to the New Jerusalem by "one of the seven angels who had the seven bowls full of the seven last plagues" (21:9; see Revelation 15–16). Second, the angel invites John to come with him to see "the bride, the wife of the Lamb" (21:9) which is a reference to the church first introduced at 19:7. Lastly, the New Jerusalem itself was mentioned in the description of the new heavens and the new earth in the previous section (21:2).

The details of the description of the New Jerusalem will be spelled out in the notes to the verses below, but here we take special note of the description of God's presence, his glory, that permeates the city. It "shone with the glory of God" (21:11) and thus it does not need a sun or moon "for the glory of God gives it light, and the Lamb is its lamp" (21:23).

Overall, we are struck by several qualities of the New Jerusalem: first, its symmetry communicates order over against chaos; second, the size of its defensive features (walls in particular), emphasizing that it is a place of safety and security; third, its immense dimensions suggesting a large population in a spacious place; fourth, the abundant precious metals and jewels used in its construction, gesturing toward its preciousness; fifth, the lack of a temple, again because God dwells throughout it and not in one place; and then finally, its inhabitants—"only those whose names are written in the Lamb's book of life" (21:27).

The New Jerusalem came down from heaven in the context of the new heavens and the new earth (21:2). Still the new heavens and the new earth dominate the description of the first part of John's final vision (21:1–8) giving way to a more detailed description of the New Jerusalem (21:9–27) which symbolically takes us back to the beginning, before the entry of sin into the world and humanity's expulsion from the garden of Eden. A river that gives life is found in both scenes (Ge 2:10 and Rev 22:1) as is abundant fruitfulness (Ge 1:11–12). In both we find trees of life (Ge 2:9 and Rev 22:2). The presence of two trees means that this is more than a return or a simple restoration. Life after the judgment goes beyond the goodness of the garden. Even more, the curses of Genesis 3:16–19 are reversed (Rev 22:3). The new heavens and new earth remind us of the original garden, yes, but they will be even better than Eden.

21:1 Then I saw *"a new heaven and a new earth."* Isaiah is the first one to introduce the idea of a new heavens and a new earth to picture a restored better future after judgment. Isaiah may be pointing primarily to life after the Babylonian judgment,[1] but his rhetoric suggests something even more than that, and it is this expectation that the book of Revelation picks up in this section. As R. L. Schultz tells us, "Rev 21 serves to clarify and complete the eschatological vision of Isaiah."[2] John likely quotes Isaiah 65:17 here (as the NIV footnote indicates). He imagines a future time after the judgment when there will be prosperity and happiness again. God had created the heavens and the earth and then declared them very good (Ge 1), but afterward humans sinned (Ge 3) with negative cosmic consequences. Note, for instance, how Paul, alluding to Genesis 3, observes that "the creation was subjected to frustration" and was presently in "bondage to decay" (Ro 8:20–21), a view that would have been held earlier by Isaiah. But neither Isaiah nor Paul believe that God's creation would stay in this sorry state. Paul spoke of the creation waiting with expectant hope to be "brought into the freedom and glory of the children of God" (Ro 8:21). Isaiah pictured this as the introduction of a new heavens and a new earth. There is also the expectation in this passage in Isaiah that Jerusalem will be renewed as well ("I will create Jerusalem to be a delight and its people a joy," Isa 65:18), a picture that John will develop at length below.

Again, it appears that Isaiah's vision looks primarily to the nearer future, the restoration of God's people from exile or a better future for the disappointed exiles after the return. He does not speak of eternal life in the new heavens and the new earth, for instance, but of his people having a long and satisfying life ("never again will there be in it an infant who lives but a few days, or an old man who does not live out his years; the one who dies at a hundred will be thought a mere child; the one who fails to reach a hundred will be considered accursed"—65:20). At the very end of Isaiah, the prophet picks up the topic of the new heavens and the new earth once again as he cites God who proclaims that these new heavens and the new earth "will endure before me" as well as the name and descendants of his faithful people (66:22). When the new heavens and the new earth arrive, all humanity will worship God constantly and "look on the dead bodies of those who rebelled against me; the worms that eat them will not die, the fire that burns them will not be quenched, and they will be loathsome to all mankind" (66:23–24). John goes beyond this limited perspective, seeing this as a fitting image for bringing all history to a close.

In the New Testament, besides John in Revelation, 2 Peter speaks of the new heavens and the new earth. In a context where Peter is talking about the final judgment against sin, he warns, "the present heavens and earth are reserved for fire, being kept for the day of judgment and destruction of the ungodly" (3:7). He envisions that everything will be destroyed, but that "in keeping with his promise we are looking forward to a new heaven and a new earth, where righteousness dwells" (3:13).

This idea that the present deeply troubled cosmos will pass away and give way to a new heavens and a new earth intends to comfort and give hope to God's people, who presently suffer at the hands of evil. However, we must be careful not to think that this picture leads to the conclusion that the present heavens and earth are useless and can be neglected or maligned any more than the fact that we will have resurrection bodies mean that our present bodies are useless and should be exploited. Like our bodies we should think in terms of transformation into something much better ("by the power that enables him to bring everything under his control" he "will transform our lowly bodies so that they will be like his glorious body," Php 3:21, see also 1 Co 15:20–28). As we read on, we will see through the imagery employed in the next chapter and a half that the new heavens and new earth will not simply be a reversion to God's creation as it was before the fall, but something much, much better.

There was no longer any sea. Repeatedly throughout Revelation (and before that in many biblical books stretching back to the Old Testament, which itself has a connection with ancient Near Eastern mythological language) the sea stands for chaos and evil (see notes at 12:15 as well as 4:6–8). In this figurative depiction of life after the final judgment, the lack of a sea signals the lack of chaos and evil.

Going Deeper into the New Heavens and the New Earth: Revelation 21:1

As Christians put their future hope in life after death, they often think in terms of intangible souls leaving bodies behind and going up to an ethereal place called heaven that is a spiritual realm. That is not the picture that the Bible, and in particular the book of Revelation, gives us of our future life.

The final chapters of Revelation rather picture our eternal future not in terms of going up to heaven, but as living in a new heavens and a new earth. Rather than God's original creation being destroyed and replaced by some kind of spiritual reality, the future is that of a creation that was marred by sin now being transformed into its original creation beauty. Indeed, Revelation 22:1–5 will describe this new heavens and a new earth as a restored—yet better—garden of Eden. Indeed, Revelation 21:1–4 pictures a melding of sorts of the heavens and the earth so that God's presence permeates the earth. As Tom Wright puts it, "In Revelation 21–22, we find not ransomed souls making their way to a disembodied heaven but rather the new Jerusalem coming down from heaven to earth, uniting the two in a lasting embrace."[3] This future reality for God's faithful people is described figuratively as having no sea (21:1, because there will be no chaos or evil) and no temple (because God's presence is now pervasive).

What a glorious future awaits God's people when Jesus returns and sets all things right again. The creation itself, according to Paul, groans in hopeful expectation for this future day of liberation from the frustration of the present (Ro 8:18–25). (See also "Going Deeper into Judgment and the Environment: Revelation 16.")

And so do we. We look forward not to the liberation of our souls from our husk of a body, but rather for the "resurrection of the dead" where "the body that . . . is perishable . . . is raised imperishable," the body that is "in dishonor" will be "raised in glory," the body that is now weak will be raised "in power." In short, our "natural body" will be "raised a spiritual body" (1 Co 15:42–44a). In other words, we can expect "the redemption of our bodies" (Ro 8:23). Make no mistake about it, we will be given a future resurrection body.

We cannot be dogmatic about the details of our future life with God, but we know it will be good. We can also be sure that we will not spend our endless days sitting on a cloud strumming harps, as so many cartoons have pictured it over the years. Rather, we will be in harmonious relationship with God and with each other and with the creation. We will have the time and capacity to enjoy God fully, to know each other more deeply, and perhaps to explore not just our world, but perhaps the whole cosmos with its billions and billions of solar systems that include countless stars, and as we are discovering for the first time, countless other planets.

21:2 *The Holy City, the new Jerusalem.* In the Old Testament, the city of Jerusalem was set apart or holy because God chose to make his name dwell there on Mount Zion (Dt 12:8–14; Ps 78:65–72), and so Solomon built the temple on Mount Zion. Psalm 46:4 celebrates Jerusalem as "the holy place where the Most High dwells." In Psalm 48, the psalmist speaks of Jerusalem as "the city of our God, his holy mountain" (v. 1). As we noted in the previous verse, Isaiah speaks of the new heavens and the new earth also in terms of a newly created Jerusalem.

Prepared as a bride beautifully dressed for her husband. The new Jerusalem is hereby equated with the church which had earlier been described as the bride of Jesus, her husband (see note at 19:7).

21:3 *God's dwelling place is now among the people.* At the beginning of creation, God dwelt with humanity (Ge 2), but sin fractured the relationship between them, so that humans could no longer easily enter the presence of God (Ge 3). Special locations were set apart (consecrated, made holy) and surrounded by restrictions so that God's people could meet with God in safety. At first, when they were an extended family, they built simple altars where they could "call on the name of God." But after the exodus, when they grew from a large extended family to be a nation, a larger facility was needed and so God directed them to build the tabernacle (Ex 25–31, 35–40), a mobile tent that fit with the fact that God's people were not yet established in the land. That moment came when David completed the conquest by subduing the last of Israel's internal enemies, so his son built the temple (1 Ki 7–8). To meet with God, that is to come into his presence, Israelites would have to come to the temple in Jerusalem. Due to their sin, the first temple was destroyed by the Babylonians and the city was destroyed (586 BC), though after the exile was over, God encouraged the building of a second temple (completed in 515 BC). This was the temple, aggrandized by Herod the Great, that Jesus knew.

With the coming of Jesus, however, the temple was no longer necessary. After all, in Jesus "the Word became flesh and made his dwelling among us" (Jn 1:14). When Jesus ascended to heaven, he sent the Holy Spirit to dwell in his people. Jesus also promised his disciples: "I am with you always, to the very end of the age" (Mt 28:20).

In this vision of the new Jerusalem, however, we are learning that God's people will have a fully restored intimate relationship with God. Again, the theme of the vision is that at the end the relationship between God and his people will be as it was in the garden of Eden—only better.

They will be his people, and God himself will be with them. Jesus is named Immanuel, which means "God is with us" (see background in Isa 7:14 and Mt 1:23). The promise that they will be God's people and God would be with them, expressing the mutuality of the relationship, is at the heart of the covenant idea.

The idea is connected to what is sometimes called the covenant promise expressed pithily in anticipation of the new covenant ("I will be their God, and they will be my people," Jer 31:33), fulfilled in Christ (Lk 22:20; Heb 10:7–13).

21:4 *Wipe away every tear from their eyes. There will be no more death.* For a second time, John quotes Isaiah 25:8 (see note at 7:17).

21:5 *He who was seated on the throne.* The one who sits on the throne is later identified as none other than God himself. (See "Revelation 4 Through Old Testament Eyes: God on His Throne.")

I am making everything new! Since the "old order" (21:4) is passing away along with the old earth and the old heavens, God is making everything new by bringing into being the new heavens and the new earth (21:1). From the description to follow, we cannot comprehend the details of this transformation, but the imagery given makes clear that what is new will both be in continuity with the old, but also better. We can imagine that what will be new will be like Eden, only better. Eden was a place where humans enjoyed a harmonious relationship with God and thus with each other and creation. There was mutuality and equality between the man and the woman. They were enjoying the fruit of the trees of the garden of Eden (with, of course, the exception of the tree of the knowledge of good and evil). They lived a wonderfully satisfying life—at least until tempted by the serpent.

Perhaps there is an allusion here to Isaiah 43:19 where God proclaims, "See, I am doing a new thing! Now it springs up; do you not perceive it? I am making a way in the wilderness and streams in the wasteland." In the same way that God transforms the wilderness into a place that can support life, so God here transforms the cosmos into a place that sustains an abundant, eternal life.

Write this down. See notes at 1:11; 14:13. The impetus to write this down is that it is "trustworthy and true," therefore important to preserve (see also 19:9).

21:6 *It is done. I am the Alpha and the Omega, the beginning and the end.* Here Alpha (the first Greek letter of the alphabet) and Omega (the last) are used to indicate a temporal sense. God began everything with creation, and he now ends time (see note at 1:8). The same thought is communicated by stating the poles of "beginning" (of time) and "end" (of time).

I will give water without cost from the spring of the water of life. God's people are spiritually thirsty, as the psalmist expressed:

As the deer pants for streams of eater,
    so my soul pants for you, my God.
My soul thirsts for God, for the living God. (Ps 42:1–2a)

The idea that God would provide water without cost is reminiscent of Isaiah's oracle in which God invites his people to a great feast paid for by someone else (see Rev 19:9) by saying:

> Come, all you who are thirsty,
>   come to the waters;
> And you who have no money,
>   come, buy and eat!
> Come, buy wine and milk
>   without money and without cost. (Isa 55:1)

The language of the spring of the water of life is first of all echoing the idea of the fountain of life in the Old Testament, which according to the psalmist is found in God himself: "for with you is the fountain of life" (Ps 36:9).

In the Gospels, Jesus tells the woman at the well that he can offer water that will mean she will never be thirsty again: "whoever drinks the water I give them will never thirst. Indeed, the water I give them will become in them a spring of water welling up to eternal life" (Jn 4:14, see also 6:35, and note on "springs of living water" at Rev 7:17).

21:7 *Those who are victorious.* See note at 2:7.

Will inherit all this . . . they will be my children. Those who are victorious, persevering through the persecution and staying faithful until the very end, will be God's children. The analogy of God as his people's father (and in the Old Testament mother; Dt 32:18; Ps 131:2; Isa 42:14; 49:15; 66:13) is found throughout the Bible. Israel was often referred to as the children of God and God addressed them as his children. In the New Testament too, those who follow Christ are also called his children (Ro 8:14–17; 9:8), and just like a parent's children inherit his property, so God's children will inherit the new heavens and the new earth.

21:8 *Magic arts.* See note at 9:21, where we have a similar though not identical list of those who will be judged by God.

The fiery lake of burning sulfur. See note at 19:20.

The second death. See note at 20:6.

The New Jerusalem (21:9–27)

21:9 *One of the seven angels who had the seven bowls.* See Revelation 15–16 and the note at 15:1. The continuing role of an angel involved with the bowls of God's wrath connects this earlier part of Revelation with its conclusion (see also 17:1).

The bride, the wife of the Lamb. The Bride of the Lamb, Jesus, is the church (see "Revelation 5:6 Through Old Testament Eyes: The Lamb Who Was Slain" and notes at 19:7 and 21:2).

21:10 *In the Spirit.* This is the final of four (see also 1:10; 4:2; 17:3) appearances of the phrase that highlights John's prophetic inspiration. He does not speak on his own authority but as a divine spokesperson. We have seen in the earlier occurrences that they introduce new sections, and this one contrasts with the previous section headlined by "in the Spirit," in that it introduces the description of the New Jerusalem in contrast with the depiction of Babylon as a prostitute riding the back of a beast.

To a mountain great and high. In the ancient Near East, gods were thought to dwell on mountains. We might think of the Canaanite god Baal who dwelled on a mountain called Zaphon. Even Greco-Roman religions, heavily influenced by ancient Near Eastern ideas, thought their chief god Zeus dwelt on Mount Olympus. That mountains were associated with the divine realm is not surprising, considering their grandeur and seeming permanence. This contrasts with the sea, which we have seen throughout the book of Revelation (also with an Old Testament and ancient Near Eastern background) was associated with divine beings who represented chaos and evil, for instance Baal's rival Yamm (the name means "Sea"). In the Old Testament the writers often used ancient Near Eastern ideas to communicate important theological truths, and thus we should not be surprised that Yahweh often appeared to his people on mountains. God met Moses and the Israelites, for instance, on Mount Sinai (Ex 19) as they departed Egypt and travelled to the promised land. Solomon built the temple on Mount Zion in Jerusalem, rendering the mountain holy space. In Revelation's figurative depiction of the future dwelling place for God's people then, it also does not surprise that the place is figuratively described as on a great and high mountain. Williamson reminds us that "many Old Testament prophecies said that the future Jerusalem would be located on a high mountain (Isa 2:2–3; 25:6–26:2; Mic 4:1–2)."[4]

The Holy City, Jerusalem, coming down out of heaven. See note at 21:2.

21:11 *It shone with the glory of God.* The Greek word translated "glory" (*doxa*) is the same word translated "splendor" in 18:1 (see note). The difference in English translation may be because the NIV translators felt that the translation "glory" should only be used for God and in chapter 18 an angel was said to exhibit *doxa*.

In any case, the Greek word *doxa* as applied to God surely reflects the frequent use of *kabod* ("glory") for God in the Old Testament, and indeed, *doxa* is typically used to translate "glory" in the Greek version of the Old

Testament. *Kabod* has the meaning "weight" (1 Sa 4:18), and when used of human beings (1 Ki 3:9) has a sense similar to what we mean today in English when we say a person is weighty, that is substantial in prestige, reputation, and honor.[5] God's glory, of course, exceeds that of even the most honored human being. God's glory accompanies his appearance and is often associated with great or brilliant light as here.[6] In the final analysis, though, it must be admitted that the "glory of God" is not reducible to a simple definition. John Piper is surely correct when he says that though the "term 'glory of God' in the Bible generally refers to the visible splendor or moral beauty of God's manifold perfections . . . it is an attempt to put into words what cannot be contained in words—what God is like in his unveiled magnificence and excellence."[7]

   Like a jasper, clear as crystal. See note at 4:3.

21:12 *A great, high wall with twelve gates.* City walls provide security, so if you are inside the wall, you are in a place of safety. This wall has twelve gates protected by twelve angels, representing the twelve tribes of Israel, thus figuratively signaling the inclusion of the ancient people of God in the New Jerusalem, namely the descendants of Abraham who put their trust in and were faithful to Yahweh. The book of Ezekiel ends with a description of a future new Jerusalem as having twelve gates, three facing each direction, each named for one of the twelve tribes of Israel (Eze 48:30–34). See "Revelation Through Old Testament Eyes: Ezekiel" at 20:7.

21:13 *East . . . north . . . south . . . west.* As we hear the dimensions of this figurative city, we should be struck by its symmetry, being a well-ordered cube. Here we have three gates on each side of the city, beginning with the east.

21:14 *On them were the names of the twelve apostles of the Lamb.* The names of the twelve tribes of Israel are on the gates of the city (see 21:12). Now the names of the twelve apostles of Jesus (the Lamb) are on the foundations, showing that the church too is part of the city. The people of both the Old and New Testaments will join at the end of history to live in the presence of God. See note at 4:4.

21:15 *A measuring rod of gold.* At the end of the book of Ezekiel, the prophet reports a vision that came to him during the Babylonian exile ("in the fourteenth year after the fall of the city," Eze 40:1). In his vision Ezekiel is transported to the land of Israel and is placed on a high mountain where he sees an angel ("whose appearance was like bronze") who stood with a "linen cord and a measuring rod in his hand" (40:3). As he looked, the angel goes out and measures a building identified as the temple and its outer court. Of course the temple that Solomon built had been destroyed by the Babylonians, so this vision gives hope that a future temple might be built. That hope finds at least initial fulfillment in the building of the second temple some decades later as described in Ezra 1–6. That temple too was ultimately destroyed by the Romans in AD 70, but from a New Testament perspective by that time a temple was obsolete since the reality that it anticipated had been fulfilled in the coming of Jesus ("the word became flesh and made his dwelling [tabernacle] among us," Jn 1:14). See "4. Measuring the Temple" in "Revelation Through Old Testament Eyes: Ezekiel" at 20:7.

Thus, the description of an angel measuring a future holy place where God makes his presence known associates these two visions together, but we can clearly see how the picture here in Revelation intensifies and expands upon the earlier vision and thus renders improbable that we are to see the measuring of the New Jerusalem as a fulfillment of the vision of measuring the temple in Ezekiel. The latter scene more likely inspired a literary and theological vehicle for expressing the future expectation of the final place where God will dwell with his people.

The intensification and expansion may be seen in the fact that the angel measures a city, not just the temple and its outer court. It may also be seen in the immense proportions and precious materials used to build the city in contrast to Ezekiel's future temple (see next verses).

21:16 *12,000 stadia in length, and as wide and high as it is long.* Again, we should note the symmetry of the city emphasizing its order, lacking chaos. It is not only, as the verse says, a "square," it is a cube. It is an immense cube at that, since 12,000 stadia (notice the use of a multiple of 12, mirroring the 12 gates and 12 foundation stones) is 14,000 miles.

21:17 *The wall . . . was 144 cubits thick.* The walls were incredibly substantial, being 200 feet thick, perhaps emphasizing the security and safety of the place (see note at 21:12).

21:18 *The wall was made of jasper.* Jasper is a precious stone, see note at 4:3.

The city of pure gold, as pure as glass. See note at 21:21. Tabb rightly points out that the cubelike dimensions of the New Jerusalem, along with the description of the city as made of pure gold makes us think of the Holy of Holies of the temple. He quotes the Greek text of 1 Kings 6:20: "the length twenty cubits and twenty cubits the width and twenty cubits its height, and he covered it with overlaid gold."[8]

21:19 *The foundations of the city walls were decorated with every kind of precious stone.* The foundations, which represent the apostles and thus the church (21:14), are ornamented with precious stones, a different type for every foundation. Though the list is not exactly the same,[9] these precious stones remind us both of the high priest's breastpiece which had twelve different precious stones (Ex 28:17–21; 39:8–14) as well as the picture of Adam before the fall in all his glory (Eze 28:13–14, in the context over an oracle against the king of Tyre). The Old Testament connects the spiritual realm with semiprecious and precious stones.

In Isaiah, a Jerusalem restored after the coming judgment is described in similar terms:

> Afflicted city, lashed by storms and not comforted,
>   I will rebuild you with stones of turquoise,
>   your foundations with lapis lazuli.
> I will make your battlements of rubies,
>   your gates of sparkling jewels,
>   and all your walls of precious stones. (Isa 54:11–12)

21:21 *The twelve gates were twelve pearls.* The gates represent the twelve tribes of Israel. Here they are ornamented with pearl, a rare and therefore expensive object, thus showing the preciousness of the Old Testament people of God.

The great street of the city. This large city has one dominant street in it, and it is described as gold, and not just any gold, but pure gold, as pure as transparent glass is pure. Pure gold would be rarer and therefore more expensive.

21:22 *I did not see a temple in the city.* The temple was a place where God made his presence known in the world in a special way. Sin created the need for such a separate sacred place (preceded by the tabernacle from the time of Moses to Solomon and altars from the time of Adam to Moses). But with the coming of Jesus there was no longer a need for a special sacred spot because in Jesus "the Word became flesh and made his dwelling among us" (Jn 1:14). And when he departed the earth, he both promised to be with us (Mt 28:20) as well as to send the Spirit who would dwell in us, rendering us temples of God. But in the New Jerusalem, which we will see is also restored Eden, God's presence permeates the place where humans dwell, thus making it even more unnecessary for a holy place like the temple. See also "Revelation 11:1–2 Through Old Testament Eyes: The Temple" (as well as notes at 21:3, 15).

Revelation 21 Through Old Testament Eyes: The Heavenly Temple

John in Revelation often describes heaven as a temple. On several occasions heaven is a temple from which angels come and go (14:15, 17; 15:5–6) and from which God and his representatives speak (16:1). God's glory fills this heavenly temple (15:8) and God receives the worship of the martyrs in the heavenly temple (7:15).

He also mentions the furniture of the temple, most often the incense and/ or the sacrificial altar. For example, in the description of the fifth seal, John sees those who had been martyred under the altar in heaven crying out for justice against those who killed them (6:9–11). As the note in the commentary explains, it is not certain which of the two temple altars this intends, but some references to the altar are more definitely a reference to the incense altar. In Revelation 8:3–5, we read that an angel stood at the altar and offered incense (Ex 30:1–10, 34–38) which are the prayers of all God's people (see also Rev 9:13), while others are most likely references to the sacrificial altar (Rev 14:18; 16:7; see also Ex 27:1–8).

In addition, we have one mention of the ark of the covenant (Rev 11:19), the most potent symbol of God's presence within the Old Testament temple. It was also taken out of the temple to represent God the warrior's presence on the battlefield, and thus is mentioned appropriately in connection with the climatic judgment that follows the blowing of the seventh trumpet (Rev 11:19).

Of particular import, we should note the description of the New Jerusalem, which descends from heaven (Rev 21:2). John goes out of his way to say that this city, which represents the new heavens and the new earth, has no temple (21:22). Why? "Because the Lord God Almighty and the Lamb are its temple" (21:22). All of heaven is a temple and when heaven (God's abode) comes to earth, there is no need for temple language anymore.

The temple built by Solomon, and the tabernacle built by Moses before it, represent heaven on earth. The reality is heaven, the symbol is the earthly buildings that point to it. Thus, Revelation can use temple language to refer to God's heavenly presence. (See also "Revelation 4 Through Old Testament Eyes: God on His Throne" and "Revelation 11:1–2 Through Old Testament Eyes: The Temple.")

21:22 *Lord God Almighty*. See note at 11:17.

21:23 *The city does not need the sun or the moon to shine on it*. Light and dark can be used symbolically for God's presence and absence or even the conflict between good and evil (Job 24:13-17; 38:12-18). In the context of the Lord bringing judgment and coming to reign as king, Zechariah looked forward to this day when there "will be neither sunlight nor cold, frosty darkness. It will be a unique day—a day known only the LORD—with no distinction between day and night. When evening comes, there will be light" (Zec 14:6-7). God is associated with light (Ps 4:6; 104:2) and here his presence gives the New Jerusalem all the light it needs. In one of his salvation oracles, Isaiah describes how Israel will be the key to the destiny of all nations. He then tells God's people:

> The sun will no more be your light by day,
>> nor will the brightness of the moon shine on you,
> for the LORD will be your everlasting light,
>> and your God will be your glory.
> Your sun will never set again,
>> and your moon will wane no more;
> the LORD will be your everlasting light,
>> and your days of sorrow will end. (Isa 60:19-20)

Likewise, as described in the following verses (Rev 21:24-26), the people of God are the key not only to who will receive judgment but also to the future blessing that the nations will enjoy.

21:24 *The nations will walk by its light*. The picture of the path or the way is best known in wisdom literature where the father teaches his son to stay on the well-lit path that leads to life (Ps 56:13; Pr 4:18; 6:23). The path represents the journey of life, and a well-lit path means smooth traveling. The prophet Micah foresaw that in the last days the nations will say, "Come, let us go up to the mountain of the LORD, to the temple of the God of Jacob. He will teach us his ways, so that we may walk in his paths" (Mic 4:2). In John's vision of the end, the ultimate fulfillment is even better than a journey to a physical temple. Rather, the nations will walk into the very presence of God himself in a New Jerusalem that does not need a temple because God's presence permeates the whole city. According to Isaiah, God proclaims that "instruction will go out from me; my justice will become a light to the nations" (Isa 51:4). Isaiah also provides an Old Testament background to the picture of the nations walking by light (see note at 18:1).

Arise, shine, for your light has come,
    and the glory of the Lord rises upon you.
See, darkness covers the earth
    and thick darkness is over the peoples,
but the Lord rises upon you
    and his glory appears over you.
Nations will come to your light,
    and kings to the brightness of your dawn. (Isa 60:1–3)

The kings of the earth will bring their splendor into it. In the ancient world, vassal kings would bring tribute to their sovereign ruler. Here the picture is of the kings of the earth, rather than raging against God (Ps 2; as echoed in Rev 2:27; 12:5; 19:15), bringing gifts to God in the New Jerusalem to honor him.

The psalmist calls on God to subdue the nations so that they will bring tribute to him at the temple:

Summon your power, God;
    show us your strength, our God, as you have done before.
Because of your temple at Jerusalem
    kings will bring you gifts.
Rebuke the beast among the reeds,
    the herd of bulls among the calves of the nations.
Humbled, may the beast bring bars of silver.
    Scatter the nations who delight in war.
Envoys will come from Egypt;
    Cush will submit herself to God. (Ps 68:28–31; see also Isa 60:5; 61:6)

Just as the Gentile wise men brought gifts to the infant Jesus (Mt 2:1–12), in John's vision the nations come streaming to the New Jerusalem with tribute in hand.

21:25 *On no day will its gates ever be shut.* A walled city closes its gates, particularly at night, for security reasons. But because there will be no night in the New Jerusalem, there will be no need to shut the gates. More to the point, because there will be no threat to the city from evil forces after they have all been thrown into the lake of fire, there will be no need to shut the gates. Here we see the continuing influence of Isaiah 60 (see note in previous verse where Isaiah 60:1–3 is quoted) since in his anticipation of restoration after judgment God declares:

Foreigners will rebuild your walls,
　　and their kings will serve you.
Though in anger I struck you,
　　in favor I will show you compassion.
Your gates will always stand open,
　　they will never be shut, day or night. (Isa 60:10–11a)

21:26 *The glory and honor of the nations will be brought into it.* Isaiah continues (see previous note) to go on to give the reason why the gates of the city will stay open: "so that people may bring you the wealth of the nations" (Is 60:11b). At the end of time, the nations will no longer rage against the Lord, but will come and bring him tribute.

21:27 *Only those whose names are written in the Lamb's book of life.* God's presence permeates New Jerusalem, so nothing impure or anyone who is shameful can enter that city. Only those whose name is written in the Lamb's (Jesus') book of life (see notes at 3:5; 13:8; 17:8; 20:12).

A Return to Eden—Only Better (22:1–5)

22:1 *The river of the water of life.* Now the New Jerusalem is described as having a river that flows though the city, actually right down the middle of the great street described in 21:21 (as we learn from 22:2). We will soon see that the New Jerusalem is also a restored Eden, and of course four rivers flowed out of Eden (Ge 2:10–14). We have seen that often in Revelation and in many other parts of Scripture, water (the sea, many waters, etc.) represented chaos and evil, but water also is life-giving to vegetation, animals, and humanity. Jesus, for example, claimed that he had "living water" that if drunk would "become in them a spring of water welling up to eternal life" (Jn 4:10, 14).

The passage that provides the most important background to this picture of the river is found in Ezekiel 47, where an angel showed Ezekiel in a vision a river that flowed out from under the threshold of the temple toward the east. As his angelic guide led him further and further to the east, the waters become deeper and deeper. Eventually, the waters enter the Dead Sea, a Sea that has no life in it due to its high salt content and is situated in a desolate area. But in his vision Ezekiel notes "a great number of trees on each side of the river" (47:7) and now "large numbers of fish" in the Dead Sea "because this water flows there and makes the salt water fresh; so where the river flows everything will live" (47:9).

Ezekiel speaks figuratively about the future of the land, which at the time of his ministry was languishing because of the sin of God's people. The river that flows out of the temple indicates that God will bring his people life again after the judgment.

In his vision of the coming "day of the LORD" (Zec 14:1), the prophet Zechariah also envisions "living water" that "will flow out from Jerusalem, half of it east to the Dead Sea and half of it west to the Mediterranean Sea, in summer and winter" (14:8).

John's vision goes further than either Ezekiel's or Zechariah's and uses the river imagery to point toward the ultimate restoration. We might also remember the powerful picture of Jerusalem, the city of God, where there is a "river whose streams make glad the city of God, the holy place where the Most High dwells" (Ps. 46:4), a passage particularly relevant to this picture of the future New Jerusalem. After the judgment, God will bring life, indeed, eternal life to his people.

From the throne of God and of the Lamb. In Ezekiel's vision of the river of life, the waters flowed from the temple. Here the waters flow from the throne of God, which was in heaven, but now is in the city (see 22:3). Earlier throughout Revelation the throne was God's, and the Lamb was next to it (Rev 4), though sometimes the Lamb was described as in the "center of the throne" (Rev 5:6; 7:17). But here the throne is occupied jointly by God (the Father) and the Lamb (the Son). See "Revelation 4 Through Old Testament Eyes: God on His Throne."

22:2 *The great street of the city.* See note at 21:21.

On each side of the river stood the tree of life. Here is the indicator that the New Jerusalem represents a restored and even better Eden. In Genesis 2, we learn that God placed the first man and woman in a garden called Eden. In this garden there was a tree, called the tree of life (Ge 2:9). As the name implies, the tree informs us that Eden was a place of life, even robust life, which was enjoyed by Adam and Eve. That is it was until they demonstrated their refusal to follow God's command not to eat the fruit of the other prominent tree in the garden, namely the tree of the knowledge of good and evil. The result was a banishment from the garden of Eden so that they may no longer eat from the tree of life, indeed God placed two cherubim at the entrance of the garden "to guard the way to the tree of life" (Ge 3:22, 24). But here in the restored Eden, in the New Jerusalem, we also have a tree of life, signaling that God's faithful people will return to Eden, a place of harmony between God and humans as well as harmony with each other and the creation. But this tree of life seems to surpass even that in the original garden story. Though one tree, it is found on both sides of the river, and it produces twelve crops of fruit, in other words every month. And then leaves of the tree are for healing. It appears that this vision of restored Eden, only better, is mediated through Ezekiel's vision of a river flowing from the temple to the Dead Sea where "fruit trees of all kinds will grow on both banks of the river. Their leaves will not wither, nor will their fruit fail. Every month they will bear fruit, because the water from the sanctuary flows to them" (Eze 47:12). We cannot be specific about what this new Eden will be like; we can only trust that it will be wonderful.

Twelve crops of fruit, yielding its fruit every month. And the leaves of the tree are for the healing of the nations. Another indication that restored Eden will surpass the fruitfulness of the original Eden is the frequency and abundance of the produce from the tree of life. In the previous verse, we noted the connection between this description of the river that flows through the New Jerusalem and the river that Ezekiel saw in his vision that flowed from under the threshold of the temple to the east and eventually to the Dead Sea. While the tree of life is not mentioned, we get a similar description that "fruit trees of all kinds will grow on both banks of the river. Their leaves will not wither, nor will their fruit fail. Every month they will bear fruit because the water from the sanctuary flows to them. Their fruit will serve for food and their leaves for healing" (Eze 47:12).

22:3 *No longer will there be any curse.* After Adam and Eve sinned, God brought punishment against the three parties involved. The serpent will now crawl on its belly and there will be enmity between the serpent "and the woman, and between your offspring and hers," pointing to the struggle between those who follow God and those who do not and so follow the serpent, who represents evil, indeed Satan himself (Ge 3:14–15). God then informs the woman that she will be punished in her most important relationships: in childbearing, where there will be increased pain; and in her relationship with her husband where she will desire (that is, try to control) him, but he will push back to rule her (Ge 3:16). To Adam, God says that he will punish him in his labor. He worked before, but now it will be filled with frustration because "cursed is the ground because of you; through painful toil you will eat food from it" (Ge 3:17–19). And then most significantly, death enters the experience of humans created in God's image (Ge 3:21–24; Ro 5:12–20). But here in the New Jerusalem, the serpent (the dragon) has been thrown into the lake of fire (20:7–10), human relationships will be restored, and work will no longer be filled with frustration. And most important of all, death will not be a part of the experience of God's people.

The throne of God and of the Lamb. See note at 22:1. The throne that was in heaven (Rev 4) now is found in the midst of the New Jerusalem, where God's redeemed people dwell.

22:4 *They will see his face, and his name will be on their foreheads.* To see God's face is to be in his presence (e.g., Ps 4:6; 11:7; 17:15). Conversely, when God hides his face from someone indicates that God is not present (Ps 13:1; 27:9; 30:7). To have God's name on their forehead demonstrates their allegiance to God (see notes at 7:3; 14:1, 9). The combination of seeing God's face and having his name on the forehead indicates an intimate relationship with God.

22:5 *There will be no more night . . . for the Lord God will give them light.* See note at 21:23.

They will reign for ever and ever. See notes at 5:10 and 20:4.

Conclusion (22:6–21)

Final Angelic Instructions (22:6–11)

What the Structure Means: Announcements, Warnings, and Rewards (22:6–21)

The visions have concluded. The book closes with a series of announcements and warnings. The primary announcement is repeated three times as Jesus says, "I am coming soon!" (22:7, 12, 20). The primary warning is to heed the words of the prophecy, to stay faithful and obedient. And the reward for those who do so is entrance into the city, the New Jerusalem, and access to the tree of life, something denied to those who do not listen and obey (22:15, 19).

The section begins with the angel who has accompanied John in these final visions (21:9), telling John that it was God himself who directed him to show John these visions that revealed "the things that must soon take place" (22:6), and therefore is able to assure John that the words he has heard are "trustworthy and true" (22:6).

At this point, Jesus gives the first announcement of his imminent return (22:7) at which point John makes as if to worship the angel, perhaps because he confuses the angel with the glorified Christ. In any account, the angel stops John and directs his worship toward God himself. He then concludes by telling John not to seal up the prophecy of the scroll because the time is near. This is in contrast with the command that the angel gave to Daniel (12:9) to seal up his prophecy because the time was not yet (see note at 22:10).

The focus then moves from the angel to Jesus himself, who announces again "I am coming soon" (22:12). He then encourages those who remain faithful and obedient that their reward is coming, warning those who are not faithful and are disobedient that their punishment is coming. Jesus affirms that he is the one who sent the angel to give him the prophecy so John could carry the message to the churches.

After warning people not to add or take away words of this prophecy, Jesus announces for the third time, "I am coming soon," to which John responds "Amen. Come, Lord Jesus" (22:20). The book then concludes with a blessing on God's people (see "What the Structure Means: The End of John's Letter [Rev 22:21]").

Going Deeper into Hope: Revelation 21–22

Many people find the book of Revelation disturbing, scary, even depressing. The images of evil are indeed frightening (dragon, beasts), as are the pictures of judgment (four horsemen, earthquakes, storms, hybrid locusts from the Abyss). The book announces God's certain and inevitable judgment at the end of time.

But for the intended readers of the book, this was not a message of despair. Quite the opposite. The book has a message of hope.

Perhaps those of us who live in the comparatively tranquil present don't have the same reaction as the oppressed and often persecuted original readers would have, but the idea that God was coming to judge those who had them by the neck was nothing short of incredibly optimistic. The book of Revelation intends to give hope to the faithful, who are the intended readers of the book.

J. J. Collins gets this when he points out that "a catastrophic imagination alone is not genuinely apocalyptic." He goes on to say, "We should give it credit for its indomitable hope, which is not always supported by rational analysis of human affairs, but may well be indispensable to human flourishing."[1] Rational analysis of John's contemporary situation as he sits in exile on the island of Patmos would indeed lead to despair, but the purpose of the book is not to be irrational but to pull aside the curtains to show that the truth of God's future victory is certain. God's people will be rescued, while those who harm them will be punished. In a word, justice will win out at the end.

Many readers of this commentary will not get it right away, but others will. The latter includes those who live in countries where Christianity is presently marginalized or persecuted. But, truth be told, Christianity is always marginalized in every society. Some, like in the United States now, live by the delusion that our country is Christian. But this is not true, never has been, and never will be. Christians are always "exiles scattered" (1 Pe 1:1) throughout the world. Our citizenship is in heaven. While we should work to make our world a better place, we need to do so as pilgrims, exiles, those wandering through the wilderness.[2] Living in the light of the message of the book of Revelation, we can do so with a sure hope.

22:6 *Trustworthy and true.* See also 21:5. Here at the end of the book the emphasis is placed on the fact that the picture of the end presented in this book is absolutely true because it comes from heaven.

The God who inspires the prophets. God inspires his prophets, including John, who four times asserted that he was speaking "in the Spirit" (1:10; 4:2; 17:3; 21:10), mimicking a claim made also by Ezekiel (see note at 1:10). But all the prophets claimed to be speaking the "word of the Lord," often punctuating their message with phrases like "thus says the Lord." Peter also tells his readers to remember that "prophecy never had its origin in the human will, but prophets, though human, spoke from God as they were carried along by the Holy Spirit" (2 Pe 1:21).

Sent his angel to show his servants the things that must soon take place. See note at 1:1.

22:7 *Blessed is.* This blessing is the sixth of seven in the book of Revelation (see note at 1:3). Here the blessing is pronounced on those who keep the prophecy, which means that they persevere during the present troubles and do not compromise the faith.

22:9 *Don't do that!* As on a previous occasion (Rev 19:10), John falls at the feet of an angel. We have seen descriptions of angels that communicate their awesome splendor (see note at 18:1), but here the angel tells John that he is not God, indeed he is a fellow servant (equally subservient to God) along with all God's followers ("all who keep the words of this scroll"). Only God deserves worship, the worship of both humans as well as angels.

22:10 *Do not seal up the words of the prophecy of this scroll.* At the end of the book of Daniel, when an angel gives that prophet his final instructions, he tells him: "Go your way, Daniel, because the words are rolled up and sealed until the time of the end" (Da 12:9). But now the situation has changed; the prophecy which had been unsealed by Jesus (Rev 5–6) should remain open because, unlike at the time of Daniel, "the time is near" (see note at 1:3).

22:11 *Let the one who does wrong continue to do wrong.* There comes a time when it is too late to change. Those who do wrong will continue to do wrong, a vile person will continue to be vile. But in the same way a person who does right will continue to do right and a holy person will continue to be holy. Still there is also an implicit assumption of choice and a challenge to change one's ways along with the idea that "the wicked will continue to be wicked" (Da 12:10).

Jesus' Final Announcements and Warnings (22:12-21)

22:12 *I am coming soon.* See note at 22:20–21.

According to what they have done. John's visions have highlighted the importance of deeds that flow from faith because they call on God's people to remain obedient despite their present struggles.

22:13 *I am the Alpha and the Omega.* God had earlier described himself as the Alpha and the Omega, the first and last letters of the Greek alphabet, as a way of saying he was the beginning and end of all things (see notes at 1:8 as well as 21:6).

The First and the Last. See note at 1:17 (in reference to Jesus).

The beginning and end. See 21:6.

22:14 *Blessed are those.* The seventh and climactic announcement of blessing (see note at 1:3). On this occasion, the blessing is pronounced on the saints who live a faithful and obedient life (they have washed their clothes, see note at 7:13–14) so their reward is the tree of life (see note at 22:2) to which they gain access by passing through the gates of the city, the New Jerusalem (see note at 21:12).

22:15 *Outside are the dogs.* The blessed saints who were faithful and obedient were inside the New Jerusalem (22:14), but outside are found those who practice evil defined by a list similar to that found in 9:20–21, see notes. For the first time, though, these sinners are called dogs. In the ancient world, dogs were not the lovable companions that they are today but were typically scavenger animals that were not only a nuisance, but a threat. To call someone or oneself a dog might express a low opinion or contempt (2 Sa 9:8; 16:9), but it can also be used to describe people who are dangerous and evil predators (Ps 22:20; 59:6, 14; Isa. 56:11). In the New Testament Paul warns the Philippians concerning false teachers to "watch out for those dogs, those evildoers, those mutilators of the flesh" (Php 3:2). These are those whom John sees outside the gates of the New Jerusalem.

22:16 *Sent my angel to give you this testimony for the churches.* See note at 1:1. As the NIV footnote explains, "you" is plural here and therefore addresses not just John but the church at large. The testimony refers to the contents of the book of Revelation.

I am the Root and the Offspring of David, and the bright Morning Star. Jesus is the Root (see note at 5:5) and Offspring of David. To say that he is the Offspring of David means that he is the expected descendant of David who fulfills the expectation generated from 2 Samuel 7 regarding David's house (dynasty) and kingdom that "will endure forever before me; your throne will be established forever" (7:16). For "bright morning star," see note at 2:28.

22:17 *The Spirit and the bride say, "Come!"* The bride is the church (see note at 19:7, also 21:2, 9). The Spirit is the Holy Spirit that dwells in his people (1 Co 3:16; 6:19), and they both call for the return of Christ.

Let the one who is thirsty come; and let the one who wishes take the free gift of the water of life. See note at 21:6.

22:18-19 *If anyone adds anything to them . . . if anyone takes words away from this scroll of prophecy.* The scroll containing the book of Revelation is God's word to the church. To add or subtract from it would defame its sacred character that would lead to punishment. The book of Deuteronomy contains a similar warning concerning adding to or subtracting from the law that God was giving Israel at the time (see Dt 4:2). Tabb, therefore, rightly concludes that "by invoking Deuteronomy's warning about adding to or taking from the words of the Law in 22:18–19, Jesus boldly asserts that 'the authority of the book of Revelation parallels and exceeds that of the Torah.'"[3]

God will take away from that person any share in the tree of life and in the Holy City. Such people would remain outside the New Jerusalem (21:9–27) and therefore not live in the restored, yet better, Eden (22:1–5), in which is the tree of life (see note at 22:2).

22:20-21 *I am coming soon.* The glorified Christ had announced his imminent arrival to the church at Philadelphia (3:11), and he has repeated this note three times here at the very end of the book (see also 22:7, 12). The readers of the visions of John should thus live in the light of the reality that Jesus might appear at any time.

Amen. From the Hebrew, meaning "so be it."

The grace of the Lord Jesus. The letter ends with a benediction that God's people be characterized by his grace, his free gift of salvation.

What the Structure Means:
The End of John's Letter (Rev 22:21)

Toward the beginning of our commentary on Revelation, we noted that John writes in the form of a letter addressed to the seven churches in Asia (see "What the Structure Means: A Letter, an Apocalypse, and a Prophecy [Rev 1:1–8]") and in Revelation 2–3 we have seven distinct letters to the churches in Ephesus, Smyrna, Pergamum, Thyatira, Sardis, Philadelphia, and Laodecia (1:11). However, from Revelation 4 on there has really been no hint of a letter form, leaving the reader with the idea that the book of Revelation simply drops the letter form in favor of an apocalypse. But letters often end with benedictions (Ro 16:25–27; 1 Co 16:23; 2 Cor. 13:14, etc.), so John's benediction in 22:21 both reminds us that the book as a whole is a letter and tells us that the apocalyptic visions that compose the bulk of the book are included in the letter and that Revelation 4 and following is not simply an apocalypse. John uses the letter form to communicate the vision that he received to the seven churches and beyond.

Going Deeper into Jesus the Divine
Warrior Who Defeats Evil

In the book of Revelation, Jesus appears at the end of history to defeat evil and save his people. This picture brings to conclusion God's battle against evil people and spiritual powers.

The Bible begins not with conflict but in harmony. In contrast to other creation accounts of the ancient Near East that envision creation emanating from divine conflict (Enuma Elish), the opening chapter pictures Yahweh bringing order out of disorder, not in conflict but by divine fiat. Genesis 2 pictures a world in harmony. The first man and the first woman live in harmony with God, with each other, and with creation.[4]

Genesis 3 describes the disruption of creation harmony and the entry of conflict into the experience of humans who have been given the status of image bearers by God.[5] Of course a previous cosmic disharmony and conflict is suggested by the appearance of the serpent, a symbol of evil in the ancient Near East identified as Satan in the New Testament (see note at 12:9). We will see that spiritual conflict, while hinted at in the Old Testament, becomes a major focus in the New Testament.

The Bible's depiction of conflict and God's role as a warrior begins in Genesis 3 and extends through Revelation 20. We will now describe this conflict as unfolding in five phases, three in the Old Testament and two in the New Testament.

What we call the first phase of the battle refers to those accounts where God fights the flesh-and-blood enemies of Israel. Examples of such battles may be found throughout Israel's history at least through the monarchical period. One particularly notable instance is the battle of Jericho. After Joshua, the leader of Israel, meets with God who appears to him in the form of a soldier (Jos 5:13–15), he leads the army in a march around the city for six days. Then on the seventh day, on God's instructions they marched around the city seven times. Finally the marchers blew trumpets (replicating thunder and announcing the appearance of God). At this point the walls fell and the Israelite army took the city (Jos 6).

The second phase of divine warfare against evil overlaps with the first in terms of a timeline. Phase two refers to those battles where God fought not Israel's enemies, but Israel itself. God fought Israel when Israel disobeyed God and he came to judge them. The most striking instance of this phase was when Israel fell to the Babylonians. As the poet of Lamentations saw clearly, the real aggressor standing behind the human army was none other than God himself, who came against Jerusalem "like an enemy" (La 2:4–5 and throughout the chapter)

However, the destruction of Jerusalem and the following exile to Babylon was not the end of the story of Israel. Not only were the Jewish exiles allowed to return to Jerusalem, if they chose to, after the Persian defeat of Babylon (539 BC), but God also promised his people, who were still living under foreign oppression, that he would come again as a warrior to save them. This future expectation of the divine warrior is what we will call phase 3 of God's fight against evil.

A number of exilic and postexilic prophets anticipated this future coming of the divine warrior, but we will focus on Daniel 7, which has played such a key role within Revelation for reasons that will become clear as I summarize the contents of Daniel's first vision and its angelic interpretation.

In his vision, Daniel observes a turbulent sea, whipped up by the four winds of heaven. Out of this sea, four horrific beasts emerge one at a time (Da 7:1–2). The first beast was like a lion, but it also had eagle's wings. Suddenly, the beast's wings were torn off and it walked like a human and was given a human mind. The second beast was a vicious bear pictured as standing on one foot. It was chewing on three ribs and was commanded to "get up and eat your fill of flesh!" (7:5). The third beast looked like a leopard but had four birdlike wings and four heads (7:6). The final beast is not even compared to a regular animal like the previous three, but rather is said to have "iron teeth" (and later "bronze claws," 7:19). This beast used those teeth to crush its victims and its claws to trample them.

The fourth and final beast also had ten horns. Three of these horns were uprooted by a little horn that had "eyes like . . . a human being and a mouth that spoke boastfully" (7:8).

Much ink has been spilled over the precise identity of the beasts and the horns over the years. But for our purposes we simply report that in the second half of the chapter an angel tells Daniel that "the four great beasts are four kings that will rise from the earth" (7:17). Later he will refer to them as "kingdoms" (7:23). He will also say that the ten horns "are ten kings" who come from the fourth kingdom. Climactically, the focus is on the little horn who is also a king who subdues three of the ten kings and "will speak against the Most High and oppress his holy people and try to change the set times and the laws. The holy people will be delivered into his hands for a time, times, and half a time" (7:24–25).

Again, for our present purpose we will not get into the potential specific references to which these symbols point.[6] What is important for us to realize is that these beasts and the horns represent evil human kings and kingdoms who oppress the people of God into the far future.

But not forever. The second half of the vision shifts to a throne on which sits "the Ancient of Days" (7:9–10). Clearly the Ancient of Days represents Yahweh who is ready to judge as he is surrounded by myriads of his servants. Into his presence "one like a son of man" rides a cloud (7:13–14). This picture of heaven is quite striking in the Old Testament in that we have one figure representing God, the Ancient of Days, encountering another figure also representing God. After all, the narrator does not say he is a "son of man" (which always means human being in the Old Testament), but rather he is "one *like* a son of man." That he is more than human is clear in that he rides a cloud, the prerogative of God in the Old Testament.

While the battle between the one like the son of man and the beasts is not detailed, there is no doubt that the former defeats the latter. It is God's kingdom that will conquer the kingdoms of the world that oppress God's people and God's kingdom is "an everlasting kingdom," 7:27).

We have spent more time on phase 3 because, as we will see, it anticipates the next two phases. But to summarize, what we are calling phase 3 looks to the future when God the warrior will come to save his people and destroy those powers that oppress God's people.

The story of God's fight against evil continues in the New Testament, beginning with what we will call phase 4. As mentioned, the Old Testament ends with the people of God still living under foreign oppressors, but with the hope expressed by exilic and postexilic prophets that God will come as a warrior to rescue them and to judge those who oppress them. In this context, we should listen to the words of John the Baptist as he is in the wilderness awaiting the coming of the Messiah:

> The ax is already at the root of the trees, and every tree that does not produce good fruit will be cut down and thrown into the fire. I baptize you with water for repentance. But after me comes one who is more powerful than I, whose sandals I am not worthy to carry. He will baptize you with the Holy Spirit and fire. His winnowing fork is in his hand, and he will clear his threshing floor, gathering his wheat into the barn and burning up the chaff with unquenchable fire. (Mt 3:10–12)

In short, John echoes the message of the late Old Testament prophets. The warrior is coming soon!

When John sees Jesus, he recognizes him as the one he was expecting and so he baptizes him. Afterwards, John goes to jail and Jesus begins his ministry. While in jail, John hears reports about Jesus that he is healing the sick, restoring sight to the blind, getting the lame to walk, raising the dead, and preaching the good news to the poor. In response, John sends two disciples to Jesus with the question, "Are you the one who is to come, or should we expect someone else?" (Mt 11:3). In other words, why aren't you chopping out the rotten wood? Why aren't you burning the chaff? We thought you were the expected warrior!

Jesus answers John's disciples by doing more of the same and telling them to go back to tell John what they have seen (Mt 11:4–6). From what happens later in Jesus' life, we can understand Jesus' actions to say: "John, I am the divine warrior! But I have heightened and intensified the battle, so that it is directed not toward flesh-and-blood, but toward the spiritual powers and authorities. And, John, this battle is not won by killing but by dying."

Indeed, this battle will take Jesus to the cross. We recognize this in the account of his arrest in the garden of Gethsemane. As the armed crowd advances to arrest him, Peter draws his sword and cuts off the ear of the High Priest's servant. Jesus instructs him: "Put your sword back in its place . . . for all who draw the sword will die by the sword. Do you think I cannot call on my Father, and he will at once put at my disposal more than twelve legions of angels? But how then would the Scriptures be fulfilled that say it must happen in this way?" (Mt 26:52–54).

No wonder then that Paul could describe Jesus' redemptive acts in terms of a military victory over the powers and authorities. Regarding his crucifixion and resurrection, we read that Jesus "disarmed the powers and authorities" and "made a public spectacle of them, triumphing over them by the cross" (Col 2:15). When speaking of Jesus' ascension to heaven, Paul quotes Psalm 68, which in its Old Testament context was a hymn celebrating God as warrior: "But to each one of us grace has been given as Christ apportioned it. This is why it says, "When he ascended on high, he took many captives and gave gifts to his people" (Eph 4:7–8).

In sum, phase 4 relates to Jesus' earthly ministry where he battles the powers of evil by dying on the cross and being resurrected in power and ascending to heaven. But was John the Baptist wrong in his understanding of the Messiah as warrior? No, and in answer, we move on now to the final phase, the phase that the book of Revelation and other parts of the New Testament anticipate.

No, John the Baptist was not wrong, but he did not understand the full import of what he was saying. He did not realize that Jesus was coming not once, but twice. The first time took him to the cross where he defeated the spiritual forces of darkness, but this was an "already-not yet" victory. As we explained at Revelation 20:1–3, the crucifixion and resurrection resulted in the "binding" of Satan so he could not deceive the nations, but not in Satan's complete defeat. In Revelation (as well as in Mt 24, Mk 13, Lk 21:5–38, and elsewhere), we learn that Jesus will come again, and in a number of places, but perhaps nowhere more clearly than Revelation 19:11–21 and 20:7–10, we learn that at that future time the glorified Christ will compete his conquest over evil by sending Satan and the two beasts that supported him (the unholy trinity) into the lake of burning fire/sulfur, to be followed by those not found in the book of life and even death and Hades itself (20:11–15).

We read the book of Revelation in the "already-not yet" period between the resurrection and the second coming of Christ. Now that we have a sense of God's long fight against evil, how should we think and act?

The "already-not yet" period is what we have called phase 4, and so our first observation is that we are in the midst of a battle, a spiritual battle, not a physical one. Paul says this most clearly in his letter to the Ephesians where he begins by exhorting his readers:

> Finally, be strong in the Lord and in his mighty power. Put on the full armor of God, so that you can take your stand against the devil's schemes. For our struggle is not against flesh and blood, but against the rulers, against the authorities, against the powers of this dark world and against the spiritual forces of evil in the heavenly realms. (Eph 6:10–12).

He then describes the weapons and armor that Christians should use in this battle, which include truth, righteousness, the gospel of peace, faith, and the word of God (Eph 6:13–18).

This battle is not against flesh and blood like it was during the Old Testament period. But note that this spiritual battle is not a new battle but an intensification of the calls for participation of God's followers. We know that the spiritual battle has been going in heaven for eons. We get glimpses of it in various ways in the Old Testament like when the angel Gabriel told Daniel that the angel Michael had to fight the prince of Persia so he could come to Daniel and that he would now have to go and fight the prince of Greece (Da 10). But it is only after Jesus came the first time that God's followers are invited into that fight.[7] We can enter that battle with full confidence thanks to the vision of Jesus' ultimate victory given to us by the book of Revelation.

While we are called to spiritual warfare, we should not disown God's warfare in the Old Testament (phases 1 and 2).[8] After all, Jesus, who fully embraced what we call the Old Testament, did not. And, of course, those who do distance themselves from the Old Testament due to its depiction of divine violence typically end up disowning the vision of the future given in the book of Revelation as well. We engage in a spiritual battle now as we live in a fallen, troubled world, and we cry out along with John: "Amen. Come, Lord Jesus" (22:20).

ACKNOWLEDGMENTS

As a long-time professor and scholar of the Old Testament, I have had the pleasure over the past couple of years telling people that I am writing a commentary on the book of Revelation. After I let them wonder why for a short period of time, I tell them that it is for a series that looks at the New Testament through Old Testament Eyes, and they finally understand. I want to begin by thanking Andy Le Peau, the one who conceived the series which he now edits, for the invitation to participate in this series and for giving me an early choice of which book I would cover. As someone who has worked on the book of Daniel for years, Revelation was the natural choice. Indeed, my contention is that Revelation, though mystifying to most modern readers, was much more readily interpreted by its contemporary audience that would have been more fully immersed in the Old Testament imagery that John employs in his writing.

I want to also thank Andy for his excellent and careful reading of the manuscript that saved me from several errors and enriched my interpretation. I also want to thank the anonymous second reader who also gave me several very helpful suggestions. Still, as is traditional and only right to say, any remaining errors or misunderstandings are mine.

I am pleased to publish a book with Kregel for the first time. I thank them, and in particular Robert Hand and his team, for their help in putting my book in shape for final publication.

I have enjoyed and profited from spending the last several years looking closely at Revelation. I believe that its message is always relevant to the church. That message is that though it looks like evil is in control, God is really in control, and he will have the final victory. Therefore, remain faithful to Jesus in a culture that is toxic to your faith. Though addressed to John's contemporaries, every generation thinks that the book is especially speaking to their predicament. And they are all right.

I am dedicating this book to my six beautiful granddaughters. Alice and I have three sons, and each of them have, at the time of writing, two daughters each. Thank you, girls, for bringing joy in the lives of your Nanny and Poppy. Though it was hard to leave friends and beautiful weather in Santa Barbara, California, to move east, you made it all worthwhile. And, having made the move, we are rediscovering the joys of living again on the East Coast.

My hope is that this book aids readers in gaining a deeper appreciation and understanding of the last book of the Bible. I harbor no illusions that it is a thorough discussion (no commentary achieves that), nor that I am correct in all my interpretations. Even if it simply whets the reader's appetite for further study, I have accomplished my goal.

LIST OF WHAT THE STRUCTURE MEANS

LIST OF THROUGH OLD TESTAMENT EYES

LIST OF GOING DEEPER

ABBREVIATIONS

BBR	*Bulletin for Biblical Research*
BCOTWP	Baker Commentary on the Old Testament Wisdom and Psalms
BECNT	Baker Exegetical Commentary on the New Testament
COS	*Context of Scripture*
DBI	*Dictionary of Biblical Imagery*
ESV	English Standard Version
JBL	*Journal of Biblical Literature*
JETS	*Journal of the Evangelical Theological Society*
MT	Masoretic Text
NICOT	New International Commentary on the Old Testament
NICNT	New International Commentary on the New Testament
NIV	New International Version of the Holy Bible
NIVAC	NIV Application Commentary
NRSV	New Revised Standard Version
TOTC	Tyndale Old Testament Commentaries
UNCS	Understanding the Bible Commentary Series
WBC	Word Biblical Commentary

YAB	Yale Anchor Bible
ZIBBCNT	Zondervan Illustrated Bible Backgrounds Commentary New Testament

SELECT BIBLIOGRAPHY

Bauckham, Richard. *The Theology of the Book of Revelation*. Cambridge: Cambridge University Press, 1997.

Beale, G. K. *Revelation: A Shorter Commentary*. Grand Rapids: Eerdmans, 2015.

Blackwell, B. C., ed. *Reading Revelation in Context: John's Apocalypse and Second Temple Judaism*. Grand Rapids: Zondervan, 2019.

DeSilva, David A. *Discovering Revelation: Content, Interpretation, Reception*. Grand Rapids: Eerdmans, 2021.

Hoskins, Paul M. "Another Possible Interpretation of the Seven Heads of the Beast (Revelation 17:9–11)." *BBR* 20 (2020): 86–102.

Johnson, Alan F. "Revelation." In *The Expositor's Bible Commentary*, edited by David Garland and T. Longman III. Rev. ed. Grand Rapids: Zondervan, 2006.

Keener, C. S. *Revelation*. NIVAC. Grand Rapids: Eerdmans, 2002.

Koester, Craig R. *Revelation and the End of All Things*. 2nd ed. Grand Rapids: Eerdmans, 2018.

Longman, Tremper III. *How to Read Daniel*. Downers Grove, IL: InterVarsity Press, 2020.

———. *The Bible and the Ballot: Using Scripture for Political Decisions*. Grand Rapids: Eerdmans, 2020.

———. *Confronting Old Testament Controversies: Pressing Questions about Evolution, Sexuality, History, and Violence*. Grand Rapids: Baker Books, 2019.

———. *The Fear of the Lord Is Wisdom: An Introduction to Wisdom in Israel*. Grand Rapids: Baker, 2017.

———. *Psalms*. TOTC. Downers Grove, IL: InterVarsity Press, 2014.

_____. "The Messiah: Explorations in the Law and Writings." In *The Messiah in the Old and New Testaments*, edited by S. E. Porter, 13–34. Grand Rapids: Eerdmans, 2007.

_____. *Immanuel in Our Place: Seeing Christ in Israel's Worship*. Phillipsburg, NJ: P&R, 2001.

_____. *Daniel*. NIVAC. Grand Rapids: Zondervan, 1999.

Metzger, Bruce M., with David A. deSilva. *Breaking the Code: Understanding the Book of Revelation*. Nashville: Abingdon, 2019.

Mounce, R. H. *Revelation*. NICNT. Grand Rapids: Eerdmans, 1977.

Moyise, Steve. *The Old Testament in the Book of Revelation*. London: T&T Clark, 2015.

Mulholland, M. Robert, Jr. "Revelation." In *James/1–2 Peter/Revelation*. CBC. Carol Stream, IL: Tyndale House, 2001.

Osborne, G. R. *Revelation*. BECNT. Grand Rapids: Baker Academic, 2002.

Paul, Ian. "Introduction to the Book of Revelation." In *The Cambridge Companion to Apocalyptic Literature*, edited by C. McAllister, 37–41. Cambridge: Cambridge University Press, 2020.

Tabb, Brian J. *All Things New: Revelation as Canonical Capstone*. Downers Grove, IL: IVP Academic, 2019.

Williamson, Peter S. *Revelation*. Catholic Commentary on Sacred Scripture. Grand Rapids: Baker Academic, 2015.

Wright, N. T. *Revelation for Everyone*. Louisville: Westminster John Knox, 2011.

_____. *Surprised by Hope: Rethinking Heaven, the Resurrection, and the Mission of the Church*. San Francisco: HarperSanFrancisco, 2007.

END NOTES

INTRODUCTION AND MAIN THEME OF THE BOOK OF REVELATION

1. Not surprisingly, the themes of Daniel, Revelation's Old Testament counterpart, are similar. See T. Longman III, *How to Read Daniel* (Downers Grove, IL: InterVarsity Press, 2020).

2. This view was held by Justin Martyr (AD 165), Tertullian (AD 220), Origen (AD 254) among others in the early church. See the helpful discussion by I. Paul, "Introduction to the Book of Revelation," in the *Cambridge Companion to Apocalyptic Literature*, ed. C. McAllister (Cambridge: Cambridge University Press, 2020), 37–41.

3. There were early church thinkers who also denied that the apostle wrote Revelation starting with Dionysius in the early third century in Alexandria. While he nonetheless believed Revelation was Scripture, others in the eastern church (e.g., Cyril of Jerusalem, John Chrysostom), and some also questioned its canonical authority.

4. Bruce M. Metzger with David A. deSilva, *Breaking the Code: Understanding the Book of Revelation* (Nashville: Abingdon, 2019), 22.

5. I became interested in the critical hermeneutical issue of genre as early as my doctoral dissertation, published as *Fictional Akkadian Autobiography: A Generic and Comparative Study* (Winona Lake, IN: Eisenbrauns, 1991). See my recent comments in "The Scope of Wisdom Literature," in *The Cambridge Companion to Wisdom Literature* (Cambridge University Press, forthcoming).

6. See my *The Bible and the Ballot* (Grand Rapids: Eerdmans, 2020), 81–100.

7. Indeed, a good case can be made for the church to engage in culture care rather than culture war. See Makoto Fujimura, *Culture Care: Reconnecting with Beauty for Our Common Life* (Downers Grove, IL: IVP Books, 2017).

8. David A. deSilva, *Discovering Revelation: Content, Interpretation, Reception* (Grand Rapids: Eerdmans, 2021), 3.

9. DeSilva, *Discovering Revelation*, 57, may be correct that, since John would already have been called as a prophet, this passage may be more like a commission to a particular mission.

10. As pointed out by de Silva, *Discovering Revelation*, 8.

REVELATION 1

1. G. R. Osborne, *Revelation*, BECNT (Grand Rapids: Baker, 2002), 54.

2. The connection with the Septuagint of 3:14 is made clear by the unusual use of the nominative rather than the genitive after the preposition "from" (*apo*).

3. Brian J. Tabb, *All Things New: Revelation as Canonical Capstone* (Downers Grove, IL: IVP Academic, 2019), 30–31, though he does not argue for seeing the reference to the "seven spirits" as a reference to the Holy Spirit but seems to assume it, putting his emphasis on an excellent discussion of the phrase "I am."

4. He cites Psalm 104:4, quoted in Hebrews 1:7 to show that angels can be referred to as "spirits." Bruce M. Metzger with David A. deSilva, *Breaking the Code: Understanding the Book of Revelation* (Nashville: Abingdon, 2019), loc. 272.

5. Tabb, *All Things New*, 53.

6. The combination of reference to Daniel 7:13 and Zechariah 12:10 in Matthew 24:30 shows that the combination of these two Old Testament passages had "become traditional in the church," so M. Eugene Boring, *Revelation*, Interpretation (Louisville: Westminster John Knox, 1989), 79.

7. See M. Boda, *Haggai, Zechariah*, NIVAC (Grand Rapids: Eerdmans, 2004) for an illuminating discussion of Zechariah 12; see 486–87 for the issue of Hadad Rimmon.

8. It is a mistake to think that the prophet himself or his original audience would have recognized a gesture to the doctrine of the Trinity as thought by some who believe that the Trinity is suggested by the change of pronouns from "me" to "him." R. D. Phillips (*Zechariah* [Phillipsburg, NJ; P&R, 2007], 268) makes this error when he points out the change from "they will look on me . . . and they will mourn for him," implying that me is a reference to the Father and the him has to be a reference to the Son who is crucified. Besides the fact that a shift from me to him is not unusual in the Old Testament as a reference to the same person (see Boda, *The Book of Zechariah*, NICOT [Grand Rapids: Eerdmans, 2016], 488), in Phillips' reading it would be the Father who was crucified since the "me" is the one who was pierced, not the "him."

9. A. J. Köstenberger, "The Use of Scripture in the Pastoral and General Epistles and the Book of Revelation," in *Hearing the Old Testament in the New Testament*, ed. S. E. Porter (Grand Rapids: Eerdmans, 2006), 252.

10. Exactly when to date the composition of the book of Daniel is a matter of scholarly debate. This essay will presume my view that, even if the book were written later, that the visions of Daniel originate in the sixth century BC (see Longman, *How to Read Daniel*, 30–35).

11. Osborne, *Revelation*, 54.

12. As G. Osborne (*Revelation*, 71–72) points out, "I am" is "used throughout the Gospel of John to emphasize the deity of Christ and to recall the sacred tetragrammaton YHWH of Ex 3:14."

13. See also Rev 21:6 and 22:13.

14. R. H. Mounce, *Revelation*, NICNT (Grand Rapids: Eerdmans, 1977), 68.

15. As shown by the Septuagint translation of the title in places like 2 Sa 5:10; Jer. 5:14; Amos 3:13; see G. Osborne, *Revelation*, 72.

16. For details, see T. Longman III, *Immanuel in Our Place: Seeing Christ in Israel's Worship* (Phillipsburg, NJ: P&R Publishing, 2001), 163–84.

17. Tabb, *All Things New*, 89.

18. See Longman, *Immanuel in Our Place*, 55–57.

19. For this reason I am not convinced by those who would argue that Zechariah 4 lies behind this text (see G. K. Beale, *Revelation: A Shorter Commentary* [Grand Rapids: Eerdmans, 2015], 47).

20. Alan F. Johnson, "Revelation," in *The Expositor's Bible Commentary: Revised Edition* (Grand Rapids: Zondervan, 2006), 606.

21. Contra G. A. Boyd, *Crucifixion of the Warrior God: Interpreting the Old Testament's Violent Portraits of God in the Light of the Cross*, 2 vols. (Minneapolis: Fortress, 2017).

22. See also Peter S. Williamson, *Revelation*, Catholic Commentary on Sacred Scripture (Grand Rapids: Baker Academic, 2015), 53.

23. Osborne, *Revelation*, 93.
24. P. Johnston, *Shades of Sheol* (Downers Grove, IL: InterVarsity Press, 2002).

REVELATION 2

1. M. W. Wilson, "Revelation," in ZIBBCNT, ed. C. Arnold (Grand Rapids: Zondervan, 2002), 262.
2. Richard Bauckham, *The Theology of the Book of Revelation* (Cambridge: Cambridge University Press, 1997), 124.
3. G. K. Beale, *Revelation: A Shorter Commentary* (Grand Rapids: Eerdmans, 2015), 58.
4. Osborne, *Revelation*, 122.
5. Going with the NIV footnote that follows the Septuagint and DSS, which most scholars recognize as a superior text.
6. Bruce M. Metzger with David A. deSilva, *Breaking the Code: Understanding the Book of Revelation* (Nashville: Abingdon, 2019), loc. 422.
7. For the latter, see Ryan E. Stokes, *Satan: How God's Executioner Became the Enemy* (Grand Rapids: Eerdmans, 2019).
8. Metzger and deSilva, *Breaking the Code*, loc. 449.
9. Metzger and deSilva, *Breaking the Code*, loc. 475.
10. In Philippi, Paul met a woman from Thyatira who was a seller of purple cloth (Ac 16:14). She and her family responded to Paul's message, and he lodged at her house. Though living in Philippi, she likely represented Thyatiran trade interests.
11. Metzger and deSilva, *Breaking the Code*, loc. 469–76.
12. See T. Longman III, *Psalms*, TOTC (Downers Grove, IL: InterVarsity Press, 2014), 59–64; T. Longman III, "The Messiah: Explorations in the Law and Writings," in *The Messiah in the Old and New Testaments*, ed. S. E. Porter (Grand Rapids: Eerdmans, 2007).
13. Metzger and deSilva, *Breaking the Code*, loc. 508.
14. Ian Paul, *Revelation*, TOTC (Downers Grove, IL: InterVarsity Press, 2018), 96.
15. Craig Keener, *Revelation*, NIVAC (Grand Rapids: Zondervan, 2000), 136.

REVELATION 3

1. J. Oswalt, *Isaiah*, NIVAC (Grand Rapids: Zondervan, 2003), 264.
2. Longman, *Immanuel in Our Place*, 46–48.
3. Williamson, *Revelation*, 91.
4. Carmen Joy Imes, *Bearing God's Name: Why Sinai Still Matters* (Downers Grove, IL: InterVarsity Press, 2019), 49.
5. T. Longman III, *Proverbs*, BCOTWP (Grand Rapids: Baker, 2006), 67–69. As to the precise way in which the New Testament authors associate Jesus with Woman Wisdom, see T. Longman III, *The Fear of the Lord is Wisdom: A Theological Introduction to Wisdom in Israel* (Grand Rapids: Baker, 2017), 246–50.
6. Though not relevant to the present book, we take note that the Song of Songs, in which an unnamed man and woman enjoy intimacy with each other—they are naked and not ashamed—in garden settings, signals that there is indeed what we might call an already-not yet redemption of sexuality possible. See D. Allender and T. Longman III, *God Loves Sex: An Honest Conversation about Sexual Desire and Holiness* (Grand Rapids: Baker, 2014).
7. Osborne, *Revelation*, 210, citing C. J. Hemer, *The Letters to the Seven Churches of Asia in Their Local Setting* (Sheffield: JSOT Press, 1986), 196–99.
8. Cited in Hebrews 12:5–6.
9. Christopher J. H. Wright, *Exodus*, Story of God Commentary (Grand Rapids: Zondervan, 2021), 461–62.
10. Quotes from "Eating," in L. Ryken, et al., eds., *The Dictionary of Biblical Imagery* (Downers Grove, IL: InterVarsity Press, 1998), 227.

REVELATION 4

1. Tabb, *All Things New*, 73.
2. Tabb, *All Things New*, 37.
3. Jasper seems to be mentioned in the list. The first jewel mentioned might be a ruby (so NIV 1984) but has recently been rendered carnelian (NIV 2011). We should also mention that these three stones are mentioned in connection with the cherub that guarded Eden (probably a reference to Adam in his created glory) like the later priests would guard the temple precincts (see Eze 28:13–14).
4. Tabb, *All Things New*, 41.
5. See the helpful description of the Roman imperial cult that permeated Asia Minor in David A. deSilva, *Discovering Revelation: Content, Interpretation, Reception* (Grand Rapids: Eerdmans, 2021), 45–50.
6. Paul, "Introduction to the Book of Revelation," 50–51, citing D. Aune, *Apocalypticism, Prophecy, and Magic in Early Christianity*, 119.
7. With the NIV alternate reading as in the footnote. Hebrew has *'elohim*, which can be rendered "angels," thus undermining our point, but such a translation is not the most natural.

REVELATION 5

1. Not only is the baptism followed by the forty days and nights in the wilderness like Israel spent forty years in the wilderness, but Paul signals that at the time of the New Testament people thought of the crossing of the Sea as a type of baptism (1 Co 10:2).
2. In the wilderness, Jesus experienced the same temptations (hunger, testing God, and worshiping a false god) that the Israelites experienced in the wilderness. In contrast to Israel, Jesus resisted the temptations, and he signals this by citing the book of Deuteronomy three times. Deuteronomy is the book warning the second generation of Israelites not to sin as their ancestors did in the wilderness.
3. T. Longman III, "Psalm 98: A Divine Warrior Victory Song," *Journal of the Evangelical Theological Society* 27 (1984): 267–74.
4. Kingdom of heaven is Matthew's preferred way of referring to the kingdom of God. The two phrases are basically synonymous.

REVELATION 6

1. M. Boda, *The Book of Zechariah*, NICOT (Grand Rapids: Eerdmans, 2016), 379.
2. G. R. Osborne, *Revelation*, BECNT (Grand Rapids: Baker, 2002), 274.
3. Craig R. Koester, *Revelation and the End of All Things*, 2nd ed. (Grand Rapids: Eerdmans, 2018), 81.
4. The phrase "sword, famine, and plague" (and its variant "sword and famine") is formulaic in the book of Jeremiah (5:12; 11:22; 16:4; 21:7, 9; 24:10; 27:8, 13; 29:18; 32:24, 36; 34:17; 38:2; 42:16–17; 44:12–13, 18, 27). It may flow from Deuteronomy 32:24–27, which describes the types of divine punishment that would come on Israel for their idolatry.
5. DBI, 944.
6. M. Robert Mulholland Jr., "Revelation," in *James, 1–2 Peter, Revelation*, CBC (Carol Stream, IL: Tyndale House, 2001), 471–72.
7. Koester, *Revelation and the End of All Things*, 82–83.
8. See note at 3:12.
9. Robert D. Miller II, *The Dragon, the Mountain, and the Nations: An Old Testament Myth, Its Origins, and Its Afterlives* (Winona Lake, IN: Eisenbrauns, 2017), 277.
10. For a full critique, see T. Longman III, *Confronting Old Testament Controversies: Pressing Questions about Evolution, Sexuality, History, and Violence* (Grand Rapids: Baker Books, 2019), 158–68.

11. See his argument presented in G. A. Boyd, *Crucifixion of the Warrior God: Interpreting the Old Testament's Violent Portraits of God in the Light of the Cross*, 2 vols. (Minneapolis: Fortress, 2017).
12. NIV 2011 for some reason misleadingly translates *sheol* "Death" rather than "grave" (as it did in the 1984 version).
13. DBI, 944.
14. R. Ryan, "Eighth-Century Levantine Earthquakes and Natural Disasters," in *Behind the Scenes of the Old Testament: Cultural, Social, and Historical Contexts*, ed. J. S. Greer, J. W. Hilber, and J. H. Walton (Grand Rapids: Baker, 2018), 308.
15. Interestingly Psalm 104 speaks of God "stretching out the heavens like a tent" (v. 2).
16. G. Von Rad, "The Origin of the Concept of the Day of Yahweh," *Journal of Semitic Studies* 4 (1959): 103; also P. D. Miller Jr., "The Divine Council and the Prophetic Call to War," *Vetus Testamentum* 18 (1968): 100–107; F. M. Cross, Jr., "The Divine Warrior," in *Canaanite Myth and Hebrew Epic* (Cambridge, MA: Harvard University Press, 1973), 91–111; D. Stuart, "The Sovereign's Day of Conquest," *Bulletin of the American Schools of Oriental Research* 221 (1976), 159–64; T. Longman III and D. G. Reid, *God Is a Warrior* (Grand Rapids: Zondervan, 1995), 69–71.

REVELATION 7

1. Craig R. Koester, *Revelation and the End of All Things*, 2nd ed. (Grand Rapids: Eerdmans, 2018), 90.
2. Peter S. Williamson, *Revelation*, CCSS (Grand Rapids: Baker Academic, 2015), 139.
3. S. Noegel, "On the Wings of the Wind: Towards an Understanding of Winged *Mischwesen* in the Ancient Near East," *Kaskal: Rivista di Storia, Ambienti e Culture del Vincino Oriente Antico* 14 (2019), 15–54.
4. See John H. Sailhamer, "Genesis," in *Expositor's Bible Commentary*, rev. ed. (Grand Rapids: Zondervan, 2008), 75–76 speculates that Eden is a larger area than the garden and that the garden is planted in the eastern portion of Eden.
5. Note that after Adam and Eve are forced to leave Eden that the cherubim who guard the garden are stationed in the east (Ge 3:24).
6. Ezekiel 47:1 describes the eastward orientation of the prophet's eschatological temple, but it is likely that Solomon's temple also faced east.
7. Once again we need to remember that apocalyptic literature, like we have here in Revelation, uses symbolic language, especially when it comes to numbers. That there are only 144,000 who have the seal on them does not mean that there will only be 144,000 people on God's side at the end of time. This point is particularly true if we are right to see the 144,000 and the "great multitude" as the same group of people.
8. Interestingly, the idea that all humans are intimately related has been supported by recent DNA studies. See Jeremiah Stout and Georgia M. Dunston, "Scientist Spotlight: Georgia M. Dunston," BioLogos, https://biologos.org/articles/scientist-spotlight-georgia-m-dunston. For how the statement that we all descend from one man comports with recent evolutionary theory, see Longman, *Confronting Old Testament Controversies*, 25–77.
9. Esau McCauley, *Reading the Bible While Black* (Downers Grove, IL: IVP Academic, 2020), 101–2.
10. See the chapter on "Racism," in T. Longman III, *The Bible and the Ballot: Using Scripture in Political Decisions* (Grand Rapids: Baker, 2020), 275–99.
11. W. W. Hallo, "'As the Seal upon Thy Heart': Glyptic Roles in the Biblical World," *Biblical Research* 1 (1985): 20–27.
12. R. Herms, "Psalms of Solomon and Revelation 7:1–17: The Sealing of the Servants of God," in *Reading Revelation in Context: John's Apocalypse and Second Temple Judaism*, eds. B. C. Blackwell, et al. (Grand Rapids: Zondervan, 2019), 73.
13. Williamson, *Revelation*, 139.

14. J. G. McConville, *Deuteronomy*, AOTC (Downers Grove, IL: InterVarsity Press, 2002), 467.
15. See Longman, *Immanuel in Our Place: Seeing Christ in Israel's Worship* (Phillipsburg, NJ: P&R, 2001 139–50.
16. Brian J. Tabb, *All Things New: Revelation as Canonical Capstone* (Downers Grove, IL: IVP Academic, 2019), 102.
17. In agreement with Tabb, *All Things New*, 103, who sees these two groups as two descriptions of the same people.
18. Palm branches are used, along with the branches of other trees, to construct shelters at the Festival of Booths (Lev 23:40).
19. D. Carson, *The Gospel according to John*, PNTC (Grand Rapids: Eerdmans, 1991), 432.
20. Though Genesis 10 precedes Genesis 11, the content clearly shows that the action of Genesis 11, which generates multiple languages, must chronologically precede the description of humanity divided into different languages. See T. Longman III, *Genesis*, SOG (Grand Rapids: Zondervan, 2016), 138–55.
21. See Longman, *Immanuel in Our Place*, 39–48.
22. DBI, 784.

REVELATION 8

1. C. S. Keener, *Revelation*, NIVAC (Grand Rapids: Eerdmans, 2002), 255.
2. For the relationship between the seven seals, the seven trumpets, and the seven bowls, see "What the Structure Means: Seals, Trumpets, and Bowls (Rev 6:1–7:5; 8:7–11:19; 15:1–16:21)" after 16:21.
3. B. S. Childs, *Isaiah*, OTL (Louisville: Westminster John Knox), 126.
4. R. J. Clifford, "The Use of Hoy in the Prophets," *Catholic Biblical Quarterly* 28 (1966): 458–64; E. Gerstenberger, "The Woe-Oracles of the Prophets," *Journal of Biblical Literature* 81 (1962): 249–63; W. Janzen, *Mourning Cry and Woe Oracle*, BZAW (Berlin: de Gruyter, 1972).

REVELATION 9

1. It is true that human death was implied in the second judgment (8:9) and in the third (8:11), but humans were not the focus.
2. B. R. Foster, "Epic of Creation," COS 1:399 (tablet 5, lines 1–2).
3. Longman, *Immanuel in Our Place: Seeing Christ in Israel's Worship* (Phillipsburg, NJ: P&R Publishing, 2001), 139–50.
4. Or perhaps God is the head of a human army (like the Babylonian army) that he uses for his own purposes of judgment. That locust hordes are sometimes used to describe human armies maybe be seen in Judges 6:5; 7:12; Jer 46:23; Na 3:15–16.
5. DBI, 514.
6. T. Longman III, *How to Read Daniel* (Downers Grove, IL: InterVarsity Press, 2020), 41.
7. Steve Moyise (*The Old Testament in the Book of Revelation* [London: Bloomsbury T. And T. Clark, 2015], 56) detects an allusion back to Daniel 5:20 where Daniel confronts Belshazzar for praying "the gods of silver and gold, of bronze, iron, wood and stone which cannot see or understand" (Dan 5:23).
8. G. Osborne, *Revelation*, BECNT (Grand Rapids: Baker Academic, 2002), 387.
9. C. John Miller, *Repentance: A Daring Call to Real Surrender*, rev. ed. (Fort Washington, PA: CLC, 2009).

REVELATION 10

1. I wish to thank Shannon Williamson, my student at Regent College in the summer of 2020, for a paper that insightfully discussed this question, though I ended up going a different direction than her conclusion on the matter.

2. For instance, R. Bauckham, *The Theology of the Book of Revelation* (Cambridge: Cambridge University Press, 1997), 80–82; and Koester, *Revelation and the End of All Things*, 2nd ed. (Grand Rapids: Eerdmans, 2018), 104–5.
3. Bauckham, *The Book of Revelation*, 80–82, and Koester, *Revelation and the End of All Things*, 104–5.
4. Contra Bauckham, *The Book of Revelation*, 81, who argues that this ending "need not differ in meaning from *biblion*."
5. The even more frequent picture of God riding a cloud, also seen in Revelation (see note at 1:7 with reference to Old Testament background) seems less relevant here.
6. This is the view of Koester, *Revelation and the End of All Things*, 102.
7. B. Wold, "Words of the Luminaries and Revelation 15:1–16:21," in *Reading Revelation in Context*, eds. Ben C. Blackwell, et al. (Grand Rapids: Zondervan, 2019), 134.

REVELATION 11

1. M. Lloyd-Jones, *Faith on Trial* (London: InterVarsity Press, 1965), 63.
2. John E. Goldingay, *Daniel*, WBC (Dallas: Word, 1989), 144.
3. Longman, *How to Read Daniel* (Downers Grove, IL: InterVarsity Press, 2020), 36–47.
4. For an excellent analysis that has informed my understanding of Zechariah's fifth night vision, see M. Boda, *The Book of Zechariah*, NICOT (Grand Rapids: Eerdmans, 2016), 263–319.
5. These are the views held by A. Hill, *Haggai, Zechariah and Malachi* (Downers Grove, IL: IVP Academic, 2012), 154–62, and Boda, *The Book of Zechariah*, 314–20, respectively.
6. P. Williamson, *Revelation*, CCSS (Grand Rapids: Baker Academic, 2015), 191.
7. Williamson, *Revelation*, 191.
8. Leviathan too, as described by God, breathes fire (Job 41:18–21), but this passage does not appear to have connection with the two prophets.
9. Though when they cut themselves (1 Ki 18:28–29), they were mimicking the god El as described in the Baal Myth who cut himself when Baal went into the underworld.
10. Williamson, *Revelation*, 194.
11. Except for a brief mention in the Hamite genealogy in a description of the borders of the Canaanite tribes (Ge 10:19).
12. Daniel I. Block, *The Book of Ezekiel: Chapters 1–24*, NICOT (Grand Rapids, 1997), 504–22.
13. The Greek version of Genesis 2:7 does not use *pneuma* either.
14. For how this conforms to the Babylonian practice of dream interpretation, see Longman, *How to Read Daniel*, 56.
15. See Longman, *How to Read Daniel*, 68–70.
16. Or as stated in Longman (*How to Read Daniel*, 37–44) "in spite of present troubles, God is in control, and will have the final victory."
17. Johnston, *Shades of Sheol*.

REVELATION 12

1. Besides a simple "and" (*kai*), untranslated by the NIV.
2. D. DeSilva, *Discovering Revelation* (Grand Rapids: Eerdmans, 2021), 129, who also has a helpful discussion of the Greco-Roman background to this chapter in the myth of Leto, Apollo, and Tryphon.
3. Williamson, *Revelation*, 206.
4. But substituting the name Yahweh for Baal.
5. Email correspondence, January 2, 2021.
6. T. Longman, "The Messiah: Explorations in the Law and Writings," in *The Messiah in the Old and New Testaments* (Grand Rapids: Eerdmans, 2007), 13–34.

7. T. Longman III, "Psalm 98: A Divine Warrior Victory Song," *Journal of the Evangelical Theological Society* 27 (1984): 267–74.

8. I am citing the NRSV because it follows the superior text attested by the Dead Sea Scrolls and the Greek. The NIV follows the Masoretic Text, but the evidence provided by DSS and the Greek is a strong indication that the MT changes "gods" to "sons of Israel" for theological reasons.

9. Ryan E. Stokes, *Satan: How God's Executioner Became the Enemy* (Grand Rapids: Eerdmans, 2019).

10. See T. Longman III, *Job*, BCOTWP (Grand Rapids: Baker, 2012), 91–92. See also John H. Walton and Tremper Longman III, *How to Read Job* (Downers Grove, IL: IVP Academic, 2015), 50–56.

11. We should also take note of the fact that God raises up various human satans (in the NIV translated "adversary") in the aftermath of Solomon's apostasy (1 Ki 11:14, 23, 25).

12. N. T. Wright, *Revelation for Everyone* (Louisville: John Knox Westminster, 2011), 115.

13. Wright, *Revelation for Everyone*, 116, 120.

14. In the Gilgamesh Epic, Gilgamesh seeks to get life by getting a certain plant from the bottom of the sea, but it is stolen by a snake. In the Adapa Epic there is a serpent-shaped gatekeeper, Ningishzida. In Egyptian mythology the snakes represent death and wisdom (like the serpent in Genesis 3, who is said to be "crafty"). And then there is the Egyptian god Apophis, a snakelike representative of chaos who is defeated nightly by the sun god. These examples come from John Walton, "Serpent," in *Dictionary of the Old Testament: Pentateuch*, eds. T. D. Alexander and D. W. Baker (Downers Grove, IL: InterVarsity Press, 2003), 736–39. I would add a fourth reference to Tiamat, the primeval deity who represents the sea and thus the forces of chaos, defeated by the creator god Marduk in the Enuma Elish.

15. See the excellent survey and analysis by Robert D. Miller II, *The Dragon, the Mountain, and the Nations: An Old Testament Myth, Its Origins, and Its Afterlives* (Winona Lake, IN: Eisenbrauns, 2017).

16. T. Longman III, *Job*, BCOTWP (Grand Rapids: Baker, 2012), 82–82, 91–92.

17. O. Cullmann, *Christ and Time: The Primitive Christians Conception of Time and History* (Philadelphia: Westminster, 1964), 3.

18. T. Jacobsen, "The Battle between Marduk and Tiamat," *Journal of the American Oriental Society* 88 (1968): 104–8.

19. COS, 1:249, translation by Dennis Pardee.

REVELATION 13

1. See T. Longman III, "God's Law and Mosaic Punishment Today," in *Theonomy: A Reformed Critique*, eds. W. S. Barker, and W. Robert Godfrey (Grand Rapids: Zondervan, 1990), 41–58.

2. P. Williamson, *Revelation*, CCSS (Grand Rapids: Eerdmans, 2015), 224.

3. D. Bryan, *Cosmos, Chaos, and the Kosher Mentality* (Sheffield: Sheffield Academic Press, 1995), 239.

4. Williamson, *Revelation*, 223.

5. T. Longman III, *Jeremiah/Lamentations*, UBCS (Grand Rapids: Baker, 2008), 121–23.

6. T. Longman III, *Job*, BCOTWP (Grand Rapids: Baker Academic, 2016), 454–56.

7. T. Longman III, *Daniel*, NIVAC (Grand Rapids: Zondervan, 1999), 94–112.

8. See D. B. Allender and T. Longman III, *Breaking the Idols of Your Heart: How to Navigate the Temptations of Life* (Downers Grove, IL: InterVarsity Press, 2007).

9. James K. A. Smith, *Awaiting the King: Reforming Public Theology* (Grand Rapids: Baker, 2017), 216.

10. Williamson, *Revelation*, 233.

11. Williamson, *Revelation*, 233.
12. See T. Longman III, *The Fear of the Lord Is Wisdom: An Introduction to Wisdom in Israel* (Grand Rapids: Baker, 2017).
13. B. Metzger and D. DeSilva, *Breaking the Code: Understanding the Book of Revelation* (Nashville: Abingdon, 2019), 96

REVELATION 14

1. T. Longman III, *The Fear of the Lord Is Wisdom: An Introduction to Wisdom in Israel* (Grand Rapids: Baker, 2017).
2. T. Longman III, *How to Read Daniel* (Downers Grove, IL: InterVarsity Press, 2020), 37–44.
3. T. Longman III, *Jeremiah/Lamentations* (Grand Rapids: Baker, 2012), 174–78.
4. Robert D. Miller II, *The Dragon, the Mountain, and the Nations: An Old Testament Myth, Its Origins, and Its Afterlives* (Winona Lake, IN: Eisenbrauns, 2017), 277.
5. Williamson, *Revelation*, 253.

REVELATION 15

1. R. Bauckham, *The Theology of the Book of Revelation* (Cambridge: Cambridge University Press, 1997), 71.
2. B. Metzger and D. DeSilva, *Breaking the Code: Understanding the Book of Revelation* (Nashville: Abingdon, 2019), 103.
3. For more, see Longman, *The Fear of the Lord is the Beginning of Wisdom: An Introduction to Wisdom in Israel* (Grand Rapids: Baker, 2017).
4. The priestly sash was not golden but rather "made of finely twisted linen and blue, purpose and scarlet yarn—the work of an embroiderer" (Ex 39:29), the same material as the innermost curtain of the tabernacle (Ex 26:1).
5. As for instance, in G. A. Boyd, *The Crucifixion of the Warrior God: Interpreting the Old Testament's Violent Portraits of God in the Light of the Cross* (Minneapolis: Fortress, 2017).
6. Metzger and DeSilva, *Breaking the Code*, 104.

REVELATION 16

1. I am citing the NRSV because it follows the superior text attested by the Dead Sea Scrolls and the Greek. The NIV follows the Masoretic Text, but the evidence provided by DSS and the Greek is a strong indication that the MT changes "gods" to "sons of Israel" for theological reasons.
2. See T. Longman III, *Job*, BCOTWP (Grand Rapids: Baker Academic, 2016), 90–91.
3. For a more substantial discussion of this topic, see the chapter on the Environment in T. Longman III, *The Bible and the Ballot: Using Scripture in Political Decisions* (Grand Rapids: Eerdmans, 2020), 233–53.
4. See the excellent work by N. T. Wright, *Surprised by Hope: Rethinking Heaven, the Resurrection, and the Mission of the Church* (San Francisco: HarperOne, 2008); also Sandra L. Richter, *Environmentalism and the Bible: What Scripture Says about Creation and Why It Matters* (Downers Grove, InterVarsity Press, 2019); and Ian K. Smith, *How the Renewal of the Earth Fits into God's Plan for the World* (Wheaton, IL: Crossway, 2019).
5. Longman, *Song of Songs*, NICOT (Grand Rapids: Eerdmans, 2001), 63–67 and D. Allender and T. Longman III, *God Loves Sex* (Grand Rapids: Baker, 2014), 133–45.
6. T. Longman III, "Nahum," in *The Minor Prophets: An Exegetical and Expository Commentary*, vol. 2 (Grand Rapids: Baker, 1993), 814–17.
7. Some Greek manuscripts have Harmagedon.

8. Brian J. Tabb, *All Things New: Revelation as Canonical Capstone* (Downers Grove, IL: IVP Academic, 2019), 164.

9. R. Bauckham, *The Theology of the Book of Revelation* (Cambridge: Cambridge University Press, 1997), 40.

REVELATION 17

1. H. G. Mays, "Some Cosmic Connotations of *mayim rabbim*, 'Many Waters,'" *Journal of Biblical Literature* 74 (1955): 9–21.

2. As defined in the passage in Genesis 2 just cited. That God permitted polygamy later in Israel's history (Ex 21:7–11) does not undermine God's creation intention but is rather an act of divine concession by which he took his sinful people where they were and moved them toward his creation ideal; see comments in T. Longman III, *Confronting Old Testament Controversies: Pressing Questions about Evolution, Sexuality, History, and Violence* (Grand Rapids: Baker Books, 2019), 229–33.

3. See the helpful article by Paul M. Hoskins, "Another Possible Interpretation of the Seven Heads of the Beast (Revelation 17:9–11)," *Bulletin for Biblical Research* 20 (2020): 86–102 for various interpretive options. His interpretation has greatly influenced my understanding, though I don't follow him in all matters.

4. Hoskins, "Another Possible Interpretation," 95.

5. See comment at 13:12.

6. Hoskins, "Another Possible Interpretation," 102.

7. Longman, *Old Testament Controversies*, 123–206, for a more detailed exposition of the theme of divine warfare in the Bible.

REVELATION 18

1. T. Longman III, "Glory in the Old Testament," in *The Glory of God*, ed. C. W. Morgan and R. A. Peterson (Wheaton, IL: Crossway, 2010), 47–48.

2. Thus changing the first edition rendition which had "demons." Also note Leviticus 17:7 which most versions render "goat demons," but NIV 2011 has "goat idols." In this case I do not believe the change in 2011 improved the translation.

3. Though it is not always the case that the "shades" (*rephaim*) are of the wicked dead.

4. P. Williamson, *Revelation*, CCSS (Grand Rapids: Baker Academic, 2015), 73.

5. See D. B. Allender and T. Longman III, *Breaking the Idols of Your Heart: How to Navigate the Temptations of Life* (Downers Grove, IL: InterVarsity Press, 2007), 62–87.

6. Uriah the Hittite died in a similar fashion (2 Sa 11:21), but as the result of David's attempt to cover up his sin with Bathsheba, not as punishment or judgment.

7. Williamson, *Revelation*, 301–02.

8. T. Longman III and D. G. Reid, *God Is a Warrior* (Grand Rapids: Zondervan, 1995), 45.

REVELATION 19

1. See T. Longman III, *Daniel*, NIVAC (Grand Rapids: Zondervan, 1999), 247.

2. P. Williamson, *Revelation*, CCSS (Grand Rapids: Eerdmans, 2015), 320.

3. T. Longman III, "Psalm 98: A Divine Warrior Hymn," *Journal of the Evangelical Theological Society* 27 (1984): 267–74.

4. G. Osborne, *Revelation*, BECNT (Grand Rapids: Baker Academic, 2002), 681–82.

5. Koester, *Revelation and the End of All Things*, 2nd ed. (Grand Rapids: Eerdmans, 2018), 177–78.

6. Osborne (*Revelation*, 683) points out that is how "word of God" is used in Revelation generally (1:2, 9; 6:9; 17:17; 19:9 and 20:4).

7. Osborne, *Revelation*, 686.

REVELATION 20

1. P. Williamson, *Revelation*, CCSS (Grand Rapids: Baker Academic, 2015), 324.
2. S. L. Cook, *Ezekiel 38–48*, Yale Anchor Bible (New Haven, CT: Yale University Press, 2018), 74.
3. While Ezekiel refers to Gog as a person, Revelation takes it as a place name parallel to Magog. This is in keeping with other Jewish texts. Brian J. Tabb, *All Things New: Revelation as Canonical Capstone* (Downers Grove, IL: IVP Academic, 2019), 132, lists 3 En. 45:5; Sib. Or. 3.319; 5.512; 4Q523 2.5.
4. S. L. Cook, *Ezekiel 38–48*, Yale Anchor Bible (New Haven, CT: Yale University Press, 2018), 74.
5. Iain M. Duguid, *Ezekiel*, NIVAC (Grand Rapids: Eerdmans, 1999), 448.
6. Notice too how Revelation turns the person Gog into another place name.
7. Though it is suggestive that Revelation 20:10 describes the torment suffered by the devil, and beast and the false prophets as being thrown into the lake of fire and lasting "day and night for ever and ever." Evil human beings are likewise said to be thrown into the lake of fire, though no mention is made of duration (20:15).
8. T. Longman III, *Job*, BCOTWP (Grand Rapids: Baker, 2012), 324–34.

REVELATION 21

1. Or perhaps even speaking directly to the returned exiles who would still be grappling with the disappointment of returning to a life still under the thumb of a foreign oppressor. See T. Longman III, "Isaiah 65:17–25," *Interpretation* 64 (2010): 72–73.
2. R. L. Schultz, "Intertextuality, Canon, and 'Undecidability': Understanding Isaiah's 'New Heavens and New Earth' (Isaiah 65:17–25)," *Bulletin of Biblical Research* 20 (2010): 37.
3. N. T. Wright, *Surprised by Hope* (San Francisco: HarperSanFrancisco, 2010), 18.
4. P. Williamson, *Revelation*, CCSS (Grand Rapids: Baker Academic, 2015), 348.
5. Sometimes it means specifically "wealthy" (Ge 13:2).
6. See T. Longman III, "Glory in the Old Testament," in *The Glory of God*, eds. C. W. Morgan and R. A. Peterson (Wheaton, IL: Crossway, 2010).
7. J. Piper, *Desiring God: Meditations of a Christian Hedonist*, 2nd ed. (Multnomah, 1966), 255.
8. Brian J. Tabb, *All Things New: Revelation as Canonical Capstone* (Downers Grove, IL: IVP Academic, 2019), 178.
9. Comparing the Greek words in Revelation with the Greek words used in the Greek translation of the book of Exodus, contra Williamson, *Revelation*, 352.

REVELATION 22

1. J. J. Collins, "Apocalypticism as a Worldview in Ancient Judaism and Christianity," in *The Cambridge Companion to Apocalyptic Literature*, ed. C. McAllister (Cambridge: Cambridge University Press, 2020), 35.
2. For more, see T. Longman III, *The Bible and the Ballot: Using Scripture in Political Decisions* (Grand Rapids: Eerdmans, 2020).
3. Brian J. Tabb, *All Things New: Revelation as Canonical Capstone* (Downers Grove, IL: IVP Academic, 2019), 220.
4. While Genesis 1–2, and indeed the first eleven chapters of Genesis, are figurative depictions of origins, these chapters point to a historical reality behind the figures in this case that there was a period of human innocence and harmony. See T. Longman III, *Confronting Old Testament Controversies: Pressing Questions about Evolution, Sexuality, History, and Violence* (Grand Rapids: Baker Books, 2019), 1–78.

5. This section reflects my views, explained in *Confronting Old Testament Controversies*, the story of Adam and Eve reflects not the origin of homo sapiens but what has been called *homo divinus*, the first humans granted the status of image-bearing.

6. For more, see Longman, *Daniel*, 185–86.

7. For what that fight looks like in more detail, see D. Allender and T. Longman III, *Bold Love* (Colorado Springs, CO: NavPress, 1992).

8. As we see in P. Enns, *The Bible Tells Me So: Why Defending Scripture Has Made Us Unable to Read It* (San Francisco: HarperOne, 2014); G. A. Boyd, *Crucifixion of the Warrior God: Interpreting the Old Testament's Violent Portraits of God in the Light of the Cross* (Minneapolis: Fortress, 2017); E. A. Seibert, *Disturbing Behavior: Troubling Old Testament Images of God* (Minneapolis: Fortress, 2009).

SCRIPTURE INDEX

Note: All Scripture references are indexed except for those in the book of Revelation.